THE GENERAL HISTORY OF PERU

THE GENERAL HISTORY OF PERU

Book 1 by Martín de Murúa

WITH AN INTRODUCTION BY BRIAN S. BAUER

TRANSLATED AND EDITED BY

Brian S. Bauer, Eliana Gamarra C.,
and Andrea Gonzales Lombardi

UNIVERSITY PRESS OF COLORADO
Denver

© 2024 by University Press of Colorado

Published by University Press of Colorado
1580 Market Street, Suite 660
PMB 39883
Denver, Colorado 80203-1942

 The University Press of Colorado is a proud member of
the Association of University Presses.

The University Press of Colorado is a cooperative publishing enterprise supported, in part, by Adams State University, Colorado State University, Fort Lewis College, Metropolitan State University of Denver, University of Alaska Fairbanks, University of Colorado, University of Denver, University of Northern Colorado, University of Wyoming, Utah State University, and Western Colorado University.

∞ This paper meets the requirements of the ANSI/NISO Z39.48-1992 (Permanence of Paper).

ISBN: 978-1-64642-653-9 (hardcover)
ISBN: 978-1-64642-654-6 (paperback)
ISBN: 978-1-64642-655-3 (ebook)
https://doi.org/10.5876/9781646426553

Library of Congress Cataloging-in-Publication Data

Names: Murúa, Martín de, author. | Murúa, Martín de. Historia general del Piru. Libro del origen y descendencia de los Ingas. | Bauer, Brian S., editor, translator, writer of introduction. | Gamarra Carrillo, Eliana, editor, translator. | Gonzáles Lombardi, Andrea, editor, translator.
Title: The general history of Peru. Book 1 / by Martín de Murúa : with an introduction by Brian S. Bauer ; translated and edited by Brian S. Bauer, Eliana Gamarra C., and Andrea Gonzáles Lombardi.
Other titles: Historia general del Piru. Libro del origen y descendencia de los Ingas. English
Description: Denver : University Press of Colorado, [2024] | Includes bibliographical references and index. | Text in English and Spanish.
Identifiers: LCCN 2024012275 (print) | LCCN 2024012276 (ebook) | ISBN 9781646426539 (hardcover) | ISBN 9781646426546 (paperback) | ISBN 9781646426553 (ebook)
Subjects: LCSH: Murúa, Martín de—Criticism and interpretation. | Incas—Early works to 1800. | Peru—History—To 1548—Early works to 1800. | Peru—History—Conquest, 1522–1548—Early works to 1800.
Classification: LCC F3444 .M85213 (print) | LCC F3444 (ebook) | DDC 985/.019—dc23/eng/20240430
LC record available at https://lccn.loc.gov/2024012275
LC ebook record available at https://lccn.loc.gov/2024012276

Cover illustrations courtesy of the J. Paul Getty Museum, Los Angeles.

In memory of our friends and colleagues who left us during the Coronavirus Pandemic of 2019–2023.

Contents

Figures and Tables

FIGURES

TABLE

Preface

Translators' Notes

In 2008, the Getty Research Institute published a facsimile edition of Martin de Murúa's *General History of Peru* (1616), making his important chronicle widely accessible. This publication provides the first English translation of book 1 of Murúa's immense work. Book 1 covers both the history of the Inca Empire and the first forty years of the Spanish occupation, culminating with the fall of Vilcabamba in 1572.

Although we have tried to remain faithful to Murúa throughout this translation, we have made changes to make his document more accessible to a wide readership. For example, we have divided many of his excessively long sentences into shorter, more comprehensible lengths. We have also added punctuation to lend clarity to the text and added paragraph breaks to shorten many of the longer passages. In some sentences, we have made minor grammatical changes such as correcting tenses, plurals, and similar errors. We have also removed certain sentence starters, such as *And* or *Thus*, to ensure a smoother narration. Finally, we have added a word or two or a proper name to rectify ambiguous sentences or to clarify confusing pronouns. The added words are placed within square brackets [ ].

Murúa's *General History of Peru* is an unusual document as it is the ultimate, preprint manuscript, that had passed through a series of official offices. The manuscript retains the scribal and authorial edits, most of which are contained within the text and a few of which written as margin notes. These changes are marked and included in our translation. The manuscript also contains sections selected for redaction by the Mercedarian censor, Alonso Remón, and the Royal censor, Pedro de Valencia, who were responsible for making the final publication acceptable to the Church and the Crown. We have marked and included the sections of the document that these censors crossed out. In most of the censored passages, we could read the original text. However, in the few cases where we can no longer identify individual letters, we mark spaces with a boldface dot (●). Furthermore, in a few instances, individual words were crossed out and replaced with corrections, and in other passages one or two words were erroneously copied twice. We have also reproduced these elements of the text within our translation. Fortunately, Rolena Adorno (2008; Adorno and Boserup 2008) provides detailed analyses, far beyond our skills, of Murúa's *General History of Peru*, and the various stages that the writing project passed through from its conception, sometime before 1590, to its final edited version in 1616. Respecting her fine scholarship, we defer in most cases to her paleographic reading and detailed understanding of the document.

The inclusion of Quechua words within this early Colonial text added complexities to our translation project. Additional difficulties arose when the same terms, or proper names, are spelled in different ways. These inconsistencies may mark Murúa's limited understanding of Quechua, the limitations of the scribes who produced the final manuscript, and the fact there had been no effort to standardize Quechua words in the newly introduced Roman alphabet. Furthermore, since we know that Murúa copied some of his history from other sources, variations in spelling may reflect differences between sources and Murúa's imperfect ability to read and transcribe these unfamiliar terms. As our English translation is intended for a general readership, we have attempted to standardize the spellings of the most common Quechua terms, toponyms, and proper names to match the Hispanic spelling found in other Spanish documents. We have tried to follow Murúa's spelling for the more obscure terms, places, and names. For the more common terms and names, we have tried to use the most common spellings currently found in the literature. This has been a difficult task, and we have certainly done it imperfectly.

We have included folio numbers in brackets within the text, noting that on a few occasions a word starts on one folio and ends on the next. Murúa generally left the folio after the end of a chapter blank. We have marked the presences of blank folios in the footnotes, but the blank sheets themselves are not reproduced in this printing.

We also provide a general glossary to help readers understand the various Quechua and Spanish terms in the manuscript. Readers who are interested in learning more about the original Quechua and Spanish spellings and the Spanish grammar and syntax used in the *General History of Peru*, or other highly specialized aspects of the text, should consult the facsimile edition (Murúa 2008 [1616]).

Acknowledgments

We thank Valentin Ubidio Maldonado Allcca, who helped us during our visit to Yanaca, and César Astuhuamán, who assisted us throughout the project.

THE GENERAL HISTORY OF PERU

Introduction

BRIAN S. BAUER

In 1613, Martín de Murúa, a Mercedarian friar, finished writing his magnum opus *General History of Peru* (*Historia General del Piru*),[1] writing across its ornate cover page "In La Plata,[2] in the year [of] our [lord] 1613."[3] A draft of this immense manuscript had already passed through more than two years of reviews and had been approved by numerous officials of the Church in different cities of what are now Peru and Bolivia. Murúa also produced an earlier version of this work in 1590 titled *History and Genealogy of the Inca Kings of Peru*.[4] In the more than twenty years that had passed since the 1590 and the 1613 versions, the form of the chronicle had dramatically changed, with large sections added and other parts removed (Adorno and

1   The full title is *Historia General del Piru origen i descendençia de los incas, donde se trata, assí de las guerras çiviles suyas, como de la entrada de los españoles, descripçión de las çiudades i lugares del, con otras cosas notables*. [General History of Peru: Origin and descent of the Incas: Which deals with their civil wars, as well as the arrival of the Spaniards, description of the cities and place within it, with other notable things.]

2   Now called Sucre (Bolivia). At that time, La Plata was one of the largest cities of South America, its growth fed by the vast mineral wealth of the Bolivian highlands.

3   "En La Plata por N. Ano de 1613." The last page of the document also contains the date of 1613 (Murúa 2008 [1616]:383v).

4   The full title is *Historia de origen, y genealogía real de los reyes ingas del Piru. De sus hechos, costumbres, trages y manera de gouierno*. [History and genealogy of the Inca kings of Peru. Of their works, customs, clothes, and manner of governing.] Sometime later Murúa may have produced another version, or he may have simply changed the title to *General History and Book on the Origin and Lineage of the Inca Lords of This Western Kingdom of Peru*.

https://doi.org/10.5876/9781646426553.c000b

Boserup 2008:9).[5] The final manuscript, totaling around 775 pages, included thirty-four new illustrations that had been created specifically for this work, as well as four other illustrations,[6] which had been removed from an earlier draft that Murúa had written and were repurposed for new uses in his *General History of Peru*.[7]

As Murúa set aside his quill pen and polished brass inkwell (Borja de Aguinagalde 2019:244), and removed his glasses (244), he couldn't help but reflect on the arduous journey his *General History of Peru* had yet to endure. Decades of tireless dedication had brought him to this moment, but he knew there were still additional offices of the Church in Potosí and the Crown in Buenos Aires, as well as the more demanding offices in Spain, through which his manuscript had to pass. Little did he know that he would die only two years later in Spain, only a few months after his return, and that his manuscript, after having passed through all the necessary steps and having been approved by King Felipe III in 1616 for publication,[8] would disappear from public view for almost 350 years. Its first printing finally took place between 1962 and 1964, certainly an unimaginable date and cultural context for Murúa.

The final version of Murúa's *General History of Peru* is divided into three books and includes both front and back materials. The manuscript begins with a cover page featuring an elaborate coat of arms drawn by an unknown artist and calligraphed by Murúa (2008 [1616]:2r).[9] The front materials also include two short epigraphic poems written by Murúa (2008 [1616]:2v), and fourteen letters of support,[10] concluding with a statement signed by King Felipe III, and a ten-year license for

---

5   It is believed that Murúa produced several other intermediate versions, now lost, between the two surviving manuscripts (Adorno and Boserup 2008). For a detailed discussion of the various possible manuscripts produced by Murúa, both before and after 1590, see Adorno and Boserup (2008).

6   Three of the four illustrations that were removed from an earlier version and inserted into the *General History of Peru* were drawn by Felipe Guaman Poma de Ayala, while one was produced by an individual referred to as Galvin Artist 1 (Adorno and Boserup 2008). For a detailed description of how the illustrations were removed and inserted into the *General History of Peru*, and the effect that these migrations had on both manuscripts, see Adorno and Boserup (2008:31–36).

7   As these illustrations were reused from an earlier version, their opposite sides contained text from the earlier manuscript. This problem was resolved by pasting blank sheets over the outdated texts. The "lost" texts were revealed in 1979, when the pasted sheets were removed (Adorno and Boserup 2008:12).

8   Although Murúa's *General History of Peru* contains the date of 1613 on its cover page, the book continued to be edited and was finally approved for publication in Spain in 1616. For this reason, we use the date 1616 when referring to this work.

9   Throughout this project, we have relied on the works of Adorno (2008) and Adorno and Boserup (2008) for the identification of different individuals' handwriting.

10   Some of the letters of support may have once been loose and were later included as front materials when the volume was rebound.

the book to be published (Murúa 2008 [1616]:3r–11r).[11] Following these materials, Murúa (2008 [1616]:13r) presents what he claims to be the coat of arms of the Inca,[12] along with a dedicatory message to the prince of Spain and his unnamed bride,[13] and a message to the reader (Murúa 2008 [1616]:14r–15r).

The first book of Murúa's *General History of Peru* is titled "Book One on the origin and descent of the Incas, lords of this Kingdom of Peru, the conquests they made in different provinces and nations and [their] civil wars until the arrival of the Spaniards. . . ."[14] It is the largest of the three books comprising the manuscript and contains all but two of the illustrations. The book spans 410 pages, thirty of which feature illustrations, and is organized into ninety-three chapters.

The second book is titled "Of [the] Inca's government in this kingdom and the rites and ceremonies that they kept."[15] This middle section consists of forty chapters written across approximately 190 pages and includes no illustrations. As implied by the title, this book provides descriptions of various aspects of the kingdom, as well as the rites and celebrations of the Inca. Large amounts of book 2 have been taken directly from other sources.

The third book is titled "The Kingdom of Peru and its principal cities and towns."[16] Similar in length to the second book, it spans some 190 pages and is divided into thirty-one chapters.[17] It features one reused drawing as its cover page, labeled by Murúa as "The Coat of Arms of the Inca Kingdom." Originally created by Felipe Guaman Poma de Ayala for an earlier text, this illustration was removed from the abandoned work and inserted into the *General History of Peru*. The third book includes additional information on the functioning of the former Inca Empire and descriptions of the most important Spanish cities in the Viceroyalty of Peru.

11 These pages are not reproduced in this translation (see Murúa 2008 [1616]).
12 A similar coat of arms appears in *The First New Chronicle* (Guaman Poma de Ayala 2004 [1615]:83).
13 Murúa dedicated his work to Prince Felipe (1605–1665), the future king of Spain (Felipe IV), and his bride, whose name is left blank in the manuscript. Since Felipe married Elisabeth (Isabel) of France, in 1615, it is curious that the place remained blank.
14 "Libro sobre el origen y descendencia de los Incas, señores de este Reino del Perú, las conquistas que hicieron en diferentes provincias y naciones y [sus] guerras civiles hasta la llegada de los españoles . . ."
15 "Del gobierno que los incas tuvieron en este reino y ritos y ceremonias que guardaban."
16 "Donde se trata en general y particular de este reino del Perú y las ciudades principales y villas de él."
17 Chapters 11 and 12 of book 3 were later removed, but their former existence is recorded in the table of contents. Furthermore, a new unnumbered chapter was added between chapters 8 and 9 of book 3, which provides detailed information on the Mercedarians in Peru (Murúa 2008 [1616]:329r–330r). The removal of the old chapters and the insertion of new chapters appear to have been done on the advice Alonso Remón after Murúa arrived in Spain.

The manuscript ends with a table of contents, which lists several chapters that are no longer held within the work. The table of contents also does not list one chapter that appears to be a last-minute addition. These discrepancies serve as evidence of critical final modifications made to the manuscript after Murúa's arrival in Spain.

Because of its late publication (1964), and the absence of translations, Murúa's masterwork on the history of the Incas has been underused by scholars interested in the Indigenous history of the Andes and the early Colonial Period of Peru.[18] However, in the past two decades, because of the extensive research of a core set of scholars, led by Juan M. Ossio, Thomas B. F. Cummins, and Rolena Adorno, the contents of Murúa's works, both his 1590 and 1616 manuscripts, have come under intensive study. Ossio's and Cummins's investigations, and the dedicated work of their colleagues, have produced two groundbreaking, edited volumes (Cummins and Anderson 2008; Cummins and Ossio 2019) that provide a vast corpus of new information on the life and times of Murúa and the production of his works. These authors have also overseen the production of unprecedentedly accurate facsimiles of Murúa's manuscripts. A facsimile of Murúa's earlier work, *History and Genealogy of the Inca Kings of Peru* (2004 [1590]), which is currently held in a private collection, was edited by Ossio and published by Testimonio Compañía Editorial in 2004.[19] Later, Cummins and Ossio (2019) arranged that all the drawings from Murúa's *History and Genealogy of the Inca Kings of Peru* and his *General History of Peru* be published and placed online.[20] We also now have access to both a printed

---

18   Before the Getty Research Institute printed a facsimile of the *General History of Peru* and provided a digital copy online, there had been only two earlier printed editions, both produced by Manuel Ballesteros Gaibrois (1964, 1987). The first edition, now long out of print, is a two-volume set that carefully reproduces the original document from photostatic images produced when the manuscript was briefly in the Oxford University Library (Anderson 2008:3). The second edition is a far inferior version that contains many transcription and copyediting mistakes.

19   This document is generally called the Galvin Murúa Manuscript, in respect to its current owner. At some time, this manuscript was removed from the Jesuit College in Alcalá de Henares (Spain) and relocated to the Jesuit archive in Poyanne (France). Sometime in the 1950s, the manuscript entered the complex network of rare book dealers and was eventually purchased by John Galvin. It was recognized as a missing work of Martín de Murúa by Juan Ossio in the early 1980s, and he has published widely on it. Since this manuscript has a title page, we prefer to refer to it by the name assigned to it by Murúa, the *History and Genealogy of the Inca Kings of Peru*. For a full history of this manuscript and its recent rediscovery, see Anderson (2008), Adorno and Boserup (2008), and Ossio (2008a, 2008b, 2009, 2019a, 2019b).

20   For the drawings from the *History and Genealogy of the Inca Kings of Peru* (2004 [1590]), see https://assets.ey.com/content/dam/ey-sites/ey-com/es_pe/topics/growth/ey -manuscrito-galvin-vi.pdf.

and a digital facsimile of Murúa's *General History of Peru* published by the Getty Research Institute (2008),[21] which now owns the manuscript.[22]

The recently published facsimiles of Murúa's works have provided unprecedented access to them, resulting in a flurry of investigations, many conducted by renowned Andean researchers.[23] Numerous articles have focused on Murúa's writings, examining the physical production of his manuscripts and the illustrations. Adorno (2008), Adorno and Boserup (2008), Turner (2019), and Ossio (2004 [1590], 2019a) have explored the intricate way in which the *History and Genealogy of the Inca Kings of Peru* (2004 [1590]) was created, expanded, illustrated, dismantled, and then reassembled. They have also highlighted how specific illustrations from this work were utilized to enhance Murúa's *General History of Peru*. Adorno (2008) and Adorno and Boserup (2008) have also analyzed the handwriting of the surprisingly large number of individuals involved in the production of Murúa's works, most importantly in the corrected sections and in the passages marked for removal by the Mercedarian and Royal censors.

Phipps, Turner, and Trentelman (2008) and Trentelman (2019) have examined the colors and the composition of the paints used in the illustrations, along with Cummins (2008b, 2019a, 2019b), who discussed the different artists involved in creating the illustrations. Phipps (2019) has also compared the clothing shown in the manuscripts with those that continued to be used in the Andes. Notably, Adorno (2008), Adorno and Boserup (2008), Ossio (2001, 2008a, 2008b, 2019b), among other researchers, have provided detailed comparisons between the various surviving drafts of Murúa's two works and that of Guaman Poma de Ayala.[24] Furthermore, Francisco Borja de Aguinagalde (2019) has discovered a wealth of new archival data on Murúa and his family. These chapters, articles, and numerous others written in

---

21   For the facsimile, see https://www.getty.edu/publications/resources/virtuallibrary
      /9780892368952.pdf. For the drawings from *General History of Peru*, see https://assets.ey
      .com/content/dam/ey-sites/ey-com/es_pe/topics/growth/ey-manuscrito-getty-vi.pdf or
      www.getty.edu/art/collection/object/105SX6.

22   For this study, we have relied on both the printed and the online versions of Murúa's
      Historia General del Piru produced by the Getty Research Institute. Accordingly, when
      we refer to specific folios, we use their folio numerations. Murúa's *General History of Peru*
      was formerly known as the Wellington Manuscript and is now referred to by many as the
      Getty Murúa Manuscript. Since this work has a title page, we refer to it as the *General
      History of Peru*, the name given to it by its author.

23   Other especially noteworthy early articles on Murúa's works include Álvarez-Calderón
      (2007), Ballesteros Gaibrois (1964), Pärssinen (1989), Pease (1992), and Rowe (1987).

24   Adorno and Ossio have spent much of their careers studying the works of Murúa and
      Guaman Poma de Ayala. I have provided references to some of their most recent articles
      and leave the reader to explore their vast contributions to Andean historiography.

the past decade have transformed our understanding of the life, times, and works of Martín de Murúa.

Murúa's *History and Genealogy of the Inca Kings of Peru* (2004 [1590]) and his *General History of Peru* (2008 [1616]) are particularly thought provoking, as Murúa's primary artistic collaborator was the now famous Andean author Felipe Guaman Poma de Ayala. Guaman Poma de Ayala completed his own chronicle in 1615 titled *First New Chronicle and Good Government*.[25] Guaman Poma de Ayala's work is a vast, nearly 1,200-page letter to the king of Spain that includes nearly 400 illustrations. Although it was completed around the same time that Murúa finished his own history, it was discovered in the Danish Royal Library in 1908 by the German scholar Richard Pietschmann. Thanks to Rolena Adorno and the Danish Royal Library, a digital facsimile of the *First New Chronicle* is now available online.[26]

It is evident that Guaman Poma de Ayala worked with Murúa for a period of time, as several of Guaman Poma de Ayala's illustrations are included within Murúa's *General History of Peru*. Moreover, many of the illustrations found in Guaman Poma de Ayala's the *First New Chronicle* are based on drawings that he previously made for Murúa's *History and Genealogy of the Inca Kings of Peru*. In other words, these three manuscripts, which are among the most important works to survive from the early Colonial Period of Peru—and describe the history of the Incas, the invasion of the Andes by the Spanish, and the major cities of the Viceroyalty of Peru—have a complex and overlapping history, just like their authors' lives.

Martín de Murúa's *General History of Peru*, perhaps due to its large size, remains one of the last early works on the history of the Incas to be translated from Spanish into English.[27] In this work, we translate the first book of Murúa's magnificent manuscript and offer extensive footnotes to provide scholarly contexts to many his observations. We also provide this brief introduction on the life of Martín de Murúa and his works, acknowledging our indebtedness to those authors listed in the preceding passages, and particularly those included within Cummins and Anderson's (2008) and Cummins and Ossio's (2019) edited volumes.

---

25   *El primer nueva corónica y buen gobierno.*
26   See http://www5.kb.dk/permalink/2006/poma/info/en/frontpage.htm.
27   To add to the complexity of Murúa's works, a third manuscript, now known to be a late, poor copy of the *History and Genealogy of the Inca Kings of Peru* (2004 [1590]), was found in the Casa Mayor de la Campania in Loyola (Guipúscoa, Spain). This copy is referred to as the Loyola Manuscript and was published in 1911, 1922, and 1946 (see Ossio 2008b). In this work, we do not directly deal with the Loyola Manuscript.

THE EARLY LIFE OF MARTÍN DE MURÚA

Less than two decades ago, our knowledge of Martín de Murúa's life was limited (Ossio 2004 [1590]). However, thanks to the dedicated scholarship of Adorno, Cummins, Ossio, and their colleagues, our understanding of Murúa has significantly expanded. As mentioned, we now have two edited volumes that examine the life and works of Murúa (Cummins and Anderson 2008; Cummins and Ossio 2019), along with numerous independent scholarly studies, some decades old, but most written more recently.

Despite these recent advancements, the documentation of Martín de Murúa's life remains inadequate, with significant periods for which information is scarce. Given his extended stay in Peru and the important positions he held within the Mercedarian Order, the lack of information on his life is surprising. Murúa briefly mentions the positions he held in Peru and Bolivia in his written works, and researchers have extensively discussed a series of official letters found in the *General History of Peru*, which document his visits to various cities between 1611 and 1615. Nevertheless, the number of clear and specific details is frustratingly limited. Fortunately, Francisco de Borja de Aguinagalde (2019), working in the archives of Escoriaza and elsewhere, provides the first comprehensive overview of Murúa's formative years and his final months in Spain. As a result of Borja de Aguinagalde's work, we now know far more about Murúa's early and late life in Spain, compared to the many decades he spent in Peru.

Martín de Murúa was born in the Gipuzkoa region in the town of Escoriaza, part of the autonomous Basque Country of northern Spain. Although his exact date of birth is not known, baptismal records indicate that an unnamed male child from the Murúa family was baptized in the town of Escoriaza on 3 November 1566. Borja de Aguinagalde (2019:205) suggests that this record may correspond to the birth and baptism of Martín de Murúa. Furthermore, documents found by Borja de Aguinagalde reveal that Murúa returned to his hometown of Escoriaza on 5 November 1615, just a month before his death on 5 December 1615. If the day of baptism is correct, Murúa lived just under fifty years, the majority of which were spent in the Andes.

Martín de Murúa was one of six children (four sons and two daughters) born to Pedro de Murúa, a barber and surgeon of Escoriaza, and María Ruiz de Gallaistegui (Borja de Aguinagalde 2019:200). The Mercedarians became active in the Basque area in the late 1400s and later established monasteries in Gipuzkoa and Bizkaia, overseen by a larger facility in Burcena (i.e., Baracaldo). In 1562, the head of the Mercedarian Order of the region initiated the construction of a *beaterio*, named Santa Ana, for devout women. This *beaterio*'s construction is significant for this

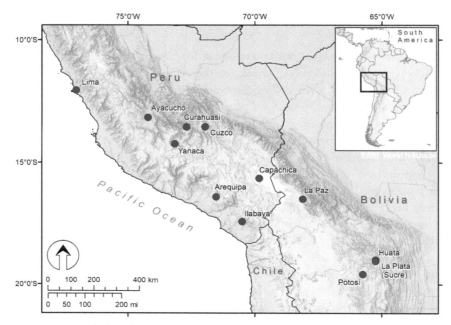

Figure 0.1. Map of southern Peru and northern Bolivia (drawn by David Reid).

study because Martín de Murúa's younger sister, Cataline de Espiritu Santa, would also become a Mercedarian and joined the Santa Ana Beaterio as a prominent member. In addition, Martín de Murúa provided substantial contributions for the *beaterio*'s construction, sending at least three large payments while he was overseas. Presumably, based on these contributions, he requested and received permission to be its first chaplain upon his return to Spain from Peru (Borja de Aguinagalde 2019:202–203, 243).[28]

MARTÍN DE MURÚA'S ARRIVAL IN PERU AND HIS FIRST POSITIONS

Martín de Murúa joined the Orden de Nuestra Señora de la Merced y la Redención de los Cautivos, better known as the Mercedarian Order, in Spain at an unknown date. However, in a deleted section of his *General History of the Incas*, Murúa notes that Fray Pedro Guerra "placed the habit upon me" (Murúa 2008 [1616]:327v).

---

28   In August 1592, Martín de Murúa's mother, Maria Ruiz de Gallaistegui, proudly recorded that two of her sons belonged to religious orders: Martín was a Mercedarian, and his younger brother Andrés (n. 1572) was a Franciscan (Borja de Aguinagalde 2019:206).

Although Murúa's departure from Spain and his arrival in Peru are unrecorded, Ossio (2008a:93, n11) convincingly suggests that Murúa traveled with Pedro Guerra to Peru in 1577, making him eleven at the time if we accept the unnamed baptismal record.[29] Some suggest that his first posting as priest was in the early 1580s in the town of San Salvador de Capachica on the shores of Lake Titicaca (Ballesteros Gaibrois 1987:6; Morrone 2019; Ossio 2008b:436).[30] While his early movements in Peru are not well defined, we know that he was in Cuzco by 1585 (Adorno 2008:116; Barriga 1942; Palacio 1999) and he most likely left for Arequipa in late 1599 (figure o.1).

MARTÍN DE MURÚA AND THE WRITING OF THE *HISTORY AND GENEALOGY OF THE INCA KINGS* (2004 [1590])

During his time in Cuzco, Murúa rose to become the *procurada del convento* and may have held other important positions as well. His position as the head administrator of a religious community in Cuzco provided Murúa access to a wide range of Indigenous elites and Spanish officials, and perhaps to Church scribes who could help him produce his first work. Murúa appears to have finished his first work, *History and Genealogy of the Inca Kings*, in May 1590, as indicated by the date on its cover page.[31] Several months later, he submitted this manuscript (or a slightly different version) to a group of local lords (*curacas* and *caciques*) for reading and commentary. However, for unknown reasons, their response took several years. By 1595, Murúa still held official positions within the Mercedarian Order in Cuzco, but he was also representing the Mercedarians over a land dispute in the village of Curahuasi (Adorno 2008:116; Ossio 2008b:436). The following year, on 15 May 1596, six years after it was completed, Murúa's work was returned to him by the local lords of Cuzco.[32] Their response was very positive, and Murúa received

---

29   Others hold different opinions; e.g., Ballesteros Gaibrois (1964:xxxiv) speculates that Murúa arrived in Peru between 1550 and 1560, dates that predate Murúa's possible birthdate as suggested by Borja de Aguinagalde (2019).

30   The time that Murúa spent in Capachica is unclear, although he does mention that he worked there in the *History and Genealogy of the Inca Kings of Peru*.

31   The cover page of the *History and Genealogy of the Inca Kings of Peru* contains the words, "[finished] in the month of May 1590." The production history of this manuscript is surprisingly complex and spanned more than a decade. I offer a short summary here, based on a far more detailed history presented by Adorno and Boserup (2008).

32   We know of this late response by the *curacas* and *caciques* of Cuzco from a reused illustration now contained within the *General History of Peru* (Murúa 2008 [1616]:307v). This sheet was removed from its original text and placed within the *General History of Peru* so that the drawing made by Guaman Poma de Ayala, which shows the coat of arms of the

their strong endorsement for the publication of his work (Adorno and Boserup 2008:9–12).[33]

Rather than finishing his book after receiving the recommendations of the *curacas* and *caciques* of Cuzco, Murúa continued to expand it over the next decade: taking notes, rewriting parts, adding new sections, and having illustrations drawn. We know that Murúa was still making significant changes to the work in 1598 when he added an entirely new book to the manuscript (Adorno and Boserup 2008:10; Ossio 2008b:436) and that he continued to make other changes over the next several years, even after he left Cuzco.

Murúa was the procurator of the Mercedarian Friary, San Juan Letrán, in Arequipa in late 1599 (Ballesteros Gaibrois 1964:34n5; Ossio 2008b:436; Pease 1992). He provides a day-to-day description of the now-famous 19 February 1600 eruption of Huaynaputina, suggesting that he witnessed it. Relatively soon afterward, in the early 1600s, Murúa was sent to the Province of Aymaraes, where, according to Guaman Poma de Ayala (2004 [1615]:648 [662], 781 [795]), he served as the priest of the town of Yanaca and of three nearby villages, Pocohuanca, Pacica, and Pichiua (figure 0.2).[34]

Sometime, presumably toward the end of his work on the *History and Genealogy of the Inca Kings*, Murúa hired two artists to develop illustrations for the manuscript (Adorno and Boserup 2008:43). The first artist, whose name is not known, drew portraits of the ten royal Incas and Coyas. Guaman Poma de Ayala was the second

---

Kingdom of Peru, could be reused. The other side of the folio contains a copy of a letter of recommendation from the Cuzco elite, dated 15 May 1596, written by the same scribe who transcribed the *History and Genealogy of the Inca Kings of Peru*. However, a slightly different title is provided for the work below the letter of recommendation. Written by Murúa, it reads *General History and Book on the Origin and Lineage of the Inca Lords of This Western Kingdoms of Peru*. This different title may simply represent a last-minute title change introduced by Murúa, or it may indicate that Murúa had produced a modified version of his work that is now lost. Adorno and Boserup (2008:11–17) strongly argue in favor of the former existence of a now lost version of Murúa's work that they call "The Cuzco Version." (It should also be considered that since the letter from the Indigenous leaders of Cuzco and the new title are written by different individuals, it is possible that they were composed on different dates and thus do not have the close association that is generally presumed.)

33 This act of public reading is similar to that undertaken by Pedro Sarmiento de Gamboa in 1572 after he completed his *History of the Incas*. If Murúa knew of Sarmiento's work, he may have wanted to also include such a public confirmation.

   This letter was addressed to King Felipe II (1556–1598), while the final version of the *General History of Peru* was approved by King Felipe III (1578–1621) and dedicated to the future Felipe IV (1605–1665).

34 Guaman Poma de Ayala (2004 [1615]:607 [621]) certainly visited Yanaca and the nearby village of Tiapara.

Figure 0.2. An early colonial bell tower stands near the center of Yanaca, perhaps marking the location where Murúa once preached (photograph by Valentin Ubidio Maldonado Allcca).

artist to provide drawings for the *History and Genealogy of the Inca Kings*. He added coats of arms to the already drawn portraits of the Coyas and contributed more than 100 other illustrations to the rest of the manuscript. Guaman Poma de Ayala's illustrations are found on pages that were left blank within the already written manuscript, or they were added in margin spaces—frequently at the end of chapters. Murúa added captions and other notes to the illustrations provided by both of these artists, indicating that he reviewed their contributions and continued working on the manuscript, at least in small ways, after the drawings had been added. Years later, when Murúa completed his *General History of Peru*, the illustrations contained within the *History and Genealogy of the Inca Kings*, particularly those of the Incas and the Coyas, served as a source of inspiration for yet another anonymous artist to illustrate Murúa's final manuscript.

After more than a decade and a half of collecting information and having two artists draw illustrations, Murúa stopped working on his *History and Genealogy of the Inca Kings*, and began writing a new, expanded work. This new manuscript would conclude with his now-famous *General History of Peru*. The work would contain a fresh set of thirty drawings and a complex cover page. The work would also contain four old illustrations that were removed by Murúa from the abandoned *History and Genealogy of the Inca Kings* manuscript and repurposed to be included in the new writing project. Of the four repurposed illustrations that were taken from the *History and Genealogy of the Inca Kings* and inserted into the *General History of Peru*, three were works of Guaman Poma de Ayala and one was from the anonymous artist who had also worked on the first manuscript.

THE RELATIONSHIP BETWEEN MARTÍN DE MURÚA AND FELIPE GUAMAN POMA DE AYALA

The relationship between Martín de Murúa and Felipe Guaman Poma de Ayala has long captivated scholars' interests, even more so with the voyeuristic knowledge that their relationship began with cooperation and ended in acrimony. Interpretations of their relationship are sometimes also clouded by racial and nationalist sediments and the understandable concern that European colonization efforts unquestionably elevated the achievements of westerners and diminished the contributions of Indigenous peoples.

When only Murúa's *General History of Peru* and Guaman Poma de Ayala's *The First New Chronicle* were known, it was widely assumed that Guaman Poma de Ayala had worked closely with Murúa, as both an illustrator and informant, and that their collaboration had taken place over a long time. However, the discovery and publication of Murúa's *History and Genealogy of the Inca Kings* have clarified the production sequence of the different manuscripts and the distinct contributions of these two writers (Ossio 2008a, 2008b). In an unprecedentedly detailed study of Murúa's and Guaman Poma de Ayala's manuscripts, Adorno and Boserup (2008) suggest that the collaboration between these two individuals was later, shorter, and more restricted than assumed.

As outlined above, Murúa's *History and Genealogy of the Inca Kings* was the first of the three manuscripts to be completed and it was presented to a group of local leaders in Cuzco in 1590. This Cuzco manuscript most likely did not contain illustrations, since artwork is generally added during the final stages of manuscript preparation (Adorno and Boserup 2008:23, 43) and the Cuzco elite made no mention of illustrations when they wrote their note of approval in 1596. Murúa continued to work on this manuscript, or more likely a later and more extended version of it, after 1596 (Adorno and Boserup 2008:9). We know that Murúa was still working on the manuscript after he left Cuzco in the late 1590s, as it provides a seemingly eyewitness description on the February 1600 Huaynaputina eruption in the Arequipa region. The fact that remarkably similar illustrations of this eruption are included in both Murúa's *History and Genealogy of the Inca Kings* and Guaman Poma de Ayala's *The First New Chronicle* pushes their encounter into the early 1600s, a time after Murúa had left Arequipa and was working in the Aymaraes region.

While Murúa was stationed in Arequipa, Guaman Poma de Ayala lost a series of lawsuits in Ayacucho focused on the recovery of family lands (Prado Tello and Prado Pardo 1991). On 19 December 1600, Guaman Poma de Ayala was sentenced to 200 lashes and forced into exile for two years. This exile may account for his movement into the Aymaraes around the same time that Murúa also entered the region to start a new assignment in the town of Yanaca.

Guaman Poma de Ayala (2004 [1615]:729 [743]) places himself in the Aymaraes sometime between 1604 and 1606, during the short time that Gaspar de Zúñiga Acevedo y Velasco (aka Carlos Monterrey) was the viceroy of Peru (Ossio 2001; 2004 [1590]:18, 50; 2008a:77, 84, 92). His detailed account of the abuses of Murúa in Yanaca, and his references to other individuals who lived in that town, suggest that Guaman Poma de Ayala visited the community, and it was there, perhaps, that the collaborative work between the two authors took place. We also know that Murúa was absent from the Aymaraes for part of 1606 as he was attending the birth of Felipe IV in Cuzco, reducing their overlap even more. This leaves a relatively narrow window of two, perhaps three, years when we know that both men were in the Aymaraes.

As Ossio (2008a:84) posits, we may never know "what happened between 1604 and 1606 in the Province of Aymaraes to produce the enmity that led Guaman Poma to refer in such derogatory terms to someone who was formerly his friend and employ." Nevertheless, there are some clues. While Murúa makes no direct mention of Guaman Poma de Ayala in either of his surviving texts, the same cannot be said for Guaman Poma de Ayala (2004 [1615]:517 [521], 647–649 [661–663], 906 [920], 1080 [1090]), who directly attacks Murúa in four different sections of his work (Ossio 2008a:78). Guaman Poma de Ayala states that Murúa fathered illegitimate children,[35] and was a cruel parish priest who frequently abused members of his parish. To emphasize that later point, he provides a drawing of Murúa beating a woman for not weaving fast enough—an event that most likely took place in Yanaca (figure 0.3).

---

35   When discussing the possibility that Murúa fathered children in the Andes, it is worth noting that among Murúa's possessions when he died was a "a shiny ribbon that is said to be the insignia worn by the Creole daughters of Spaniards in the Indies" (Borja de Aguinagalde 2019:244). Perhaps the ribbon was a keepsake from a daughter.

Figure 0.3. Guaman Poma de Ayala's illustration from his *First New Chronicle* (2004 [1615]:647 [661]) showing the ill treatment of a woman weaver by Martín de Murúa. The caption reads "Fathers/Fry Mercedario Morua. They are violent and authoritative and treat Indians so poorly that they use a stick to make them work in the doctrines of this Kingdom, there is no solution" (courtesy of Det Kongelige Bibliotek).

Guaman Poma de Ayala also charges Murúa with being an incompetent historian. In a direct criticism of Murúa's *History and Genealogy of the Inca Kings*, which he had helped to illustrate, Guaman Poma de Ayala accuses Murúa of failing to research the entire history of the Incas and for being a racist writer:

> Fray Martin de Murúa, of the order of Our Lady of Mercy of the Redemption of Captives, wrote another book about the history of the Incas. He began to write it but did not finish—better said—he neither began nor finished—because he does not explain where the Inca came from, how, in what way, or from where. He also does not explain if [the Inca] had the right to rule nor how his lineage ended. He did not write about the ancient kings, the great lords or other matters; instead, he wrote entirely against the Indians. (Guaman Poma de Ayala 2004 [1615]:1080 [1090])

Elsewhere, Guaman Poma de Ayala (2004 [1615]:906 [920]) reveals even more personal grievances he harbored against Murúa, accusing him of both wife stealing and dismissing his views on Andean history:

> Look Christian, at all that I have suffered, even to the extent that a Mercedarian friar named Murúa attempted to take my wife away from me in the town of Yanaca. These are the offenses, harms, and misfortunes [I have encountered]. They refuse to tolerate [a] Christianized Indian who speaks in Spanish; they became frightened and ordered my immediate expulsion from these towns. They pretend that we are fools, donkeys, in order to take away everything. (Guaman Poma de Ayala 2004 [1615]:906[920])

It seems clear that after working for some time with Murúa, Guaman Poma de Ayala dissolved the relationship, having seen Murúa's abusive behavior, his lust, and his disregard for Indigenous people, even for those individuals who had learned to read and write in Spanish. It is even possible that his exposure to Murúa's manuscript, and his intense dislike of the man, motivated Guaman Poma de Ayala to begin his own chronicle, which grew to be filled with 400 drawings.

Within this scenario, the likelihood of Guaman Poma de Ayala being a key informant in the production of the *History and Genealogy of the Inca Kings* is reduced. While the contents of the *History and Genealogy of the Inca Kings* and the *First New Chronicle* differ considerably, the outlines of the two are similar, indicating that Guaman Poma de Ayala used Murúa's *History and Genealogy of the Inca Kings* as a general guide for his own work. It is also not surprising that many features of Murúa's first book were repeated in his second book project, the *General History of Peru*. All three works, for example, share the same general organization: beginning with precontact times, followed by the conquest, and concluded with a description of various Spanish cities. They each also include separate chapters on the different Incas and Coyas as well as on important "captains," a feature unique to these two

Figure 0.4. Two illustrations, both drawn by Guaman Poma de Ayala, showing the encounter between Inca Sayri Tupa Yupanqui and Viceroy Andrés Hurtado de Mendoza in Lima. The left illustration comes from Murúa's (2004 [1590]:49v) *History and Genealogy of the Inca Kings*. The right drawing is from Guaman Poma de Ayala's (2004 [1615]:440 [442]) *The First New Chronicle* (courtesy of Det Kongelige Bibliotek and EY).

writers. Perhaps the largest, overlapping sections between the two authors, in these three works, are their descriptions of what they call "*calles*," or what we now call male and female age groups (Rowe 1958). Furthermore, it can be noted that many of the illustrations drawn by Guaman Poma de Ayala for the *History and Genealogy of the Inca Kings* are similar to drawings found in his *First New Chronicle*. This is not surprising, since Guaman Poma de Ayala would have remembered many of the drawings he had produced while working for Murúa and then selected to reproduce them within his own work (figure 0.4).

There is also the occasional phrase or description that can be found in all three works. Nevertheless, given the massive size of the works and the fact that Guaman Poma de Ayala worked with Murúa in Yanaca, there is surprisingly little overlap between the written texts of these two authors. In other words, one author did not copy large sections from the other, nor did one serve as the single informant or source of information for the other. The evidence suggests that these two authors wrote their works separately, with little direct collaboration beyond the work that Guaman Poma de Ayala did as an illustrator for Murúa.

It should be emphasized that while three drawings by Guaman Poma de Ayala were eventually included in Murúa's second work, the *General History of Peru*, this does not indicate that Guaman Poma de Ayala had a hand in its production. On the contrary: their relationship had dissolved at least a decade earlier, after Guaman Poma de Ayala finished illustrating the *History and Genealogy of the Inca Kings*. Guaman Poma de Ayala would have had no knowledge of the *General History of Peru* or that three of his drawings would eventually be repurposed and included within it.[36] In other words, it is likely that Murúa never knew that Guaman Poma de Ayala began formally writing his own chronicle after their work together ended and that Guaman Poma de Ayala never knew that Murúa had started on a new version of Inca history after their collaboration had finished.

MARTÍN DE MURÚA AND THE WRITING OF
THE *GENERAL HISTORY OF PERU*

Although we do not know when Murúa abandoned the *History and Genealogy of the Inca Kings* and started drafting the *General History of Peru*, we do know that the latter was begun after the working relationship between Murúa and Guaman Poma de Ayala ended (ca. 1604 or 1606) and that the final version was completed in La Plata in 1615. Filling in this timeline, I believe that there is evidence that large parts of the *General History of Peru* were written while Murúa was in the city of Cuzco. For example, while describing the trophies brought to Cuzco after Tupa Inca Yupanqui's conquest of the islands of Avachumpi and Niñachumpi, Murúa (2008 [1616]:50v) writes, "He also brought back horse hides, heads, and bones, all to be shown here [in Cuzco] as an ancient custom among the Incas to showcase unusual items that could cause wonder and astonishment." Another example can be found within Murúa's description of the works built by Huayna Capac in the city of Tomebamba. Murúa (2008 [1616]:63v) writes, "In addition to this, [Huayna Capac] placed the most venerated and respected *huaca* here in Cuzco, called Huanacauri, [in Tomebamba]." A third case occurs where Murúa (2008 [1616]:76v) discusses a fabled gold chain of the Incas: "Some old and elderly people say that this wondrous

---

36   It can also be noted that Guaman Poma de Ayala's manuscript was sent to the king of Spain from Lima around 1615, while Murúa spent that year traveling from what is now Bolivia to Buenos Aires. Accordingly, there is little chance that they met after their working relationship ended in the Aymaraes or knew of their separate manuscripts.

chain was thrown in a large lake that is in Huaypo,[37] three leagues from this city of Cuzco, when the Spaniards arrived." A fourth case is found within Murúa's (2008 [1616]:180v) description of Vilcabamba: "[Toledo] was unaware of [Cusi Titu Yupanqui's] death because the Indians of Vilcabamba had carefully concealed it, preventing anyone from that area or here in Cuzco to leave or enter." While it is difficult to know how much scrutiny should be given to these lines, we do know that Murúa did visit Cuzco toward the end of his time in the Aymaraes, as he describes the celebrations that took place in Cuzco in 1606 with the birth of Felipe IV. Perhaps it was during that time that Murúa began his second manuscript, which is, interestingly, dedicated to Prince Felipe.

A newly discovered document may also provide a possible date for when Murúa ended his time in the Aymaraes. Among the documents found in his possession when Murúa died was a receipt dated 29 June 1609, indicating that he owed nothing to the inhabitants of an unnamed town (Borja de Aguinagalde 2019:243). It is likely, given what we know about his life, that the unnamed town was that of Yanaca and that Murúa secured this document as a form of personal protection at the end of his turbulent time in the Aymaraes.

Evidence that Murúa was in Lima on 15 February 1610, about seven months after the receipt was issued, has been found independently in the archives in Lima (Lohmann Villena 2004 cited by Ossio 2008a:93 n.21) and in Spain (Borja de Aguinagalde 2019:216, 243). On that day he sent 1,000 pesos to the Santa Ana Beaterio in northern Spain. Within this donation, 200 pesos were for the direct benefit of his sister, Cataline de Espiritu Santo, who was already a member of that religious community. This was the first of at least three large donations that Murúa sent to the Santa Ana Beaterio (Borja de Aguinagalde 2019:216–217). Although the sources of his funds are unknown, his wealth appears surprising, and this substantial transfer of funds seems to support the common complaint, voiced by Guaman Poma de Ayala, that certain priests misappropriated funds intended for the Church or the *corregidor* for their own purposes. The donation also suggests that Murúa was already laying the groundwork for his return to Spain, since years later, he would seek and receive specific favors from the Mercedarians based on his history of contributions to this *beaterio*.

A set of letters now included within the front materials of the *General History of Peru* provide information on Murúa's movements within Peru and what is now Bolivia between the years 1611 and 1615. These letters were most likely once loose, but they are now included within the modern binding, grouped out of chronological order, in the front of the chronicle (Adorno and Boserup 2008:29). Eleven of these letters are copies made by Murúa, while the final four are originals, written

---

37   Modern Lake Huaypo.

in Spain after Murúa's return. Some of the letters were a formal part of the publication process, as the highest-ranking members of the Mercedarian Order needed to approve the work, along with specific offices of the Crown. Other letters are from various important individuals and appear to have been included by Murúa to document that there was widespread support for the publication of his manuscript.

From these letters, we know that on 25 August 1611, Murúa was in the town of Ilabaya in southern Peru. At that time, he may have been on his way to his new assignment as the priest of the small town of Huata near La Plata.[38] In Ilabaya, Murúa met with Martín Domínguez Jara, the commissioner of the Holy Office. Apparently, the archbishop of the city of La Paz, Domingo de Centeno y Valderrama, had asked Jara to read and provide comments on Murúa's work. Jara specifically mentions the work as being titled the *General History of Peru*, and he praises the contents of the book and notes that its publication would be a great service to God. These words of praise would be copied, almost verbatim, by several other officials who read the document over the next two years. This letter also provides evidence that Murúa had completed a readable draft of his magnum opus before he began his journey into Bolivia.

Murúa appears to have traveled from Ilabaya and arrived at the city of La Paz in early September of 1611. On 6 September, his book was read and approved by Pedro González, the inspector general for the bishop in La Paz. Two days later, on 8 September, the book was reviewed by Diego Guzmán, a leading cleric of the same city. Both officials strongly encouraged its publication.

From La Paz, Murúa traveled on to La Plata and perhaps the nearby village of Huata. Apparently, sensing that his time in the Americas was coming to an end, Murúa sent a second installment of funds to the Santa Ana Beaterio, from La Plata on 22 December of 1611. The funds were sent to Spain on the first convoy of ships to sail in the new year (1612), and they were delivered by his brother to the convent with a statement by Martín de Murúa requesting that he would be appointed as the first chaplain of the Santa Ana Beaterio on his return to Spain (Borja de Aguinagalde 2019:216).[39]

Although one would think that a career that included a high position in Cuzco but that ended with a posting in the small town of Huata would have been a cause

---

38   Huata was formally named Limpia Concepción de Nuestra Señora de Huata. Not to be confused with Santiago de Huata on the shores of Lake Titicaca. During Inca times, the city of La Plata was called Chuquisaca. The Spaniards changed its name, and La Plata became the capital of the Audiencia de Charcas. After independence, the city was renamed Sucre after Antonio José de Sucre.

39   At the time of his death, Murúa had an official letter from the Mercedarian Order naming him as the foundational priest of the Santa Ana Beaterio (Borja de Aguinagalde 2019:243).

for disappointment, Murúa shows no qualms with his new posting and on the cover page of his *General History of Peru*, he proudly documents his authorship, stating that it was written by "Fry Martín de Murúa, Elector General, of the Order of Our Lady of Mercy and the Redemption of the Captives, priest of Huata." He also mentions his position in Huata in the final chapter of book 2, writing that he was the priest and the commander of an "Indian town," one league from the city of La Plata, called Huata. In addition, several of the later letter writers mention Murúa as the priest of Huata. Therefore, he must have served in that position during the final years of the manuscript preparation.

One advantage of the location of Huata is that it provided Murúa with relatively easy access to a series of important individuals within the Church, located in La Plata, La Paz, and Potosí—the three most important towns of the Charcas, the political unit of the Viceroyalty for what is now Bolivia. All three of these towns also had Mercedarian complexes that no doubt facilitated his stays while different officials were reviewing his manuscript.

Murúa may have spent part of 1612 in Huata, fulfilling his duties for his new parish. However, in early February of that year, Murúa seems to have traveled the short distance from Huata to the city of La Plata seeking the penultimate round of approvals for his manuscript by members of the Church. On 8 February 1612, on the orders of Alonso de Peralta, the archbishop of La Plata, Francisco Bázquez, read and approved Murúa's work. In his letter of approval, Bázquez notes that Murúa had lived in Peru for more than fifty years. He also notes that Murúa was currently the priest of Huata, indicating that Murúa was already installed in his new assignment (Murúa 2008 [1616]:6r).

On 10 May 1612, in the same town of La Plata, the manuscript was read by Alexo de Benavente Solís, the canon of the Cathedral and City of La Plata, and he added his approval to the growing number of letters praising the book. Four days later, on 14 May 1612, Gutiérrez Fernández [Hidalgo], the conductor of the Cathedral of La Plata, read and approved the *General History of Peru*. In his letter, Fernández Hidalgo specifically mentions that Murúa had spent a long time serving in Cuzco. Since Fernández Hidalgo had been the conductor of the Cuzco Cathedral (1591–1597), perhaps this is a reference to the years that they spent together working in Cuzco.

Some ten months later, Murúa was in the immense city of Potosí, to gather the approval of the highest members of his own order. There the manuscript was read and approved of by three different individuals. On 3 March 1613, Luis Carrillo, the examiner for the General Language of Peru, approved the work. The following day Baltasar de los Reyes, the commander of the Mercedarian Convent in Potosí, and Pedro de Arze, the head of the Mercedarians in Cuzco, Charcas, and Santa Cruz de la Sierra, praised the book. Being a cautious administrator, Arze gave his recommendation for printing, adding the condition that the manuscript needed to gain approval of the Crown in Madrid. Adorno (2008:117) notes that Murúa had served under Arze during his time in Cuzco, so these two men already knew each other. Murúa may have stayed in Potosí for some five months, past 3 August 1613, when he sent additional funds to the Santa Ana Beaterio (Borja de Aguinagalde 2019:217).

After completing his work in Potosí, it can be assumed, Murúa returned to La Plata. There, he elicited the help of two scribes to produce a clean, final version of the manuscript intended for presentation to the Crown. These scribes most likely copied the penultimate version that had been read in Ilabaya, La Paz, La Plata, and Potosí but that is now lost. The task of writing was divided equally between the two scribes to such an extent that they switched turns midway through a specific page (Murúa 2008 [1616]:191v). Adorno (2008:100) writes, "Two scribes produced the bulk of the text, and their work is neatly divided at the approximate midpoint of the manuscript. Getty Scribe 1 started at folio 18r . . . and, with the exception of folio 20 (a latter addition set down by Getty Scribe 2), carried on through the sixth line of folio 191v. Getty Scribe 2 took over at the seventh line of folio 191v and calligraphed the text through folio 382r." As they were working on the final version, both scribes occasionally stopped and corrected minor errors in their work.[40]

When the transcription was completed, Murúa carefully read over the work, making several adjustments. For example, he inserted a few words into different chapters to provide clarification. He also corrected spelling and grammatical errors, and addressed cases of dittography and other scribal mistakes. Furthermore, he filled in blank spaces the scribes had left, perhaps because of illegible words in the draft document, and addressed other minor issues within the text. In total, more than 100 corrections were made at that time and later (Adorno 2008:101–102). Nevertheless, the scribes did a remarkable job in producing such a long manuscript. It also evident that while in La Plata, Murúa added a table of contents to the back of the work (Murúa 2008 [1616]:384r–387v) and copied the letters that he had collected up to that point (Adorno and Boserup 2008:29).[41]

After the scribes produced a clean copy of the *General History of Peru*, Murúa engaged an artist to create illustrations for the narrative. These illustrations were meant to be placed on pages that been intentionally left blank at the ends of chapters.[42] This artist had access to the *History and Genealogy of the Inca Kings* as they

---

40   We have marked the most notable of these corrections.

41   It is possible that Murúa retained the originals of the letters, and they were among the items in his possession when he died (see Borja de Aguinagalde 2019:240–246). The fact that the final letters from Potosí were copied suggests that the production of the final manuscript occurred after he had spent time in La Plata. See also Adorno (2008), Adorno and Boserup (2008), and Ossio (2019b) for detailed descriptions of the two Murúa manuscripts.

42   There are two additional blank folios within the manuscript, folios 94 and 121, which may have been intended to hold additional drawings that were never executed.

Figure 0.5. The four illustrations that were removed from the *History and Genealogy of the Inca Kings* and inserted into the *General History of Peru*. From left to right: A. Mama Rahua Ocllo (Murúa 2008 [1616]:79r), B. Huascar Inca (Murúa 2008 [1616]:84r), C. Coya Chuqui Llanto (Murúa 2008 [1616]:89r), and D. The coat of arms for the Kingdom of Peru (Murúa 2008 [1616]:307r). The first drawing was produced by an unknown illustrator, although the coat of arms in the upper left was later added by Guaman Poma de Ayala. The other three illustrations were drawn by Guaman Poma de Ayala (courtesy of The J. Paul Getty Museum, Los Angeles. Ms. Ludwig XIII 16 [83.MP.159]).

copied the coat of arms that accompanied the Coyas,[43] and incorporated them within the drawings of the Incas in the *General History of Peru* (figure 0.5). In certain portraits, the artist also chose to reproduce other aspects of the Incas and Coyas found in the *History and Genealogy of the Inca Kings* to include in their own illustrations of the Inca nobility.

However, for some unknown reason, the illustration project stalled after the drawing of Huayna Capac in book 1, chapter 31 (Murúa 2008 [1616]:64r). To complete the planned set of illustrations, Murúa returned to his *History and Genealogy of the Inca Kings* and removed four drawings that had been created decades earlier, for reuse in the *General History of Peru*. Since these four illustrations—three of which were by Guaman Poma de Ayala and one by a different artist—already had texts written on their opposite sides, sheets of blank paper were pasted over the old texts to hide them.

The first of these illustrations (Murúa 2008 [1616]:79r), drawn by the unknown artist, contained a portrait of Mama Rahua Ocllo and a coat of arms that had been added by Guaman Poma de Ayala. The opposite side of the drawing contained chapter 29 from the *History and Genealogy of the Inca Kings*. This folio was pasted over with a blank page to conceal the old text (figure 0.5).

---

43   These coats of arms were initially incorporated into the Coya drawings in the *History and Genealogy of the Inca Kings of Peru* by Guaman Poma de Ayala, after an unknown artist had completed them. For additional insights into the two Murúa manuscripts, see Adorno (2008), Adorno and Boserup (2008), and Ossio (2019b).

The second relocated illustration was inserted right before chapter 42 of book 1 (Murúa 2008 [1616]:84r). This illustration is meant to provide a portrait of Huascar Inca; however, the original drawing, created by Guaman Poma de Ayala, was intended to depict a more general scene titled, "How the Inca kings traveled" in the *History and Genealogy of the Inca Kings*. To bridge the transition from its previous usage to its new purpose, Murúa (2008 [1616]:84r) added a new title at the top of the drawing, stating that it was illustrating Huascar Inca. The opposite side of the illustrated page featured the title page of book 3 of the *History and Genealogy of the Inca Kings*, so this folio was concealed by a blank sheet.

The third relocated illustration was inserted just before chapter 43 of book 1 (Murúa 2008 [1616]:89r). Murúa modified this drawing, suggesting that it was a portrait of Coya Chuqui Llanto, the wife of Huascar Inca. However, it was originally drawn by Guaman Poma de Ayala for a more general use in the *History and Genealogy of the Inca Kings*, depicting "How the Coyas and Queens, women of the Inca, went about." To aid the reader in understanding its new usage, Murúa (2008 [1616]:89r) added a new title at the top of the drawing, indicating that it illustrated "Chuquillanto, wife of Huascar Inca." The opposite side of the illustrated page contains chapter 9 of the *History and Genealogy of the Inca Kings*, titled "The costume and dress that all the *ñustas*, Coyas, and married women worn." This folio was covered with a blank sheet to hide the text.

The fourth relocated illustration, showing the "coat of arms for the Kingdom of Peru," was inserted in the *General History of the Incas* as the frontispiece for book 3 (Murúa 2008 [1616]:307r).[44] This illustration was originally drawn by Guaman Poma de Ayala for use in the *History and Genealogy of the Inca Kings*. On the opposite side of the page is the letter of recommendation from the Cuzco elite, dated 15 May 1596.[45] A blank sheet of paper was pasted over this letter so that the illustration could be reused, and the text hidden.[46]

---

44 The coat of arms of the Kingdom of Peru is composed of four smaller coats of arms representing the four *suyus*.

45 The date of this letter has caused confusion in understanding Murúa's and Guaman Poma de Ayala's collaborative efforts. Because the letter is dated 1596 and concerns a submission that occurred some five years earlier, some scholars have logically suggested that the submission date can be used to date Murúa's and Guaman Poma de Ayala's working relationship. However, Adorno and Boserup (2008) propose that the verso of the letter was originally blank and that Guaman Poma de Ayala illustrated this blank side years after the letter was written. If this is the case, then, the date of the letter marks a time after which the working relationship between the author and the illustrator began.

46 It is worth noting that by 1613, when this sheet was removed from the *History and Genealogy of the Inca Kings of Peru* and inserted into the *General History of Peru*, the letter of recommendation from the *curacas* and *caciques* of Cuzco was seen as less valuable than the artistic work contained on its opposite side.

At some time during its production, perhaps once the illustrations were completed, Murúa wrote the title of his new book, *General History of Peru*, on the top of the elaborately decorated cover page. At the bottom of the page, he wrote, "In La Plata, in the year [of] our [lord] 1613" (Murúa 2008 [1616]:2r).[47] The same date was also placed at the bottom of the final page of the manuscript. Nevertheless, his work was far from over. Even though the text and the illustrations for the manuscript were now complete, and Murúa had assembled an impressive collection of supporting letters, he still needed approval from his order (both in the Viceroyalty and in Spain) and from the Spanish Crown before his work could be published.

Murúa began his journey back to Spain in mid-1614.[48] Instead of traveling from the village of Huata to the port of Arica on the Pacific, where he could board one of the many Spanish ships transporting silver from the mines of Potosí to Spain, Murúa chose to travel eastward across the Andes to set sail on the Atlantic from Buenos Aires. On 28 September 1614, Murúa was in the city of Córdoba, in modern-day Argentina, where he obtained another letter of support. His book was read and praised by Luis de Quiñones Osorio, the governor of Tucumán. While this reading was not necessary for the publication process, it's possible that Murúa wanted to accumulate additional letters of support.

Upon reaching the Spanish seaport of Buenos Aires, Murúa's book was read, praised, and approved on 17 December 1614 by Francisco de Irujo, the head of the Holy Office of the Inquisition. This step must have been a great relief to Murúa, as it was the last approval required before he departed for Spain, where he hoped his book would be printed with the assistance and support of the Mercedarian Order.

MARTÍN DE MURÚA'S RETURN TO SPAIN

Until just a few years ago, little was known about Murúa's return to Spain and even the year of his death was unknown. However, thanks to the archival work of Francisco Borja de Aguinagalde (2019), the situation has changed. It is now known that Martín de Murúa departed from Buenos Aires in a convoy of six ships, carrying silver, perhaps from Potosí. Several of these ships, carrying Murúa and an Andean servant from Potosí, arrived in Lisbon on 15 August 1615. Over a month later, on 20 September 1615, Murúa sent a message to his brother Diego de Murúa in Escoriaza, indicating that he was still in Lisbon but short on money. Although Murúa must

---

47 This sentence was crossed out when the manuscript was reviewed for printing in Spain.
48 It has been suggested that Murúa needed to travel to Spain to attend a meeting of the Mercedarians in Calatayud, Zaragoza, which was to be held on 5 June 1615 (Álvarez-Calderón 2007; Placer 1987). If this is correct, he arrived too late to attend this meeting.

have been looking forward to returning to his hometown after spending so many decades abroad, there were several crucial steps in the publication process that needed to be completed first (Borja de Aguinagalde 2019:218). These included contacting the head of his order in Madrid so that they could review the manuscript, after which it could be submitted to the Crown for a publication license. Murúa also needed to find a professional artist to transform the drawings in the *General History of Peru* into printable illustrations.

From Lisbon, Murúa traveled to Madrid, where his work was reviewed by the Mercedarian fray Alonso Remón, who recommended a series of important changes.[49] Remón served as a supportive editor and censor, modifying the manuscript to make it more acceptable to the Spanish Court. These "recommendations" were most likely made before Murúa left Madrid, since Murúa rejected a few and offered alternative phasing for others. Adorno (2008:103) writes, "Remón may rightly be called an editor . . . because of the many instances where Remón corrected Murúa's word choice, deleted his expressions of excessive praise, excised his self-referential statements, and substituted the past tense for the present . . . Moreover, in at least two instances we see Remón and Murúa working in sequence if not in concert."[50]

Remón's editorial changes generally included crossing out words, lines, or paragraphs with a single or a few pen strokes. The original text can still be seen beneath these marks, unlike the later heavy redactions made by the Court's censor, Pedro de Valencia, which aimed to obscure the original text. Adorno (2008:104–105) also notes, "His was what I would call a 'friendly censorship,' designed not to condemn Murúa's work but to secure its passage through the complex channels of publications. It was, after all, Remón's signed, formal recommendation of the manuscript for publication that set off in Madrid the series of events that culminated in the granting of the royal license to print."

In addition to numerous small changes, Remón also demanded some large alterations to the manuscript. For example, it appears that at this time, the original chapter 1 was removed and replaced with what appears to be a hastily written text (Murúa 2008 [1616]:16r–16v), a large section of book 1, chapter 63, describing Francisco Pizarro's encounter with Atahualpa, was marked for removal (Murúa 2008 [1616]:134v–137r), and the first page of chapter 5 was removed from book 3 (Adorno 2008:113). Two other major changes likely took place at this time: chapters 11 and 12 of book 3 (Murúa 2008 [1616]:329r–330r), which described a large celebration that occurred in Cuzco in 1606, were removed, and an unnumbered chapter, written

---

49   Later, in 1618, Alonso Remón wrote a history of the Mercedarians, titled *Historia general de la orden de Nuestra Señora de la Merced, redención de cautivos* (Cummins 2008a:5, n2).

50   For a detailed analysis of the many editorial changes that were introduced into the text during its various stages of preparation, see Adorno (2008).

by Murúa, describing the works of the Mercedarians in Peru, was inserted between chapters 8 and 9 of book 3 (Adorno 2008:101). Other last-minute changes made at this time, revealed by the watermarks of the pages, include the copying of the support letters written in Córdoba and Buenos Aires, Murúa's dedicatory epistle to the Spanish crown prince, and his prologue to the reader (Adorno 2008:101).

Remón also reviewed the illustrations in the manuscript. He approved some, but on others he wrote "do not paint" and on others simply "no." It seems that Remón wanted to reduce the number of drawings, so that there was only one drawing per Inca and Coya (Adorno 2008:104; Adorno and Boserup 2008:32). In total, Remón marked nine drawings for removal (Murúa 2008 [1616]:40v, 42v, 44v, 49r, 51v, 57v, 60r, 62r, and 64r).

Having carefully reviewed the manuscript, Alonso Remón signed his letter of approval in Madrid on 22 October 1615 (Murúa 2008 [1616]:8r). On that same day Francisco de Rivera, the newly appointed head of the Mercedarians, signed and sealed a letter approving that the manuscript be sent on to the Crown (Murúa 2008 [1616]:10r).

Once the number of drawings had been decided upon and the manuscript had been approved by the Mercedarian Order, Murúa may likely have begun to search for a professional artist to create the final illustrations for publication. This search seems to have been quickly resolved, as among his personal belongings inventoried after his death was a signed contract between Murúa and the well-known Flemish artist and printer Pedro Perete,[51] who was then living in Madrid, to create the illustrations for the book (Borja de Aguinagalde 2019:218–219, 241).

Murúa then entrusted his prized work with the Mercedarians so that they could oversee the final steps of the publication process, while he returned to his hometown of Escoriaza (Borja de Aguinagalde 2019:219). It must have been a difficult decision for Murúa, as he had carried different versions of the manuscript across much of the Andes since 1590. However, he must have had great faith in the power of the Mercedarians to see his lifelong project to the end, and certainly he was eager to visit his hometown after so many decades abroad.

As Murúa and his Andean servant departed Madrid and made their way toward Escoriaza, they encountered Murúa's brother Diego in the port city of Somosierra, walking in the opposite direction to meet him in Madrid (Borja de Aguinagalde 2019:220). It must have been an emotional reunion, considering Murúa had spent most of his life separated from his family. By 5 November 1615, the two brothers had reached the house of Diego in Escoriaza, and shortly afterward, Murúa, accompanied by two of his brothers, made the short trip to the city of Vitoria-Gasteiz to

---

51   Also known as Pieter Perret.

visit the bishop of the diocese. Along the way, Murúa surely thought of the Santa Ana Beaterio that he was to lead and his younger sister, Cataline de Espiritu Santa, who was in residence there.

However, on 22 November 1615 Murúa fell ill with a fever in his hometown (Borja de Aguinagalde 2019:220). Martín de Murúa, who had left Escoriaza some fifty years before and had spent his adult life in the service of the Mercedarians in Peru died on 6 December 1615 from typhoid, less than three months after returning to Spain. The Andean servant who was traveling with him also fell ill but appears to have recovered (Borja de Aguinagalde 2019:248).

Although Murúa had arrived in Lisbon, the ship carrying his personal items from Peru, docked at Laredo (Portugal). The responsibility for and the cost of transporting Murúa's luggage from Laredo to Escoriaza fell to his brother Diego. Murúa's goods arrived after his death, and the final arrangements for the inheritance were not completed until 15 April 1616 (Borja de Aguinagalde 2019:247). Several objects of special note are listed among the items that arrived in Escoriaza, including two live macaws, certainly exotic animals to have in Spain at that time. Murúa also owned a fine wool shirt, so fine that it was thought to be the shirt of an Inca King.[52] The inventory also listed a handwritten manuscript described as "a draft of his book with some figures of the Indians."[53] It is likely that this was the *History and Genealogy of the Inca Kings*, first completed in Cuzco in 1590 and later abandoned in the early 1600s, possibly while Murúa was in the Aymaraes region, after Guaman Poma de Ayala had filled it with drawings. After the payment of debts, which had been incurred by his brother Diego, the remaining possessions of Murúa, including the *History and Genealogy of the Inca Kings*, were turned over to the Mercedarians and sent to their monastery in the nearby town of Logroño (Borja de Aguinagalde 2019:226).[54]

THE FINAL PREPARATION OF THE *GENERAL HISTORY OF PERU*

After Murúa's death, his *General History of Peru* continued its path toward publication. On 28 April 1616, the manuscript passed through the office of Pedro de Valencia,

---

52   This shirt may be the same one that Murúa collected while in the town of San Salvador de Capachica and that he mentions in his *History and Genealogy of the Inca Kings of Peru* (Murúa 2004 [1590]:73v). It may also be the royal Inca tunic that is now owned by Dumbarton Oaks (Hamilton 2024).

53   "Un boron de su libro con algunas figures de las yndias" (Borja de Aguinagalde 2019:223).

54   The *History and Genealogy of the Inca Kings of Peru* disappeared into the archives for several centuries and then embarked on a long journey, ending in the private library of Sean Galvin. A facsimile was made available to the public in 2004 through the work of Juan M. Ossio.

the royal censor. His redactions are made with closely spaced loops, making it very difficult to read the underlying text, as was his intention.[55] After reading and redacting the manuscript, Valencia gave his formal approval for its publication:

> By order of Your Highness, I have read the book entitled General History of Peru, origin and descent of the Incas, etc. composed by Father Fray Martín de Murúa, Redemption of Captives, Commander, and Priest of Huata, and it seems to me that the request license can be given so that it may be printed because it does not contain [any]thing against [our] faith or good customs and will greatly help to fill the history of Peru. (Murúa 2008 [1616]:9r)

About a month later, the manuscript successfully passed its final prepublication steps, which entailed the issuing of a license by Felipe III (Murúa 2008 [1616]:11r)[56] and the final rubrication of the text by the Crown notary, Gerónimo Núñez de León. The royal license granting "Fray Martín de Murúa of the Order of Our Lady of Mercy" permission to print the *General History of the Kingdom and Provinces of Peru*[57] for a period of ten years was signed by Felipe III himself (I, the king) in Madrid on 26 May 1616 and was notarized by Núñez de León. Then, after practicing his rubric several times on the blank side of the royal license (Murúa 2008 [1616]:11v), Núñez de León placed his mark at the bottom of each page of the manuscript, indicating that they had been individually approved for publication.

Even with the manuscript licensed for publication by the king, several critical steps remained before it could be printed and sold. The next step would have involved the author, after receiving the final illustrations, finding investors willing to support the publication project. Once a printer had been contacted, the financial arrangements agreed upon, and the typesetting completed, a printed version of the book would be checked against the Court-approved manuscript. A final approval decree would have then been issued by the Court and the price assigned (Adorno 2008:120).

However, these final steps never occurred, because the royal license for publication was issued in May of 1616, almost six months after the death of Murúa.[58] It

---

55   Valencia made only five redactions: two in book 1, which are included in this translation, and three in book 3. See Adorno (2008:113–115) for a more complete description of Valencia's censorship.

56   Adorno (2008:120) notes that these three individuals—Valencia, Núñez de León, and Felipe III—also approved the publication of the second part of Garcilaso de la Vega's *Royal Commentaries* in January 1614, and by November 1616 the typeset version of that work was approved.

57   It is worth noting that the Court may have required a slight change of title for Murúa's work.

58   It is possible that the Crown was unaware of Murúa's death when the publication license was approved.

seems that without the driving force of the author to continue pushing the process forward, Murúa's work, which was first conceived of in Cuzco, perhaps in the mid- to late 1580s, and had evolved through several different versions and illustrators, was set aside.

THE RECENT HISTORY OF THE *GENERAL HISTORY OF PERU*

Although the recent history of the *General History of Peru* has been described by various authors (e.g., Adorno and Boserup 2008; Ballesteros Gaibrois 1987; Hemming 1970; Ossio 2008b; and perhaps most completely by Anderson 2008), it is appropriate to provide a brief summary here.[59]

At some point after the Court granted the publication license, the manuscript was returned to the Mercedarians. Later, it was placed in the library of the Colegio Mayor de Cuenca in Salamanca, Spain (Anderson 2008:2). Its presence in that library was first recorded in 1782 by the historian Juan Bautista Muñoz. Charles IV ordered the consolidation of the major works in the libraries in Spain into the holdings of the Royal Library, so the *General History of Peru* was moved to Madrid (2008:2). When Charles IV was deposed by Napoleon Bonaparte in 1808, Napoleon's brother, Joseph Bonaparte, took control of the Crown's holdings, which included the Royal Library (2008:2).[60] Joseph Bonaparte's rule over Spain was short lived. In less than five years, he was forced to flee the region taking a wagon train of materials from the Royal palace with him. Under the leadership of Arthur Wellesley (the future first duke of Wellington), a coalition of forces defeated the French and captured the wagon train in the Battle of Vitoria on 21 June 1813. Although Wellesley strongly denounced the looting of the kingdom's treasures that followed, he had many items shipped back to England. Years later, after Ferdinand VII declined to accept the return of the book, it ended up in Wellesley's personal library. It was there that Manuel Ballesteros Gaibrois's researcher, Miguel Enguídanos Requena, gained access to it, leading to its first publication in 1964 (2008:3). As a result, for a period, the manuscript was known as the Wellington Manuscript. Starting in 1979, the manuscript changed hands several times,[61] until it was acquired by the J. Paul

---

59   For the complex history of the *History and Genealogy of the Inca Kings of Peru* (i.e., the Galvin Manuscript and the Loyola Copy), see Cummins (2008b) and Ossio (2008b, 2019b).

60   Anderson (2008:2, citing Ballesteros Gaibrois 1964:xxvii) notes that the seal of Joseph Bonaparte could still be seen on the manuscript as late as 1961.

61   As the manuscript was being prepared for sale in 1979, John Rowe was commissioned to write an evaluation of the work (Anderson 2008).

Getty Museum in Los Angeles in 1983, when it purchased the Ludwig collection of European illuminated manuscripts.[62] The manuscript is now commonly referred to as the Getty Murúa Manuscript, although we prefer to refer to it by its author's title, the *General History of Peru*.

MURÚA'S SOURCES

Juan Ossio (2008a:93n11) suggests that Murúa traveled to Peru with his mentor, Pedro Guerra, in 1577. If correct, this would place Murúa's arrival approximately forty-six years after Pizarro landed on the shores of the Inca Empire and only five years after the fall of Vilcabamba and the execution of Tupac Amaru Yupanqui. It suggests that early on, Murúa may have had access to a few surviving soldiers who had traveled with Pizarro, such as Martín Alonso de Mesa (d. 1587) or Mancio Sierra de Leguizamo (d. 1589).[63] He may also have had access to a few aging Andeans who could remember the era of Huascar and Atahualpa. However, by the time Murúa finished the first version of his work, the *History and Genealogy of the Inca Kings of Peru* (1590), there may have been no surviving eyewitnesses of the Inca Empire at its height or the Spanish invasion.

Between his arrival in Peru and his departure, approximately fifty years later, Murúa had access to many Spaniards who had arrived soon after the tragic events of Cajamarca, as well as individuals of mixed birth and Andeans who continued to follow the traditions of their parents and grandparents. One Spaniard, who many earlier scholars have passed over, was the Mercedarian friar Nicolás de los Ríos. He may have provided much of Murúa's information on the Spanish raid into Vilcabamba and the execution of Tupac Amaru. We know of de los Ríos through Baltasar Ocampo Conejeros's (2013 [1611]) description of Vilcabamba, in which he provides a detailed account of Tupac Amaru's execution. Ocampo Conejeros credits de los Ríos as an eyewitness and his major informant to the events on that eventful day. Since de los Ríos and Murúa were both members of the same order and were living in Cuzco at the same time, it is likely that Murúa and de los Ríos discussed the final years of the Incas.[64] In fact, there are many sections within Murúa's description

---

62   Therefore, the book carries the record number of "Ms. Ludwig XIII 16 (83.MP.159)" within the Getty Collection.

63   E.g., Mancio Sierra de Leguizamo, the last of the men who were with Pizarro in Cajamarca, died in 1589.

64   Other Mercedarian eyewitnesses to the execution of Tupac Amaru were Gonzalo Ballesteros, who is known to have overlapped with Murúa in Cuzco, as well as Gonzalo de Mendoza (Ocampo Conejeros 2016 [1611]:130).

of the Vilcabamba raid and Tupac Amaru's execution that resemble those found in Ocampo Conejeros's (2013 [1611]) account, suggesting that Murúa paid careful attention to the information that de los Ríos recounted. Or alternatively, Ocampo Conejeros and Murúa met in Lima sometime during 1610 or 1611, when we know that they were both in that city.

ANDEAN SOURCES

In addition to interviewing both Spaniards and Andean officials, Murúa had access to other remembrances of the past. There is ample evidence, for example, that the deeds of the Incas were recorded in epic songs or told in official narratives, which were presented on special occasions, such as when an Inca returned from a conquest. Murúa (2008 [1616]:40r) records such a case as he describes Pachacuti Inca Yupanqui's return to Cuzco: "Upon [Pachacuti Inca Yupanqui's] return, he ordered epic songs of their victory over their enemies to be sung as he entered [the city] until he reached the House of the Sun." These songs were also sung during the mourning rituals for an Inca or when his body was brought out for the public to see on special occasions. Murúa (2008 [1616]:87v) provides the following description of the return of Huayna Capac's body to Cuzco after his death in Ecuador: "Many lords and people left Cuzco just to accompany the body of Huayna Capac and to enter with him in the triumph. They sang sad and melancholy songs, recounting Huayna Capac's heroic deeds and praying to the Creator for him." These songs were also performed by members of his kin group on other occasions. For example, when telling of the life of Inca Yupanqui, Murúa (2008 [1616]:46r) writes, "He was accompanied by a great multitude of people, lords, *orejones*, as well as commoners, all painted with different colors and designs, dancing and twirling without pause, some singing and others responding, [reciting] the stories and deeds of [Pachacuti] Inca Yupanqui."

In his earliest work, Murúa provides a detailed account of these epic songs:

> These Indians had neither letters nor laws nor statutes nor ordinances but only the songs and dances, which they called and continue to call arabic. They memorized and retold the past and ancient things in this way: many of them gathered together, both male and female Indians, and they joined hands or crossed arms, and one of them led, and [the others] sang in chorus. The guide would begin, and all the others would respond, and this would last for three or four hours, until the guide finished their story, and sometimes they would mix a drum in with the singing, and in this way they would tell their stories and past memories, how their Incas died, how many

[there were], what [offices] they [held], what deeds they did, and other things. They communicated to young and old the things which they did not want to be forgotten in this way. (Murúa 2004 [1590]:58r)

Therefore, some of the information that Murúa includes in his history may have been obtained from individuals who remembered songs or other types of oral history recounting the deeds of each Inca. And it is possible that some of the similarities between Murúa and those of other writers stem from their exposure to the same songs.

At times, the information that Murúa received from different Indigenous sources would have been complementary, but on other occasions there was no consensus about what had occurred. An example of Murúa receiving mixed information about a specific event is seen within his discussion of a rope that was made in honor of Huascar Inca's birth. Murúa (2008 [1616]:76v) writes, "Some old and elderly people say that this wondrous chain was thrown into a large lake that is in Huaypo, three leagues from this city of Cuzco, when the Spaniards arrived. Others say that [it was thrown] into the lake near the town and *tambo* of Urcos, on the royal road to Potosí, six leagues from this city [i.e., Cuzco]." Murúa also indicates that he often did not understand the relationship between various narratives that he heard. He writes, "This [mixing] causes great difficulties for those who hear them and are trying to recover information" (Murúa 2008 [1616]:23v).

Besides conducting interviews with individuals and groups, Murúa claims that much of his information came from the reading of *quipus*.[65] For example, as a statement of authenticity, he writes:

> They had no written letters and did not know how to write or [record] history, more than what was recorded on their quipus. These [quipus] are strings on which they tie knots, recording anything they want. These [quipus are the sources] of what I have said and shall say in all of this history. (Murúa 2008 [1616]:22v)

The Incas used *quipus* as mnemonic counting devices, meaning that specific numbers were recorded in the form of knots on *quipu* cords, and those numbers could be deciphered by trained individuals. However, the specific context to which those numbers referred had to be memorized by the *quipu* reader. In other words, if we find the number 14 recorded on a *quipu* cord, we will not know what that number corresponds to: days? alpacas? tribute? or towns?

Some *quipus* may have also contained other information beyond numbers, recorded in mnemonic form, including what we might call histories. For example, we have the

---

65   Additional information may have come from other Indigenous sources, such as a series of painted boards that were stored in a temple in the Cuzco Valley. These boards are mentioned by Cristóbal de Molina (2011 [ca. 1575]) and Sarmiento de Gamboa (2007 [1572]), both of whom worked on their own histories of the Incas in the early 1570s.

reading of one account of the conquests of Tupa Inca Yupanqui that was originally recorded on *quipus* (Rowe 1985) that matches much of what Murúa reports.

While discussing the coastal city of San Marcos de Arica, Murúa describes how he believed these more "event-based" *quipus* worked as mnemonic devices:

> As they did not know how to read or write, they used their *quipus* instead of writing, which, as we have said, are very elegant and well-made cords, and in them, they tie many large knots [representing] conquered towns, and in other smaller [knots represent] the number of defeated Indians, and in a black cord, those who had died in the war. (Murúa 2008 [1616]:367r).

Accordingly, it seems likely that Murúa did collect some of his information about the Inca from *quipucamayocs* (*quipu* readers), especially during the period that he lived in Cuzco. However, it is also certain that his sources were far more complex than what he was willing to admit to the reader.

SPANISH SOURCES

Despite Murúa's (2008 [1616]:22v) claim of historical authenticity, stating that all of his information came from Indigenous sources, we have found, like many other researchers who have studied Murúa (Adorno 2008; Adorno and Boserup 2008; Álvarez-Calderón 2007; Bayle 1946; Duviols 1962; Pärssinen 1989; Porras Barrenechea 1986; Rowe 1987, to name only a few), that large parts of his chronicle were copied or paraphrased from earlier Spanish documents. Murúa alludes to having read some Spanish sources, but he is ungenerous in acknowledging the sources from which he copied substantial amounts of specific details.

Murúa copied large amounts of information from Cristóbal de Molina's lost *History of Peru* (ca. 1571) for use in books 1 and 2 of his *General History of Peru*. We know this because much of the same material also appears in Miguel Cabello Valboa's *Miscelánea antártica* (1951 [1586]), and Cabello Valboa, unlike Murúa, states that he had access to Molina's *History of the Incas*. Similar information also appears in Pedro de Sarmiento de Gamboa's chronicle (2007 [1572]), although the source of Sarmiento de Gamboa's overlapping information is less well understood. Murúa also appears to have had access to a second manuscript of Molina's titled *Account of the Fables and Rites of the Incas* (2011 [ca. 1575]), which describes various ceremonies conducted in Cuzco during the last years of the Inca Empire. Much of this information is contained in book 2 of Murúa's *General History of Peru*.

It will be evident to most who are familiar with the early chronicles of Peru that Murúa copied, as so many other earlier writers did, large sections from two critically important manuscripts written by Juan Polo de Ondegardo: "De los errores y supersticiones de los indios" (2012 [n.d.]) and *Notables daños de no guardar a los indios sus fueros* (2021 [1571]). Small sections of these works were copied into book 1, while Murúa copied dozens of pages for use in book 2.

The earliest printed book that Murúa extracted information from is Francisco López de Gómara's *Historia general de las Indies* (1552). Although López de Gómara lived in Spain, he is best known for his description of Hernán Cortés's invasion of Mexico. Some of Murúa's descriptions of the Coyas, especially that of Chimpo Ocllo, reflect Aztec practices taken from López de Gómara (Álvarez-Calderón 2007:115; Bayle 1946; Rowe 1987:753–761).

Murúa also copied sections from Diego Fernández de Palencia's *Primera y segunda parte de la Historia del Piru* (1963 [1571]). Fernández lived in Peru for several decades and wrote largely about the civil wars among the Spaniards following the Spanish invasion. Murúa (2008 [1616]:168r) appears to refer to Fernández's book, writing, "As a book has [already] been written about them [i.e., the Spanish civil wars], I touch upon all these things briefly, since my intention here is to discuss only the Incas." Murúa mentions explicitly his use of Fernández when describing the journey of Sayri Tupac to Cuzco, "At the time when they went, as is stated in the Chronicle of Peru, Sayri Tupac had not [yet] received the tassel" (Murúa 2008 [1616]:f.136r). While a few scattered sentences from Fernández are contained within book 1, much larger sections are present in book 2.

Murúa also copied sections from Jerónimo Román y Zamora's *Repúblicas del Mundo*, first published in 1575 (Pärssinen 1989; Rowe 1987). Román y Zamora, an Augustinian, copied some of his information from Bartolomé de Las Casas's work *Apologética historia sumaria* (1988 [1566]), as pointed out by Adorno (2008:123n15). However, Román y Zamora's book was quickly denounced by the Council of the Indies for its criticism of Spanish actions in the Americas and was banned from being printed. As a result, Román y Zamora was forced to rewrite large sections of his work and a second edition, one that met the requirements of the Crown, was published in 1595. Fine sleuthing by Adorno and Boserup (2008:19) indicates that Murúa had access to the 1595 approved edition of Román y Zamora, and not the earlier 1575 work. Most of the information taken from Román y Zamora appears in book 3 of Murúa's manuscript.

Murúa also copied information from Jerónimo de Oré's *Símbolo católico indiano* (1598), or they shared a common source, for inclusion within book 1. Oré was a Franciscan from Huamanga (Adorno 2008; Rowe 1987). Since the two men were contemporaries, it is possible that they knew of each other and attended some of the same important events.

Furthermore, we know that Murúa had access to the results of two investigations conducted by the Augustinians in 1595 and 1599–1600 regarding the death of Padre Diego Ortiz in Vilcabamba. During their failed effort to nominate Ortiz for sainthood, the Augustinians conducted a series of interviews in the Vilcabamba region and in the city of Cuzco (Bauer et al. 2014). Murúa copied much of the information contained in various testimonies into his work.[66] Since the investigations of Padre Diego Ortiz started in 1595, they are not included in Murúa's *History and Genealogy of the Inca Kings of Peru* (2004 [1590]), but they are included with his *General History of Peru* (1616).[67]

There is further indirect evidence suggesting that Murúa integrated other documents into his narrative. This becomes apparent through abrupt shifts in tone and style within the text. This phenomenon is most prominently demonstrated when Murúa initiates a chapter with a meandering treatise or moral tale, only to subsequently transition into a straightforward historical account. In such instances, it seems as though he briefly departs from the historical framework he was employing to introduce a metacommentary, aimed at aiding the reader in contextualizing the events within a broader perspective.

REGARDING MURÚA'S *GENERAL HISTORY OF PERU* AND THE WORKS OF MOLINA [CA. 1571, 1575], CABELLO VALBOA [1586], SARMIENTO DE GAMBOA [1572], AND COBO [1653]

Since the first printing of Murúa's *General History of Peru*, scholars have explored the complex relationship that exists between his manuscript and the works of Cristóbal de Molina (ca. 1571, ca. 1575), Miguel Cabello Valboa (1586), Pedro Sarmiento

---

66 Parts of the Augustinian reports were also copied by Antonio de la Calancha for inclusion in his *Corónica moralizada del Orden de San Agustín en el Perú* (1981 [1638]).

67 There are also small sections throughout Murúa's *General History of Peru* that overlap with information provided by Juan de Betanzos (1996 [1557]) and a few sections that match information provided by Juan de Santa Cruz Pachacuti Yamqui Salcamaygua in his work *Relación de las antigüedades deste reyno del Piru* (1993 [ca. 1613]). So, there has been some questioning about whether Murúa had access to these works. Juan de Betanzos was an early Spanish settler in Cuzco, who married an Inca noblewoman and wrote one of the earliest detailed reports on Inca society. Santa Cruz Pachacuti Yamqui Salcamaygua was an Indigenous writer who lived in the Cuzco region during the late 1500s and early 1600s. Nevertheless, there is no clear evidence that Murúa had access to either Betanzos's or Santa Cruz Pachacuti Yamqui Salcamaygua's work. The overlaps can easily be accounted for by widely shared oral traditions within the Inca capital.

de Gamboa (1572), and Bernabé Cobo (1653) (e.g., Álvarez-Calderón 2007; Araníbar 1963; Julien 2000; Ossio 2008a; Pärssinen 1989; Pease 1992; Rowe 1985, 1987).[68]

Cristóbal de Molina's writings serve as a crucial starting point in understanding the interweaving of these different but related historical narratives. Molina was born in Spain and arrived in Cuzco in 1556. He served as the priest of the Hospital for the Natives of Our Lady of Succor in Cuzco for many years, and he also held the position of the preacher general of the city for nearly twenty years.[69] Molina was an outstanding Quechua speaker, and his advanced language skills allowed him to record the history, prayers, and the religious celebrations of the Inca in unprecedented detail.

Sometime between February 1571 and October 1572, Molina was ordered by Viceroy Toledo to write a work on the history of the Incas. This was the first of two important manuscripts that Molina wrote within a relatively short time. Although no copy of Molina's first report, commonly referred to as the *History of the Incas* (ca. 1571), survives, we know of its existence because Molina specifically mentions that he gave a copy of it to Bishop Sebastián Lartaún. Molina's report on the history of the Incas must have impressed Lartaún, as sometime between 1573 and 1575 the bishop requested that Molina write a second report, this one focused on the rituals of the Incas. This second report, *Account of the Fables and Rites of the Incas* (ca. 1575), describes various ceremonies conducted in Cuzco during the last years of the Inca Empire and has been widely published.

There are numerous sections in books 1 and 2 of Murúa's *General History of Peru* that contain overlapping information with materials found within Molina's *Account of the Fables and Rites of the Incas*, indicating that Murúa had access to it. However, there is also evidence that Murúa, along with two or three other early writers, had access to Molina's earlier *History of the Incas*, and they all copied large sections from it into their own chronicles.

In the opening statement of Molina's *Account on the Fables and Rites of the Incas* (ca. 1575), he provides a summary of his now lost *History of the Incas* (ca. 1571).

> The account that I gave to Your Most Illustrious Lordship [described] the dealings, origin, lives, and customs of the Incas who were the lords of this land; how many there were, who their wives were, and the laws they made, [the] wars that they waged, and [the] people and nations that they conquered. Because, in some parts of the account, I discussed the ceremonies and rituals that they established, although not in

---

68   Bauer has explored these relationships in two earlier publications, and his views continue to evolve (see Sarmiento de Gamboa 2007 [1572]:25–34 and Molina 2011 [ca. 1575]:xix–xxii).

69   Both Antonio de la Calancha (1981 [1638]:1883) and Baltasar de Ocampo Conejeros (2013 [1611]:39) note that Molina was with Tupac Amaru on the day of his execution. Molina died in Cuzco in 1584.

much detail, I thought it was proper now, principally because Your Most Reverend Lordship has requested it of me, to expend additional effort so that Your Most Reverend Lordship [can] learn about the ceremonies, rituals, and idolatries that these Indians had. (Molina 2011 [ca. 1575]:3)

From this brief description we can see how valuable Molina's *History of the Incas* would have been to other early writers researching the history of the Incas.

A copy of Molina's *History of the Incas* must have been archived somewhere in Cuzco, as Vasco Jacinto López de Contreras y Valverde, writing in Cuzco in 1649, specifically mentions it as an important source for his overview of the history of the city. He writes:

They give the same origin of the city's foundation as they attribute to the descent and royal blood of the Incas. I have found another version that mentions it, and in/at? some length, in a manuscript that, by command of Viceroy Don Francisco de Toledo, was written by the Father Cristóbal de Molina. [He was an] elderly priest [and] a scrutinizer of the intricate *quipus*, annals of those times, or, better said, labyrinths where the Indians would barbarically imprison the memories of their ancient past. (López de Vasco de Contreras y Valverde 1982 [1649]:43)

Some researchers have assumed, based on the opening line of the *Account of the Fables and Rites of the Incas*, that Molina wrote his *History of the Incas* at the request of Lartaún when he arrived in Cuzco (Calvo Pérez and Urbano 2008; Urbano 2008a, 2008b; Urbano and Duviols 1989). However, it should be noted that Molina only indicates that he had given a copy of his history to Lartaún and that the bishop had then requested a second study to be made concerning the rituals of the Incas. In contrast, López de Vasco de Contreras y Valverde's reference to Molina's *History of the Incas*, provided above, specifically states that Molina's first work was written at the request of Viceroy Toledo. The request would have been made during Toledo's relatively brief stay in Cuzco (February 1571–October 1572).[70] Murúa must have also found a copy of this work during his stay in Cuzco (before 1585–1599).

Now let us turn to Miguel Cabello Valboa and his *Miscelánea antártica* (1591 [1586]). Miguel Cabello Valboa arrived in Peru in 1566 and traveled widely, although it is not clear if he visited Cuzco. Cabello Valboa was ordained as a priest in Quito in 1571 and started writing his work soon afterward. His *Miscelánea Antártica* was completed in Lima, some fifteen years later, in 1586. Researchers (Loayza 1943; Markham 1873:viii–ix) have long suggested that parts of Molina's *History of the*

---

70   The request for Molina to write a history of the Incas was among several other similar requests that Toledo made to different Spaniards then in Cuzco, including Sarmiento de Gamboa (2007 [1572]) and Ruiz de Navamuel (1882 [1572]).

Incas are preserved within the *Miscelánea antártica*, as Cabello Valboa specifically notes that he used the work of the "venerable Father Cristóbal de Molina," along with that of several other writers, to research the origins of the Inca Kings (Cabello Valboa 1951 [1586]:259–260). Both Cabello Valboa and Molina were in Lima for the Third Provincial Council (1582–18 October 1583) some three years before Cabello Valboa finished his work, so perhaps this is when Cabello Valboa gained access to Molina's *History of the Incas* (Núñez Carvallo 2008:91). Some researchers suggest that Murúa had direct access to Miguel Cabello Valboa's work, since numerous passages in the *General History of Peru* duplicate passages in the *Miscelánea antártica*. However, it is more likely that both Murúa and Cabello Valboa had access to Molina's *History of the Incas* and that they both used it as a common source of information (Julien 2000; Rowe 1985).

Pedro Sarmiento de Gamboa also wrote a well-known work titled the *History of the Incas* in Cuzco in 1572. Sarmiento de Gamboa, a sea captain and cosmographer of the viceroyalty, traveled with Viceroy Francisco de Toledo on his general inspection of Peru. When they arrived in Cuzco, Toledo asked Sarmiento de Gamboa to write a history of the Incas.[71] Sarmiento de Gamboa's brief time in Cuzco overlapped with Molina's long-term tenure in the city, and there are numerous passages within Murúa's *General History of Peru* that overlap with information presented in Sarmiento de Gamboa's *History of the Incas* and Cabello Valboa's *Miscelánea antártica*, suggesting that the information came from Molina.

While it is known that Cabello Valboa copied information directly from Molina's *History of the Incas*, establishing the relationship between Sarmiento de Gamboa's and Molina's works is more difficult to assess. The problem lies in the fact that both Sarmiento de Gamboa's and Molina's times in Cuzco overlapped, and they were both charged by Viceroy Toledo to write histories of the Inca. Sarmiento de Gamboa and Molina also must have known each other and attended some of the same public events, and it is even possible that they shared sources and informants on Inca history. Therefore, the many passages in Sarmiento de Gamboa's *History of the Incas* that overlap with information found in Cabello Valboa's *Miscelánea antártica* may be the result of Molina and Sarmiento de Gamboa sharing the same sources and informants, or may be the result of Sarmiento de Gamboa having access to, and copying information from, Molina's *History of the Incas*.[72]

---

71   Like Molina's Account of the *Fables and Rites of the Incas* (ca. 1575) and Cabello Valboa's *Miscelánea antártica* (1586), Sarmiento de Gamboa's *History of the Incas* (1572) has been widely published.

72   Both Cabello Valboa (1951 [1586]) and Sarmiento de Gamboa (2007 [1572]) end their chronicles with the death of Atahualpa, so it is likely that Molina's *History of the Incas* also ended with this event.

TABLE 0.1. Martín de Murúa and the *General History of Peru*.

1552	Francisco López de Gómara finishes his *General History of the Indies*, a source used by Murúa.
3 November 1566	An unnamed male child of the Murúa family is baptized in the town of Escoriaza.
ca. 1571	Cristóbal de Molina finishes his now lost work titled *History of the Incas*, a source used by Murúa.
1571	Diego Fernández de Palencia finishes his *First and Second Part of the History of Peru*, a source used by Murúa.
1572	Pedro Sarmiento de Gamboa finishes his *The History of the Incas*.
	The town of Vilcabamba is burned and Tupac Amaru, the last Inca ruler, is captured and executed in Cuzco. The Mercedarian Nicolás de los Ríos witnesses the execution.
ca. 1575	Cristóbal de Molina finishes his now lost work *Account of the Fables and Rites of the Incas*, a source used by Murúa.
1577	Pedro Guerra, and perhaps Murúa, sails to Peru.
Early 1580s	Murúa is stationed in San Salvador de Capachica.
1585	Murúa has relocated and is stationed in Cuzco.
1586	Miguel Cabello Valboa completes his *Miscelánea antártica*. Like Murúa, Cabello Valboa had access to Molina's 1571 document on the history of the Incas.
1590	Murúa finishes a draft of his work titled *History and Genealogy of the Inca Kings of Peru*. He submits the manuscript to a group of local lords in Cuzco for review.
1595	Murúa represents the Mercedarians in a land dispute in Curahuasi. Jerónimo Román y Zamora finishes his revised edition of *Republics of the World*, a source used by Murúa.
15 May 1596	The *History and Genealogy of the Inca Kings of Peru* is returned to Murúa after being approved of by the local lords of Cuzco. Murúa continues to conduct research.
1598	Jerónimo de Oré finishes *Símbolo católico indiano*.
1599	Murúa relocates to Arequipa.
1599–1600	Augustinians in Cuzco finish their second investigations concerning the death of Padre Diego Ortiz in Vilcabamba.
19 February 1600	Murúa witnesses the eruption of Huaynaputina.
12 December 1600	Guaman Poma de Ayala is banished from Huamanga.
Early 1600s	Murúa relocated to the town of Yanaca, where he continues to work on the *History and Genealogy of the Inca Kings*.
Early 1600s	Guaman Poma de Ayala and an unknown artist provide drawings for Murúa's *History and Genealogy of the Inca Kings*. Sometime later, Murúa sets this work aside and begins writing his *General History of Peru*.

continued on next page

TABLE 0.1.—*continued*

1606	Murúa attends the birth celebrations of Felipe IV in Cuzco. He may have begun to draft his *General History of Peru* during this visit.
29 June 1609	Murúa leaves an unnamed town (most likely Yanaca) with a letter indicating that he owed nothing to the community.
15 February 1610	Murúa is in Lima and sends funds to the Santa Ana *beaterio* in Spain.
1611	Baltasar Ocampo Conejeros finishes his *Description of the Province of Vilcabamba* in Lima.
25 August 1611	Murúa is in the town of Ilabaya, and the *General History of Peru* is read by Martín Domínguez Jara, the commissioner of the Holy Office.
6 September 1611	Murúa is in La Paz, and his *General History of Peru* is read by Pedro González, inspector general for the bishop.
8 September 1611	Murúa is in La Paz, and his *General History of Peru* is read by Diego Guzmán.
22 December 1611	Murúa is in La Plata, and he sends funds to the Santa Ana *beaterio*.
8 February 1612	Murúa is in La Plata, and his *General History of Peru* is read by Francisco Bázquez. Bázquez notes that Murúa is the Mercedarian priest of the nearby town of Huata, indicating that he was already installed in this new assignment.
10 May 1612	Murúa is in La Plata, and his *General History of Peru* is read by *Alexo de Benavente Solís*, canon of the Cathedral and City of La Plata.
14 May 1612	Murúa is in La Plata, and his *General History of Peru* is read by Gutiérrez Fernández Hidalgo, the conductor of the cathedral. In his letter, Fernández Hidalgo specifically mentions that Murúa had spent a long time serving in Cuzco.
3 March 1613	Murúa is in Potosí, and his *General History of Peru* is read by Luis Carrillo, the examiner for the general language of Peru.
4 March 1613	Murúa is in Potosí, and his *General History of Peru* is read by Baltasar de los Reyes, commander of the Mercedarian Convent, and by Pedro de Arze, the head of the Mercedarians in the Viceroyalty of Peru.
3 August 1613	Murúa is in Potosí, and he sends funds to the Santa Ana *beaterio*.
Late 1613?	Two scribes produce a final version of the *General History of Peru*.
Late 1613?	The illustrations for the *General History of Peru* are completed. Murúa removes four illustrations, three of which were drawn by Guaman Poma de Ayala, from his *History and Genealogy of the Inca Kings* for inclusion in the *General History of Peru*.
Late 1613?	Murúa is in La Plata. He declares the *General History of Peru* completed and writes the date and the location on the illustrated cover page and on the last page of the manuscript.
Mid-1614?	Murúa leaves La Plata and begins his trip back to Spain.
28 September 1614	Murúa is in Córdoba, and his *General History of Peru* is read by Luis de Quiñones Osorio, the governor of Tucumán.

continued on next page

TABLE 0.1.—*continued*

17 December 1614	Murúa is in Buenos Aires, and his *General History of Peru* is read by Francisco de Irujo, the head of the Holy Office of the Inquisition.
1615	Felipe Guaman Poma de Ayala completes his *First New Chronicle and Good Government*.
Mid-1615	Murúa and an Andean servant from Potosí sail from Buenos Aires to Lisbon.
15 August 1615	The ship carrying Murúa arrives in Lisbon.
20 September 1615	Murúa sends a message to his brother Diego de Murúa in Escoriaza stating that he was still in Lisbon.
22 October 1615	Murúa is in Madrid and the *General History of Peru* is read, edited, and approved by the Mercedarian censor Alonso Remón. Francisco de Rivera, the head of the Mercedarians, writes a letter approving Murúa's manuscript be sent on to the Crown for review.
Late October 1615	Murúa recruits Pedro Perete to create the final illustrations for the book. He leaves the *General History of Peru* in Madrid for the Crown to review and begins a trip to visit his hometown of Escoriaza.
Early November 1615	Murúa and his Andean servant meet Diego de Murúa in Somosierra.
5 November 1615	Murúa arrives in Escoriaza. Soon afterward, Murúa, accompanied by two of his brothers, travel to Vitoria-Gasteiz.
22 November 1615	After returning to Escoriaza, Murúa and his Andean servant become sick.
5 December 1615	Murúa dies of typhoid in Escoriaza. The Andean servant recovers.
15 April 1616	An inventory is made of Murúa's possessions, which include "a draft of his book with some figures of the Indians," a likely reference to the *History and Genealogy of the Inca Kings*. Murúa's goods are given to the Mercedarians.
28 April 1616	The *General History of Peru* is read, edited, and approved by Pedro de Valencia, the royal censor.
26 May 1616	A royal license to print the *General History of Peru* is signed by Felipe III, and the manuscript is notarized by Gerónimo Núñez de León. They seem unaware of Murúa's death.
1782	Juan Bautista Muñoz records that the *General History of Peru* is held by the Colegio Mayor de Cuenca in Salamanca, Spain.
Early 1800s	The *General History of Peru* is moved from Salamanca to the Royal Library in Madrid.
1808	Charles IV is forced off the throne and replaced by Joseph Bonaparte.
21 June 1813	Arthur Wellesley defeats Joseph Bonaparte in the Battle of Vitoria. Among the spoils is the *General History of Peru*. Wellesley takes the manuscript to England, and it is placed in his personal library.
1964	Manuel Ballesteros Gaibrois publishes the *General History of Peru* after it was found by Miguel Enguídanos Requena in the Wellesley library.

continued on next page

TABLE 0.1.—*continued*

2004	A facsimile of Códice Murúa, *Historia y genealogía de los reyes incas del Perú del padre mercenario Fray Martín de Murúa*, Códice Galvin, is published after being identified by Juan Ossio.
2008	A facsimile of *Historia General del Piru* is published.

In 1653, Bernabé Cobo, a Jesuit priest and formidable naturalist, finished one of the last and most important chronicles of Peru, *The History of the New World* (*Historia del Nuevo Mundo*). Cobo traveled extensively in Peru, and he spent several years in Cuzco. Like most writers of his time, Cobo was inconsistent in acknowledging his sources. Nevertheless, in the introduction to book 12 of his *History of the New World*, Cobo (1979 [1653]:98–102) describes the three major sources that he used while writing his overview of Inca history and religion. Cobo states that his most importance source on the Incas was Polo de Ondegardo's report "De los errores y supersticiones de los indios." In fact, Cobo had the original manuscript with Polo de Ondegardo's own signature, which, like so many other documents, had been sent to Archbishop Jerónimo de Loayza. Cobo also acknowledges his debt to Cristóbal de Molina, indicating that he used a "copious account of the rites and fables that the Peruvian Indians practiced in pagan times." This is an unmistakable reference to Molina's *Fables and Rites of the Incas*, which we know was sent to Loayza. Cobo also states that he made extensive use of a report on the history and government of the Incas written for Viceroy Toledo.[73] However, it is unclear whether he is referring to Sarmiento de Gamboa's *History of the Incas*, Molina's *History of the Incas*, or another manuscript.[74] Nevertheless, it is clear that there is a complex relationship, and much overlap, between Murúa's *General History of the Incas* and Cobo's *History of the New World*, the details of which remain to be explored.

---

73 Cobo writes: "Viceroy Francisco de Toledo took great care in obtaining a true history of the origin and form of government of the Inca kings, and to this end, since he was in the city of Cuzco himself, he ordered all the old Indians who remained from the time of the Inca kings to be brought together. To ensure that the proceedings were conducted with less danger of misunderstanding in an undertaking whose ascertainment was so much desired, each Indian was interrogated separately; they were not allowed to communicate with each other. The person entrusted by the viceroy to make this inquiry, who was one of those working under him on the general inspection, made the same careful inquiry with all the old Incas he found in the Provinces of Charcas and Arequipa, and with former Spanish conquistadores who were in this land, not a few of whom still lived at that time" (Cobo 1979:100 [1653:bk. 12, ch. 2]).

74 The reference to the "provinces of Charcas and Arequipa" suggests that Cobo was working from Sarmiento de Gamboa's manuscript; however, it has not been documented that there was a copy of this work in Cuzco after the author sent the final version to Spain in 1572.

Figure 1.1. The coat of arms of the Inca Kings (courtesy of The J. Paul Getty Museum, Los Angeles, Ms. Ludwig XIII 16 [83.MP.159], f.13r).

The General History of Peru

MARTIN DE MURÚA

TRANSLATED AND EDITED BY
*Brian S. Bauer, Eliana Gamarra C.,
and Andrea Gonzales Lombardi*

https://doi.org/10.5876/9781646426553.c001

[f.16r] Book One on the origin and descent of the Incas, lords of this Kingdom of Peru, the conquests they made in different provinces and nations and [their] civil wars until the arrival of the Spaniards . . .

CHAPTER I

How in earlier times there was no king or universal lord in this kingdom until the Incas[75]

Many people have inquired and tried to establish who the first inhabitants of these provinces of Peru were and the origin of the Incas who ruled this kingdom. Among them was Don Francisco de Toledo,[76] [the] brother of Don Juan de Toledo, Count of Oropesa, of the custom and Order of Alcántara,[77] commander of Acebuche.[78] [Toledo] was the Viceroy of these kingdoms. He governed them with great prudence and just laws, worthy of such a gentleman.[79] The most certain thing he found was that there had been no general ruler of all these provinces [before the Incas]. Instead, each province, nation, and family was governed by the most prominent individual, without organized villages or politics as they now have and as they were in the Inca times. Their villages, or rather populations, were dispersed, located on hills or [in] valleys where *[f.6v]* they were most comfortable establishing their fields,

---

75   This chapter replaces an earlier chapter 1, now lost, which was most likely removed at the request of Alonso Ramón. The replacement chapter is written in Murúa's own hand (Adorno and Boserup 2008). A blank page follows this chapter, perhaps intended to hold an illustration.

76   Francisco Álvarez de Toledo, Viceroy of Peru: November 1569–May 1581. Murúa repeats this information in chapter 78.

77   A religious order in Spain.

78   An area of Spain.

79   Murúa provides a description of the various viceroys of Peru and its political organization under Spanish rule in book 3 and chapters 5 and 6 of his chronicle.

close to some river or spring. They fought with each other, using slings which they call *huaracas*, to expand and defend their boundaries and *chacras*.[80]

Cuzco did not exist nor was there any other political unity, for that was all later created and established by the Incas. [The Incas] were so courageous and intelligent, that they brought order and structure [to the region] and new ways of living, establishing, and enforcing boundaries, as will be described later. They only strictly punished, among other things, men engaged in sexual relations with their daughter, sister, or [some other] very close relative. When something like this happened, they saw it as a bad omen, and believed it would bring droughts, hardships, illnesses, pestilences, and [poor] harvests. Those who [committed these acts] received exemplarily punishment; they were killed and buried in the roads and boundary markers, with white stones marking their graves.[81] Furthermore, men who had sexual relations with their stepmothers, sisters-in-law, or close kin were tortured by having their arms pulled back and then repeatedly struck with a stone. [The couple] was then separated so they could never get together again.

Some used certain *huacas*[82] and they only sacrificed the heads of sheep of the land,[83] blew *coca*,[84] [poured] *chicha*,[85] and [offered] other foods. As described below, these practices continued until the time of the Incas, when they were reformed and organized into a single kingdom.[86]

[F.18R] CHAPTER 2

The beginning and origin of the Incas and where they came from

The Indians tell various stories and amusing fables about the appearance of the first Incas and how they entered, conquered, and populated the city of Cuzco.[87] Yet none of them are certain or confirmed. The most popular, common, and widely

---

80   This word is underlined (Murúa 2008 [1616]:16v).
81   A spelling mistake may have been corrected in the manuscript (Murúa 2008 [1616]:16v).
82   This word is underlined (Murúa 2008 [1616]:16v).
83   A llama or alpaca.
84   This word is underlined (Murúa 2008 [1616]:16v).
85   This word is underlined (Murúa 2008 [1616]:16v).
86   This same chapter can also be found written on the back of Murúa (2008 [1616]:19r). Folio 19 was removed by Murúa from his *History and Genealogy of the Inca Kings of Peru* (Murúa 2004 [1590]) and used within his 1616 manuscript because of its illustration. Folios 17r and 17v are left blank.
87   A space was left blank and later filled with the words "Cuzco and the" (Murúa 2008 [1616]:18r).

believed is that the first Inca was named Manco Capac, though some assert he was the last of [four] Inca brothers. Whatever happened, I will present in this history the most likely that I have been able to collect and deduce.

According to the Indians, when[88] the [universal] flood destroyed humanity, the [first] Incas [emerged] from a cave,[89] like a window, in the town of Pacariqtambo,[90] five leagues from Cuzco.[91] These [were the first] Incas, and they were four brothers. The eldest was Manco Capac, [and the others were] Ayar Cachi, Ayar Auca, and Ayar Uchu. There were also four sisters: Mama Huaco, who was very masculine and she fought and conquered some Indians,[92] Mama Cura,[93] Mama Ocllo, and Mama Rahua. Additionally, some elderly Indians claim that a group of male and female siblings emerged from the great Lake Titicaca,[94] in the province of Collao, arriving at the cave of Pacariqtambo. These siblings were noble and courageous and had gold earplugs. One of these was Manco Capac.[95] Either of these accounts can be accepted as the origins of the Incas since neither can be proven to be more valid than the other;[96] as they are both only fables.

The brothers and sisters left Pacariqtambo at night and arrived at the town of Pachete,[97] where they looked for suitable land to settle. But not satisfied, they

---

88   The word "with" has been added to the text (Murúa 2008 [1616]:18r) by Remón (Adorno 1980:103).

89   This cave is generally called Tambotoco. The Inca town of Pacariqtambo, now called Maukallaqta, and the outcrop of Tambotoco, now called Puma Orco, are located south of Cuzco (Bauer 1991).

90   A spelling error has been corrected (Murúa 2008 [1616]:18r).

91   For a review of the Pacariqtambo Origin Myth and a retracing of the mythical journey of Manco Capac and his siblings from Pacariqtambo to Cuzco, see Bauer (1991, 2004). Both Cabello Valboa (1951 [1586]:261–264) and Sarmiento de Gamboa (2007 [1572]:60–68) present similar versions of the Pacariqtambo Origin Myth, although some details differ. For other versions of the myth, see Betanzos (1996 [1557]), Cieza de León (1976 [1553–1554]), Cobo (1979 [1653]:103–104), and Santa Cruz Pachacuti Yamqui Salcamaygua (1993 [1613]), among many others.

92   Mama Huaco is believed to have defeated the original inhabitants of the Cuzco Valley (Bauer 1996).

93   Sarmiento de Gamboa (2007 [1572]:61) notes that Mama Cura was also called Mama Ipacura.

94   For a review of the Lake Titicaca Origin Myth, see Bauer and Stanish (2001).

95   This version of the Inca Origin Myth has been copied from Oré (1598:39r–39v). Also see Fernández de Palencia (1963 [1571]:83) for another reference to earplugs and Manco Capac.

96   The final part of this sentence has been changed from "So there is not much reason to believe one and not the other" by Remón (Murúa 2008 [1616]:18r; Adorno 1980:103).

97   Pachete is a small hill between Puma Orco and Maukallacta (Bauer 1991). It is also mentioned by Cabello Valboa (1951 [1586]:261) but not by Cobo (1979 [1653]:104) or Sarmiento de Gamboa (2007 [1572]:63).

returned along the same road and arrived at Huayna Cancha,[98] where Manco Capac had intercourse with his sister Mama Ocllo (or, according to some, his sister Mama Huaco). As they traveled the road, they realized that the sister was pregnant, and asked, "Which of us has done this evil?" After discovering the truth, they traveled to Tambuqui,[99] where Sinchi Roca was born. They celebrated [his birth] by thanking the Creator and the Sun, and [then] they proceeded to Chasquito.[100] There they decided that their brother, Ayar Auca,[101] the most courageous of them all, should go back to the cave of Pacariqtambo,[102] from which they had emerged and be sealed inside it. Calling out to him, they said: "Brother, you know that we left some golden drinking vessels called *topacusi* and some seed[s][103] in the cave we emerged from; you must return for them so that we can gather [the] people together and be [their] rulers." Ayar Auca refused, saying he did not want to [return], but Mama Huaco told him that he should be ashamed of being such an insolent young man [and] not wanting to return for the relics. Shamed by this, [Ayar Auca] agreed, and he took a servant, Tambo Chacay, with him. On arriving at the cave, Ayar Auca went inside to get the drinking vessels that he had been asked to bring, and while he was looking inside the cave, Tambo Chacay sealed the door with a large stone, as he had been instructed to do by the [other] brothers. As Ayar Auca was trapped inside, he began to scream, attempting to escape. He shouted so loudly that the *[f.18v]* mountain shook and [split open] in many places, and Tambo Chacay [sat] on top of the stone that he had used to close the entrance. Then, Ayar Auca cursed him from inside the cave, saying, "You traitor! You [think you will] return from here and tell of this? You will [always] remain there, [just] as I am trapped inside." With this, Tambo Chacay was turned into stone and can be seen there to this day.

[The Indians] tell a ridiculous tale and story to explain the reason why the other brothers had Ayar Auca return to the cave and had him locked inside. [They say that] while [the brothers] were walking, [Ayar Auca] was throwing stones and knocking down hills, and because he was so fierce, they did not dare to continue

---

98   The Hacienda of Huayna Cancha is located close to Puma Orco (Bauer 1991). Both Cabello Valboa (1951 [1586]:261) and Sarmiento de Gamboa (2007 [1572]:65) suggest that Manco Capac had sex with Mama Ocllo there.

99   Sarmiento de Gamboa (2007 [1572]:65) writes "Haysquisrro," which could be the modern town of Yaurisque.

100   Cabello Valboa (1951 [1586]:261) writes "Tambo," while Sarmiento de Gamboa (2007 [1572]:63) writes "Tamboquiro."

101   Sarmiento de Gamboa (2007 [1572]:65) states that it was Ayar Cachi who was entombed in Tambotoco, while Murúa and Cabello Valboa (1951 [1586]:261) suggest it was Ayar Auca.

102   A spelling error has been corrected (Murúa 2008 [1616]:18r).

103   Cobo (1979 [1653]:104) indicates that these were maize seeds.

with him. They feared that when they arrived where there were [other] people, he might dare to commit an excessive [act], so they would all be killed.

They left [Tambuqui] and arrived at the hill now called Huanacauri.[104] There they saw in the morning at dawn a rainbow from afar, because it was the rainy season, with one end fixed on the hill [of Huanacauri]. They asked one another, "Do you see that rainbow?," and they all answered, "Yes." Then Manco Capac, the eldest, said: "This is a good sign; the world shall not be destroyed by water. Let us go there, and from there see where we can establish our town." So, they cast lots to decide what to do, and they saw that it was good to go to the hill and to see what was there and what land could be seen. As they walked toward the hill, they spotted a *huaca*[105] in the distance shaped like a person, seated atop a rock and the rainbow's arch emerging from it. This was Chimpo Ycahua,[106] the *huaca* of a small town called Sañu,[107] which was a little less than a league away.

After discussing the matter, they decided to try to capture [the *huaca*], and if they failed, no harm would be done. Ayar Cachi[108] approached the huaca, and as he arrived, he grabbed it and said: "What are you doing, brother? Let's stay together." The *huaca* turned its head to see who was [speaking], but because [Ayar Cachi] was on top of it, [the *huaca*] could not see him. When [Ayar Cachi] tried to leave, he could not, as the soles of his feet were stuck to the back of the *huaca*. The [other] brothers, realizing that [Ayar Cachi] was trapped, ran to help him. However, when they arrived, [Ayar Cachi] said to them, "You have done me a great evil. I can no longer go with you [and] I am now separated from your company. I know that you will become great rulers. I beg you to remember me in all your feasts and sacrifices and make me the first to receive your offerings, for I will remain here. And when you hold the[109] *Huarachico*[110] celebration for your boys, let them worship me as their father who will remain here forever." With these [words], Ayar Cachi was transformed into [the] stone known as Huanacauri.[111]

---

104   Huanacauri is the highest mountain on the south side of the Cuzco Valley. It was one of the most important shrines for the Inca (Bauer 1998).

105   This word is underlined (Murúa 2008 [1616]:18v).

106   Cabello Valboa (1951 [1586]:263) also uses the name Chimpo Ycahua.

107   Sañu (clay) was a small town within the Cuzco Valley known for its ceramic production (Bauer 1998:103).

108   In Sarmiento de Gamboa's (2007 [1572]) telling of the myth, it is Ayar Auca who climbs Huanacauri and is converted into stone, while Cabello Valboa (1951 [1586]:262) and Murúa have Ayar Cachi climbing the hill.

109   A correction has been made (Murúa 2008 [1616]:18v).

110   Cabello Valboa (1951 [1586]:263) and Sarmiento de Gamboa (2007 [1572]:67) both mention the Huarachico at this point in their chronicles. The word is underlined (Murúa 2008 [1616]:18v).

111   Huanacauri is underlined (Murúa 2008 [1616]:18v).

Figure 2.1. The figure reads "Manco Capac," written by Murúa (Adorno 2008:101.) It depicts Manco Capac at the top of a hill wearing a pectoral as the people of Cuzco see him. The cave of Tambotoco is visible near the base of the hill, with the Ayar siblings emerging from it. Near the center of the illustration, Ayar Auca is depicted returning to Tambotoco. The two figures in the forefront may represent Manco Capac and Copalimayta meeting at a stream just outside of Cuzco. For a slightly different interpretation of this drawing, see Adorno and Boserup (2008:39). This illustration has been removed from Murúa (2004 [1590]) and inserted into Murúa (2008 [1616]:19r); on the reverse side of this illustration is a version of chapter 1 from Murúa (2004 [1590]) (courtesy of The J. Paul Getty Museum, Los Angeles. Ms. Ludwig XIII 16 [83.MP.159], f.19).

The brothers sadly descended the hill and arrived at a place called Matahua, located at the foot of Huanacauri.[112] There, they pierced the ears of Sinchi Roca,[113] which is [part of the] *Huarachico* [celebration]. They wept the loss of their brothers, saying, "Oh, if only our brothers could see this youth, how they would rejoice with him." And so, they began to weep. This is when they invented the [tradition] of mourning for the dead and [other] ceremonies where they cry, imitating the cooing of doves. There they also invented the *raymi*[114] ceremonies: *Quicochico*,[115] *Rutuchico*[116] and the festival of *Ayuscay*,[117] which will be described in their respective places.

[F.20R] CHAPTER [BLANK][118]

The first king and Inca, Manco Capac, father and founder, from whom all the other [Incas] descended, and his wonderful works

Manco Capac[119] began ruling the great city of Cuzco in one of the aforementioned ways.[120] Because he had a strong and generous spirit and a sharp, wise, and subtle wit, he governed in a way that quickly won the hearts of all. The first thing he did was to organize the town's laws,[121] establishing a settlement in what was previously *chacras* and farmhouses. He divided it into two *ayllus* or neighborhoods, as will be described in the section on the city of Cuzco.[122] With [these changes], he sanctioned his position, making himself more respected by the general populace. He

---

112 Matahua is mentioned by several other writers, including Cabello Valboa (1951 [1586]:263), Cobo (1979 [1653]:109), and Sarmiento de Gamboa (2007 [1572]:68), as well as by more recent researchers (Bauer 1998:110; Rowe 1944:43).
113 Cabello Valboa (1951 [1586]:263–264), Cobo (1979 [1653]:109), and Sarmiento de Gamboa (2007 [1572]:68) also note that these important rituals occurred at Matahua.
114 This word is underlined (Murúa 2008 [1616]:18v).
115 The female initiation rite for the Inca. This word is underlined (Murúa 2008 [1616]:18v).
116 A rite held by the Inca at the time of the first hair cutting of a child. This word is underlined (Murúa 2008 [1616]:18v).
117 The birth rite held by the Inca. This word is underlined (Murúa 2008 [1616]:18v).
118 The *General History of Peru* (Murúa 2008 [1616]:20r) contains an unnumbered chapter between chapters 2 and 3.
119 A textual error has been corrected (Murúa 2008 [1616]:20r).
120 In this chapter, Murúa diverts from his discussion of the arrival of the Incas to provide additional comments on Manco Capac.
121 A textual error has been corrected (Murúa 2008 [1616]:20r).
122 Murúa provides a detailed description of Cuzco in book 3, chapter 10 of his chronicle.

Figure 2.2. The figure reads: "Sinchi Roca," written by Murúa (Adorno 2008:101). It shows Manco Capac giving the youth Sinchi Roca the royal arms (courtesy of The J. Paul Getty Museum, Los Angeles, Ms. Ludwig XIII 16 [83. MP.159], f.21r.).

appointed his son Sinchi Roca as the captain of one of the *ayllus* he founded so that after his death, Sinchi Roca would succeed him as king. He [also] distributed the rest [of the people] among his direct descendants, establishing a law that the second sons of the living Inca would serve as the heads and general captains of their father's *ayllus* and kin groups.

The practice of dividing the settlements by their *ayllus* and neighborhoods, which was done in Cuzco, was replicated in all the other towns of his kingship and continues to this day in the kingdoms of Peru.[123] As Cuzco was a town and a city, [Manco Capac] ordered that no one should enter after sunset or leave before dawn, so they [had to] leave during daylight hours. This was done to track who was leaving and entering the city, for a tyrant fears plots against him. This [demonstrates] that no matter how much dread a tyrant inflicts upon his vassals, the fear he experiences within himself is greater. As [Claudio] Claudiano writes in his *Institutio Principis*: "The tyrant is more terrified of himself than of those he oppresses."[124]

Having established these laws and organized Cuzco (which I will return to), Manco Capac pursued *[f.20v]* greater things that awakened his generous heart. Wanting a larger empire and monarchy, he established general courts, summoning all the *caciques*, ~~chiefs~~[125] captains, and the most distinguished people in his realm. On a chosen day, they all gathered in Cuzco, and he outlined how the courts would be formed and operated and what would be done one in [each of] them.

Many other measures were ordered to ensure good government and laws. Above all, he sought and wanted to establish a dynasty and courts for a Western empire. So, he had his son Sinchi Roca sworn in as his legitimate successor and natural lord through these courts, and he personally knighted him. [margin note: with the ceremonies and insignia, which will be described later.][126] With this his generous spirit was content, and considering what Aristotle says in *The Politics*,[127] that a sure way to remain a tyrant is to not do all one wants or can during their lifetime, [Manco Capac] governed the rest of his life with such great prudence and gentleness that he was [both] feared and loved by all his vassals. Manco Capac lived many years, and upon his death, he left only one legitimate son, who succeeded him. In the end, Sinchi Roca became the second Inca King of the western Kingdom of Peru.

---

123 Murúa discusses the origin of the word "Peru" and the arrival of Francisco Pizarro in book 3, chapter 1 of his chronicle.

124 This section is written in Latin: "*qui terret plus ipse timet sors ista tyranis*," within which several corrections have been made (Murúa 2008 [1616]:20r).

125 The word "mandones" has been crossed out by Remón (Adorno 1980:107).

126 "Con las ceremonias e insignias que dire adelante" is written in the margin of the manuscript by Remón (Adorno 1980:103).

127 "Aris[toteles] polit[ica]" is written in the margin by Remón (Adorno 1980:103).

The coronation of Sinchi Roca, and the body and face of[128] Manco Capac, well as the first weapons that he held and used, being the first of the Incas, can be seen in figures 2.1 and 2.2.[129]

[F.22R] CHAPTER 3

How Manco Capac armed his son Sinchi Roca as a knight and forced his way into Cuzco and took it over

Manco Capac, his brother, sister, and son remained in Matahua for a long time.[130] His sister, Mama Huaco (although others claimed she was his wife), cast two golden staffs towards Cuzco. One landed at Colcapampa,[131] which was two harquebus shots away, but it did not stick. The second [staff] landed at Huacaypata,[132]

---

128   A textual error has been corrected (Murúa 2008 [1616]:20r).

129   This last sentence was added by Murúa (Adorno 2008:103).

　　　Guaman Poma de Ayala's drawings of the kings of Peru are generally very different than those found in the *History and Genealogy of the Inca Kings of Peru* (Murúa 2004 [1590]) and the *General History of Peru* (Murúa 2008 [1616]). However, a few show close similarities. For example, this drawing is similar in many ways to the drawing of Manco Capac in the *History and Genealogy of the Inca Kings of Peru* (Murúa 2004 [1590]:9v) and to the drawing of Manco Capac provided by Guaman Poma de Ayala (2004 [1615]:86). Furthermore, the coat of arms shown on this drawing is similar to the coat of arms shown on the figure of Mama Uaco, or Mama Ocllo, in the *History and Genealogy of the Inca Kings of Peru* (Murúa 2004 [1590]:22v).

　　　It is also worth noting that most of the Incas and Coyas illustrated in the *General History of Peru* (Murúa 2008 [1616]) are shown standing on tile floors while the Incas and Coyas in both the *History and Genealogy of the Inca Kings of Peru* (Murúa 2004 [1590]) and *The First New Chronicle* (Guaman Poma de Ayala 2004 [1615]) are shown standing on the ground (Ossio 2008:88). One can also note that the Murúa manuscripts tend to show both the Incas and Coyas standing alone, while *The First New Chronicle* (Guaman Poma de Ayala 2004 [1615]) tends to show the Incas standing alone while the Coyas are generally surrounded by servants.

130   Cabello Valboa (1951 [1586]:268–270), Cobo (1979 [1653]:104), and Sarmiento de Gamboa (2007 [1572]:68–73) all present similar accounts of the arrival of Manco Capac and his siblings at the Cuzco Valley. Sarmiento de Gamboa tends to provide more information than the others.

131   Colcapampa was a shrine on the Cuzco Ceque System and was where the plaza of San Sebastián is now (Bauer 1998:90–91). Also see Cobo (1990 [1653]:68); Santa Cruz Pachacuti Yamqui Salcamaygua (1993 [1613]:214–215); Sarmiento de Gamboa (2007 [1572]:68); and Cabello Valboa (1951 [1586]:269), who writes "Cullca Bomba."

132   The field of Huacaypata was a shrine within the Cuzco Ceque System (Bauer 1998:103). It

about three-quarters of a league from the Arch [de la Plata on the road] to Our Lord Sebastián, sinking deep into the ground. This was interpreted as a good sign.

In Matahua, which is a league from Cuzco, Sinchi Roca was knighted and given the gold *tupayauri*, which is like a scepter, which was given to those who were to be Inca lords. There, Sinchi Roca and Mama Coca, [the] daughter of [Sutic] Huamán[133] from the village of Sañu, had [a son named] Manco Sapaca before they walked to Cuzco. When they arrived at Colcapampa,[134] where the first rod landed, they took the earth in their hands and saw that it was not good for sowing. So, they continue to Guamantiana[135] and [then to] Huacaypata, where the second staff had landed. Seeing that it had sunk in deep and that the soil was good and fertile, they planted [corn] there.

At that time, Cuzco was called Acamama[136] and was inhabited by Lares, Poques, and Guaylas Indians; [who were] ordinary, poor, and miserable people. [The Incas] captured a Poque or Guayla and killed him, taking out his lungs and inflating them, and then with their mouths still bloody, they continued to the town of the[137] Guaylas.[138]

On seeing them, the Guaylas fled, believing they were cannibals. The Incas continued until they reached an arch near a small stream,[139] where Copalimayta, a native of Cuzco, came to stop them from entering [the city]. Faced with this opposition, the Incas returned to Huanaypata, which translates to "a precious thing." As the land was so good and productive, they found that their sowing had produced an abundance of corn, with ears even at the top of the stalks.[140] After discussing

---

is also mentioned by Cabello Valboa (1951 [1586]:269) and Sarmiento de Gamboa (2007 [1572]:68, 69, 71, 227). It was a large, terraced area on the outskirts of Cuzco where the first planting ritual took place each year (Bauer 1996).

133   Cabello Valboa (1951 [1586]:274), Cieza de León (1976 [1553–1554]:194), Cobo (1979 [1653]:109), and Sarmiento de Gamboa (2007 [1572]:68) all write, "Sutic Huamán." Murúa misread the name Sutic as "su tia" in the text he was copying and wrote, "hija de su tia Huamán [daughter of his aunt Huamán]." We have corrected this error, writing, "the daughter of Sutic Huamán."

134   A mistake within the word "Colcapampa" was corrected.

135   Cabello Valboa (1951 [1586]:269) also mentions this location. Guamantiana was a spring on the Cuzco Ceque System (Bauer 1998:90). Its location is still known today.

136   Murúa again mentions that Cuzco was first called Acamama in book 3, chapter 10 of his chronicle. It is worth noting that Cabello Valboa, Cobo, and Sarmiento de Gamboa do not mention this name; however, Guaman Poma de Ayala (2004 [1615]:31, 84, 86) mentions Acamama three times in his chronicle.

137   The word "the" has been inserted into the text (Murúa 2008 [1616]:22r).

138   For additional information on these mythic actions, see Bauer (1996).

139   This may be a reference to Tullumayo.

140   This field was called Sausiro and is listed as a *huaca* in the Cuzco Ceque System: "[In

Figure 3.1. The figure reads: "Manco Capac the first Inca," written by Murúa (Adorno 2008:101) (courtesy of The J. Paul Getty Museum, Los Angeles, Ms. Ludwig XIII 16 [83.MP.159], f.21v.).

their options, they decided to take Cuzco by force, and due to their courage and [hard] work, they captured the [city] and Copalimayta himself. Finding himself imprisoned and fearing for his life, [Copalimayta] offered to give them his lands and make a cession of all that he possessed. So, they released him. Upon seeing that he was no longer able to drive [the Incas] out of his land, and that they were a war-like, fierce, and industrious people, [Copalimayta] left his house, land, and *[f.22v]* family to Mama Huaco, Manco Capac's wife. He said to them, "I am going away, and wherever you see much snow, you will say, there he is." With that, he vanished, and they never saw or heard of him again.[141]

Manco Capac and Mama Huaco, his wife, Sinchi Roca, and Manco Sapaca[142] then founded the city of Cuzco, and constructed the Coricancha,[143] a temple dedicated to the Sun, where the convent of Santo Domingo is now. As the first king and lord, Manco Capac instructed the people in their religion and how to worship, although not as perfectly as they later did. After ruling for many years, [Manco Capac] died, leaving Sinchi Roca, his son, as his successor and heir, along with Mama Huaco, his wife and sister, a daughter named Chimpo Coya, and a bastard son named Pachacuti.[144]

Others describe the arrival of this brave Manco Capac in Cuzco in a different way, saying that after arriving with his brothers, son, and wife, he made two very thin gold disks. He put one on his chest and the other on his back and [he wore] a diadem, which the Indians call a *canipu*,[145] on his head. Manco Capac sent some Indian to announce in Cuzco that he was the son of the Sun, and that they should receive him and obey him as their lord and that they could see him on a high hill.[146] He showed himself there and was seen by the Poques Indians, natives of Cuzco, as he walked the hill. As the sunlight reflected off the disks and diadem, they shone brightly. On

April] those who had been knighted, would go to the field of Sausiro to bring in the corn that had been harvested there, which is below the arch, where they sat Mama Huaco, sister of Manco Capac, the first Inca, sowed the first maize. They cultivated that field every year for the mummy of Mama Huaco, producing from it the chicha necessary for the service of her mummy" (Bauer 1998:101).

141   Cabello Valboa (1951 [1586]:269) and Sarmiento de Gamboa (2007 [1572]:71) present similar accounts of Copalimayta.

142   The final "a" in the name Sapaca appears to have been removed (Murúa 2008 [1616]:22v).

143   Additional details concerning the Coricancha are provided by Murúa in book 3, chapter 10 of his chronicle.

144   See book 1, chapter 86 for a description of this son. He should not be confused with Pachacuti Inca Yupanqui, who ruled many generations later.

145   It is interesting to note that the Oré text, which Murúa was copying in this section, does not include the word "canipu"; however, Molina (2011 [ca.1575]) does use this word.

146   Cabello Valboa (1951 [1586]), Cobo (1979 [1653]), and Sarmiento de Gamboa (2007 [1572]) do not mention this alternative myth.

seeing him, the Indians were frightened. Believing he was the son of the Sun and a divinity, they accepted him as their absolute lord, offering him obedience and innumerable riches, treasures, and all that he desired. This made him rich and powerful, and he went on to conquer some nearby villages that defied his authority.[147]

Be either of these [stories] true, both versions are told and discussed among the Indians, and they[148] treat them as fact. There is no other known origin, or foundation [story], for the lordship of the Incas, who founded the great city of Cuzco, [the] capital of these kingdoms, [and] who led, conquered, and ruled over these kingdoms, apart from the one that is presented here, for they had no written letters and did not know how to write or [record] history, more than what was recorded on their *quipus*.[149] These [*quipus*] are strings on which they tie knots, recording anything they want. These [*quipus* are the sources] of what I have said and shall say in all of this history.[150]

The departure of the brothers from the cave and Manco Capac's trick using silver[151] disks to make himself be worshipped can be seen in the following figure (figure 3.1).[152]

[F.23V] CHAPTER 4

Coya Mama Huaco, the wife of Manco Capac, and her rule

Ordinarily, when recounting [the history] of the Inca lords of this kingdom, some things and events concerning the Coyas, their queens [and] wives, are mentioned. However, to provide more details and clarity to this story, I will give each Coya and queen, as well as their husband, their own chapters, rather than mixing them within a single text and confusing the reader, which I am striving to avoid.[153] It will, and

---

147   This myth of the arrival of Manco Capac at Cuzco is taken from Oré (1598:39r–39v). Cobo (1979 [1653]:103) contains a similar, although not identical, version of this myth.

148   The word "they" has been inserted into the text by Murúa (Adorno 2008:22).

149   Murúa (2008 [1616]) includes more information on *quipus* in book 3, chapter 23 of his chronicle.

150   We know that Murúa copied a great deal of his chronicle from other writers, so this statement is questionable at best.

151   Earlier in this chapter, these plates were described as made of gold.

152   This final sentence was added by Murúa (Adorno 2008:101). However, the figure is now found at the end of chapter 2.

153   Both the *General History of Peru* (Murúa 2008 [1616]) and *The First New Chronicle* (Guaman Poma de Ayala 2004 [1615]) provide chapters on the Coyas. However, there is little overlap in the information that they contain. They also differ in that the *General History*

Figure 4.1. Untitled. Presumed to be Mama Huaco Coya (courtesy of The J. Paul Getty Museum, Los Angeles, Ms. Ludwig XIII 16 [83.MP.159], f.23r).

has, cost me more work and effort, but because the Indians mix and confuse certain things and events with others, it ensures more accuracy. This [mixing] causes great difficulties for those who hear them and are trying to recover information.

This Coya and Lady, Mama Huaco, was renowned for her courage, understanding, and discretion. Some attribute the death of the Poques Indian, who was killed on their arrival at Cuzco, to her.[154] She removed his lungs and inflated them, which horrified and frightened the local inhabitants.[155] She was, as it is said, the wife and sister of Manco Capac, the first Inca and Lord of this land. It is possible that among them, marriage with their full sisters was not abhorred nor detested, but instead it was licit and permitted, or perhaps as kings and powerful people, they believed that nothing was forbidden to them, and everything was licit and just. Or the sensual and lure of the vice and weakness of the flesh, defeated and trampled them, and they made a law to cover up their faults and vices. [Whatever the case may be] it was established and ordered that [only] the sister of the Inca and lord would be his true and legitimate wife, and that her son or sons would succeed him as the universal ruler of the kingdom. Thus, this custom and abuse was continued ~~against our natural law of which according to the~~ ●●●●●●●aga ●●●●●●●●●●●ta is ~~marriages between siblings~~.[156]

It would take forever to describe the greatness of Mama Huaco, the legitimate wife of Manco Capac, and the majesty of the service and riches of her house. She was very beautiful, with a somewhat brown complexion, which is generally true of all the Coyas and *ñustas* of this noble line. They wore dresses of the finest *cumbi*, which looks like silk, decorated with many various figures of birds and flowers. They [adorned themselves with] gold and silver *tupus*[157] and *tipqui*,[158] which they still use today, with small bells. These [shawl pins] were used to fasten and secure *lliclla*[*s*][159] across their chests.

of Peru (Murúa 2008 [1616]) discusses the Coyas together with the reigning Inca, while in *The First New Chronicle* (Guaman Poma de Ayala 2004 [1615]), all the Incas are discussed first, followed by all the Coyas. There is, however, much overlap between some of the descriptions of the Coyas provided in the *History and Genealogy of the Inca Kings of Peru* (Murúa 2004 [1590]) and those of *The First New Chronicle* (Guaman Poma de Ayala 2004 [1615]).

154   Cabello Valboa (1951 [1586]:182–194) also describes the actions of Mama Huaco and the conquest of the Cuzco Valley by the first Incas. Also see information collected by Toledo during his 26 January 1572 meeting with Native leaders in Cuzco (Levillier 1940:182–194).

155   The Incas inflated the lungs of sacrificed animals as a form of divination.

156   The censor, Alonso Remón, felt uncomfortable with the topic of sibling marriage (Adorno 2008:103; Murúa 2008 [1616]:23v).

157   This word is underlined (Murúa 2008 [1616]:23v).

158   This word is underlined (Murúa 2008 [1616]:23v).

159   This word is underlined (Murúa 2008 [1616]:23v).

[Mama Huaco], out of nobility and pretention, changed garments three times a day, never wearing the same clothes twice. This Coya was served with great fanfare and music, and she usually had fifty *ñustas*,[160] daughters of lords, in addition to other commoners. She usually ate maize in *locros*[161] *anca*[162] *[f.24r]* and *mote*[163] mixed in different ways with [other] foods, cooked or otherwise. Although these foods may seem coarse and crude to us, to them, they were as elegant and tasty as the most refined meals served to the monarchs and kings of our Europe. They drank *chicha*,[164] which was held in high regard, much like the smooth and aged wines of Spain. This *chicha* was made in countless ways, thanks to the efforts of the expert *ñustas* and maidens in her household. [Mama Huaco] was a woman of great authority, and when the people entered [her presence] they performed endless observances, and they knelt when talking to her. As mentioned, she and Manco Capac, her brother and husband, had two children: Sinchi Roca and Chimpo Coya. ~~She looked like this.~~[165]

Her drawing appears at the beginning of this chapter (figure 4.1).[166]

[F.25R] CHAPTER 5

The life of Sinchi Roca, the first Inca lord

As mentioned, Manco Capac was succeeded by Sinchi Roca, the son of him and Mama Huaco, his wife and sister.[167] Sinchi Roca was a brave and warlike man. He was frank, generous, and friendly to those whom he held in high esteem. He was the first to command that everyone in his lineage should have their ears pierced as a sign of their nobility, as his [ears] had been pierced by his nephew Manco Hinga during a war. Although others say that the [tradition] of ear piercing began with the first Incas, who had pierced ears upon arriving in Cuzco, and from that time [this practice] was passed to Inca Sinchi Roca's lineage, to identify them as royal nobility.

160   This word is underlined (Murúa 2008 [1616]:23v).
161   This word is underlined (Murúa 2008 [1616]:23v).
162   This word is underlined (Murúa 2008 [1616]:23v).
163   This word is underlined (Murúa 2008 [1616]:24r).
164   This word is underlined (Murúa 2008 [1616]:24r).
165   This sentence, written by Remón, was later removed since the illustration of Chimpo Coya is located at the front of the chapter, not at the end (Adorno 2008:104, 107; Murúa 2008 [1616]:24r).
166   This final sentence was added by Murúa (Adorno 2008:102).
167   Cabello Valboa (1951 [1586]:274), Cobo (1979 [1653]), Guaman Poma de Ayala (2004 [1615]:89), and Sarmiento de Gamboa (2007 [1572]:78) each provide very different details on the life of Sinchi Roca.

Figure 5.1. The figure reads: "The likeness of Sinchi Roca, who was the first lord and Inca" and "this Inca's coat of arms." (courtesy of The J. Paul Getty Museum, Los Angeles: Ms. Ludwig XIII 16 [83.MP.159], f.24v).

This was done with great ceremony, as will be detailed later. Sinchi Roca married his sister Chimpo Coya, in accordance with the law.[168] He had many children, the foremost of whom was Lloque Yupanqui, [the] son of his wife and sister, who succeeded him as lord. This is what he looked like (figure 5.1).[169]

[F.26R] CHAPTER 6

The life of Chimpo[170] Coya, [the] wife of Inca Sinchi[171] Roca

Chimpo Coya, the wife and sister of Sinchi Roca, was the daughter of Manco Capac, the first Inca King, and his wife Mama Huaco.[172] Her face was very similar to that of her mother's and she [exuded with the same] pomp and majesty when she was served, and in how she conducted herself. Sinchi Roca had many children with her, but we know only the names of two: Cusi Huanan Chiri[173] and Lloque

---

168   Cabello Valboa (1951 [1586]:274), Cieza de León (1976 [1553–1554]:194), Cobo (1979 [1653]:109), and Sarmiento de Gamboa (2007 [1572]:68) all mention that Sinchi Roca married Mama Coca, who was the daughter of Sutic Huamán, the leader of the nearby town of Sañu. However, Guaman Poma de Ayala (2004 [1615]:89) states that Sinchi Roca married Chimpo Urma.

169   This final sentence was added by Murúa (Adorno 2008:103).
      In the History and Genealogy of the Inca Kings of Peru (Murúa 2004 [1590]), it is the Coyas who are shown with coats of arms, while in the General History of Peru (Murúa 2008 [1616]) the coats of arms have been copied from the History and Genealogy of the Inca Kings of Peru and placed with the appropriate Inca. This indicates that the artist of the General History of Peru had access to the History and Genealogy of the Inca Kings of Peru.
      The drawing in figure 5.1 shares some similarities with the drawing of Sinchi Roca in the History and Genealogy of the Inca Kings of Peru (Murúa 2004 [1590]:10rv) and with the drawing of Sinchi Roca provided in The First New Chronicle (Guaman Poma de Ayala 2004 [1615]:88). However, the figures in the History and Genealogy of the Inca Kings of Peru (Murúa 2004 [1590]) and The First New Chronicle (Guaman Poma de Ayala 2004 [1615]) are extremely similar. The coat of arms shown on this drawing is the same coat of arms shown on the figure of Mama Cura (the third Coya) in the History and Genealogy of the Inca Kings of Peru (Murúa 2004 [1590]:24v).

170   A spelling mistake has been corrected by Murúa in the text (Adorno 2008:101).
171   A spelling mistake has been corrected by Murúa in the text (Adorno 2008:101).
172   Cabello Valboa (1951 [1586]:283–284), Cobo (1979 [1653]:115–117), and Sarmiento de Gamboa (2007 [1572]:80–81) tell somewhat similar stories of the life of Lloque Yupanqui as presented in this chapter. Sarmiento de Gamboa tends to provide more information than the others. Some of this information also appears in Fernández de Palencia (1963 [1571]:80).
173   Guaman Poma de Ayala (2004 [1615]:158 [160]) also mentions Cusi Huanan Chiri; however, he suggests that he was the son of Lloque Yupanqui, not his brother.

Yupanqui, with the latter inheriting his father's [position].[174] She generally lived in Cuzco and had many *ñustas* and females serving her. She dressed them ostentatiously in fancy clothes and gold anklets. They considered thick thighs and calves as signs of elegance and beauty, and so they tastefully and stylishly [wore adornments] below and above their knees.

When a captain or governor *orejón*[175] visited this Coya, she would receive them in a round *buhío*, like a chapel. She would command them to sit down and have the *ñustas* bring out carved, black, palm-wood benches, which they called *duhos*. The captains and *orejones* held these [seats] in high esteem, and they sat down before her with great humility. She treated all her vassals with the same respect and affection as she had a noble and generous heart.

She is [shown] on the opposite page (figure 6.1).[176]

[*F.27R*] CHAPTER 7

Lloque Yupanqui, the third Inca

Lloque Yupanqui, the third Inca, son of Sinchi Roca and Chimpo Coya, married [his] sister, Mama Cura, who was also known as Anahuarque. He was left-handed, which is "*lloque*" in his language. He lived in great peace and prosperity, as [the leaders from] nations in different areas came to visit him; such as Huamac Samo of Huaro and Pachachulla Viracocha of the Ayarmacas and the Quilescaches.[177] They say one day during a large celebration, the Sun appeared to Lloque Yupanqui in the form of a person and told him that he would become a great lord, and have a son in his old age. Since he was already [old] and he had no son to succeed him in the kingdom, the Indians, his vassals, thought that it was impossible for him to have or produce [a son]. Nevertheless, his *orejon*[178] servant, or some say his bastard brother Manco Sapaca,[179] took him one day to his wife, Coya Mama Cura,[180] and they had intercourse.

---

174   Guaman Poma de Ayala (2004 [1615]:123) provides the names of several other children of Sinchi Roca and Chimpo Coya.

175   A high-ranking person from Cuzco.

176   This final sentence was added by Murúa (Adorno 2008:101).

177   These leaders and groups are also mentioned by Cabello Valboa (1951 [1586]:283), Cobo (1979 [1653]:115), and Sarmiento de Gamboa (2007 [1572]:80). We have used the names recorded in these works, since those of Murúa are poorly copied.

178   This word is underlined (Murúa 2008 [1616]:27r).

179   Manco Sapaca is also mentioned in Cabello Valboa (1951 [1586]:283) and Sarmiento de Gamboa (2007 [1572]:80).

180   Cabello Valboa (1951 [1586]:283), Cobo (1979 [1653]:117), and Sarmiento de Gamboa

Figure 6.1. The figure reads: "Chimpo Coya," written by Murúa (Adorno 2008:101) (courtesy of The J. Paul Getty Museum, Los Angeles, Ms. Ludwig XIII 16 [83.MP.159], f.25v).

She became pregnant and bore a son named Mayta Capac. He had no other sons, although some believe that he had other [sons] but they were poisoned in their youth. When civil war broke out in the empire, they fled to the *Andes*,[181] to avoid being killed. One of their father's brothers hid them there, and one of them died.[182]

The truth is that Lloque Yupanqui was succeeded by his son Mayta Capac. Lloque Yupanqui was so feared and respected by his [people] that they would turn their backs on him unable to even look at his face. If he spat, one of the principal persons would kneel, and he would spit into a small gold or silver cup that the Indians call "*chua*." Lloque Yupanqui ordered his people to fast for two months each year, during which time they were forbidden to consume salt and chili, or to touch their women. He would harshly [punish] public sins such as theft, killing, and sodomy, using methods such as whipping, cutting off their ears and noses, and hanging. He would [punish] nobles and other important people by cutting their hair or ripping off their shirts. When he died, his son Mayta Capac succeeded him.[183]

This is what he looked like (figure 7.1).[184]

[F.28R] CHAPTER 8

The Coya Mama Cura, also called Anahuarque, wife of Lloque Yupanqui Inca

The Coya and Lady Mama Cura, also known as Anahuarque, was the oldest sister of her husband Lloque Yupanqui. She was wise, discreet, and serious in her demeanor. She was highly esteemed, especially when she left the palace accompanied by *curacas*, important Indians, lord *orejones*, and common people. She dressed in fine clothes, and tried to imitate Chimpo Coya, her husband's mother. She wore an abundance

---

(2007 [1572]:80) call her Mama Cava (Cachua) and note that she was from the town of Oma. Cieza de León (1976 [1553–1554]:197) calls her Mama Cahua Pata. Guaman Poma de Ayala (2004 [1615]:96) states that Lloque Yupanqui married Mama Cura Ocllo.

181   This word is underlined (Murúa 2008 [1616]:27r).

182   This information is not provided in Cabello Valboa (1951 [1586]), nor in Sarmiento de Gamboa (2007 [1572]).

183   This information is not provided in Cabello Valboa (1951 [1586]), nor in Sarmiento de Gamboa (2007 [1572]).

184   This final sentence was added by Murúa (Adorno 2008:101).
        There is no coat of arms provided for the second Coya (Coya Chimpo) in the *History and Genealogy of the Inca Kings of Peru* (Murúa 2004 [1590]), so the artist of the *General History of Peru* (Murúa 2008 [1616]) used the same coat of arms for the second and third Coyas (see figure 7.1).

Figure 7.1. The figure reads: "Lloque Yupanqui, third Inca" and "this Inca's coat of arms," written by Murúa (Adorno 2008:101) (courtesy of The J. Paul Getty Museum, Los Angeles, Ms. Ludwig XIII 16 [83.MP.159], f.26v).

of *chaquira* and gold over her chest. She was well liked and loved by her vassals and was so serious that when some *ñustas*, or other female Indians, spoke to her, they were required to kneel, look down, and whisper without looking at her face. She enjoyed banquets and parties and frequently invited the principal lords of Cuzco; offering them, with a rare magnificence, splendid food, and abundant drink, and allowing them to take away whatever remained. This Coya rarely conversed with common people or ordinary female Indians, but she highly respected important female Indians, such as the wives of governors and *orejones*, whom she deemed to be honest. She honored them so much that she sometimes called them Coyas, which means "lady," but with all the seriousness and respect described above. They called her Sapa Coya, which means "unique lady." She was married, as mentioned, to Lloque Yupanqui, and they had a son name Mayta Capac, but no other children.[185]

This is what she looked like (figure 8.1).[186]

CHAPTER 9

Mayta Capac, [the] fourth Inca and king

Mayta Capac was the son of Lloque Yupanqui and Mama Cura. He was handsome, [had] a good disposition, great courage, strength and daring. [However,] during his father's life, he [was involved in] some misconduct, which caused him to be both hated and feared. [Mayta Capac] was feared because when playing with other boys of his same age and some natives of Cuzco, called Alcabiza and Culunchimas, he killed some boys and broke the legs [of others], and chased them to their homes. This caused the Alcabiza to hold a great enmity and hatred toward the Incas. They agreed one day to kill Lloque Yupanqui and his son Mayta Capac because they could not tolerate this poor treatment and insolence and [wanted to] completely destroy that lineage. So, they sent ten Indians to kill them in their house, the Coricancha. Upon arrival, they found Mayta Capac in the patio, playing with other boys[187] and two dogs[188] using balls called *cuchu*.

---

185   Fernández de Palencia (1963 [1571]:80) provides similar information on Mama Anahuarque. Guaman Poma de Ayala (2004 [1615]:125) provides the names of two of her children and suggests that there were others.

186   This final sentence was added by Murúa (Adorno 2008:101).

187   Cabello Valboa (1951 [1586]:284) notes that these boys included two of Lloque Yupanqui's cousins, Apu Conde Mayta and Tacachungay.

188   Cabello Valboa (1951 [1586]:284) also mentions these dogs and provides the name of the ball.

Figure 8.1. The figure reads: "Mama Cuya Coya," written by Murúa (Adorno 2008:101) (courtesy of The J. Paul Getty Museum, Los Angeles, Ms. Ludwig XIII 16 [83.MP.159], f.27v).

When [Mayta Capac] saw them entering his house with weapons, he seized a ball and killed two of the Indians with it. The other [boys] he was playing with ran to tell his father, Lloque Yupanqui. Lloque Yupanqui came out with other Indians and the dogs, chasing after the retreating Indians. They killed five of them; but the others escaped and went to tell the *caciques* of the Culunchimas and Alcabiza, who were close by. The *caciques*, seeing how Mayta Capac had killed their Indians, said: "If he is capable of such actions as a child, what will he do when he grows up? He will surely kill us! We should kill him and his father." So, they asked their nearby friends for help and support.

Upon seeing this, Lloque Yupanqui called his son and asked, "Why do you do these things? Do you want me to die at the hands of my enemies now that I am old?" [However] his captains told [Lloque Yupanqui] to leave [Mayta Capac] alone [as] there was a reason for [his actions], so [Lloque Yupanqui] kept silent.[189]

Seeing that the Alcabiza were coming to attack him, Mayta Capac went out to fight with his people and they thwarted them. The Alcabiza gathered more people to fight Mayta Capac again and encircled the Coricancha on three sides. Mayta Capac left through the door of Coricancha with a few people, and they fought and defeated [the Alcabiza] again. Mayta Capac then held the *Huarachico*, which is a festival or a celebration for a battle and victory. The Alcabiza then returned for a third time to try their luck and challenge Mayta Capac to battle. He faced the Alcabiza with great courage and bravery, and while fighting they say it hailed[190] so hard that he destroyed them. He won and destroyed them. His father, Lloque Yupanqui, was very pleased with the battle's outcome, and afterward held grand celebrations, gatherings, and feasts. When the people of the region saw the [Inca's] overwhelming victory, they came to obey and recognize [Lloque Yupanqui] as their lord.

When his father, Lloque Yupanqui, died, [Mayta Capac] expanded his kingdom and rule even more. As a result, the Incas grew more powerful every day, winning and conquering new lands and adding them to their crown, known as the *mascapaicha*. It was a red wool head band with very fine tassels, which they wore from temple to temple.[191] They also used the royal scepter, the *champi*, and the *sunturpaucar*,

---

189   Cabello Valboa (1951 [1586]:274, 284–286), Cobo (1979 [1653]:118–120), and Sarmiento de Gamboa (2007 [1572]:81–84) provide similar versions of the life of Lloque Yupanqui. Sarmiento de Gamboa tends to offer more information than the others. Cieza de León (1976 [1553–1554]:195–197) also narrates the life of Mayta Capac and his conflicts with the locals of the Cuzco region, but there is no overlap between his telling and that of Cabello Valboa, Cobo, Sarmiento de Gamboa, or Murúa.

190   Sarmiento de Gamboa (2007 [1572]:83) also mentions hail.

191   It is interesting to note that this section, which describes the *mascapaicha*, appears in both Cabello Valboa and Oré (1598:41r), suggesting that there was a common source.

Figure 9.1. The figure reads: "Mayta Capac [the] fourth Inca" and "this Inca's coat of arms," written by Murúa (Adorno 2008:101). The coat of arms shown on this drawing is the same coat of arms shown on the figure of Coya Mama Coca Chimpo Urma (the fourth Coya) in the *History and Genealogy of the Inca Kings of Peru* (Murúa 2004 [1590]:25v) (courtesy of The J. Paul Getty Museum, Los Angeles, Ms. Ludwig XIII 16 [83.MP.159], f.28v).

which was [made] of very elegant flower[s],[192] which was the ancient insignia used and painted on weapons in service of Inca Mayta Capac.[193]

When he died, he ordered that he be buried with much gold, silver, and precious stones, and a tomb be made as his[194] grave, and that his weapons be hung there, along with many featherworks and a vast array of food and drink. Some of his dearest women, pageboys, and [other] people [who were] close were to be buried with him. Mayta Capac was married to Chimpo Urma,[195] his first cousin, with whom he had eight sons and three daughters. The eldest was named Capac Yupanqui, another Tarco Guaman,[196] and one of the daughters was called Chimpo Ocllo.[197]

This is what he looked like (figure 9.1).[198]

[F.30R] CHAPTER 10

The Coya Chimpo Urma, the wife of the courageous Mayta Capac, who was also called Mama Yacche

Chimpo Urma was [the] wife and first cousin of Mayta Capac. [She was] very beautiful and since her childhood she was very calm, funny, and beloved by her people. She enjoyed pleasures and recreation, for which she had lions, tan tigers,[199] deer, monkeys, cats, guanacos, [and] vicuñas. She had raised them all since they were young, so they were tame and domesticated. She also owned a variety of birds,

192   The *sunturpaucar* is generally described as being made of bird feathers, not flowers.

193   Some of this paragraph was copied from Oré (1598:41r).

194   The word "his" has been inserted into the text by Murúa (Adorno 2008:101).

195   Both Cabello Valboa (1951 [1586]:286) and Sarmiento de Gamboa (2007 [1572]:83) state that Mayta Capac was married to Mama Tuacaray, from the town of Taucaray, which is near Cuzco. Cobo (1979 [1653]:119) states that her father was from the Collaguasi. Guaman Poma de Ayala (2004 [1615]:99, 129) lists the wife of Mayta Capac as Chimpo Urma Mama Machi and Chimpo Mama Yachi Urma.

196   Cabello Valboa (1951 [1586]:274, 284–286), Cobo (1979 [1653]:120), and Sarmiento de Gamboa (2007 [1572]:130) mention Capac Yupanqui and Tarco Huamán. Acosta (2002 [1590]:368), in a short and unusual listing of the Inca Kings, states that Tarco Huamán and his unnamed son became Incas. Polo de Ondegardo (2012 [1571]:346) also list Tarco Huamán within his list of Inca Kings.

197   Cabello Valboa (1951 [1586]:286), Cobo (1979 [1653]), and Sarmiento de Gamboa (2007 [1572]:83) do not mention Chimpo Ocllo.

198   Guaman Poma de Ayala (2004 [1615]:98) provides a drawing of Mayta Capac Inca that is similar in many ways to the one found in the *General History of Peru* (Murúa 2008 [1616]). This final sentence was added by Murúa (Adorno 2008:101).

199   The term "lions" may refer to pumas, and the term "tan tigers" may refer to jaguars.

Figure 10.1. The figure reads: "Chimpo Urma Coya," written by Murúa (Adorno 2008:101) (courtesy of The J. Paul Getty Museum, Los Angeles, Ms. Ludwig XIII 16 [83.MP.159], f.29v).

especially parrots. She [also] had salamanders, which were deadly poisonous and clucked like chickens at night. She had *guacamayos*, nightingales, thrushes, gold-finches, hawks, partridges, and numerous other varieties [of birds]. She had many fishermen who fished in different ways with nets, hooks, and arrows. In contrast, others could not fish without a license from the Inca and his captains; otherwise they would be subject to a fine. In the same way, she had many women to sow her *chacras* and diligently attended the most[200] productive cornfields. She [had] all kinds of *ají*; the most precious and finest were called "*asnac uchu*,"[201] meaning "fragrant chili pepper." She had many fruit trees, including prickly pears, *guavas*, bananas, *pacaes*, and all the other genres and types that grow in these provinces.

All of this was in this Coya's garden, where there was [also] a tree from which a milk-like liquor flowed, becoming a white gum which served as incense for their idols. Another liquor was distilled from a different tree, which when curdled, was a deadly poison. Instruments [such as] deer-bone flutes, large wooden flutes, pan-pipes, painted wooden drums, shell horns, and shell rattles were used to make music for this Coya. They danced with snails and shells attached to their legs, producing a bell-like sound. It is said that this Coya had many pastimes, enjoyed herself greatly, and was well-served and respected by her people. As mentioned, she left many sons, the eldest being Capac Yupanqui and [a] daughter [named] Chimpo Ocllo.[202]

She looked like this (figure 10.1).[203]

[F.31R] CHAPTER 11

Capac Yupanqui, the fifth Inca

Capac Yupanqui succeeded his father, Mayta Capac, as lord.[204] He was brave and bellicose. When he began his reign, he made all his brothers swear to accept [him] as lord and king, and they did so.[205] He lived peacefully in the Coricancha and con-

200   A spelling mistake has been corrected by Murúa (Adorno 2008:101).
201   Guaman Poma de Ayala (2004 [1615]) also mentions "asnac uchu" (i.e., *rocotos*, hot peppers).
202   Guaman Poma de Ayala (2004 [1615]:127) provides the names of many other children.
203   This final sentence was added by Murúa (Adorno 2008:101).
204   At this point in his narrative, Murúa moves away from information also presented in Cabello Valboa and Sarmiento de Gamboa and provides a nonoverlapping description of the life of Capac Yupanqui and later Incas. Interestingly, this chapter contains information also found in Molina (2011 [ca. 1575]).
205   Sarmiento de Gamboa (2007 [1572]:84) provides more information on this coronation.

quered the Cuyos²⁰⁶ in the province of Antisuyu. This Inca was the wisest, the most knowledgeable, and the best orator of all his ancestors. It was he who, by natural reasoning, began to question why the sun, with all its rays and brightness, could be obscured by something as small as a small cloud. He concluded that [the sun] could not be [the most powerful] God,²⁰⁷ but rather a messenger of the Creator who sent it to fertilize the earth and to visit the world every day.²⁰⁸ To prove this, he sent two important Indians to visit [the temple of] the Creator of the World, known as Pachacamac or Pacha Yachachic in their language. Upon arriving at Pachacamac,²⁰⁹ which is near the sea, four leagues from the city of Lima, they received an answer and guarantee from the people of that land that the Creator was invisible. When Capac Yupanqui understood this, he made the admirable and wonderful buildings that are at Pachacamac, dedicating them to the true and immense Creator God, to whom he made this elegant prayer:²¹⁰

> O Creator, you are [eternal]; from the foundation and beginning of the world to its end. You are powerful, rich, and merciful, and You gave being and spirit to all humanity, saying "[let] this [one] be a man and [let] this [one] be a woman" as You created, shaped, and painted all men and women. To all those that²¹¹ you made and have given life; guard them, [give them] safe and sound lives of peace and without danger. Wherever You are, be it high in the sky or lower in the clouds or in the darkness or in the abysses, hear me, answer me, and grant me what I ask! Give us eternal life. Hold us in Your hand and receive this sacrifice wherever You are.²¹²

When Capac Yupanqui finished saying this, he raised his eyes to Heaven and exclaimed, "O Creator!" with great emotion and reverence.²¹³

He explains that Conde Mayta was the eldest son of Mayta Capac. Nevertheless, Capac Yupanqui was selected to be ruler with the approval of his brothers. Cobo (1979 [1653]:121) also suggests that there were issues between these brothers.

206 Located near Pisac. Cabello Valboa (1951 [1586]:290) and Sarmiento de Gamboa (2007 [1572]:86) also mention this campaign. Also see Bauer and Covey (2002) and Covey (2006).

207 Molina (2011 [ca. 1575]:15) also discusses this cloud observation and attributes it to Pachacuti Inca Yupanqui.

208 Murúa further explores this issue in book 2, chapter 35 of his chronicle. Similar information is presented in Molina (2011 [ca. 1575]:15) and Cobo (1979 [1653]:134–135).

209 The site of Pachacamac is also described by Murúa in book 3, chapter 19 of his chronicle.

210 Murúa has written "prayer" in the margin (Adorno 2008:101).

211 The word "that" has been inserted into the text (Murúa 2008[1616]:31r).

212 This same prayer is recorded by Molina (2011 [ca. 1575]:49), and a much shorter version is presented by Guaman Poma de Ayala (2004 [1615]:54).

213 Much of this first paragraph, including the prayer, comes directly from Oré (1598:39v–40v).

Figure 11.1. The figure reads: "Capac Yupanqui" and "this Inca's coat of arms," written by Murúa (Adorno 2008:101). The coat of arms shown on this drawing is the same one shown on the figure of Coya Chimpo Ocllo Cahua (the fifth Coya) in the *History and Genealogy of the Inca Kings of Peru* (Murúa 2004 [1590]:26v) (courtesy of The J. Paul Getty Museum, Los Angeles: Ms. Ludwig XIII 16 [83. MP.159], f.30v).

During the time of this Inca, a miraculous event occurred. The town of Cache in Canas and Canchis was devastated by fire from the sky, as will be described later.[214] It is said that Capac Yupanqui died due to herbs that a sister, Cusi Chimpo,[215] gave him during a meal. He was married to Chimpo Ocllo,[216] his sister, with whom he had Inca Roca, who succeeded him, and Apu Mayta, who was very brave as will be mentioned later. They also had a daughter named Cusi Chimpo.

This is what he looked like (figure 11.1).[217]

CHAPTER 12

Chimpo Ocllo, also known as Mama Cahua, [the] wife of Capac Yupanqui Inca

Chimpo Ocllo, also known as Mama Cahua, [the] wife of Capac Yupanqui, was of medium height, thin, dark,[218] and had long black hair. She was agreeable, affable, sane, and serious, which is why they called her Mama Cahua, meaning "a sane and serious woman." She was a friend of [the] *chacras* and fields and [enjoyed] working in them. She was also a friend of the poor, to whom she gave many alms. Above all, she was known as a great ruler, when her husband, Capac Yupanqui, was not in Cuzco. She never wore a dress two times and changed [clothes] twice or thrice daily. Afterward, these clothes were distributed to the *ñustas* in her service. [Mama Cahua] bathed twice daily [and] always ate alone.[219] Her table was carved [and] about three to four feet [long]. The tablecloths and napkins were [brightly] colored. As in Spain, her palace was full of nimble and agile jesters, dancers, and tumblers.

---

214 See chapter 88.
215 No other writer mentions the death of Capac Yupanqui by poisoning.
216 Sarmiento de Gamboa (2007 [1572]:86) notes that Capac Yupanqui married Curihilpay from the Ayarmaca or from Cuzco itself. Cabello Valboa (1951 [1586]:90) and Cobo (1979 [1653]:122) state that Capac Yupanqui married Curihilpay (Curi Ilpayachua) and that she was from Cuzco. Cieza de León (1976 [1553–1554]:202) suggests that Capac Yupanqui married his sister named Micay Cuca. Guaman Poma de Ayala (2004 [1615]:99, 129, 197) writes that Capac Yupanqui married his sister named Chimpo Mama Cahua, also called Chimpo Mama Ocllo Cahua, and then, after her death, Capac Yupanqui married her younger sister named Cusi Chimpo Mama Micay, also called Coya Curi Ocllo.
217 This final sentence was added by Murúa (Adorno 2008:101).
218 A spelling mistake has been corrected by Murúa (Adorno 2008:101).
219 Rowe (1987:753) suggests that this description represents a summation of information presented in López de Gómara, in his work *Historia general de las Indias* (1552), concerning the court of Moctezuma (also see Álvarez-Calderón 2007).

They performed a thousand different feats and dances for the Coya, which they called "*saynatas*," akin to night parties among us.

When she went out of her house, she traveled under a canopy of feathers of different colors adorned with silver tassels which was carried by two of her *ñusta* nieces. Her *ojotas* were made of gold with stones set in them. These are just soles worn with straps as they are painted [being used] in the olden days. Walking in pairs, her servants laid blankets on the earth in front of her so she would not step on the ground. She died at a young age, and her death was deeply felt and mourned by her vassals. Her funeral rites were held in accordance with the custom of that time. She left behind a daughter, Cusi Chimpo.

This is what she looked like (figure 12.1).[220]

[F.33R] CHAPTER 13

Inca Roca, the sixth lord, who made the two divisions of Hanan Cuzco and Hurin Cuzco

Inca Roca, son of Capac Yupanqui, succeeded his father as lord and king. He was serious, peaceful, and ruled peacefully, maintaining harmonious relationships with his sons and vassals. He discovered the waters of Hurin Chacán and Hanan Chacán, which still irrigate the entire Cuzco Valley today, and his descendants [still] possess them.[221] He also divided and ordered the [city into] two parts, Hanan Cuzco and Hurin Cuzco, to better govern and rule his kingdom.[222]

He was generous, magnificent, and commanded that drinking parties and feasts be held as public gatherings, fearing that he would be killed [during one].[223] This brave Inca also commanded that certain stones and statues be erected so that

---

220   This final sentence was added by Murúa (Adorno 2008:101).

221   Cabello Valboa (1951 [1586]:294), Cieza de León (1976 [1553–1554]:202), and Sarmiento de Gamboa (2007 [1572]:88) mention the waters of Chacán in their accounts of Inca Roca. Cobo (1979 [1653]:125) notes that the body of Inca Roca was associated with rain and that it was brought out and carried through the fields during droughts. Both Albornoz (1984 [ca. 1582]:204) and Cobo (1979 [1653]) list Chanan Huanacauri as a shrine within the Cuzco Ceque System (Bauer 1998:61–62).

222   Cabello Valboa (1951 [1586]:294), Cobo (1979 [1653]:124), and Sarmiento de Gamboa (2007 [1572]:88) mention the creation of Hanan and Hurin Cuzco in their accounts of Inca Roca. Murúa (2008 [1616]) provides additional information on Hanan and Hurin Cuzco in book 3, chapter 10 of his chronicle.

223   In this next chapter, Murúa suggests that this Inca was poisoned in one such event.

Figure 12.1. The figure reads: "Chimpo Ocllo Coya," written by Murúa (Adorno 2008:101) (courtesy of The J. Paul Getty Museum, Los Angeles: Ms. Ludwig XIII 16 [83.MP.159], f.31v).

the Inca Kings would be venerated and honored, in life and death. Thus, every *ayllu* and lineage have statues of their Incas, and there were a great many in the city of Cuzco and its surroundings.[224] The statue of Inca Roca was the first to be discovered.[225] He was the head of Hanan Cuzco, and by his order, he was succeeded by Yahuar Huacac, Viracocha Inca, Tupa Inca Yupanqui, Huayna Capac, Huascar Inca, and Manco Inca. He was highly respected and feared. When the Indians spoke to him, they averted their gaze, looking at the ground, and when they entered his presence, they did so and on their knees. Before speaking, they asked for permission, and often, in a state of great emotion, they found it difficult to talk. When they [did] speak [to Inca Roca], it was in very low voices. Being an eloquent man, he spoke to them with a pleasant expression, granting many favors. He conquered Wimpillay and Quisallay,[226] near Cuzco and Caytomarca.[227] He was married to Cusi Chimpo,[228] and their first son, Yahuar Huacac, inherited the rule. Beside him, there were four [*sic*] other [sons]: Paucar Inca, Huamantassi Inca, Vicaquirao Inca,[229] Cacachicha Vicaquirao and Apu Mayta,[230] and a daughter named Ipa Huaco, also known as Mama Chiquia. They were comrades-in-arms of [Pachacuti] Inca Yupanqui. After a battle with some Indians near Cuzco, who were fortified in some high places near the town of Ocongate, he was hit on one side by an arrow. A female Indian herbalist from Hualla healed him but he died shortly afterward of a fever.

---

224   This may be a reference to the Cuzco Ceque System (see Bauer 1998).
225   This refers to when Polo de Ondegardo discovered the remains of all the Inca kings and queens in different areas of Cuzco (see Bauer and Coello Rodriguez 2007).
226   Wimpillay and Quisallay are two areas close to Cuzco. Cabello Valboa (1951 [1586]:294) also notes their fall under Inca Roca.
227   Cobo (1979 [1653]:124) and Sarmiento de Gamboa (2007 [1572]:88) mentioned that Inca Roca captured Caytomarca. Cieza de León (1976 [1553–1554]:211) attributes the fall of Caytomarca to Viracocha Inca. While Wimpillay and Quisallay are both near the city of Cuzco, Caytomarca is in the Urubamba Valley above Calca. See Covey (2006:109–136) for a comparison of different accounts of early Inca expansionism.
228   Cabello Valboa (1951 [1586]:293), Cobo (1979 [1653]:124), and Sarmiento de Gamboa (2007 [1572]:88) mention that Inca Roca married Mama Micay from the town of Huayllancan. Guaman Poma de Ayala (2004 [1615]:103) states that he married Cusi Chimpo Mama Micay, which is the same name that he gives for the second wife of Capac Yupanqui.
229   Cabello Valboa (1951 [1586]:293, 294) mentions Yahuar Huacac and Vicaquirao, and later notes Inca Paucar, Inca Huaman, Vicaquirao Inca, and Inca Cazachicha. Cobo (1979 [1653]:124) also notes Yahuar Huacac, Vicaquirao, and Apu Mayta. Sarmiento de Gamboa (2007 [1572]:88) writes of Yahuar Huacac, Paucar Inca, Guaman Taysi Inca, Vicaquirao Inca, and Apu Mayta.
230   Guaman Poma de Ayala (2004 [1615]:152) writes of two captains of Mayta Capac named Apu Mayta and Vilcac. The *History and Genealogy of the Inca Kings of Peru* (Murúa 2004 [1590]:40v) contains a drawing showing Captain Mayta.

Figure 13.1. The figure reads: "[the] sixth" and "this Inca's coat of arms," written by Murúa (Adorno 2008:101) (courtesy of The J. Paul Getty Museum, Los Angeles, Ms. Ludwig XIII 16 [83.MP.159], f.32v).

This is what he looked like (figure 13.1).[231]

[F.34R] CHAPTER 14

The Coya Cusi Chimpo, also called Mama Micay

The Indians say that Coya Cusi Chimpo, Inca Roca's wife, was cruel, had a bad temperament, enjoyed punishing others, and was inclined to drunkenness and feasts. Some say that she was the sister of Capac Yupanqui and that she killed him using poison in a golden *mate*. Others say that she was his daughter and was, nevertheless, married to Inca Roca. Due to [her] advice, drinking parties [became] public, as mentioned in the previous chapter. She had a thousand Indians as personal guards, who ate from the Inca's stores. Whenever anyone entered the palace, they were required to take off their shoes and never look at her face, and when they left, they were not allowed to turn their backs to her.

The palace where she lived was magnificently carved and she had more than a thousand, some say more than three thousand, women for her service, confined within it. The coat of arms of this great lady included the *mascapaicha*, which was the royal crown of the Inca, a bird called *cori quinqui*, a jaguar, [which they call] *otorongo*, with its tongue out profiled standing beside the trunk of a large tree, and two large snakes.[232] Another coat of arms was painted above a different palace door, including

---

231   This final sentence was added by Murúa (Adorno 2008:101).
   The coat of arms shown on the drawing in figure 13.1 is the same coat of arms shown on the figure of Coya Cuci Chimu Mama Micai (the fifth Coya) in the *History and Genealogy of the Inca Kings of Peru* (Murúa 2004 [1590]:27v).
   This drawing is similar to that of Inca Roca provided in *The First New Chronicle* (Guaman Poma de Ayala 2004 [1615]:102) and in the *History and Genealogy of the Inca Kings of Peru* (Murúa 2004 [1590]:14v). All three illustrations show Inca Roca with his son Huaman Capac Inca. Interestingly, although the drawings of Guaman Poma de Ayala are in black and white, he describes the clothing worn by Manco Capac Inca: "Inca Roca loved his son very much and kept him close because the boy was very young. [He] used a pink cloak, a black tunic with two tocapos and a red llautu" (2004 [1615]:103). This description documents that Guaman Poma de Ayala could remember the illustration that had been completed while he worked for Murúa, and that that same drawing serviced as inspiration for the new drawing that was composed for the *General History of Peru*.

232   This reference to the coat of arms of Coya Cusi Chimpo is interesting. This coat of arms is now within the front materials of the *General History of Peru* and is titled "The Royal Coat of Arms of the Incas" (Murúa 2008 [1616]:13r). An identical drawing can be found in *The First New Chronicle* (Guaman Poma de Ayala 2004 [1615]:83). See Ossio (2008:93n22) for a more detailed discussion concerning the appearance of this coat of arms in the works of Murúa and Guaman Poma de Ayala.

Figure 14.1. The figure reads: "Cusi Chimpo Coya," written by Murúa (Adorno 2008:101) (courtesy of The J. Paul Getty Museum, Los Angeles, Ms. Ludwig XIII 16 [83.MP.159], f.33v).

a rainbow with a two-headed eagle above it, which they called *cuichi cuntur*, and an Indian armed with a *champi* in his hand, which was called *orquetuyu*[233] *hualpa*.

This Coya had [several] children, the most important being Yahuar Huacac, along with the others that have already been mentioned, and a daughter, Ipa Huaco, who was also known as Mama Chiquia.[234]

This is what she looked like (figure 14.1).[235]

[F.35R] CHAPTER 15

Yahuar Huacac, [the] seventh Inca and king

The Inca and lord Yahuar Huacac,[236] was sick as a youth.[237] For many years he had an illness in which blood came out of his nose. Some say that when he was a boy, his enemies kidnapped him and took him to Vilcabamba to kill him, but he wept tears of blood.[238] So they released him, [and] he fled to the lowlands to find a cure, where he had three children with a *yunga* woman.[239]

Then he set out to conquer new lands, capturing their main *huaca*, and bringing it to Cuzco, thereby subjecting those people without giving them a chance to rebel. They [were] forced to contribute people and riches for sacrifices and to serve guards for the *huaca*. They put the *huaca* in the Temple of the Sun, the Coricancha, alongside many [other] altars and idols, as will be described in its proper place. [Yahuar Huacac] was married to Ipa Huaco Coya,[240] also known as Mama Chiquia.[241] They

233   Originally, this word may have ended with an "a," but it was changed to end with a "u" (Murúa 2008 [1616]:34v).

234   Guaman Poma de Ayala (2004 [1615]:131) provides a list of other children.

235   This final sentence was added by Murúa (Adorno 2008:101).

236   Sarmiento de Gamboa (2007 [1572]:89) suggests that Yahuar Huacac was also known as Titu Cusi Hualpa.

237   In this chapter, and others that follow, Murúa continues to move away from the information presented in Cabello Valboa and Sarmiento de Gamboa, providing a nonoverlapping description of the life of Yahuar Huacac and those of several other Incas. Much of Murúa's information on the later Incas appears to be taken from Fernández de Palencia (1963 [1571]).

238   Sarmiento de Gamboa (2007 [1572]:96) also speaks of Yahuar Huacac being kidnapped but provides a completely different story.

239   See Fernández de Palencia (1963 [1571]:80–81) for similar information on Yahuar Huacac.

240   Guaman Poma de Ayala (2004 [1615]:105, 133) states that Yahuar Huacac married Ipa Huaco Mama Machi.

241   Cabello Valboa (1951 [1586]:298, 296) and Sarmiento de Gamboa (2007 [1572]:92, 94) indicate that Yahuar Huacac married Mama Chiquia, who was from the Ayarmaca ethnic group. Cobo (1979 [1653]:126) suggests her name was Mama Choque Chicllayupay. Cieza

Figure 15.1. The figure reads, "Yahuar Huacac Inca," written by Murúa (Adorno 2008:101) and "this Inca's coat of arms." From this Inca forward, the coats of arms for the Incas are not included (courtesy of The J. Paul Getty Museum, Los Angeles: Ms. Ludwig XIII 16 [83.MP.159], f.34v).

had a son, Viracocha Inca, and a daughter, Mama Yunto Caya, who later became Coya.

This is what he looked like (figure 15.1).[242]

[F.36R] CHAPTER 16

Ipa Huaco Coya, also known as Mama Chiquia,[243] [the] wife of Yahuar Huacac

Coya Ipa Huaco married her brother, Yahuar Huacac. She was beautiful though somewhat brown, affable, agreeable, a friend of her subjects, especially to the poor, whom she was always eager to help. In her palace, she kept an infinite number of birds for plucking their feathers, and in another area, she had a countless number of birds to hunt.[244] In another [area], she had an infinite number of beasts, as many as one can imagine. Innumerable Indians were in charge of them.

Inside the palace, she had a chapel for her oratory, which was plated with gold and silver. Many nights she would enter this chapel to say her prayers, during which time the Devil would sometimes appear and speak to her. On one side of the chapel, she had many weapons, [such as] bows, arrows, slings, spears, truncheons, clubs, helmets, made of wood, leather, and gold. The wood for these weapons was sturdy, and their points were either sharpened or inserted with flint. These weapons were in the chapel dedicated to the idols, which she greatly ~~cared for and~~[245] venerated. Whenever there was a war, she would enter and ask the idol or *huaca* for those weapons for the Inca, her husband. She [also] pleaded [with the huaca] to grant her husband strength to defend himself from his enemies and achieve victory with those weapons. For this, she offered gold, silver, and other riches and figures.

She died young and her death caused anguish and sadness to all her vassals, both

---

de León (1976 [1553–1554]:204) differs and suggests that it was Yahuar Huacac's eldest son, whom he calls Inca Yupanqui, who married Mama Chiquia of the Ayarmaca. Fernández de Palencia (1963 [1571]:6) provides a list of six children of Mama Chiquia and Yahuar Huacac.

242 This final sentence was added by Murúa (Adorno 2008:101).

243 Fernández de Palencia (1963 [1571]:81) also calls the wife of Yahuar Huacac, Mama Chiquia. Guaman Poma de Ayala (2004 [1615]:132) lists her as Ipa Vaco Mama Machi, while the *History and Genealogy of the Inca Kings of Peru* (Murúa 2004 [1590]) refers to her as Coya Ypa Uaco Mama Machi Mama Chiquia.

244 Alternatively, the end of this sentence could read "for the house."

245 Crossed out by Remón (Adorno 2008:107). The crossed-out section reads, "obligacion y."

Figure 16.1. The figure reads: "Ipa Huaco Coya," written by Murúa (Adorno 2008:101) (courtesy of The J. Paul Getty Museum, Los Angeles, Ms. Ludwig XIII 16 [83.MP.159], f.35v).

in general and in particular. She had sons and a daughter named Mama Yunto Caya, who became [a] Coya, as is told in another chapter.[246]

This is what she looked like (figure 16.1).[247]

[F.37R] CHAPTER 17

The deeds of Viracocha, [the] eighth Inca

Viracocha Inca, [the] son of Yahuar Huacac, was brave and courageous. Some say he had a beard and conquered many villages, but later he [suddenly] disappeared. He was married to Mama Yunto Caya,[248] with whom he had five children: the first, who was the heir, was called Pachacuti Inca Yupanqui, also called Inca Yupanqui; the second [was] Urcon Inca; the third [was] Inca Mayta;[249] the fourth [was] Coropanqui;[250] [and] the fifth [was] Capac Yupanqui.[251] Others say that he never married, and that when he died without a son or successor, his brother [Pachacuti] Inca Yupanqui was selected.

[Viracocha Inca] was interested in sorcery, and he dedicated a vast number of sorcerers and soothsayers to the cult of the *huacas* and idols. To distinguish them, he ordered them to have long hair and wear long, white, narrow shirts made of cotton or *cumbi* and a blanket with balls of cotton or colored wool on the border tied across the right shoulder. On festival days, they painted [themselves] and [Viracocha Inca] ordered them to teach their ministers secrets figures, which were

246 Guaman Poma de Ayala (2004 [1615]:135) provides a list of other children.
247 This final sentence was added by Murúa (Adorno 2008:101).
248 Cabello Valboa (1951 [1586]:297–298), Cobo (1979 [1653]:131) and Sarmiento de Gamboa (2007 [1572]:98, 101, 231) state that Viracocha Inca married Mama Rondocaya from the town of Anta. Guaman Poma de Ayala (2004 [1615]:107, 135) writes that Viracocha married Mama Yunto Caya. This matches information in the *History and Genealogy of the Inca Kings of Peru* (Murúa 2004 [1590]:29v).
249 Guaman Poma de Ayala (2004 [1615]:156 [158]) also mentions Inca Mayta and Inca Urcon as sons of Yahuar Huacac, but he also lists individuals with these same names as sons of Viracocha Inca (Guaman Poma de Ayala 2004 [1615]:107). He also has an illustration of Inca Mayta fighting (Guaman Poma de Ayala 2004 [1615]:155 [157]). Furthermore, he mentions an Inca Urcon as the son of Pachacuti Inca Yupanqui who was responsible for moving stones from Cuzco to the northern provinces (Guaman Poma de Ayala 2004 [1615]:159 [161]) and includes a drawing of that Inca moving the stones. Guaman Poma de Ayala's image of Inca Urcon moving stones appears to be based on the drawing in the *History and Genealogy of the Inca Kings of Peru* (Murúa 2004 [1590]:37v).
250 Better known as Coropanqui Vicaquirao.
251 This information concerning the children of Viracocha Inca and Mama Yunto Caya appears in Fernández de Palencia (1963 [1571]:6, 81).

Figure 17.1. The figure reads: "Viracocha [the] 8th Inca," written by Murúa (Adorno 2008:101) (courtesy of The J. Paul Getty Museum, Los Angeles, Ms. Ludwig XIII 16 [83.MP.159], f.36v).

never discussed or revealed. Many of them did not marry due to their high status. Some very elderly Indians claim that Viracocha Inca also took up this craft, [and] because he had a greater mastery than the other [sorcerers] he disappeared.

[Viracocha Inca] conquered Calca,²⁵² also known as Caytomarca, Piñacapay, Caquiamarca [which was] ruled by Tocay Capac,²⁵³ and [he defeated the towns of] Huaypomarca,²⁵⁴ Maras,²⁵⁵ and Mullaca.²⁵⁶ Although [some] attribute [these conquests] to Inca Urcon, his son, as they occurred during his father's lifetime.

This is what he looked like (figure 17.1).²⁵⁷

[F.38R] CHAPTER 18

Mama Yunto Caya, [the] wife of Viracocha Inca

The elderly say that Mama Yunto Caya,²⁵⁸ [the] wife of Viracocha Inca, was one of the most beautiful and gracious women in all this kingdom. Her beauty surpassed that of all the previous Coyas, making her deeply cherished by her husband, Viracocha Inca, and all his subjects. She lived a long time, and her palace and home had a thousand kinds of entertainments, gardens, [and] orchards. She also had a place called Manan Huañunca, which means "will never die," a quarter league outside the city of Cuzco.²⁵⁹ It had a forest and path, where there were many different kinds of wild and tame animals. It is now [owned] by the religious order of Our Lady of Mercy in that city. This Coya died when she was very old and left the sons mentioned in the

---

252   Cobo (1979 [1653]:131) also mentions the conquest of Calca by Viracocha Inca. Cabello Valboa (1951 [1586]:298) mentions several of these towns. Sarmiento de Gamboa (2007 [1572]:96, 103) lists several of these towns in addition to many others.
253   Guaman Poma de Ayala (2004 [1615]:148) also mentions a Tocay Capac.
254   Sarmiento de Gamboa (2007 [1572]:103) mentions the town of Guayparmarca, presumably near Lake Huaypo.
255   The modern town of Maras.
256   Modern Mullaca, near Moray (Covey 2006).
257   This final sentence was added by Murúa (Adorno 2008:101).
258   Garcilaso de la Vega reports seeing the mummy of Mama Rondocaya in the house of Polo de Ondegardo in 1560. Soon afterward, it was set to Lima (Bauer and Coello Rodriquez 2007).
259   Manan Huañunca is described within the Cuzco Ceque System document as the house of an unnamed Coya, and it is listed as "on the site which the monastery of La Merced now has." Manan Huañunca is located along the Huancaro River, just outside the city of Cuzco (Bauer 1998:25, 128). Because Murúa was a Mercedarian, this place may have held special importance to him. Murúa provides information on how this place gained its name in book 1, chapter 89 (f.210v).

Figure 18.1. The figure reads: "Mama Yunto Coya," which was written by Murúa (Adorno 2008:101). Note the drawing is labeled "Mama Yunto Coya," rather than "Mama Yunto Caya" (courtesy of The J. Paul Getty Museum, Los Angeles, Ms. Ludwig XIII 16 [83.MP.159], f.37v).

previous chapter, and a daughter named Mama Anahuarque Coya.²⁶⁰
This is what she looked like (figure 18.1).²⁶¹

[F.39R] CHAPTER 19

The courageous Inca Yupanqui, also called
Pachacuti Inca, [the] ninth [Inca]

As we approach modern times, information about the Incas and their accomplishments become clearer and more reliable, since their memories of them are fresher and more vivid. The more recent the event, the more certain older people can be about the details. This is especially [true] for the [life] of [Pachacuti] Inca Yupanqui, who is credited with bringing order and consensus throughout the entire kingdom. He is also [remembered] as the most courageous and bravest in conquering new lands and extending the boundaries of their kingdoms and lordships. [His accomplishments] overshadow those of all his ancestors and push their deeds and feats into obscurity. Therefore, moving forward, it is essential for us to provide a clear narrative of their history, recognizing and attributing the many conquests and achievements of the Incas.

[Pachacuti] Inca Yupanqui, as said, was the son of Viracocha Inca.²⁶² He was cruel, severe, ambitious, honorable, and even envious man, as will be shown. He married Mama Anahuarque²⁶³ and completed the conquest of the entire region of Cuzco and the Cuyo Indians,²⁶⁴ whom he destroyed and devastated. The conquest happened like this: the entire province of Cuyo Capac, Chahua[ytire], and Chuchuca²⁶⁵ was vast and had many people. Their leaders were Cuyo Capac, Yanqui

---

260 Guaman Poma de Ayala (2004 [1615]:107, 135) also states that Mama Yunto was the mother of Mama Anahuarque.
261 This final sentence written by Murúa (Adorno 2008:101).
262 In the chapters that follow, it appears that Murúa returned to the same source that was shared with Cabello Valboa, Cobo, and Sarmiento de Gamboa.
263 Cabello Valboa (1951 [1586]:303), Cobo (1979 [1653]:133), Guaman Poma de Ayala (2004 [1615]:109, 137), and Sarmiento de Gamboa (2007 [1572]:154) all state that Pachacuti Inca Yupanqui married Mama Anahuarque. Cabello Valboa and Cobo both indicate that she was from the town of Choco, near Cuzco. Cobo (1990 [1653]:67) also notes that her mummy was kept in Pumamarca, near Cuzco.
264 The Cuyo were located near the modern town of Pisac (see Covey 2006). Cabello Valboa (1951 [1586]:300) and Sarmiento de Gamboa (2007 [1572]:123) provide similar accounts of the Cuyo and Pachacuti Inca Yupanqui.
265 Cabello Valboa (1951 [1586]:300) also mentions these three locations, while Sarmiento de Gamboa (2007 [1572]:123) only mentions the town of the Cuyo.

Lalama, and Apu Canataqui.[266] [Pachacuti] Inca Yupanqui offered one of these a daughter as a wife. During the celebration and festivity, a servant of the *curacas* [was present]. He was a foreigner who knew how to make small vessels called *ultis*,[267] in which the Indians keep *llipta*,[268] which is used while [chewing] coca. [Pachacuti] Inca Yupanqui ordered [this Indian] to make some *ultis*[269] for him.

This Indian grew close to the Inca, and he was always allowed to be in his presence. One day, while they were alone in conversation, this Indian struck [Pachacuti] Inca Yupanqui, on the head with an *ultis*, knocking him unconscious. His servants, who were outside, rushed in and found the Inca bathed in blood. They seized the Indian and tortured him until he confessed that all the leaders of the Cuyo Capac were planning to revolt and that he had been told to kill [Pachacuti Inca Yupanqui].[270] The Inca discovered a treacherous plot that had been organized against him. However, this was a lie, as the Indian was afraid and was being tortured, so he thought that by saying this he could escape and save his life *[f.39v]*. [Pachacuti] Inca Yupanqui had all the chiefs of that province arrested and executed. After their deaths, he punished the common people. According to the elderly Indians, he killed nine thousand single males of all ages,[271] causing their downfall and devastation and they remain in ruins until today.

Then [Pachacuti] Inca Yupanqui traveled down the [Urubamba] River to Yucay and [then] to Vitcos,[272] near Vilcabamba. He conquered all those provinces, and many other towns surrendered to him without a fight, as they feared his boldness and strength as well as that of his two captains, Apu Mayta[273] and Vicaquirao.[274]

---

266   Sarmiento de Gamboa names these leaders, while Cabello Valboa (1951 [1586]:300) does not mention them by name.

267   These are small ceramic vessels used to hold *llipta*, a mixture of lime or ash that enhances the extraction of alkaloids from coca leaves. The word is underlined.

268   This word is underlined (Murúa 2008 [1616]:39r).

269   This word is underlined (Murúa 2008 [1616]:39r).

270   Cabello Valboa (1951 [1586]:300), Santa Cruz Pachacuti Yamqui Salcamaygua (1993 [ca. 1613]), and Sarmiento de Gamboa (2007 [1572]:123–124) all describe the fall of the Cuyo and this attack. This wound was later seen on the mummy of Pachacuti Inca Yupanqui (Acosta 2002 [1590]:364).

271   Cabello Valboa (1951 [1586]:300) also mentions the number 9,000.

272   The Inca town of Vitcos is now called Rosaspata (see Bauer, Santa Cruz, and Aráoz Silva 2015; Hemming 1970; and Lee 2000). Cobo (1979 [1653]:135) describes Pachacuti Inca Yupanqui's expansion into the Vilcabamba region, while many other writers do not. Sarmiento de Gamboa (2007 [1572]:125) notes his expansion into the Ollantaytambo region but not further downriver.

273   The *History and Genealogy of the Inca Kings of Peru* (Murúa 2004 [1590]:39v) includes a drawing of Apu Mayta.

274   Guaman Poma de Ayala (2004 [1615]:99) mentions several different individuals named Apu Mayta Inca and Vilca Inca as sons of different Incas.

At that same time, the Chanka[275] of the province of Andahualyas left their lands, having previously reached near Cuzco in the time of Viracocha Inca. [Pachacuti] Inca Yupanqui, seeing the damage [the Chanka] were doing in his land, went out and fought them in two battles—one in Queachili,[276] [which is] behind Ayavira,[277] and the other in Ichupampa,[278] which is behind Jaquijahuana.[279] He defeated them in both [battles] and made them retreat to their home in Andahualyas.

In these battles, the chiefs of the Chanka, Tomayhuaraca,[280] and Astuhuaraca were captured and taken to Cuzco, where [Pachacuti] Inca Yupanqui ordered them killed and drinking *mates*[281] be made of their skulls. According to some elderly Indians, [Pachacuti Inca Yupanqui] returned to Cuzco and usurped the kingship from his father, who was still alive, and [he] killed his brother, Inca Urcon, whom his father had selected heir. [Pachacuti Inca Yupanqui] killed [Inca Urcon] in Cache;[282] he had him [walk] in front of him in an orchard and then sent a captain to kill him from behind. [Pachacuti Inca Yupanqui] pretended to mourn for the death of [Inca Urcon], but when his father, Viracocha Inca, learned of it, he died of grief, leaving [Pachacuti Inca Yupanqui] as the undisputed ruler. This is one opinion; however, others say that [he] vanished, as noted above when discussing the case of Viracocha Inca.

[Pachacuti] Inca Yupanqui[283] pursued the Chanka to Andahuaylas, and he fought and defeated them in multiple battles. He captured their lords and *curacas*, and killed any who showed signs of rebellion against his rule. He then appointed

---

275   For a description of the Chanka and the region of Andahuaylas, see Bauer, Kellett, and Aráoz Silva (2010).
276   Queachili was also a shrine within the Cuzco Ceque System (Bauer 1998:71). It is mentioned by Cabello Valboa (1951 [1586]:299) and Cobo (1980 [1653]:29) and is most likely mentioned by Albornoz (1984 [1582]:204) as Oma Chilliguas (Bauer 1998:71).
277   The small town of Ayaviri is located near the Vilcaconga Pass (now call Huillque Pass).
278   Ichupampa is located near the town of Ancahuasi on the Pampa de Anta. It was a shrine within the Cuzco Ceque System (Bauer 1998). There are many descriptions of the Inca-Chanka war. One of the most detailed is contained within Cieza de León (1976 [1553–1554]).
279   Murúa writes Sacsahuana, which could be Sacsayhuaman but is more likely to be Jaquijahuana. Cabello Valboa (1951 [1586]:299) also mentions that Queachili.
280   Cabello Valboa (1951 [1586]:300) and Sarmiento de Gamboa (2007 [1572]:107) mention that the heads of Tomayhuaraca and Astuhuaraca were made into drinking vessels.
281   These are drinking vessels are often made of gourds. This word is underlined (Murúa 2008 [1616]:39v).
282   Cabello Valboa (1951 [1586]:301) tells of the death of Inca Urcon in Cache. Sarmiento de Gamboa (2007 [1572]:121–122) describes the death of Inca Urcon near Yucay in a very different way. Cobo (1979 [1653]:137) mentions Inca Urcon's death but does not provide specifics.
283   A spelling error may be corrected (Murúa 2008 [1616]:39v).

Figure 19.1. Untitled. Presumed to be Pachacuti Inca Yupanqui, the ninth Inca (courtesy of The J. Paul Getty Museum, Los Angeles, Ms. Ludwig XIII 16 [83.MP.159], f.38v).

his own *curacas* and lords, selecting the sons of those who had died in battle, as well as [the sons] of those captured and killed during the initial skirmishes as previously mentioned.

[f.40r] When this was completed, he went on to conquer the Soras[284] and the Lucanas, who are located next to the Chanka. As the Soras were a larger group, they fortified themselves in Chalcomarca.[285] Yet [Pachacuti Inca Yupanqui] defeated them through strength-of-arms. After appointing lords and *caciques* of his choosing from among the [Soras] or from among the supreme governors and captains who were with him, [Pachacuti] Inca Yupanqui returned to Cuzco.

Upon [Pachacuti Inca Yupanqui's] return, he ordered epic songs of their victory over their enemies to be sung as he entered [the city] until he reached the House of the Sun. There, the most important defeated [prisoners] were thrown to the ground, and [the Incas] walked over them. As they trampled them, they shouted "We walk upon our enemies!" The prisoners were unable to lift their heads and had to lie on the ground, as previously described.[286]

[F.41R] CHAPTER 20

How [Pachacuti] Inca Yupanqui decorated the House of the Sun and other memorable things and his conquests

When [Pachacuti] Inca Yupanqui returned from the conquest of the Soras and Lucanas, as described in the preceding chapter, he [re]built and decorated the House of the Sun to its former splendor, as will be described in its place. While this very important work was being done, he left Cuzco to conquer Collasuyu, accompanied by Apu Conde Mayta.[287] As a reward for his hard work, ingenuity,

---

284   A spelling error is corrected (Murúa 2008 [1616]:40r).
    Sarmiento de Gamboa (2007 [1572]:122, 126) credits the defeat of only the Soras to Pachacuti Inca Yupanqui, while Cobo (1979 [1653]:138) mentions both the Soras and the Lucanas. Also see Cieza de León (1976 [1553–1554]:230–231).

285   This fort is mentioned by both Cabello Valboa (1951 [1586]:304) and Sarmiento de Gamboa (2007 [1572]:126).

286   See Sarmiento de Gamboa (2007 [1572]:122) for a more detailed telling of Pachacuti Inca Yupanqui's return to Cuzco.
    The drawing in figure 19.1 shares similarities with the drawings of Pachacuti Inca provided in the *History and Genealogy of the Inca Kings of Peru* (Murúa 2004 [1590]:17v) and in *The First New Chronicle* of Guaman Poma de Ayala (2004 [1615]:108). However, the latter two are far more alike than the drawing in the *General History of Peru* (Murúa 2008 [1616]).

287   Cabello Valboa (1951 [1586]:312) and Cobo (1979 [1653]:139) also mention Apu Conde Mayta.

and industry, [Pachacuti] Inca Yupanqui gave him many *chacras*, women, and servants. [Pachacuti] Inca Yupanqui conquered up to Pucará, and everywhere he conquered, he left *caciques* and lords of his own choosing to oversee the own natives, and over them, he placed governors who had been his captains so that they would never again revolt. Upon returning to Cuzco, [Pachacuti Inca Yupanqui] entered triumphantly, in the same most-solemn way as Huayna Capac did [on his return from Quito], as will be described further ahead.

We now will discuss Colla Capac, the universal Lord of all Collao.[288] In Cuzco [Pachacuti Inca Yupanqui] made sacrifices to the Sun and brought [large] quantities of gold and silver from that province, to finish the House and Temple of the Sun. [Pachacuti Inca Yupanqui] endowed it with the most precious and valuable [things] that he captured from the lands that he had conquered, including livestock, *chacras*, parcels, workers, women, and servants.[289]

He dedicated a room within the Temple of the Sun to the statue of the Pacha Yachachic, giving it all that has been described. He also constructed a group of buildings [called] Pucamarca, as the house of this *huaca*,[290] as well as of another [huaca] that he established to the Thunder, Lightning, and Sheet-lightning known as Chuqui Ylla Yllapa Inca.[291] He magnificently endowed them with farms and servants for their service.[292]

When this was finished, [Pachacuti Inca Yupanqui] began to organize all his land and dominion, giving laws to guide people's lives. He founded the main Inca *huacas* in the provinces and their capitals: the Sun, the Creator, Lightning, and his own *huaca*, Huanacauri. He destroyed the *huacas* that had been in those towns, which will be explained later in relation to *huacas*.[293]

Amaru Tupa Inca[294] and his brother, Huayna Yanqui Yupanqui, had had the task

---

288   Collao was a vast region near Lake Titicaca, from which Collasuyu gained its name. Also see Cieza de León (1976 [1553–1554]:232–233) for a detailed account of Pachacuti Inca Yupanqui's expedition south of Cuzco.

289   The last part of this paragraph also appears in Cabello Valboa (1951 [1586]:306) and in Sarmiento de Gamboa (2007 [1572]:131).

290   This was a huaca within the Cuzco Ceque System. Cobo (1990 [1653]:57) writes, "The second huaca was a temple named Pucamarca ... in it was an idol of the Thunder Chucuylla" (see Bauer 1998:58).

291   Molina (2011 [ca. 1575]:23) writes of "another idol called Chuqui Ylla Yllapa which was the huaca of lighting, thunder, and lightning bolts. This huaca was shaped [like] a person, although its face could not be seen. It also had a gold llautu, gold earplugs, and a gold medallion, which they called canipu, and it had its clothes folded next to it."

292   Cabello Valboa (1951 [1586]:308) provides similar information on the buildings of Cuzco.

293   Cabello Valboa (1951 [1586]:311) provides similar information on the founding of *huacas*.

294   Guaman Poma de Ayala (2004 [1615]:139) also lists Amaru Inca among the brothers of Huayna Capac. In the *History and Genealogy of the Inca Kings of Peru*, Murúa (2004 [1590]:41v) includes a drawing of Tupa Amaru.

of destroying the false *huacas* and dismantling others and their cults. [They gave] the *huacas* that were left, [new] instructions concerning what, *[f.41v]* when, and for what purpose, sacrifices were to be made. Their functions and sacrifices were changed, and they were given different functions, roles, and purposes. This was because [Pachacuti Inca Yupanqui] feared that the [local] sorcerers would harm him through sacrifices and spells, so he forced them to abandon their old ceremonies and rites and replaced them with new ones that he taught them.[295]

Having finished this, [Pachacuti] Inca Yupanqui dispatched his two brothers and a Captain-General named Capac Yupanqui and another brother, named Huayna [Yanqui] Yupanqui,[296] and another captain named of Apu Yanqui Yupanqui,[297] along the road to Chinchaysuyu until the provinces of Quito.[298] Their conquests included Cajamarca, where they captured Guzmanco Capac,[299] the Lord of Cajamarca, Huamachuco, Conchucos, and another province called Caraz. As a result of these [conquests], they brought large quantities of gold and silver to Cuzco, which were used in service of the Temple of the Sun and [to make a] gold band that was on the wall of the temple.[300]

The reason why they reached Cajamarca was as follows. During General Capac Yupanqui's conquest of Urcocolla, which is a fortress next to Parcos, the Chanka attacked, raided, and destroyed a nearby group of towns. In this the Chanka showed remarkable bravery, looting the best [things] and outdoing all the other nations that were there.[301] This being the case, [the Chanka] were motivated to capture the fortress [of Urcocolla]. When news of this event arrived in Cuzco, [Pachacuti] Inca Yupanqui, driven by envy, became very angry, noting that [his men] had been very brave and industrious soldiers in that war, and yet the Chanka had taken the

295   Cabello Valboa (1951 [1586]:311) and Sarmiento de Gamboa (2007 [1572]:131–132) provide similar, but not identical, information on the creation of new *huacas*. Also see Sarmiento de Gamboa (2007 [1572]:131).

296   Huayna [Yamqui] Yupanqui is also mentioned by Betanzos (1996 [1557]:143) as having been sent into Chinchaysuyu.

297   He was the uncle of Tupa Inca Yupanqui.

298   Cabello Valboa (1951 [1586]:314) provides similar information on the sending of men to Quito. Murúa describes the town of San Francisco de Quito in book 3, chapter 17 of his chronicle.

299   Sarmiento de Gamboa (2007 [1572]:134) also mentions the defeat of Guzmanco Capac.

300   This band of gold is a famous part of the Coricancha (see Bauer 2004:146–152). Juan Ruiz de Arce (1933 [ca. 1545]:372) describes the band before it was removed by the Spaniards, writing, "There was a band of gold as wide as a hand around the buildings at roof level. This was found in all the chambers of the monastery."

301   Much of this same information concerning Parcos, the fort of Urcocolla, and the Chanka can be found in Cabello Valboa (1951 [1586]:313–314) and Sarmiento de Gamboa (2007 [1572]:132–133).

advantage and seized the glory of victory and had become more venerated than the other [armies]. So [Pachacuti Inca Yupanqui] sent Captain-General Capac Yupanqui an order, that all the Chanka should be killed by sending them into a battle or by having them storm a difficult fortress in the most dangerous way. In this way, [the Chanka] would all be killed or reduced, or some other way to kill them should be found. When [Pachacuti] Inca Yupanqui's messenger arrived with the order, a sister of the captain of the Chanka,[302] who was the wife of General Capac Yupanqui, was present. Upon hearing what [Pachacuti] Inca Yupanqui had commanded; she secretly told her brother about it. When the Chanka found out, they desperately agreed one night to flee to the encampment of Huarautambo[303] near Huaylas, in an attempt to escape the imminent death. *[f.42r]*. That night, the [Chanka] army passed through the jurisdiction as calmly as they could. Believing their general was leaving, the Inca forces and many other people from different nations followed them. The next morning some wanted to flee, realizing that this [was a] mistake and that they had been deceived, but the Chanka killed them, and they then proceeded to the province of Huaylas. There, assuming that the Inca and his Captain-General were arriving, [the Huaylas] came out to receive them in peace. After staying there for several days, [the Chanka] grew suspicious and seized the opportunity to pillage the entire province, taking many people with them to the Chachapoyas. This is what is known about the Anco Ayllu and Ruparupa people who are currently living there.[304]

Later, General Capac Yupanqui noted the absence of [the Chanka] and their flight, prompting him to send inquiries to various locations. Eventually, he followed them until he arrived at Cajamarca. There, he saw the wealth of the province, its multitudes of intelligent people, and its vast [amounts of] gold and silver. Although [General Capac Yupanqui] had not received orders or instructions from [Pachacuti] Inca Yupanqui to go there, they decided to conquer them, commencing war on [the Cajamarquinos]. [The Incas] fought so expertly that [the Cajamarquinos] were defeated and subdued. After conquering the entire province, they left it under the good rulership of a governor and many soldier garrisons to hold it, before returning to Cuzco. Guzmanco Capac, Lord of those provinces, was imprisoned [in Cajamarca] and died there. Upon arriving in Cuzco, they entered with great triumph, bearing a huge quantity of gold and silver, as was said.[305]

---

302   Sarmiento de Gamboa (2007 [1572]:133) notes that this captain was named Anco Ayllu.

303   The site of Huarautambo is in Pasco.

304   Cabello Valboa (1951 [1586]:314–316) provides similar information. However, Murúa is confused here: the leader of the Chanka was named Anco Ayllu, and it is believed that he led his people into the jungle area of Ruparupa (Sarmiento de Gamboa 2007 [1572]:133–134).

305   See Sarmiento de Gamboa (2007 [1572]:134–135) for a clearer and more detailed account of the fall of Cajamarca to Capac Yupanqui and his return to Cuzco. Also see Cabello Valboa (1951 [1586]:317).

Figure 20.1. Untitled. Presumed to be Pachacuti Inca Yupanqui. The figure reads: "do not paint," indicating that it was not to be included in the final printing. These instructions and those that follow on other figures are the work of Remón. He ordered the removal of some drawings, feeling that it was necessary to include only one drawing of each Inca and Coya (Adorno 2008:102–104) (courtesy of The J. Paul Getty Museum, Los Angeles, Ms. Ludwig XIII 16 [83.MP.159], f.40v).

[F.43R] CHAPTER 21

*How [Pachacuti] Inca Yupanqui had his brother, Capac Yupanqui, killed
and [how he] sent his son, Tupa Inca Yupanqui, to conquer new lands*

Three beloved and beautiful mothers, revered by all, gave birth to three horribly
ugly daughters. However, this was not their fault, but the result of the malicious-
ness of men with depraved natures. Most importantly, [the first mother] was Truth,
an attribute of the supreme and sovereign God from whom all truth is derived.
Who does not love and seek truth, for it is so beautiful and pleasing? Yet [she] gave
birth to a child as ugly as Hate. The [second] mother, was Conversion, something
all men of sound understanding rejoice in, yet she gave birth to a son as wretched
as Disdain. The [third] mother was Happiness and Human Honor, something all
desired. Yet, [she] gave birth to a child as abominable as Envy, a vice despised by
all. Of all the vices that have the power to ensnare and deceive people, envy is the
most notorious. It saps a person of joy and contentment, leaving them with only
sadness and sorrow for the success of their friends. I am telling this because of what
happened to [Pachacuti] Inca Yupanqui.[306]

[When Pachacuti Inca Yupanqui] saw the victory and triumph of his brother and
general, Captain Capac Yupanqui, he felt saddened, sorry, and envious, that he had
not sent his male heir, Tupa Inca Yupanqui, on that conquest so that he could have
claimed the glory. Even though the honor and glory were rightfully his [as the ruling
Inca], and the profits of the conquest, the newly won territory, and all of the loot,
belonged to him and were under his power and possession. The reward and prize
that [the Inca] gave the unfortunate Capac Yupanqui for increasing his kingdom
and [for the] riches that he brought him [from Cajamarca] was to *[f.43v]* find a way
to kill him and his other brother Huayna [Yanqui] Yupanqui. To disguise his envy
and to gild this detestable vice, he used an excuse; claiming that because they had
failed to fulfill their orders to kill the Chanka, they had allowed [the Chanka] to flee
and escape, and that rather than carrying out his orders, they had exceeded his command by reaching Cajamarca and conquering that province. So, with this excuse, he
ordered them to be killed and they suffered the disgraceful prize of a death.[307]

After this sad tragedy, [Pachacuti] Inca Yupanqui sent his son, Tupa Inca Yupanqui,
who was his heir to the kingdom, to war with a large army. [The Inca] dispatched him,

---

306   Here, as in several other chapters, Murúa includes a seemingly tangential introduction
        to the chapter before he returns to copying information from other sources to move the
        history forward.

307   Cabello Valboa (1951 [1586]:317) and Sarmiento de Gamboa (2007 [1572]:135) also tell of
        the death of Capac Yupanqui and Huayna Yanqui Yupanqui.

giving him as companions, because he[308] was still young, Tupa Capac, [the Inca's] bastard son, and the captains [Apu] Yanqui Yupanqui and Tilca Yupanqui, who were Tupa Inca Yupanqui's brother and comrade in arms in this conquest.[309] Amaru Tupa Inca[310] and Tupac Yupanqui, who were brothers of Tupa [Inca] Yupanqui[311] by father and mother, and Apu Yanqui Yupanqui, a courageous captain, also went with them. During the life of his father, [Tupa Inca Yupanqui], his eldest son, conquered and expelled the natives of the Amaibamba[312] Valley, and reached [the] Pilcosuni,[313] whose descendants are currently in the Amaibamba Valley.[314,315]

Tupa Inca Yupanqui and his brothers embarked on a conquest, leaving Cuzco with a large army from various nations.[316] They first took the fortresses of Cayara[317] and Tohara, then Curamba, all in the province of Quechuas. They then took [the fortresses] of Ur[co]colla [and] Huayla Pucara in the province of Angaraes, where they arrested the *cacique*, Chuquis Guaman. Moving on to the province of Jauja, [they seized the fortress of] Siciquilla Pucara, and then [the fortresses of] Chungomarca, Pillahuamarca, and Huánuco in the province of Huaylas.[318] In the Chachapoyas, [they took the fortresses of] Pia[jajalca], Palca, Paltas, Pas[a]mayo, and Chimu,[319] and then [moved on] to the province of the Cañari. The Cañari, knowing of Tupa

---

308   A spelling mistake has been corrected (Murúa 2008 [1616]:43v).
309   Sarmiento de Gamboa (2007 [1572]:146) also mentions these two brothers.
310   Guaman Poma de Ayala (2004 [1615]:148) also mentions a Tupa Amaru Inca, but he is related to Sinchi Roca, the second Inca.
311   There seems to be an error in the listing of the names of the brothers.
312   Modern Amaibamba in Huayopata.
313   The Pilcosuni were an ethnic group that lived in the lower Urubamba River region during the Colonial Period.
314   Archival documents indicate that there were large areas of land near and within the Amaibamba Valley controlled by Pachacuti Inca Yupanqui, Tupa Inca Yupanqui, and his sister/wife, Mama Ocllo. These documents are especially interesting since they mention the town of Picchu (now called Machu Picchu) in the nearby Urubamba River Valley (Amado Gonzalez and Bauer 2022; Rowe 1985).
315   Cabello Valboa (1951 [1586]:314–316) provides similar information on the conquest of the Amaibamba region.
316   This conquest and several others to follow are also described in slightly different but overlapping accounts by Cabello Valboa (1951 [1586]:318–320), Sarmiento de Gamboa (2007 [1572]:147–148), and within the *Probanza de los Incas* (Rowe 1985). We have selected to follow Sarmiento de Gamboa's spellings for the names of people and places, as many of those recorded by Murúa appear to be incorrect.
317   Modern town of Cayara.
318   The town of Leon de Huánuco is described in book 3, chapter 16 of Murúa's chronicle.
319   Sarmiento de Gamboa (2007 [1572]:147–148) and the *Probanza de los Incas* (Rowe 1985:209) mention these provinces within the conquest of Tupa Inca Yupanqui, while Cabello Valboa (1951 [1586]) does not.

Inca Yupanqui and the punishments he imposed on those who disobeyed him, were afraid that he would destroy them. So, they came out *[f.44r]* to meet his army and submitted to his authority. [However], some of [the Cañari] rebelled, and [Tupa Inca Yupanqui] defeated them, capturing the *caciques*: Pisar Capac, Cañar Capac, and Chica Capac.[320] In order to continue subjugating them, he built a famous fortress in Quinchucajas,[321] and populated this outpost with many *mitimaes*, which are Indians from other areas, as will be described in more detail later.[322]

Continuing his conquest, Tupa Inca Yupanqui reached the powerful province of Quito, where there were great encounters and battles with the local people; in the end he defeated and subjected them, seizing their *cacique* and lord, Pillahuaso, whom he brought back to Cuzco in triumph.[323] From there he descended upon Huancavilca, where he built the fortress of Guachalla. After a difficult struggle, the courage and industry of his army enabled him to conquer the Huancavilca and their leaders, as well as the Guañapi,[324] Guamo[te],[325] Manta,[326] Tucaray, and Quisin. Then [he moved on to the island of] Niñachumpi.[327]

[F.45R] CHAPTER 22

How Tupa Inca Yupanqui returned to Cuzco and his father, [Pachacuti] Inca Yupanqui, renounced his lordship

Having completed the above conquests, in the mountains and on the coast of all the provinces of Quito, Tupa Inca Yupanqui built a fortress in Tumbes to control

320 Cabello Valboa (1951 [1586]:318–320) and Sarmiento de Gamboa (2007 [1572]:147–148) mention all three of these *caciques*, while the *Probanza de los Incas* only mentions two (Rowe 1985:210).

321 Modern San Luis de Quinchucajas.

322 This conquest is also described in detail by Cabello Valboa (1951 [1586]:321), by Sarmiento de Gamboa (2007 [1572]:147–148, 150–151), and in the *Probanza de los Incas* (Rowe 1985:211).

323 This conquest is also described in detail by Cabello Valboa (1951 [1586]:322), by Sarmiento de Gamboa (2007 [1572]:150), and in the *Probanza de los Incas* (Rowe 1985:210).

324 The island of Guañapi in Ecuador.

325 The town of Guamote in central Ecuador.

326 A coastal town in Ecuador.

327 This conquest is also described in detail by Cabello Valboa (1951 [1586]:322–323), by Sarmiento de Gamboa (2007 [1572]:151), and in the *Probanza de los Incas* (Rowe 1985:210). We have chosen to follow Sarmiento's spellings rather than Murúa's (Huacapi, Huamoy, Manta, Tucaray, Quisiri, Ahuachumpi, and Niñachumpi).

Figure 21.1. Untitled. Believed to show Pachacuti Inca Yupanqui ordering his son Tupa Inca Yupanqui to conquer new lands. The figure reads, "do not paint," written by Remón (Adorno 2008:104), indicating that it was not to be included in the final printing (courtesy of The J. Paul Getty Museum, Los Angeles, Ms. Ludwig XIII 16 [83.MP.159], f.42v).

and hold those coastal provinces. He [then] returned to Cuzco to give a complete account and narrative to [Pachacuti] Inca Yupanqui, his father, of what had been conquered and captured. He appointed governors to oversee and guard the provinces and established a garrison in each. He took the route through Cajamarca, sending his two uncles to Trujillo[328] via the coast, who seized that rich and fertile land, where they found vast riches of gold and silver including famous and splendid vessels and beams of silver and gold, which were used to construct the houses of the Chimu Capac,[329] the Lord of those provinces.[330]

This incredible feat was unmatched by any monarch in the world. The *huacas* that were discovered and found in Trujillo after the Spaniards came and seized that land are clear evidence of the wealth and power of Chimu Capac, the natural Lord of Trujillo. These were the most magnificent, opulent, and numerous [*huacas*] that have been discovered to date in the Indies. All of these gold and silver vessels were brought to Tupa Inca Yupanqui at Cajamarca and then to Cuzco, where he entered with the greatest triumph any Inca has ever had. He brought with him an assortment of people and nations he had subdued and pacified, making a pompous example of all the main *curacas* and captains he had captured in battle, which he brought from their lands for this very purpose.[331]

Since the envious heart is even envious and resentful of its own things, [Pachacuti] Inca Yupanqui received this great and majestic triumph from his son with immense sorrow and sadness, knowing that [all] the honor and glory of the victories would go to [Tupa Inca Yupanqui] and not to himself since he did not go on the conquests. Only [Tupa Inca Yupanqui] would receive the credit for the victory. As a result, [Pachacuti Inca Yupanqui] plotted to kill his two sons, Tilca Yupanqui and [Apu] Yanqui Yupanqui. [However, he] only killed Tilca Yupanqui,[332] claiming that the reason for his death was their disobedience of his orders and they had taken his son, Tupa [Inca] Yupanqui, and his army to such distant and far-flung provinces that they risked being lost.[333] When Tupa Inca Yupanqui saw the unjust and undeserved death

---

328   Murúa describes the town of Trujillo and many other towns on the northern coast of Peru in book 3, chapter 18 of his chronicle.

329   Guaman Poma de Ayala (2004 [1615]:156 [158]) briefly mentions Chimu Capac.

330   Later, while the Spaniards were marching from Cajamarca to Cuzco, they found a storehouse of silver beams that were being transported by the Inca from the site of Curamba to the Chimu.

331   Cabello Valboa (1951 [1586]:324–325) and Sarmiento de Gamboa (2007 [1572]:152–153) briefly describe the fall of the Chimu and the return of Tupa Inca Yupanqui to Cuzco.

332   Cabello Valboa (1951 [1586]:334) states that both brothers were killed. Sarmiento de Gamboa (2007 [1572]:153) notes that some people report that the Inca killed both men, while others state that the Inca only killed Tilca Yupanqui.

333   Both Cabello Valboa (1951 [1586]:333) and Sarmiento de Gamboa (2007 [1572]:153)

of *[f.45v]* his brother, he was deeply saddened and showed his grief. [Pachacuti] Inca Yupanqui commanded the gold taken in this [conquest to be used] to make the golden statues of the Sun, Viracocha, and [their wives] Palpa Ocllo and Inca Ocllo[334] and to decorate and enrich the temple of Coricancha with gold.[335]

From the gold that was brought [to Cuzco], Tupa Inca Yupanqui took the opportunity to discover more gold and silver ores. To this end, he issued [an order] across the kingdom, and an abundance of gold, silver, and emeralds began to appear, and they continued to appear in all of these provinces. To this day Peru remains the deposit of riches for the entire world, with new samples being [found] every day, more than in any other province or kingdom in the entire world. It is an astonishing and wondrous sight to behold.[336]

Knowing that he was old and wanting to see his son, Tupa [Inca] Yupanqui, in possession of the kingdom and lordship, [Pachacuti] Inca Yupanqui spoke to him as well as to all his brothers, [other] relatives, lineage [members], and the captains and governors in Cuzco. Everyone came because Tupa Inca Yupanqui was much loved and adored by the children and adults [of Cuzco]. Seeing the *orejones* so willing, his father called a general meeting and took Tupa Inca Yupanqui to the Coricancha and placed him in front of the statue of the Sun. He then spoke to the Sun, saying: "You see here your son who is to take my place in all the kingdoms and provinces that I possess." Then he[337] made [Tupa Inca Yupanqui] put on a very elaborate garment that was called *capac uncu tarco hualcay*, which means "rich and precious clothes," and then they placed the tassel on his forehead, called the *mascapaicha*, which is the royal crown made of a very fine red wool. [The priests of the Sun] also presented the *sunturpaucar* and the *tupayauri*, which as noted above, is the scepter that is given to the Inca when they crown him and pronounce him as king and lord. They [also] gave him some small golden cups, known as *tupa cusi napa*. Once these ceremonies and rites were completed, the priests of the Sun, who were present and who had the duty, lifted [the Inca] on their shoulders with great shouts, officially crowning and proclaiming him as lord.[338]

[Pachacuti] Inca Yupanqui returned to all of his lineage, captains, and governors for the purpose of announcing his successor: "You see here your lord. Since I am

---

mention these events.

334 Cabello Valboa (1951 [1586]:333) and Molina (2011 [ca. 1575]:27, 37, 100n39) mention these golden statues.

335 Much of this information is also presented in Cabello Valboa (1951 [1586]:332–333).

336 Murúa interrupts his historical narrative to relate a myth concerning the origin of gold in Peru.

337 A spelling correction has been made (Murúa 2008 [1616]:45v).

338 Cabello Valboa (1951 [1586]:314–316) provides similar information on the coronation of Tupa Inca Yupanqui.

already old and handicapped, and I cannot govern you, he will rule and command you from here on out. You must obey and respect him and follow all his orders and commands." His brothers, relatives, all the *orejones*, governors, and captains, then knelt before Tupa [Inca] Yupanqui and kissed his hands and feet with great humility. Afterward, they went out to the plaza to celebrate the coronation in their way: with many dances, parties, singing, eating, and drinking. Soon after, [Pachacuti] Inca Yupanqui died in Cuzco, although some say he died in Quito. However, the above is the truth. *[f.46r]*

He was married to Mama Anahuarque,[339] also known as Hipa Huaco, and together they had many sons and daughters, including Tupa Inca Yupanqui, who is described above, and they had [a] daughter Mama Ocllo, who married her brother. [Pachacuti] Inca Yupanqui was the [Inca] who started building the fortress of Cuzco,[340] outlining and arranging it, [and] ordering that the foundation [stones] be quarried,[341] the likes of which had never been seen before in Peru.[342] In this, the Incas showed their great power and spirit, since they did not have iron or picks to carve such hard stones, so they carved them with other harder stones, known as *higujayas*,[343] and they fitted them together in such a way that a very thin needle could not be inserted into the joints. The [stones] were brought from far-off places using only manpower and without the help of draft animals, as is the case for all other buildings of the world. [Pachacuti Inca Yupanqui] also made the famous and remarkable Vilcas[huaman] fortress.

For festivities and celebrations, he was very handsome and pompously dressed, with the *mascapaicha*[344] placed on his forehead as a sign of his kingship and lordship, adorned with many flowers and gold and silver plates. His face was painted according to the celebration, and he was accompanied by a great multitude of people, lords, *orejones*, as well as commoners, all painted with different colors and designs, dancing and twirling without pause, some singing and others responding, [reciting] the stories and deeds of [Pachacuti] Inca Yupanqui. When they arrived at the house where the party was to be held, they celebrated, and when [Pachacuti] Inca Yupanqui returned to his house, those who remained with him ate and drank with great rejoicing. Thus, like barbarians, all their happiness was related to this.

---

339   Guaman Poma de Ayala (2004 [1615]:137) also notes that Mama Anahuarque married [Pachacuti] Inca Yupanqui.

340   Sacsayhuaman.

341   Additional information on the fort of Sacsayhuaman is provided in book 3, chapter 10 of Murúa's chronicle.

342   Fernández de Palencia (1963 [1571]:81) provides similar information in his chronicle on the building of Sacsayhuaman.

343   A spelling mistake has been corrected (Murúa 2008 [1616]:46r).

344   This word is underlined (Murúa 2008 [1616]:46r).

Figure 22.1. Untitled. Believed to show Pachacuti Inca Yupanqui (right) receiving his son Tupa Inca Yupanqui (left). The drawing includes the word "no," written by Remón (Adorno 2008:104), indicating that it was not to be included in the final printing (courtesy of The J. Paul Getty Museum, Los Angeles, Ms. Ludwig XIII 16 [83.MP.159], f.44v).

[F.47R] CHAPTER 23

Mama Anahuarque Coya, wife of [Pachacuti] Inca Yupanqui

Coya Mama Anahuarque, also known as Hipa Huaco,[345] was a woman of great intelligence, sharpness, and courage. During the absence of her husband, the great Pachacuti Inca Yupanqui, who had gone to conquer the province of Quito, she ruled the city of Cuzco with admirable prudence, order, and harmony. Her incomparable courage and composure were demonstrated during the terrible earthquake that occurred in her time in the city of Arequipa; caused by a fearful volcano that was three leagues from the city.[346] They say that [the volcano] spewed so much fire, with so many frightful flares, that it astonished and held the attention of the people for many leagues.

This volcano overflowed and cast so much ash that it rained throughout the kingdom, causing universal admiration and fear. If it were not for the encouragement of Coya Mama Anahuarque, most of the people of the nearby provinces of Arequipa would have been devastated.[347] She first ordered great sacrifices be made to their idols in the temple they call Ticsi Huasi, the House of the Universe, and in many others that were in Cuzco. When [Pachacuti] Inca Yupanqui, her husband, received news of it, he quickly returned [to Cuzco] within a few days. He traveled to Arequipa with many priests, fortune tellers, and sorcerers. When he was near, he made various sacrifices, as will be described in the chapter dedicated to this city.[348] A few days later this Coya died, leaving behind sons and a daughter named Mama Ocllo, who was the wife of Tupa Inca Yupanqui, her elder brother.[349]

Although the sacrifices were sinful and vain and could not result in anything good, these people were misled, distracted, and encouraged by seeing that their kings were attempting to appease their idols.[350]

345   In the *History and Genealogy of the Inca Kings of Peru* (Murúa 2004 [1590]:28v), the name is written as Coya Ypa Mama Machi Chiquia.

346   Guaman Poma de Ayala (2004 [1615]:137) also mentions that during the rule of Mama Anahuarque and Pachacuti, "there were great punishments, hunger, thirst and pestilence sent by God."

347   Additional information concerning Arequipa and Huaynaputina is provided in book 3, chapters 21 and 22 of Murúa's chronicle.

348   Murúa is referring to his chapter on Arequipa in book 3.

349   Guaman Poma de Ayala (2004 [1615]:139) provides a list of other children.

350   This final sentence, which does not match the tone of the rest of the chapter, was added by Remón (Adorno 2008:104).

Figure 23.1. Untitled. Presumed to be Coya Mama Anahuarque (courtesy of The J. Paul Getty Museum, Los Angeles, Ms. Ludwig XIII 16 [83.MP.159], f.46v).

[F.48R] CHAPTER 24

Tupa Inca Yupanqui, [the] 10th Inca and king

We already described in chapter 23, how Tupa Inca Yupanqui was endorsed and recognized as the absolute Lord of these kingdoms by his father. When his father died, Tupa Inca Yupanqui tried to undertake new conquests to extend his lordship. As he was an Inca of great strength and courage, and was feared, [he] was respected by all his vassals. Whatever he commanded them to do, was immediately done with promptness and diligence, without delay, everywhere.[351] Since he already controlled a large number of provinces and vassals, the first thing he did was to marry his sister Mama Ocllo,[352] a daughter of [Pachacuti] Inca Yupanqui, his father, and of Mama Anahuarque, [his mother]. To celebrate the wedding, he held grand festivals and rejoiced with parties and dances, as they do, with many of his relatives joining him.

After his marriage, he assembled a massive army from all the nations subject to him and then set off from Cuzco to conquer the Andes. He took Tupac Yupanqui, his brother, Otorongo Achachi,[353] and Apu Chalco Yupanqui as captains.[354] As they entered the Andes, the conquest continued, and they reached the other side of the mountain range, which took a great deal of work, a feat that was incredibly difficult due to the mountainous terrain and its vast rivers. Because of this, their progress was extremely difficult, and more than once it seemed as though they were on the verge of getting lost. He had many encounters, that included famous battles where he demonstrated his courage and diligence.

He conquered four interior provinces in the Andes: Opatarisuyu,[355] of the Andes Indians, Manansuyu,[356] Mañarisuyu,[357] and Chunchu. He also went to the

---

351 Fernández de Palencia (1963 [1571]:6) provides similar information.
352 Guaman Poma de Ayala (2004 [1615]:139) mentions that Tupa Inca Yupanqui married Mama Ocllo.
353 Guaman Poma de Ayala (2004 [1615]:111, 154 [156], 269 [271]) lists three different individuals having the name Otorongo Achachi Inca: a son of Tupa Inca [Yupanqui], a son of Inca Roca, and a captain of Huayna Capac. Also see Betanzos (1996 [1557]:161, 162).
354 Sarmiento de Gamboa (2007 [1572]:158) and Cabello Valboa (1951 [1586]:334) also describe Tupa Inca Yupanqui's departure for the Andes with these captains.
355 This word is underlined (Murúa 2008 [1616]:48r). The Opataris are mentioned in various early Colonial documents in references to groups living on the eastern slope of the Andes in Maúrtua (1906), *Probanza de los Incas* (Rowe 1985), and Salazar (2016 [1596]).
356 This word is underlined. It may be a reference to the town of Momorí (Maúrtua 1906:3–70).
357 The Mañarís are mentioned in various early Colonial documents in references to groups living on the eastern slope of the Andes, including Ocampo Conejeros (2016 [1611]), *Probanza de los Incas* (Rowe 1985), and Salazar (2016 [1596]).

Chiponahuas[358] and to Manopampa,[359] who are people who have black mouths and paint their faces like Blacks, when needed. This was done on purpose. There were surprise attacks [which led to the] capture of the *caciques* of these provinces, Vinchi Cayna [and] Canta Guancuru. In a hard-fought battle, his brother Tupa [Inca] Yupanqui seized one of the *caciques*, Nutanguari, thus spreading his fame and name to all those regions.[360]

Although this area is largely unknown, it is believed and presumed to be vast and densely populated by diverse people. However, due to the difficulty in traversing its mountains and ridges, few in this kingdom, aside from seeking wealth, have attempted to spread the name of Christ and raise his standard within these barbarous nations ~~making it impossible [for the faith] to enter these provinces~~.[361] Supplicating to the bowels of the lord, who also died for them, that[362]●●●●●●●●●●●●●●●●●●●●●●●●●●●●●●●●[363] to enlighten the minds of those who are able to do so, despite the expenses and various inconveniences, [let us] send people to plant the Tree of the Most Holy Cross in the midst of these fierce people, so that through this, the most abundant fruit can be transplanted to the forests and streets of Heaven.[364]

While Tupa Inca Yupanqui was in the Andes and involved in the [above] mentioned conquest *[f.48v]*, a Colla left from there fleeing to Collao, spreading [the false news] that Tupa Inca Yupanqui had been killed in battle and that his entire army had been completely destroyed, with no leaders surviving. The Collas, following their nature, as all these people easily believe anything [they are told], and [because of] the ill will they held against the Incas, who had recently conquered and subjected them, [believed] the false news. [This] was enough [of a reason] to discuss in secrecy and by common consent how to rebel against the yoke [that held them] and deny obedience to the Inca's appointed governors. So, they revolted across the province of Collao,[365] preparing themselves for the start of war, since they were well aware that [the Inca] would turn against them again.[366]

358   This word is underlined (Murúa 2008 [1616]:48r).

359   *Probanza de los Incas* (Rowe 1985:212) also mentions the town of Manopampa. It is certainly related to modern Manu.

360   Cabello Valboa (1951 [1586]:335), *Probanza de los Incas* (Rowe 1985), and Sarmiento de Gamboa (2007 [1572]:158–159) also mentioned these conquests, areas, and leaders. We have generally followed Sarmiento's spellings.

361   This line has been crossed out by the royal censor, Pedro de Valencia, making it difficult to read (Murúa 2008 [1616]:48r). Adorno (2008:115) suggests that it reads "ymposibilataba la entrada en estas proviniese."

362   The word "that" has been inserted into the manuscript (Murúa 2008 [1616]:48r).

363   This is the work of the royal censor, Pedro de Valencia (Adorno 2008:107). Little remains that can be read.

364   Here Murúa interrupts the historical narrative to intercede with some spiritual thoughts.

365   A spelling mistake may have been corrected (Murúa 2008 [1616]:48v).

366   Cabello Valboa (1951 [1586]:335) and Sarmiento de Gamboa (2007 [1572]:159) also state

News of the rebellion and uprising in Collao quickly reached Amaru Tupa Inca, [the] brother of Tupa Inca Yupanqui, who had been left in Cuzco as Governor General in his absence, to deal with whatever occurred.[367] Upon learning the aforementioned, [Amaru Tupa Inca] dispatched messengers and *chasquis* to his brother, informing him of the situation, and asking him to act quickly to solve [the problem], before the enemy could become stronger [and] more difficult to defeat again. This news greatly upset Tupa Inca Yupanqui, as the uprising cut short his series of victories and conquests [in the Andes]. So, he agreed to go to Collao and remedy [the situation]. Otorongo Achachi, his brother, was appointed governor in the Andes and, with the people assigned to him, he had a good army, so he continued the conquest as much as he could. [Otorongo Achachi] was ordered to leave [the region] after the war and not to return to Cuzco in victory, but rather to wait for [Tupa Inca Yupanqui] in Paucartambo and Pillco[pata], while [the Inca] finished and returned from Collao. In this way, [the Inca] would enter Cuzco in triumph with everyone.[368]

[Tupa Inca Yupanqui] left for Cuzco, with half his army, and leaving the rest in Urcos[369] to wait. Upon his arrival in Cuzco, he called upon all the peoples of the provinces to join him in war. So, all the young men volunteered to go to war with Tupa [Inca] Yupanqui. Thus, having ordered all the [war] supplies belonging to the government of the kingdom, they set off from Cuzco with an infinite number of people bound for Collao. [Tupa Inca Yupanqui] took Hualpaya, the son of Capac Yupanqui, and Lavico, his first cousin, and Cuyuchi Yachic, his [half] brother on his father's side, with him as captains.[370] He left Cuzco and joined the army he had left in Urcos, advancing very slowly as some soldiers had not arrived yet. Once his entire army was together, and those who came from the Andes were rested and well fed from the work that they had done there, [Tupa Inca Yupanqui] entered the Collao to start a war of fire and blood.[371]

[The war] lasted several years, and [Tupa Inca Yupanqui] was involved in innumerable encounters and battles. He lost many people and destroyed and killed an infinite number of enemies. This war was arduous for [the Incas], for the Colla were

---

that the rebellion in the Collao was caused by this individual, and they described the subsequent campaign. See Cobo (1979 [1653]:143) and *Probanza de los Incas* (Rowe 1985:213–214) for much shorter versions.

367   Amaru Tupa Inca held many important positions in Cuzco. Upon his death, his body was mummified, and it was later discovered by Polo de Ondegardo and sent to Lima (Bauer and Coello Rodriquez 2007).

368   Cabello Valboa (1951 [1586]:335) provides similar information about the war in Collao and the return of the Incas to Cuzco.

369   A town southeast of Cuzco.

370   See Sarmiento de Gamboa (2007 [1572]:160) for a slightly different rendition of captains who joined Pachacuti Inca Yupanqui on the Collao campaign.

371   Cabello Valboa (1951 [1586]:335) provides similar information on the Collao campaign.

fortified in three or four places—Pucara, Asillo, Arapa, [and] Llallahua—from where they maintained and sustained themselves with great self-determination.[372] Knowing how enraged Tupa Inca Yupanqui was by their revolt, which they had committed without reason, the Collao had lost all hope of forgiveness or saving their own lives.

They knew for certain that their punishment would be harsh if they fell into his hands *[f.49r]*. This made them invent new and superb ways of defense, yet in the end, they were defeated by the multitude and courage of the Inca's army and the strong captains that [Tupa Inca Yupanqui] had with him. They were subjected, destroyed, and devastated, and their main *caciques*, Chuca Chuca and Pachacuti Coaquiri, were imprisoned. Once under the control of Tupa Inca Yupanqui, to warn others and to frighten the entire kingdom, he ordered that the *caciques* be skinned and the leather be used on his war drums; a barbaric act only a godless man could commit, which he was.[373]

Once the entire province of Collao was defeated, [Tupa Inca Yupanqui] continued to punish the rebels. He gravely punished those places which were fortified and defended so that they would always remember [their defeat] and never consider rebelling again. In this way, they would be obedient subjects, no matter if he was present or absent, in times of peace or war.[374]

This task ended so well that [Tupa Inca Yupanqui's] name and fame spread through many provinces not under his control, nor had they ever been conquered by him or his predecessors. Yet fearful of his power, the provinces of Chumbivilcas and Condesuyu came to offer him peaceful obedience and to recognize him as lord and king. [They] arrived with rich presents, offering [their obedience] in order to follow him in the war, and many people from these provinces went with him [to Chile], as will be seen in the next chapter.[375]

---

372   These forts, all modern towns, are also listed in Cabello Valboa (1951 [1586]:336), *Probanza de los Incas* (Rowe 1985:213, 214), and Sarmiento de Gamboa (2007 [1572]:160).
373   Similar descriptions of these caciques are provided by Cabello Valboa (1951 [1586]:336), *Probanza de los Incas* (Rowe 1985:213), and Sarmiento de Gamboa (2007 [1572]:160). Both Cobo (1979 [1653]:143) and Guaman Poma de Ayala (2004 [1615]:164 [166]) also mention the making of drums from the skins of these two leaders.
374   Cabello Valboa (1951 [1586]:336) provides similar information on the fall of Collao.
375   Cabello Valboa (1951 [1586]:334) and Sarmiento de Gamboa (2007 [1572]:160) provide similar accounts of the surrender of Chumbivilcas and Condesuyu.

Figure 24.1. Untitled. Presumed to be Tupa Inca Yupanqui. Murúa (2004 [1590]:18v) and Guaman Poma de Ayala (2004 [1615]:110) have similar drawings of Pachacuti Inca Yupanqui that are very different than the drawing provided within Murúa (2008 [1616] f.47v) (courtesy of The J. Paul Getty Museum, Los Angeles, Ludwig XIII 16 [83.MP.159], f.47v).

[F.50R] CHAPTER 25

How Tupa Inca Yupanqui discovered many mines and conquered until Chile and gave laws[376] to his kingdoms

Having finished punishing the province of Collao and having received the ambassadors of the provinces that came to give obedience, Tupa Inca Yupanqui issued an order to discover mines. It was at this time that the [mines] of Porco, seven leagues from Potosí,[377] were found and discovered, as well as the silver [mines] of Tarapacá, and the gold [mines of] Chuquiapo and Carabaya,[378] which were of higher quality and purity than the celebrated ancient mine of pure gold. Furthermore, many other mines [were discovered] in different provinces, from which they brought an innumerable amount of gold and silver. [Tupa Inca Yupanqui] ordered these to be used to make fine tableware and wonderfully exquisite drinking vessels for sacrifices to their idols and for the grandeur of his house.[379]

He then gave an order [for his army] to march through the highlands and provinces, conquering and dominating them to extend his name. Consequently, with a huge army, he conquered all the land as far as Coquimbo, and then entered Chile, controlling everything until he reached Arauco. There, an infinite number of his Indians and many of his *orejones* were killed, without defeating the Astunía. Thus, he set his boundary markers and limits near Arauco, settling there and in all the lands of Chile, people to guard the borders and maintain his domination over what he had conquered.[380] Aware of the courage and bravery of those people, [Tupa Inca Yupanqui] made sure to leave and keep adequate security in those provinces. He then returned to Cuzco with an infinite quantity of gold, silver, and other riches as well as captives and prisoners. When he was near Cuzco, he sent for his brother Otorongo Achachi, who was waiting for him with the spoils of the Andes conquest and with the army that he had left in Paucartambo, twelve leagues from Cuzco.[381]

---

376 The word "law" has been changed from its singular to its plural (Murúa 2008 [1616]:50r).

377 Murúa provides a detailed description of the town of Potosí in book 3, chapters 30 and 31 of his chronicle.

378 The *Probanza de los Incas* (Rowe 1985:214) also notes that Carabaya fell to Tupa Inca Yupanqui.

379 Cabello Valboa (1951 [1586]:336) provides similar information concerning the discovery of mines by Tupa Inca Yupanqui, while Sarmiento de Gamboa (2007 [1572]:160) provides only a glancing reference to them.

380 Cabello Valboa (1951 [1586]:336–337), Cobo (1979 [1653]:146–147), and Sarmiento de Gamboa (2007 [1572]:160) provide similar descriptions of Tupa Inca Yupanqui's expedition into Chile, his fight with the Aía, and the establishment of the empire's southern border.

381 Cabello Valboa (1951 [1586]:337) and Sarmiento de Gamboa (2007 [1572]:160) provide similar descriptions of Tupa Inca Yupanqui's return to Cuzco from the Andes.

With the armies combined, [Tupa Inca Yupanqui] entered Cuzco in a splendid triumph, like no one before him, making a frightful and splendid display and presentation of the many captive lords and chiefs, men and women, and a vast number of poor and common people. As he entered Cuzco, his brother Amaru Tupa Inca and all his relatives and kin came out to meet him. [Tupa Inca Yupanqui then] went to the Temple of the Sun and sacrificed many of the most important lords he had brought captive *[f.50v]* from all the conquered provinces to the Sun. Then, he began to distribute the other captives to all the lords, to his brothers, to the captains and to the soldiers, who had gone with him and had distinguished themselves with the most courage and bravery in the war. He gave each of them a quantity of gold, silver, *cumbi*, *abasca*, and spoils, as well as male and female servants according to their status,[382] lineage, and what they had done in the war. With these [gifts], [the Inca] won the goodwill of everyone, and they felt rewarded and honored. Accordingly, they ceaselessly admired and praised him, raising his name to Heaven, and showing their eternal admiration for him.[383]

When [Tupa Inca Yupanqui] had finished celebrating his victory and giving rewards to his soldiers, he established laws for all his kingdoms and lordships, as well as for the political government and the *huacas* and sacrifices.[384] He also commanded that the construction of the fortress,[385] which his father, [Pachacuti] Inca Yupanqui, had started be continued with great care, as these famous and renowned buildings[386] would make his name last forever. He [also] ordered the streets and *canchas* of Cuzco to be straightened, and new buildings be constructed. He also ordered that the royal roads be organized from Cuzco to Chile and to the mountains[387] above Charcas, and below[388] to the coast [all the way to] Quito. So much effort was expended that it was as if he were personally involved in every aspect of the project. As these efforts were underway, he went to visit the Chachapoyas[389] and other provinces.

Some elderly Indians say that on this trip [Tupa Inca Yupanqui] embarked on a sea [journey] in rafts to the Island of Puná[390] and [then] went to Manta. He spent a

---

382   The manuscript originally read "quantities." This was later change to "calidad" (i.e., status) (Murúa 2008 [1616]:50v).

383   Sarmiento de Gamboa (2007 [1572]:160) describes the triumphal return of Pachacuti Inca Yupanqui from Chile.

384   Cabello Valboa (1951 [1586]:337) and Sarmiento de Gamboa (2007 [1572]:162) provide references to Pachacuti Inca Yupanqui making a series of new laws when he returned from Chile but do not describe them in detail.

385   Sacsayhuaman.

386   Cabello Valboa (1951 [1586]:337) also mentions the continued construction of the fortress.

387   This is to say to the south.

388   This is to say to the north.

389   Cobo (1979 [1653]:144) mentions Pachacuti Inca Yupanqui entering the Chachapoya area.

390   Cabello Valboa (1951 [1586]) and Cobo (1979 [1653]:159) provide detailed descriptions of

year at sea and arrived at the islands called Avachumpi and Niñachumpi, where he conquered them and brought back people [who look] like Blacks, a large quantity of gold, and a brass chair, as a display of his victory.[391] He also brought back horse hides, heads, and bones, all to be shown here[392] [in Cuzco] as an ancient custom among the Incas to showcase unusual items that could cause wonder and astonishment. In this way, their exploits were remembered from the things that were collected from other remote provinces. It is believed that all these trophies were later burned by Quisquis[393] and Chalcuchima,[394] captains of Atahualpa, when they took Cuzco, [and] imprisoned Huascar Inca.[395] They also burned the body of Tupa Inca Yupanqui, because no evidence of these things was found when the Spanish arrived.[396]

Others assert that Tupa Inca Yupanqui conquered those lands and islands while his father, [Pachacuti] Inca Yupanqui, was alive when he went to Quito and [f.51r] conquered it with his brothers. Both opinions can be believed, as it makes no difference when it took place.[397]

the Incas reaching the Island of Puná but place this event during Huayna Capac's lifetime. Sarmiento de Gamboa (2007 [1572]:184) also makes a brief reference to this island. Murúa also describes the Island of Puná in book 3, chapter 18 of his chronicle.

391   Cabello Valboa (1951 [1586]:323) and Sarmiento de Gamboa (2007 [1572]:151) provides similar information on the discovery of these islands. We have chosen to use Sarmiento de Gamboa's spellings for their names.

392   The use of the word "here" suggests that Murúa was in Cuzco when he wrote this part of the manuscript.

393   The *History and Genealogy of the Inca Kings of Peru* (Murúa 2004 [1590]:44v) includes a drawing of Atahualpa, Quisquis, and Pizarro.

394   Guaman Poma de Ayala (2004 [1615]:162 [164]) mentions Chalcuchima and includes a drawing of this general.

395   Sarmiento de Gamboa's (2007 [1572]:152) account provides some interesting details. He writes: "When he returned from there, he brought back black people and much gold and a brass chair and the skin and jawbone of a horse. These trophies were kept in the fortress of Cuzco until the time of the Spaniards. The skin and jawbone of the horse were kept by an important Inca who is alive today named Urco Huaranca, who gave this account and was present with the others when they ratified this chronicle."

396   Sarmiento de Gamboa (2007 [1572]:199) confirms that the mummy of Tupa Inca Yupanqui was burned by Chalcuchima and Quisquis when they took over Cuzco on behalf of Atahualpa, writing, "They found that Tupa Inca Yupanqui's house had sided with Huascar. Cusi Yupanqui entrusted the punishment of this house to Chalcuchima and Quisquis, who then seized the steward of the house and the mummy of Tupa Inca and [members] of his house and hung them all. They then had the body of Tupa Inca Yupanqui burned outside the house and reduced to ashes." Then the ashes of Tupa Inca Yupanqui were placed in a jar and continued to be worshiped. For additional information, see Cobo (1979 [1653]:151), Ruiz de Navamuel (1882 [1572]:256–257), Sarmiento de Gamboa (2007 [1572]:171), and Bauer and Coello Rodríguez (2007:3–7).

397   Sarmiento de Gamboa (2007 [1572]:152) places Tupa Inca Yupanqui's journey to the Islands of Avachumpi and Niñachumpi during the life of Inca Yupanqui.

Figure 25.1. Untitled. Presumed to show Tupa Inca Yupanqui with mines on the right and his army to the left. The drawing includes the word "no," written by Remón (Adorno 2008:107), indicating that it was not to be included in the final printing (courtesy of The J. Paul Getty Museum, Los Angeles, Ludwig XIII 16 [83.MP.159], f.49v).

There is no clear information today about the islands that Tupa Inca Yupanqui conquered in the sea;[398] only confusing [accounts] from those who say that there are islands [populated] with somewhat dark people. Other old people say that before the Inca, very wealthy people dressed in cotton came to the coast of this kingdom from various islands in large canoes or rafts to trade for gold, pearls, and large shells. This [practice] has completely ceased since the Spanish entered this kingdom, [and] there is no longer any memory of such people or Indians coming from islands or from other places beyond this kingdom to exchange gold, silver, or other things. This is because they know that the Spanish have arrived and conquered this kingdom, and [are aware of] how [the Spaniards] have seized it and of their character and insatiable greed. [These people] have withdrawn and they do not want to come, as they used to. [They do] not want to subject themselves to anyone, or lose their lordship and wealth, which they want to keep in their homelands. Although this withdrawal results in them losing the greatest good and treasure, [that is] incomparable—their souls—which they would gain by receiving the Holy Baptism through the preaching of the Spanish. [May] God take pity on them and look upon them with compassionate eyes so that, when [they eventually] leave their ignorance and idolatry, they [may] come to know the sincere goodness that is found in Christ.

[F.52R] CHAPTER 26

How Tupa Inca Yupanqui organized his entire kingdom, and the treason [that] his brother, Tupa Capac, attempted against him, and of his death

No one doubts that Tupa Inca Yupanqui was the most far-sighted, informed, and wisest Inca and king. Also, of all the Incas before and after him, he was the best governor and ruler of their kingdoms because all the [empire's] organization, order, and layout are attributed to him. Although his father, [Pachacuti] Inca Yupanqui, did some things, [Tupa Inca Yupanqui] perfected them all. This chapter will present only a summary of Tupa Inca Yupanqui's accomplishments; a detailed narration of them will be provided later.[399]

Above all, he was the one who created and implemented the *mitimaes*, moving people from one place to another, taking males along with their women and

398   Sarmiento de Gamboa (2007 [1572]:152) would disagree with this statement since he writes, "These are the islands that I discovered in the South Sea on 30 November in the year [15]67, two hundred or so leagues west of Lima."
399   See *Probanza de los Incas* (Rowe 1985) for a series of interviews with the descendants of Tupa Inca Yupanqui.

children from one province and transplanting them to another, as they would not dare to rebel when living outside of their own lands. He provided [the *mitimaes*] with the best lands, pastures, and places and charged them to watch the people of that province carefully and tell him everything they did. In this way, they acted like guards, and watching and noting if the laws of the Inca, given by the government, [were being followed] and if the sacrifices were kept. When there were many such people, he settled them in abandoned towns, to repopulate them.[400]

Tupa Inca Yupanqui made the people gather in towns [on the valley bottoms], as they had previously lived in caves, hills, and mountainsides, which were more comfortable and nearer their fields.[401] He relocated those in difficult locations to flat places without defenses, so they would not be able to rebel. He selected the chief *cacique* from the natives themselves, taking into consideration their origin, class, and nature. He appointed the most capable to be the chief *cacique* of the entire province and nation, giving them servants, *chacras*, cattle, and women, all for their own use and account, according to the [number] of Indians they oversaw.[402]

[Tupa Inca Yupanqui] also appointed local natives as *caciques* of a thousand, five hundred, and a hundred Indians.[403] He assigned tasks to each cacique based on the number of servants, *chacras*, women, and cattle under their control. All these were subject to the order and command of the main *cacique* for all matters of governance.

[*f.52v*] Each town in the entire province had a *chacra* [reserved] for the main leader, according to the [number of] Indians he had, and the Inca selected its location. At harvest time, their stewards came and gathered the food. This *chacra* was [then] inherited by the successors of his official position.[404] In this same way, the [fields] of all the *curacas* and lords were planted up to the *cacique* in charge of one hundred Indians. [The *chacras*] of the [lower ranked] *caciques* of ten Indians were worked and arranged by the *cacique* themselves to assist with their tasks.

When a lord or *cacique* died, the eldest son of their [principal] wife, called Mama Huarmi, would succeed him. This was the woman that the Inca had given him because although they had other women, those children were thought to be bastards. So, the eldest son of the [Mama Huarmi] inherited his estate and chiefdom, and if he was too young to rule when his father died, the most skilled and

400 Cabello Valboa (1951 [1586]:339–340) offers a similar description of the use of *mitimaes*.
401 Here we read that the Incas relocated populations from ridge tops to valley floors. This movement is well documented by many different archaeological surveys.
402 Cabello Valboa (1951 [1586]:339–340) provides a similar description of the movements of *mitimaes*.
403 Sarmiento de Gamboa (2007 [1572]:162) goes into far greater detail concerning the decimal hierarchy of the Incas.
404 Cabello Valboa (1951 [1586]:340) provides a similar description of the organization of local townships.

self-assured brother of the deceased would remain as governor until the boy came of age to be given the lordship and estate of his father.[405] But if the deceased's brother, who assumed the role of guardian and governor for the nephew, was favored by the Inca, he [could] be ordered to remain as absolute lord, and if [the deceased] had no children, his brother would inherit the position. But if there were no [brothers] for the position, or if they were not well suited to govern, the Tucurico Apu,[406] that will be described later, choose the closest person from that lineage who had the best judgment and sent him to the Inca to be named as lord. Upon being named, he was given a woman, as described above, as well as other things according to his status.

The first Inca to impose tribute in the provinces was [Pachacuti] Inca Yupanqui, but it was this[407] Tupa Inca Yupanqui who made the taxes logical, common, and orderly, based on what was in each province and could be produced there.[408] This [tribute] was used for the general taxes as well as for the *huacas*. He divided the *chacras* of the kingdom into *topos* and ordered his governors to use this measurement. He also divided the year into months that were to be used to provide the necessities for the Sun, *huacas*, and Inca. He selected three months out of the year for the ordinary people: one month for sowing, one for harvesting, and another for holding their celebrations as well as for spinning and weaving for themselves.[409]

This Inca created the *acllas*, who were women chosen from childhood and separated [from everyone else].[410] They were only able to marry on orders of the Tucurico Apu when the Inca approved because without [permission], they could not [marry].

Tupa Inca Yupanqui ordered that merchants should traverse the provinces *[f.53r]* and towns, trading their merchandise for [precious] stone[s], emeralds, gold, and silver. Tupa Inca Yupanqui also commanded that when they found an Indian with gold, silver, or some valuable stone, they should seize him and [make] him reveal where he had found it or who had given it to him. This was a very effective means of discovering a great many gold and silver mines in each province, and it was the mission and goal that he gave to the merchants.[411]

---

405   There are numerous court documents dating to the early Colonial Period, charging that after receiving a position from this brother, that he wished, on his death, that the lordship be passed down to his son, rather than to his nephew.

406   Also see Cabello Valboa (1951 [1586]:340).

407   A correction to the text appears to have been made (Murúa 2008 [1616]:52v).

408   Sarmiento de Gamboa (2007 [1572]:166) describes the tribute demanded by Pachacuti Inca Yupanqui in more detail.

409   Sarmiento de Gamboa (2007 [1572]:166) describes the division of the year and the demands of Pachacuti Inca Yupanqui in more detail.

410   Sarmiento de Gamboa (2007 [1572]:166) describes the creation of the *acllas* and the work of the merchants by Pachacuti Inca Yupanqui in more detail.

411   Cabello Valboa (1951 [1586]:349) provides a similar description of how merchants were used to find gold mines.

CHAPTER 26   **127**

[Tupa Inca Yupanqui] had two people with the title of Suyuyoc Apu, who acted as his lieutenants and Viceroys wherever they went; one lived in Jauja and the other in Tiahuanaco. He always appointed individuals from his lineage in whom he had great trust to this position.[412]

Of the many things summarized here, longer treatises will be provided later. I will only state here, as it is necessary, that [Tupa Inca Yupanqui] ordered a general census and record of all the lands in all the provinces, from Chile to Quito, and established capitals of the *cacicazgos*. He also ordered and appointed governors from Cuzco in all the provinces, known as Tucurico Apu, as has been noted, and other [officials] called Michoc, who oversaw accounts and taxes. These [officials] acted as spies reporting back to the Inca what was happening [in the provinces].[413]

Tupa Inca Yupanqui appointed his brother, Tupa Capac, as the General-Inspector of all the provinces. He loved [Tupa Capac] very much, and he gave him servants and *chacras* and servants in all the provinces. These benefited from and planted the lands of Tupa Capac, harvesting the crops according to his orders and instructions. While Tupa Capac conducted the abovementioned General Inspection, being in charge of the accounting, he concealed [Indians] from the census and did not register them, as had been ordered, disguising [them as] the servants that his brother, Tupa Inca Yupanqui, had given him. Instead, [Tupa Capac] told them that he wanted to rebel against his brother, seize the land, and take away his lordship. Therefore, [Tupa Capac] left them out of the census, but they were to come immediately each time he called them to help him with this goal. After this great treason was forged and arranged, [Tupa Capac] went to Cuzco to report to his brother.

As [Tupa Capac] found himself rich and powerful, he wanted to set his plans in motion. Tupa Inca Yupanqui had left Cuzco to go to Pacariqtambo, where he was occupied in the festivities [and] rites *[f.53v]* celebrating the knighting of his very dear son, Tupa Ayar Manco. Tupa Capac had told and shared his plot with many people in different areas, but even a few were enough for [Tupa Inca Yupanqui] to find out, as these Indians are not discreet enough, even when it concerns their own interests. When Tupa Inca Yupanqui learned of his brother's betrayal, he immediately returned to Cuzco with great urgency and secrecy, and the first thing he did was to arrest his brother, Tupa Capac, putting him in a very dark prison. He then [arrested] all [Tupa Capac's] servants, acquaintances, and those whom he trusted. Upon investigation, the truth was discovered and [Tupa Capac] was ordered to

---

412   Sarmiento de Gamboa (2007 [1572]:166) also describes the Suyuyoc Apu, but he does not mention that they were of the Inca's lineage.

413   Both Cabello Valboa (1951 [1586]:340) and Sarmiento de Gamboa (2007 [1572]:162) also mention Tucuricos and Michocs. Fernández de Palencia (1963 [1571]:81) provides similar information on governors and other officials.

be killed, along with all his advisers and the many sorcerers who had favored and encouraged him.

Learning that [Tupa Capac] had left out many people across the land from the census, [Tupa Inca Yupanqui] left Cuzco to punish them. When he arrived at Yanayacu, which is in front of Vilcas[huaman], [he gathered the people] in large corrals there called Yanayacu.[414] Mama Ocllo, his sister and legitimate wife, was moved that so many souls were condemned to death and she begged him to stop the punishment, as he could earn so much [goodwill] with clemency and mercy, and those people could then be servants in his household. Moved by the requests of his wife, Tupa Inca Yupanqui granted a general pardon to them all. Taking the name of the place where this decision was made, the pardoned people were called Yanayacus. They were not registered in the record of the Sun or in the general census but were reserved for the Inca's household.[415]

Having completed this, Tupa Inca Yupanqui returned to Cuzco and revoked all the census work that had been done by his brother Tupa Capac. He [then] appointed Apu Achachi, another one of his brothers, to conduct the census again.[416] He instructed [Apu Achachi] not to include the Yanayacus in the census and sent him with great powers and instructions throughout the kingdom.

Tupa Inca Yupanqui died at an advanced age, purportedly from an arrow wound. He fathered an immense number of children; some say one hundred and fifty. He named his son, Capac Huaritito, as his successor due to his immense love for *[f.54r]* his mother, Chuqui Ocllo; however, this had no bearing as will be discussed in the following chapter.

Tupa Inca Yupanqui had a frank and liberal disposition, especially toward the soldiers and captains who displayed courage and hard work in battle. Consequently, he always had loyal and brave people who willingly follow him in all his journeys and conquests. His name and commands were held in such awe that even the most remote parts of his domain trembled at the mere mention of them, and his orders were quickly carried out as if he was present.

He liked learning new things, so to stay informed of events happening in different parts [of the kingdom], he instituted the *chasquis*, through which he knew everything

414   Cobo (1979 [1653]:150) mentions that Pachacuti Inca Yupanqui and his wife passed through the town of Yanayacu; however, he makes no mention of Tupa Capac or the false census.

415   Cabello Valboa (1951 [1586]:346–347) and Sarmiento de Gamboa (2007 [1572]:163) offer longer descriptions of Tupa Capac and the Yanayacu.

416   Cobo (1979 [1653]:150) states that Pachacuti Inca Yupanqui appointed his brother, Apu Achachi, to be the inspector of the coastal provinces while in the town of Yanayacu but does not link this action with Tupa Capac or the false census.

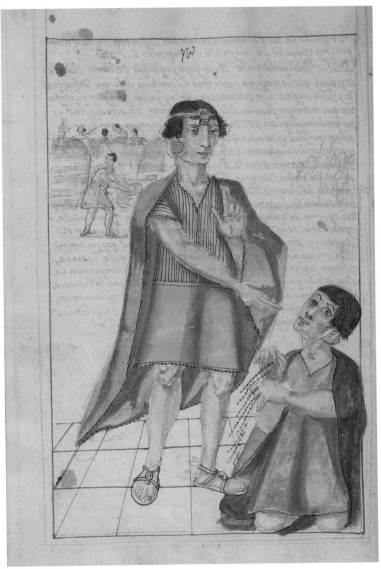

Figure 26.1. Untitled. Presumed to show Tupa Inca Yupanqui confronting Tupa Capac, who holds a false census *quipu*. The drawing includes the word "no," written by Remón (Adorno 2008:104), indicating that it was not to be included in the final printing (courtesy of The J. Paul Getty Museum, Los Angeles, Ms. Ludwig XIII 16 [83.MP.159], f.51v).

that was occurring in the entire kingdom with incredible speed. [They were] so [swift], that they delivered fresh fish from the seacoast, which is eighty leagues from Cuzco to the Inca.[417] It is incredible that the *chasquis* did not use horses or mules, nor any other animals to travel, since they had never seen or known them until the Spanish arrived. It is even more [impressive considering that] the roads are notoriously steep, rough, and difficult. In sum, he organized and improved the entire area of his lordship so wisely that even if he had read the teachings of Aristotle and everything that moral philosophy offers, no further improvements could have been made.

[F.55R] CHAPTER 27

Mama Ocllo, [the] 10th Coya, wife of Tupa Inca Yupanqui

Mama Ocllo, also known as Tocta Cuca, [was the] wife of the courageous Tupa Inca Yupanqui and [the] mother of Huayna Capac, his successor.[418] As mentioned, she was the daughter of Mama Anahuarque Coya and was said to be a native of Chincha, because she was born there. They [also] say that she was very beautiful, discreet, and wise, prudent and, above all, merciful, which was exemplified in the previous chapter. She and her husband, Tupa Inca Yupanqui, accomplished what no one [else] in the entire kingdom could do; and due to her relationship and pleas, he pardoned the Yanayacus.

Because [Tupa Inca Yupanqui] loved her, he built her a famous temple in the fortress[419] of the city of Cuzco with an infinite number of doors and a diabolically carved entrance, which was a snake's mouth, that created fear among those who looked upon it. By passing through [the door] and entering, one traveled underground to the temple and House of the Sun, called [the] Coricancha. This door is believed to still exist, and according to some old inhabitants, it is in a cave that is now called the Chincana, which means "place where one gets lost."[420]

---

417   Fernández de Palencia (1963 [1571]:81) also mentions the bringing of fresh fish from the sea.

418   Mama Ocllo is a well-known figure in Inca history. Cabello Valboa (1951 [1586]:339, 346, 357, 360), Cobo (1979 [1653]:152–153), Guaman Poma de Ayala (2004 [1615]:106), and Sarmiento de Gamboa (2007 [1572]:171) state that Mama Ocllo was the wife of Pachacuti Inca Yupanqui. After her death, her mummy was kept just outside of Cuzco in Picchu (Bauer 1998; Betanzos 1996 [1557]:172–173; Cobo 1990 [1653]:6). In 1559, Polo de Onde-gardo found the mummy of Mama Ocllo and sent it to Lima along with several others (Acosta 2002 [1590]:365; Bauer and Coello Rodríguez 2007).

419   Sacsayhuaman.

420   Or labyrinth. There is a long-standing tradition of myths of underground passages in the Andes. The connection of Sacsayhuaman and the Coricancha via a secret underground passage is still frequently told.

This Coya resided in this temple in the fortress for a long time when her husband Tupa Inca Yupanqui went on wars and conquests. More than five thousand male and female Indians served her, all sleeping inside [the temple] and eating at her expense because she was very wealthy. She had many towns to supply her and to provide for this temple. Outside the main door, there was an ossuary of Indian skulls carefully stacked, said to number one hundred and fifty thousand skulls on beams and steps, not including those on the towers, which could not be counted.

The Indians who visited Mama Ocllo's temple *[f.55v]* used to recount remarkable tales and fables: [they said that] since the creation of the world, four suns had passed before this one that shines upon us now. The first one was lost to water, the second fell from the sky onto the earth and a [race] of giants were killed. Spaniards have found their bones in various areas. The size and proportion [of the bones] suggest that they were men standing over twenty palms high. The third sun, they say, ran out of fire; the fourth [out] of air. They had an extensive account of the fifth sun, which was painted and marked in the temple of Coricancha and recorded in their *quipus* up to the year 1554.[421] It is unsurprising that people without the light of faith erred so remarkably, as one can read similar nonsense from other wiser and advanced nations. This Coya had [three] sons—Huayna Capac, Auqui Tupa[422] and Auqui Toma[423]—and a daughter named Rahua Ocllo,[424] also known as Pilli Coaco Coya, who became the wife of Huayna Capac.[425]

---

421   It is unclear why this date is mentioned in relation to the sun. By this time, the Coricancha was converted into a Dominican monastery.

422   Guaman Poma de Ayala (2004 [1615]:139) writes the name of this son as Uisa Tupa Inca.

423   Guaman Poma de Ayala (2004 [1615]:154) lists Huayna Capac and Auqui Pachacuti Inca Yupanqui as two of her sons and Rahua Ocllo as one of her daughters. Fernández de Palencia (1963 [1571]:82) provides the names of these three children.

424   Guaman Poma de Ayala (2004 [1615]:139) writes this daughter as Rahua Ocllo.

425   There are some similarities between the drawing of Mama Ocllo, in the *General History of Peru* (Murúa 2008 [1616]:54v) and in *The First New Chronicle* (Guaman Poma de Ayala 2004 [1615]:138). Also, Guaman Poma de Ayala writes of Mama Ocllo (2004 [1615]:139), "Her *lliclla* was yellow in the middle and the sides, her *chumpi oque* (waist-belt ash gray), her *acso* dark blue with stripes." This description shares similarities with the drawing provided in the *General History of Peru* (Murúa 2008 [1616]:54v). Furthermore, there are some slight similarities between the drawing of Coya Cusi Chimpo Mama Micai in the *History and Genealogy of the Inca Kings of Peru* (Murúa 2004 [1590]:27v) and that of Mama Ocllo in the *General History of Peru* (Murúa 2008 [1616]:54v) and in *The First New Chronicle* (Guaman Poma de Ayala 2004 [1615]133).

Figure 27.1. Untitled. Presumed to show Mama Ocllo (courtesy of The J. Paul Getty Museum, Los Angeles, Ms. Ludwig XIII 16 [83.MP.159], f.54v).

[F.56v] CHAPTER 28

How Inca Huayna Capac, the son of Tupa Inca Yupanqui, was coronated

The best-known Inca and king of these kingdoms, who is talked about the most by both the Spanish and Indians, was Huayna Capac, [the] son of Tupa Inca Yupanqui and his legitimate wife Mama Ocllo. Those who pride themselves on being born with the royal blood of the Incas try to show that they are his descendants, although some with falsehoods and lies. [Huayna Capac], who we are discussing now, is the one who extended his dominion the most. [He was] courageous, feared, esteemed, prudent, [and] severe, and wise. [He also] liked and understood war and was good in organizing them. In peace, he was of great magnanimity and [was a] brave and courageous person. He also [was the] first to fight on all occasions to encourage [others] to follow his example, often taking his [soldiers] on the most arduous deeds and conquests. This will be illustrated in his life and history.

When Tupa Inca Yupanqui died, in his last will and testament, he showed great love for one of his women, Guaman Ocllo, by naming their son Capac Huari[tito],[426] as his successor in the lordship and kingdom, as we mentioned. [This appointment] broke with and was against the order and custom, that had been strictly kept by the ancestral Incas, that the heir was to be the son of the legitimate wife of the Inca, who was the Coya and main queen, commonly his sister, for it was said that the Inca and king had [to be] the son of the king and queen, and as such a [direct] descendant of the first Inca, called Manco Inca [*sic*],[427] through both the line of his father and mother, as we mentioned.

The brothers of Tupa Inca Yupanqui, his relatives, captains, and governors were not willing to transgress his will, so they were ready to accept Capac Huari[tito] as king, crowning him with the [royal] headband and swearing him in as lord, as his father had commanded in his will. [However], upon seeing the wrong and injustice that were being done to Huayna Capac, their nephew and rightful heir to the kingdom, the brothers of Mama Ocllo, *[f.57r]* [the] legitimate wife of Tupa Inca Yupanqui, spoke out. They declared that such a wrong should not be allowed and that [the tradition] that had been strictly kept by all the Inca when it came to succession in the kingdom had to be followed. [They stated] that this would be fulfilled by swearing Huayna Capac, their nephew, as king since he was the real lord and successor of his father, Tupa Inca Yupanqui.

The kingdom was due to Huayna Capac by right and justice since Capac Huari[tito] was not the son of [a] Coya and queen, and for this reason the last

---

426   Here we follow Sarmiento de Gamboa's spelling.
427   This should read Manco Capac.

Figure 28.1. Untitled. Presumed to show Huayna Capac. All three drawings of Huayna Capac found within Murúa (2008 [1616]:56r), Murúa (2004 [1590]:19v), and Guaman Poma de Ayala (2004 [1615]:112) are very different (courtesy of The J. Paul Getty Museum, Los Angeles, Ms. Ludwig XIII 16 [83. MP.159], f.56r).

will of Tupa Inca Yupanqui should not be obeyed. Due to this evident argument, the coronation of Capac Huari[tito] was suspended and those who followed him agreed, and [even] more when the uncles of Huayna Capac accused, be it the truth or a lie, that Chuqui Ocllo was a sorceress and that she had killed Tupa Inca Yupanqui with spells and poison so that her son Capac Huari[tito] would take the crown. As a result, Chuqui Ocllo was killed and her son, Capac Huari[tito], was exiled by common consent to Chinchero, three leagues from Cuzco, where they allocated him plentiful food, servants, women, and *chacras*[428] so that he could live there separately and never return to Cuzco.[429]

Once this was done and Capac Huari[tito] had left Cuzco, the captains, governors, and *orejones* appointed Huayna Capac[430] as Inca and king, swearing and recognizing him in the same way that Tupa Inca Yupanqui had been crowned as Inca in front of the Sun in the temple of Coricancha. To celebrate his coronation, [Huayna Capac] hosted sumptuous parties and celebrations in Cuzco, gathering a variety of people. Since Huayna Capac was still very young and unable enough to govern such a large kingdom, with such distant and remote provinces, they all selected an uncle of his, Hualpaya, [a] son of Capac Yupanqui, and [a] brother of [Pachacuti] Inca Yupanqui, [as regent]. He was chosen among those present as the most suitable to govern, because of his great prudence and courage. It was believed he would act with great care and loyalty to protect all the kingdom, and would look after things for Huayna Capac, who was younger than him.[431]

---

428   This word is underlined (Murúa 2008 [1616]:571).

429   Cabello Valboa (1951 [1586]:358) and Sarmiento de Gamboa (2007 [1572]:171–172) also describe the actions of Chuqui Ocllo and Capac Huaritito but with additional details.

430   Sarmiento de Gamboa (2007 [1572]:172–173) also mentions that Huayna Capac was called Titu Cusi Hualpa before he became the Inca.

431   Cabello Valboa (1951 [1586]:358), Cobo (1979 [1653]:152), and Sarmiento de Gamboa (2007 [1572]:173) also state that Hualpaya was given the role of regent. Also see Betanzos (1996 [1557]:161, 162).

[F.58R] CHAPTER 29

How Governor Hualpaya wanted to usurp the rule and kill Huayna Capac, and [how] he was killed, and the marriage of Huayna[432] *Capac*

The wise apostle Saint Paul said that insatiable greed is the root, source, and origin of all evils for it can pervert and obscure the thoughts of men and cause them to do improper things and that before the eyes of the highest God and men [such sins] are judged as ugly and unworthy [acts], without excuse. Though some may claim that a king can commit treason by achieving command and power, there is no justifiable reason for such a detestable act as acting against the supreme Lord of the republic, his natural king and lord, who protects and guards his vassals, and the one who ordinarily watches over everyone. Fidelity, love, and reverence are naturally due to him.

This is especially true for anyone connected by blood and kinship, who would receive benefits and, most importantly, the trusted tutors. Just as we now see with Hualpaya, a relative of Huayna Capac, who was his tutor, governor of all his kingdoms. [Huayna Capac] had placed himself in his hands and power, to guard, protect, and teach him until he was old enough to take on the administration of his own state. [Hualpaya] forgot these many obligations that have been mentioned and became carried away by the blind desire to be the absolute lord. Perhaps he was arrogant with the power that he held at that time, or perhaps he was moved by the desire to see his own son placed on the royal throne and [to achieve] greatness.

After having ruled the lordship with fidelity for some years, [Hualpaya] ignored these many obligations as he made plans to rebel and occupy the kingship. To achieve his perverse goal, he dealt with the governors of some provinces with whom he had greater confidence, giving gifts to help him and possibly even putting them in the offices for this purpose. He arranged this all *[f.58v]* with great secrecy and they slowly came from various parts of the kingdom separately and without any indication of soldiers or anything that might be perceived or suspected as treasonous or rebelling. They brought their weapons [to Cuzco] secretly and well concealed, tucked into coca baskets and spears [disguised] as canopy poles.

Hualpaya would undoubtedly have executed his plan and killed Huayna Capac, seizing the kingdom and taking control as governor, as he had planned and calculated, all for his advantage, if his misfortune, or better said, Huayna Capac's luck, had not crossed with the betrayals and the disrupted plans that occurred. As many of his people were in route to the uprising, in Limatambo, nine leagues from

---

432   A spelling error has been corrected (Murúa 2008 [1616]:58r).

Cuzco, some thieves stole some baskets of coca. These leaves are from trees that they plant to harvest so that during work or hardships, they can eat [the leaves] and become very happy and relieved. When [the thieves] opened the baskets, they were surprised to find that there were *champis*, which are clubs, sling-stones, and other weapons. They were doubly suspicious of wrongdoing, especially since the weapons came hidden and more because they were not the result of a call to war from the Inca, as that would have been well known. They quickly went to Cuzco and denounced [Hualpaya] to [Guaman] Achachi,[433] Huayna Capac's uncle and governor of Chinchaysuyu, who was then in Cuzco. They showed him all the weapons they had found in the baskets.

Having heard and seen this, [Guaman] Achachi was surprised, not knowing or understanding who these hidden weapons were for, or for what purpose. No one could tell him. Feeling treason in his heart, he quickly and carefully sent people on the road to bring the remaining baskets, and to seize the *curacas* and lords who had them. He did this secretly without informing his nephew, Huayna Capac, or Hualpaya, or anyone else. When the baskets were before him, he found more weapons, [so] he arrested the *curacas*, placing them in a secret place in his house [where] he quickly, cruelly, and horribly tortured them. Defeated, they confessed the real reason why they were coming [to Cuzco] and [why] they had those weapons [f.59r]. They also told him of all the actions and plans of Hualpaya and the conspiracy and schemes they had hatched. [Guaman] Achachi was astounded and bewildered as he had not suspected Hualpaya, nor known that he had thoughts of taking the lordship of Huayna Capac for himself or for someone else.

[Guaman] Achachi believed that the only remedy for this conspiracy was to act swiftly and prudently. He thus assembled many of Huayna Capac's[434] relatives, servants, and close friends, and he left his house well armed and went to seize Hualpaya, before he knew what was happening. Although his intentions could have been disclosed by some spies or Indians who came with the captured *curacas*, who might have told [Hualpaya] about their imprisonment, Hualpaya did not learn that his plan had been discovered. He was determined to carry out his revolt by killing Huayna Capac before his plan became public and people could gather against it. At the time, [Huayna Capac] was in Quispicancha,[435] unaware of what his tutor Hualpaya was plotting against him, and was attending parties that Hualpaya himself was holding to celebrate and entertain him. With his people, Hualpaya set out to kill [Huayna Capac] in his own house in Quispicancha. However, at that

---

433   A spelling error has been corrected (Murúa 2008 [1616]:58v).
434   A spelling error has been corrected (Murúa 2008 [1616]:59r).
435   Sarmiento de Gamboa (2007 [1572]:172) also mentions that Huayna Capac was in danger in Quispicancha before being crowned by Guaman Achachi.

moment, Huayna Capac received word from his uncle, [Guaman] Achachi, telling him to keep himself [safe] and to leave immediately, as Hualpaya was coming to kill and execute him. Upon hearing this, Huayna Capac was worried and afraid of being killed, as were his captains and the family members who were with him.

As occurs in surprise events such as this, the first solution that came to mind was quickly put into action. With the sole purpose of saving Huayna Capac, they had him climb out of a window and shout: "Treason! Treason!" Hualpaya and his people entered the house where Huayna Capac was and searched it carefully. When [Hualpaya] did not find him and realized that [Huayna Capac] had escaped out the window, he rushed out to search for him and finish his plan the best he could, realizing that he had been discovered. [Guaman] Achachi, who had gone to Hualpaya's houses and could not find him, came with his people to where his nephew, Huayna Capac, was. As he found Hualpaya in the doorway, he and his people were easily captured, declaring: "You have committed a treacherous act against my nephew, Huayna Capac. Did you believe that your treachery wouldn't be found out? It didn't work!" They seized and beat [Hualpaya], then took him and many of his companions to the houses of [his father], Capac Yupanqui, as prisoners. They assigned guards to him so that he could not escape, nor could his relatives or friends rescue him.

After this, Huayna Capac joined his uncle [Guaman] Achachi and other relatives, including the most faithful advisers they had since his father's time. [With them] they began to investigate the traitor Hualpaya carefully, and his accomplices to discover more about their motives and uprising. They found him guilty, and he was convicted of treason, so [Huayna Capac] ordered him killed. They continued to pursue the guilty and ordered memorable punishments [f.59v] for all children and property of the traitor. The same was done across the kingdom to the accomplices and to those who had been aware of the conspiracy. [As a result], many of them requested to become *yanaconas* of Huayna Capac. Subsequently, [Huayna Capac] freed himself from the influence and authority of his tutors and assumed full control of his kingdom. Having reached the age of maturity, he began to rule alone.[436]

At the outset, [Huayna Capac] appointed Auqui Tupa Inca, his full brother by his father and mother, as his companion and advisor, since he was a wise, prudent, and courageous man.[437] He then married his full sister by his father and mother, Mama Cusi Rimay [Ocllo]. For this marriage, he hosted magnificent parties at great

---

436   Sarmiento de Gamboa (2007 [1572]:173) dedicates only two sentences to the failed rebellion of Hualpaya, while both Cabello Valboa (1951 [1586]:358–360) and Cobo (1979 [1653]:152) provide more details concerning Hualpaya's attempt to usurp the rule, the discovery of arms in coca baskets, and the execution of Hualpaya by [Guaman] Achachi.

437   Cabello Valboa (1951 [1586]:360), Guaman Poma de Ayala (2004 [1615]:85, 119, 123), and Sarmiento de Gamboa (2007 [1572]:173) mention Auqui Tupa Inca.

Figure 29.1. Untitled. Presumed to show Huayna Capac. In the background one can see the wedding of Huayna Capac (upper left) and the execution of Hualpaya (upper right.) The word "no," written by Remón (Adorno 2008:104), is written at the top of the figure indicating that it should not be printed (courtesy of The J. Paul Getty Museum, Los Angeles, Ms. Ludwig XIII 16 [83.MP.159], f.57v).

expense and pomp. To make it a bigger celebration, he called the governors and leaders of all the provinces. [Mama] Cusi Rimay [Ocllo] died in Quito. Huayna Capac then married Rahua Ocllo, mother of Huascar Inca, in the same location, as will be told in chapter 31.

[F.60V] CHAPTER 30

How Huayna Capac mourned for his father and mother, and personally visited many provinces

After Huayna Capac fulfilled his marriage and festivals, he wished to show compassion for his deceased father and mother, so he organized mourning rituals and honors for them throughout the land.[438] To make them more solemn, he proclaimed in all provinces from Quito to Chile that the expenses related to the mourning rituals would be covered by the estate left by his father, Tupa Inca Yupanqui, and his mother, Mama Ocllo, due to their great wealth, as was previously described. So, an infinite amount of gold, silver, cattle, food, drink, and clothes made of *cumbi*, *ahuasca*, and cotton were consumed and used. The lords and leaders who mourned the dead were presented with many vessels, pots, and pitchers of gold and silver, and the common people [were given] a great amount to eat and the poor were clothed according to their individual needs. Huayna Capac asked the Sun for permission to mourn his parents in Cajamarca. So, he departed Cuzco with a large entourage and paid tribute to his father with great shows of sorrow and anguish everywhere his father had been, in accordance with their traditions.

During the year, they held three memorial events for the deceased: the first was called Tioya; it was held five days after the death. [The second] was another mourning [ceremony] held six months later in Cuzco. The last one was called Cullu Huacani, which was held at the end of one year. This was universally observed throughout the land, and then they stopped mourning and discarded all displays of grief and pain. They washed off the black soot from their painted faces. Huayna Capac traveled to Cajamarca to hold this last mourning event, as noted above.

On this occasion, [Huayna Capac] left a bastard brother of his, Sinchi Roca, as governor in Cuzco. He was a man of great ingenuity and industry in buildings and architecture.[439] [Huayna Capac] ordered him to construct a grand and expensive

---

438   Much of this paragraph is included in Cabello Valboa (1951 [1586]:360–361). Cobo (1979 [1653]:152) and Sarmiento de Gamboa (2007 [1572]:173) also mention Huayna Capac mourning his father but with far fewer details.

439   Cabello Valboa (1951 [1586]:361–362), Cobo (1979 [1653]:153–154), and Sarmiento

house [named] Casana,[440] where[441] the main church in Cuzco[442] is currently because before it was in Ucchullo.[443] It was a large *buhío* in the plaza which served during heavy rains, [so that] people would gather in it to drink. It was also like a storage house where the Collas, who were the ones who owned and benefited from it, distributed rations of meat to those the Inca ordered.

[f.61r] Sinchi Roca made all the famous buildings that exist in Yucay, all for Huayna Capac. Many multitudes of Indians were occupied [in their construction].[444] At this time Huayna Capac arrived in the Chachapoyas and conquered parts of it, although not all, and he returned to Cuzco in triumph, as his predecessors had done.[445] Sometime[446] [later] [Huayna Capac] went to visit the provinces of Collao and to ensure that they were still functioning as his father, Tupa Inca Yupanqui, had ordered. Because he wanted to make the famous journey to Quito against the Caranqui and other provinces, [Huayna Capac] ordered that they go slowly, with diligence and care, selecting the most hardworking, toughest, and spirited [warriors] from that province. He went toward Charcas intending to conquer the Mojos and Chiriguano.[447] However, upon seeing that the people of the Chiriguano were poor and naked, without buildings or established houses, and realizing the little they might gain by dominating them, he ignored them. Instead, [Huayna Capac] went to Cochabamba,[448] and he saw [that] there was an abundance of fertile land, enough to support many thousands of Indians as well as the few locals. Thus, he

---

de Gamboa (2007 [1572]:174) briefly mention the architectural works of Sinchi Roca, as does Garcilaso de la Vega.

440   The Casana was located on the central plaza of Cuzco. Several chroniclers provide detailed descriptions of it. See Betanzos (1996 [1557]:190), Cabello Valboa (1951 [1586]:361), Cobo (1979 [1653]:153, 1990:58), Sarmiento de Gamboa (2007 [1572]), Pedro Pizarro (1921 [1571]:356), and Bauer (2004:17–121).

441   A textual error has been corrected (Murúa 2008 [1616]:60v).

442   Garcilaso de la Vega (1966 [1609]:799) suggests that the house of Inca Viracocha was built where the cathedral now stands. Also see Bauer (2004:122–124).

443   There is a location called Ucchullo near the Universidad Nacional San Antonio de Abad del Cuzco.

444   Huayna Capac's estate in Yucay was called Quispihuanca (see Niles 1988, 1999). Many decades later, controlling the Yucay estate became a critical part of the negotiations between the Spanish and the Incas of Vilcabamba (Covey and Amado Gonzalez 2008).

445   Cabello Valboa (1951 [1586]:361), Cobo (1979 [1653]:153), and Sarmiento de Gamboa (2007 [1572]:174) also briefly mention Huayna Capac's conquest of the Chachapoyas.

446   An error has been corrected (Murúa 2008 [1616]:61r).

447   Cabello Valboa (1951 [1586]:362) and Cobo (1979 [1653]:154) also mention Huayna Capac's interests in the Mojos and Chiriguano during this campaign.

448   Murúa also describes Huayna Capac arriving in Cochabamba in book 3, chapter 28 of his chronicle.

ordered a great number of *mitimaes* to come from other parts,[449] and settled them there, making Cochabamba the head of the province.[450] How its name was imposed will be described in the chapter on its foundation.[451]

Having done this, Huayna Capac traveled to Pocona to better organize the existing border and to rebuild the fortress which his father, Tupa Inca, had established there to keep his enemies in check. He ordered this with great support, owing to the Chiriguano, who caused great destruction in those areas, the *chacras*, and agricultural fields as robbers. Having finished, he visited all the highland provinces and arrived at Tiahuanaco, whose magnificent and astonishing buildings are admired by all those from Spain who pass through this kingdom and see them.[452] While Huayna Capac was there, he solemnly proclaimed the war that he planned to undertake in the provinces of Quito and commanded that the infinite number of soldiers and people who were appointed to serve the Inca in his conquests should come before him.[453]

So, soldiers everywhere began to prepare themselves for their journey with their traditional arms, clothes such as *ojotas* and *chuspas*, and other necessary things [including] food and rams.[454] Some were filled with joy, hoping to return rich and prosperous from the journey as others had done with Tupa Inca Yupanqui, while others were filled with ill will, sorrow, and sadness at [having to] go to such distant, rough, and unknown lands, and to fight against people renowned for their bravery, not knowing what fate awaited them. *[f.61v]* But they all complied, as [it was] the command and order of Huayna Capac, and nobody dared to disobey.

[Huayna Capac] then visited the Temple of [the Sun in] Lake Titicaca,[455] where he made infinite sacrifices to all the idols that were there for the success of his planned journey, [and] he left priests there entrusted to pray continuously to the Creator for him. Following this, he gave orders for how the Uros should live in

449 Betanzos (1996 [1557]:175) mentions Huayna Capac visiting Cochabamba. See Wachtel (1982) for an analysis of the *mitimaes* of Cochabamba.
450 Cabello Valboa (1951 [1586]:361–362), Cobo (1979 [1653]:154), and Sarmiento de Gamboa (2007 [1572]:175) provide similar descriptions of Cochabamba and Pocona.
451 Murúa describes the foundation of Cochabamba in book 3, chapter 28 (f.84r).
452 Betanzos (1996 [1557]:176) mentions Huayna Capac visiting Tiahuanaco.
453 Cabello Valboa (1951 [1586]:109) provides a similar description. Sarmiento de Gamboa (2007 [1572]:175) also states, but with fewer details, that Huayna Capac proclaimed war against the north while in Tiahuanaco. Cobo (1979 [1653]:154) suggests it occurred in Chucuito. Regardless of where the announcement occurred, much of the war in the north was fought with individuals from the Lake Titicaca region.
454 This refers to llamas.
455 Cabello Valboa (1951 [1586]:362), Cobo (1979 [1653]:144), and Sarmiento de Gamboa (2007 [1572]:175) also mention that Pachacuti Inca Yupanqui visited the Island of the Sun and the Uros before returning to Cuzco.

Figure 30.1. Untitled. Presumed to show Huayna Capac mourning the death of his parents. The drawing includes the word "no," written by Remón (Adorno 2008:104), indicating that it was not to be included in the final printing (courtesy of The J. Paul Getty Museum, Los Angeles, Ms. Ludwig XIII 16 [83.MP.159], f.60r).

the lakes, marking boundaries and indicating limits. To prevent the differences and disagreements that ordinarily arose between them about fishing, he ordered that no one should enter another's fishing area.

Having finished [this], he returned to Cuzco, leaving all the land above organized and in good order, and with [appointed] governors who [would] guard it in his absence, and [he placed] garrisons of soldiers on the borders to defend it from their enemies, in case of a sudden attack, since he believed that the journey [north] was going to be very difficult and would take many years, and it indeed proved to be so.

[F.62V] CHAPTER 31

How Huayna Capac gathered his army and left Cuzco to go to Tomebamba and the buildings he made there

When Huayna Capac arrived in Cuzco, he rested for a few days and then he called all the *orejones* of Cuzco to the plaza. There, he made a serious speech, proposing his intention to go personally and conquer the Cayambes and Caranqui in the provinces of Quito. He also [declared] that those of his lineage who wanted to join them should tell him now, so that he would have sufficient time to know who would accompany him.[456] Upon hearing this, many of the strongest and most courageous *orejones* offered to [join] him, and many of his brothers and relatives showed signs of goodwill and a strong desire to serve him. He thanked them with great kindness and benevolence, saying that those who fight alongside him in his campaigns would also have their share of the glory and honor that he would receive, and that all would benefit the rewards of victory and the spoils of their enemies, based on their performance in war. With this, all those who offered and signified [their willingness] began to collect weapons and [other] necessary items to appear more splendid and gallant.

Then the soldiers and armies that they had left prepared in the provinces of Collao and Charcas began to arrive in Cuzco. As they were arriving, they ostentatiously presented their troops, in a formidable formation and order of war. After they rested from their journey and entertained themselves at parties—rejoicing, eating, and drinking—[Huayna Capac] dispatched them little by little[457] to Quito.

---

456 Cabello Valboa (1951 [1586]:363) and Cobo (1979 [1653]:155) also provide brief descriptions of Huayna Capac's time in Cuzco. In Sarmiento de Gamboa's (2007 [1572]:175) version, Huayna Capac decides to go north because of various rebellions in areas conquered by his father.

457 A spelling mistake has been corrected (Murúa 2008 [1616]:62v).

The Inca ordered a person to accompany them, ensuring all their needs on the road, [including] food, drink, and things, were met from the Inca's storage houses, which he had for such occasions.

After having sent first, all the people of Collasuyu, Anti[suyu] and Cundisuyu,[458] so that no one was missing, [Huayna Capac] conducted a review of all the soldiers of Cuzco, who are [those of] Hanan Cuzco and Hurin Cuzco. He appointed Michi as captain of the Hurin Cuzcos and Auqui Tupa,[459] the brother of Huayna Capac, as captain of the Hanan Cuzcos.[460] [Auqui Tupa] was the most courageous captain, in spirit and strength, that the Inca had, and who was the most noted on this journey. The natives of Cuzco and the gallant and brave *orejones* then left, carrying fancy and showy weapons, [and] Huayna Capac was very pleased and satisfied with this.

At this time, the people of Chinchaysuyu were ready to go to war, having received secret orders from Huayna Capac. They traveled to Cuzco to present themselves and be inspected. The captain said *[f.63r]* to [Huayna Capac]: "Let's go, Lord. It is time to see our enemies and test them. We have been preparing for this journey for a year and now everything is ready." Hearing this, Huayna Capac was pleased, and set out from Cuzco, accompanied by the most illustrious people in his army, who were armed with great weapons and well organized for war. Huayna Capac left a son, Tupa Cusi Hualpa, also known as Huascar Inca,[461] as king and his successor after his time. However, in Quito, he chose another [son], Ninan Cuyuchi,[462] at the time of his death. He [only] lived a few [additional] days so—Tupa Cusi Hualpa inherited [the rule].[463] [He] was [Huayna Capac's] most beloved son. He was the son of Rahua Ocllo, [Huayna Capac's] full sister,[464] although not his legitimate wife. That was Cusi Rimay [Ocllo], another sister whom he had [already] married who was mentioned previously. Cusi Rimay [Ocllo] died in Quito leaving no male child,

458   It is hard to know if Murúa means Cundisuyu near Arequipa, or Cuntisuyu, the southeast quarter of the empire.

459   In his manuscript, Guaman Poma de Ayala (2004 [1615]:123, 153) provides a drawing of Auqui Tupa but associates him with an earlier Inca.

460   Cabello Valboa (1951 [1586]:363) and Sarmiento de Gamboa (2007 [1572]:177) mention these captains.

461   Originally the *General History of Peru* (Murúa 2008 [1616]) did not contain an illustration of Huascar. However, the illustrations of Huascar contained within the *History and Genealogy of the Inca Kings of Peru* (Murúa 2004 [1590]:20v) and *The First New Chronicle* (Guaman Poma de Ayala 2004 [1615]:115) are similar.

462   Ninan Cuyuchi is mentioned by Betanzos (1996 [1557]:183–184), Cabello Valboa (1951 [1586]:364), Cobo (1979 [1653]:161), Sarmiento de Gamboa (2007 [1572]:177, 185), and Santa Cruz Pachacuti Yamqui Salcamaygua (1993 [1613]) among other writers.

463   Betanzos (1996 [1557]:178) also notes that Huascar was called Tupa Cusihualpa.

464   Guaman Poma de Ayala (2004 [1615]:87, 108) writes this name as Mama Ocllo, Raura Ocllo, and Mama Rahua Ocllo.

so [Huayna Capac then] took Rahua Ocllo, [the] mother of Huascar Inca, as his legitimate wife.[465]

Huayna Capac left Cuzco with Titu Atauchi[466] [to rule] in his name after holding the solemn fast that they held. He also [named] Apu Hilaquita, his uncle, [a] brother of his father, Tupa Inca Yupanqui, and Auqui Tupa Inca, a brother of Huayna Capac by his father and mother, as governors so that they would guard the realm and watch over it.[467] [Huayna Capac] took many of his children with him, because when he went on these journeys, Huayna Capac was [already] an old man with some gray hair. Among those that he took with him was Atahualpa,[468] his son, who had no mother [because] she was already dead,[469] and he left Tupa Cusi Hualpa [also called] Huascar Inca, in Cuzco [along with] Manco Inca, Paullu,[470] and many others, and illegitimate sons who were too young to go accompany him. Thus, for this journey, he moved [north] slowly without anything remarkable occurring until he arrived at Tomebamba.[471]

---

465   Much of the above information appears in Cabello Valboa (1951 [1586]:364). Sarmiento de Gamboa (2007 [1572]:177) also discusses the relationships between Huayna Capac's wives and their sons. Guaman Poma de Ayala (2004 [1615]:108) notes that Raura Ocllo gave birth to Tupa Cusi Hualpa Huascar Inca, an illegitimate son of Huayna Capac. He also notes that she died in Tomebamba of smallpox or measles at the same time as Huayna Capac. This differs from Murúa, who has Rahua Ocllo alive and accompanying her dead husband to Cuzco. Betanzos (1996 [1557]:178) writes that Huascar was the son of Raura Ocllo and that she was related to many of the former Inca rulers of Hurin Cuzco and was a distant relative of Inca Yupanqui.

466   The son of Titu Atauchi, called Alonso Titu Atauchi, was an important figure in the early Colonial Period. As the nephew of Huascar, he represented the greatly diminished line of Huascar. He was in Cuzco for the public reading of Sarmiento de Gamboa's (2007 [1572]:202, 205, 210) chronicle. After the fall of Vilcabamba, Alonso Titu Atauchi was sent to Lima.

467   Cabello Valboa (1951 [1586]:363) and Sarmiento de Gamboa (2007 [1572]:177) also describe this complex arrangement of lordships over Cuzco. Cobo (1979 [1653]:184) also mentions that Apu Hilaquita, Tupa Inca, and Mama Coca (Huayna Capac's sister) all died in Cuzco as a result of the European diseases that would soon claim Huayna Capac.

468   Murúa writes Atao Hualpa. However, we have selected to use the more traditional spelling of Atahualpa. Betanzos (1996 [1557]:182) states that Atahualpa was thirteen years old when he left Cuzco with his father for the north.

469   Sarmiento de Gamboa (2007 [1572]:237n254) suggests that Atahualpa's mother, Tocto Coca, was Huayna Capac's cousin rather than his sister. Guaman Poma de Ayala (2004 [1615]:87) suggests she was from the Chachapoya. In contrast, Betanzos (1996 [1557]:178) calls her Pallacoca and states that she was from the lineage of [Pachacuti] Inca Yupanqui.

470   Decades later, Manco Inca and Paullu Inca held critical roles in the Spanish invasion of the Inca Empire, with Manco Inca rebelling against the Spaniards and Paullu being a supporter of Spanish rule.

471   Now called Cuenca. Much of this information is included in Cabello Valboa (1951 [1586]:364–365).

When Huayna Capac arrived at Tomebamba, he stopped with all his army, which included a vast number [of men] from various nations and provinces, and thought it was a good place to make the capital of his empire and lordship. [So] he built famous and illustrious buildings and erected a renowned *cancha* called Mullucancha, where reverently he placed the placenta[472] in which he had grown in his mother's womb.[473] For this, he ordered a carved figure of a woman be made, and he placed [the placenta] inside her womb along with a great quantity of gold and precious stones. All the walls of the house were covered with inlaid *mullu* and bands of gold.

He made a figure of his mother, Mama Ocllo, entirely of gold, and placed her [within the house]. They called her Tomebamba Pachamama. Those who served and guarded this house were Cañari, who said that it was their responsibility because Mama Ocllo was the mother and aunt of Huayna Capac, and that he had been born there when his father, Tupa Inca Yupanqui, had gone to war in Quito.[474] In memory of this, and to celebrate and empower the place of his birth, [Huayna Capac] made this frightful work there, intending to make it the capital of his kingdom.

This house had a cobblestone-like floor called by the Indians "golden roots," and the entire ground was covered with it. The walls of the courtyard were lined on the outside with worked crystals,[475] which were brought *[f.63v]* from the province of Huancavilca for this purpose. To ensure his name and to create a large town, surpassing that of all the nations that followed him from Cuzco, Charcas, Collao, and Chile, he ordered them to settle around Tomebamba. He [also] built houses for the Creator, the Sun, and Thunder just like in Cuzco, and he endowed them with farms, servants, *chacras*, and cattle in the same way and manner as in Cuzco. In addition to this, he placed the most venerated and respected *huaca* here in Cuzco,[476] called Huanacauri, [in Tomebamba]. After putting all the other *huacas* that they had around Cuzco [in Tomebamba], all in the same order and places as they were in

---

472 Murúa uses the word "pares," which we have translated as placenta.
473 Much of this information can be found in Cabello Valboa (1951 [1586]:365). Sarmiento de Gamboa (2007 [1572]:177) and Cobo (1979 [1653]:155) also tell of Huayna Capac constructing buildings in Tomebamba and him placing his placenta within one, but Murúa provides more details of the changes that occurred in the city during Huayna Capac's rule. Betanzos (1996 [1557]:182) confirms that Huayna Capac was born in Tomebamba.
474 Cobo (1979 [1653]:155) writes, "The Cañaris Indians served the statue of Mama Ocllo willingly because she had given birth in that place to Huayna Capac."
475 Perhaps Murúa is referring to cinnabar that was mined in Huancavelica.
476 This reference to Cuzco suggests that this part of the chronicle was written while Murúa was in that city.

Figure 31.1. *[f.62r]* Untitled. Presumed to show Huayna Capac in the newly constructed town of Tomebamba. The figure contains the instructions "not to be painted," written by Remón (Adorno 2008:104), indicating that it was not to be included in the final printing. Note that the buildings in the background were drawn before Huayna Capac and the floor on which he is standing (courtesy of The J. Paul Getty Museum, Los Angeles, Ms. Ludwig XIII 16 [83.MP159], f.62r).

Cuzco,[477] he built a structure in the plaza as the *usnu*, called Chuqui Pillaca by the Indians, to sacrifice *chicha* to the Sun when they drank with him.[478]

So, there was nothing that he did not do to make the new buildings in Tomebamba look like the old ones in Cuzco; [nothing] that he did not put and order in the same way and style as in Cuzco. This was because he wanted to establish the new capital of the kingdom and dominion there and divide it among his sons while remaining there with all the armies and nations that he had brought with him on this journey. Furthermore, he oversaw with his own eyes the construction of the most precious and venerated things that he had left in Cuzco, whose recollection and memory might lure people back to Cuzco, causing them to lose their will and [create a] desire to leave Tomebamba, so that they would remain permanently[479] in that land. Or he did this because [all] the buildings, temples, and *huacas* of Cuzco, were the products of all past Incas, his ancestors, with each one having done his part. As the greatest lord and most powerful, [the] richest and most feared, he alone wanted to make all the buildings that all the [other Incas] had built, to show that he could do more than them combined and that his name would be famous forever.

Regardless of his intentions, he never returned to Cuzco, and with him, it can be said that the existence and majesty of this Inca monarchy and the kingdom came to an end and perished. However, his son, Huascar, enjoyed it; but not for long due to the arrival of the Spanish, as will be told.

[F.64V] CHAPTER 32

How Huayna Capac sent part of his army to conquer Pasto and [how] they were thwarted, and [how] in the end he seized and conquered Pasto

One thing that remains to be noted and described about the conquests of the Incas, so that they will be considered unjust tyrants [and] usurpers of what is not theirs, is that before they broke with any nation or province, they would justify their actions [by arguing that] the [nation] had been warring with one another, or with the provinces subject to the Inca, or had caused damages to them. So, [the Inca] would then

477 This could be read as a reference to the Cuzco Ceque System being reproduced in Tomebamba (see Bauer 1998).

478 Much of this information can be found in Cabello Valboa (1951 [1586]:365). There are many descriptions of the Incas ritually pouring *chicha* into underground drains located on *usnus* or in the center of plazas during major celebrations.

479 There may be a correction in the text (Murúa 2008 [1616]:63v).

send his messengers to ask for amends for the grievances done to his vassals. [He] asked once, twice or [even] three times, and [if] the demands were not met, [the Inca] would proclaim a war of fire and blood and defeat them cruelly until they were forced to submit and obey. Others were summoned by [the Inca] to present gifts and presents that would cover the damages and costs of the war. If they sent them willingly, [and] accepted the rule of the Inca, he would highly esteem and honor them, granting them liberties, exemptions, privileges, and rich and precious gifts. The *caciques* and lords, [were given] wives [related] to him and relatives from his lineage, as a way of showing benevolence and goodwill to attract and defeat them. These [leaders], seeing themselves so honored and favored by the Inca, and with their hands full of gifts, spread the news of the Inca's generosity[480] and the favors that the Inca had given them far and wide. This drew other lords and *caciques* to the obedience of the Inca and enabled them to extend their lordship and empire every day, becoming more powerful and feared in the process.

After completing the large buildings and settlement of Tomebamba on the order of the Inca, [Huayna Capac] called a general meeting of all his advisers, governors, captains, and men-of-war, where he discussed and proposed which province the war and conquests should begin in, whether they should move toward the sea, the nearby Andes, or Caranqui. After many differences and a diversity of opinions, Huayna Capac decided to go to Pasto first. Upon announcing his wishes and orders, two captains, named [Mollo] Cauana from [the town] of Ilave, and Mollo Pucara from [the town of] Hatun Colla in the province of Collao, stood up, along with two others from Cuntisuyu called Apu Cauac Cauana and [Apu] Cunti Mollo.[481] All four begged Huayna Capac with much humility to let them serve him before the others, offering to take the lead and *[f.65r]* to conquer that province. They wanted to demonstrate their great determination to excel in their service, because through spies [which] they had secretly sent, they knew one thing for certain; that it was a rough land with mountains and snow, just like their own, while the Chinchaysuyus in the army were accustomed to hot areas, like where they had been born and raised. Therefore, they were not as well suited, and [those of Callao] should be chosen for the journey.[482]

---

480   A spelling has been corrected (Murúa 2008 [1616]:64v).

481   Sarmiento de Gamboa (2007 [1572]:177) and Cobo (1979 [1653]:155–156) also mention [Mollo] Cauana, Mollo Pucara, Cauac Cauana, and [Apu] Cunti Mollo.

482   This section of Murúa (2008 [1616]:64v) contains many misspellings and other mistakes. However, Cobo (1979 [1653]:155–156) provides a clearer description of these captains and where they were from. We have relied on his writings to sort out much of the information contained in this section. Cabello Valboa (1951 [1586]:366) and Sarmiento de Gamboa (2007 [1572]:177) also mention that Huayna Capac moved against the Pasto and mention the same captains.

Huayna Capac expressed his gratitude to them for their eagerness to demonstrate their abilities before the others. He warned them to consider their decision carefully, as he was aware that the terrain was treacherous and difficult, and he did not want them to risk their lives, or have their army be defeated, or diminished in such a way that it would be difficult for them to conquer the area. In resolute response, they assured him that they were prepared for the harsh and cold land, like their own, and that they wanted to perform this service and they earnestly begged him for permission.

Seeing their enthusiasm, Huayna Capac willingly granted [them permission], and to further strengthen them and give them a better chance of success, he gave them two thousand *orejones* from Cuzco. [He appointed], among others, Auqui Tupa, his brother, and Colla Topa, of the lineage of Viracocha Inca, as captains and he sent them with the Collas in good order and formation.[483]

After the four abovementioned captains left with their *orejones* to conquer the province of Pasto, they began to enter the high mountains, where there were some passes, and wide, deep canyons, where the people of that province lived. They advanced, with much effort and determination, aided by their weapons and spirits, [despite] the difficulties of the terrain. They defeated the natives, who, with great bravery [and] without hesitation, placed themselves in all [kinds of] risk and danger. When they saw that they were underpowered and that the multitude of Huayna Capac's army leveling everything, they used a trick to test if, through luck, they could gain the advantage that their strength denied them. What they did was to leave only females and elderly men and women in the towns, and the soldiers regrouped and fortified themselves in the main town. They waited there to see how and by what means the Inca's army would respond. Observing this sudden advancement or retreat and assuming that they were deserting the area, the [Inca's army] pursued them until they reached the main houses of the Lord of the province, in a very large town, which they entered with little effort, defeating the people there and seizing all the land.

Being certain that everyone had fled the province, with no one left to fight, and that all was destroyed, and that they were safe from their enemies, who had disappeared, [the Inca's army] laid down their weapons and began to recover from the previous effort. As they were hungry and they had found an abundance of food and quantities of *chicha*, all left prepared by the enemy to help achieve their plan, [the Inca's army] indulged in eating, drinking, rejoicing, and dancing without *[f.65v]* worries of the damage that might be inflicted on them.

---

483   Cabello Valboa (1951 [1586]:366) and Cobo (1979 [1653]:155–156) provide similar information on Huayna Capac's actions in forming an army.

During these festivities, as they happily enjoyed the spoils of the enemy, the people of that province of Pasto, joined together with their chief *cacique*. Knowing from their spies that their enemies were unprepared, and not wanting to lose such a good opportunity, one night just when [the Inca's army] was busy eating and drinking, they suddenly attacked the people of Huayna Capac's army, the Collas and the *orejones*, in three or four areas. The [people of Pasto], sadly and regrettably, destroyed and slaughtered them, especially the Collas, as they only fought with *ayllus*,[484] and [they] were suddenly attacked in narrow and difficult places where they were unable to take advantage of these weapons. Many of them died and after bearing the worst of the battle the rest broke ranks, with some escaping and others either killed or captured by the enemy, who rejoiced in their clear victory.[485]

Seeing this disastrous event and the destruction of the Collas, the[486] Inca *orejones* and their captains began to withdraw and collect the Collas who had managed to escape the collapse [of the army]. Among those that died fighting, as a good captain in the battle, was Apu Cunti Mollo from Cuntisuyu. All those who left [the battle] together [did so] in good order, abandoning the positions they had won, and walking slowly until they reached the rest of the army that had come with Huayna Capac, their lord, who were coming to support them, albeit late. When Huayna Capac saw his army and people broken, with so many of the leaders dead and so many outstanding soldiers missing, he felt great pain and anger. [Then], with very insulting words, he reprimanded and scolded the captains, rebuking the carelessness and negligence in not securing themselves in the main town and [not] using guards and spies, as is generally done in war to prevent just what had happened to them.

Having reviewed the facts and all the information, and not wanting to allow the enemy to rebuild and strengthen themselves in the most important locations, nor give them time to gather in greater numbers, [Huayna Capac] ordered his army to quickly re-enter [the area] where their captains had entered before. [He ordered them] to conquer [the region] anew, killing the enemy and wreaking havoc as never seen before: burning the towns, destroying the forts, *chacras*, and crops and devastating all the land. [He also ordered] that everyone found in the entire province be captured and killed, regardless of sex or age, and that they be more terrible and frightening than before. He *[f.66r]* continued in this way until, by force of arms and with many deaths

---

484   These are sets of three stones connected with leather straps that are thrown at the legs of enemies or prey.

485   Cabello Valboa (1951 [1586]:367), Cobo (1979 [1653]:156), and Sarmiento de Gamboa (2007 [1572]:180) also tell of the trick played on Huayna Capac's army and their defeat by the Pastos.

486   There is a writing mistake in the information that Murúa (2008 [1616]:65v) was copying (see Cabello Valboa 1951 [1586]:367).

Figure 32.1. Untitled. Presumed to show Huayna Capac dressed for battle with his army in the upper right. The figure contains the instructions "not to be painted," written by Remón (Adorno 2008:104), indicating that it was not to be included in the final printing (courtesy of The J. Paul Getty Museum, Los Angeles, Ms. Ludwig XIII 16 [83.MP.159], f.64r).

and bloodshed, he had conquered the entire province and subjugating all its nations and peoples. When the war was over, [Huayna Capac] exacted fearful punishments on those who had refused to submit to his obedience, and on those who had been responsible for the deaths of his captains and people, so that his name would spread through all the provinces he intended to conquer, and so the people would be afraid of him and thus obey and submit to him, recognizing him as lord. After appointing a governor of his choice in the province and installing captains and soldiers in strategic posts and fortified garrisons, as was the custom of the Incas, [Huayna Capac] returned with the rest of his army to Tomebamba, from where he had departed.[487]

[F.67R] CHAPTER 33

How Huayna Capac conquered the provinces of the Caranqui and the danger he experienced

As mentioned, Huayna Capac returned to Tomebamba and rested there for some days, giving himself to pleasures and interacting with his people. To replace those of Collao who had been lost and killed in the battle of Pasto, the *caciques* and captains of the Collas sent for new people from the province of Collao, with which they reinforced and rebuilt [the army] for new initiatives. Huayna Capac then promoted Apu Cari, the *cacique* of Chucuito,[488] as Captain-General of the entire Collao army. Huayna Capac did this because [Apu Cari] had demonstrated great courage, bravery, great diligence, and prudence in the battle, more than the other Collao captains.

Once the army had grown and been [re]equipped with the necessary weapons, clothing, and *ojotas* for the road, Huayna Capac agreed with all his captains to go and conquer the province of the Caranqui, where there is a nation called [the] Cayambes. [They were] a belligerent and brave people of great spirit and industry. [The Incas] all understood that [the Cayambes] would defend themselves with great courage and bravery, so Huayna Capac himself wanted to personally lead the incursion. He took his entire army, first conquering a great diversity of people and nations called Macas, and then the area of the Cañari, and the Quisnas, Ancasmarcas, Puruay, Nolitria, and other nearby nations.[489]

---

487 Cabello Valboa (1951 [1586]:367–368) and Sarmiento de Gamboa (2007 [1572]:180) also tell of the second conquest of the Pastos. Also, folio 66v is blank.

488 Both Cabello Valboa (1951 [1586]:386) and Cobo (1979 [1653]:157) mention Apu Cari and note that he was from Chucuito.

489 Both Cabello Valboa (1951 [1586]:368) and Sarmiento de Gamboa (2007 [1572]:180) list these same groups in the same order.

He [then] went down to Tumbes and arrived at the border of the Caranqui and Cochisque. There, Huayna Capac showed great bravery, courage, and effort, as he was usually the first of his captains to [enter] danger and [other] tasks, wanting to set an example [and] to create immortal fame for himself for centuries to come. Thus, in the battles and encounters where the enemy put up the most resistance, he personally fought bravely, accepting the greatest dangers and risks, such that everyone admired his courage and daring. His enemies feared him wherever his name was heard, and his people respected him, and called him par excellence "Sinchi Capac Inca," meaning "brave and strong, powerful lord."

[When] he arrived at the fortress of Cochisque, he found it well guarded and fortified, as many people had gathered and sheltered there, carefully arming themselves with everything necessary [for war] since they had heard *[f.67v]* of the bravery of the Inca and his army. [Huayna Capac] surrounded the fortress of Cochisque and attacked from multiple directions. He encountered great defensive [works] and obstacles and had courageous encounters where he lost many of the most valiant and brave [members] of his army, who were all trying to perform well in front of their lord. At last, he took the fortress by force of arms and slaughtered an innumerable amount of people within it. Those who could escape fled to the fortress of Caranqui, where they congregated.[490]

[After] taking the fortress of Cochisque, Huayna Capac withdrew from the forts that were near it and ordered his people to rest for some time. He then held a council of war, proposing [that] they take the Caranqui fortress. The captains expressed various views on how the conquest should be carried out, and eventually the captains Colla Topa,[491] Michi, and Auqui Tupa agreed with the other *orejones*, that the best way to achieve their goal was to conquer and destroy all the land surrounding the fortress, preventing help from arriving and making the conquest easier.

When this was agreed upon, Huayna Capac set off with his entire army, entering through Ancasmayo and Otavalo with reckless fury, destroying and ravaging the land and terrorizing its inhabitants and natives. One way or another they abandoned their places and land, retreating to the fortress of Caranqui, where they strengthened themselves with much diligence. Huayna Capac, having destroyed the area around the fortress, arrived there and stationed his army and himself in the places and areas that seemed most suitable to him and his captains, in order to pressure them more and to prevent the Caranqui rebels from aiding them.

After spending several days near the [Caranqui] fortress and attempting to persuade them to surrender peacefully to avoid their own deaths, which he knew would

---

490   Both Cabello Valboa (1951 [1586]:369–370) and Sarmiento de Gamboa (2007 [1572]:180) offer more detailed descriptions of the fall of the Cochisque fortress.

491   A spelling mistake has been corrected (Murúa 2008 [1616]:67v).

be many since the fortress was almost impregnable and the area rough and difficult, [Huayna Capac] finally tried to assault it in the best way that he knew, and with the bravest and most courageous soldiers of his army, who charged with great spirit and determination to win or die. The Cayambes received him with no less [spirit] and [despite] fighting with reckless stubbornness, many of Huayna Capac's [army] perished, so it was necessary to retreat. While doing so, the Cayambes, wanting to show their strength and determination, left the fortress in pursuit. The onslaught was so great that an infinite number of *orejones* were killed, and Huayna Capac, who was with them, fell [from his litter] to the ground, with many of his [orejones] deserting him, believing him dead. Without a doubt, this would have occurred if members of his guard, numbering around a thousand men, had not arrived with captains Cusi Tupa Yupanqui and Huayna Achachi. These captains were very brave and brothers in arms of Huayna *[f.68r]* Capac, and they helped lift him up from where he had fallen. Gathering together with their captain, Capan, the *orejones* ran back in shame, having abandoned their lord.[492] With newfound vigor, they attacked the Cayambes, slaying many, and driving them back to the fortress from which they had left. Freed from the dire straits that Huayna Capac had found himself in, which was the gravest [moment] of his life and where he lost many people of the finest [warriors] in his army, he returned to his camp, while the enemies rejoiced in their safety within the fortress.

Later, Huayna Capac considered the difficulty of the campaign, and realized that it would cost him many people that he wanted to use in other conquests. He, along with those of his council, decided to take all the roads through which [the Cayambes] could get help and food [in order] to starve the enemy in the fortress and to force them to surrender, even if the war lasted longer than he initially anticipated. Once this was ordered and done and he had set up good guards and jails, he returned to Tomebamba to organize the conquered provinces.

When he arrived at Tomebamba[493] he organized the provinces of Pasto, Macas, Quisnas, Ancasmarca, Nolitria, and Otavalo in his own way, giving them laws to rule their lives. Most of the nations did not have any *huacas* or idolatries, except for the Cayambes and Cañari, who were great sorcerers. The Sun was ordered as the main *huaca* for everyone, as it was for [Huayna Capac] and his territory. [Huayna Capac] selected natives from those provinces as lords, as was the custom. He also appointed governors from his generation and lineage. Once appointed, he received extensive information from them regarding the people who could be taken from each of the provinces, who were the warlike people within them, and who could

492 Cabello Valboa (1951 [1586]:370), Cobo (1979 [1653]:157), and Sarmiento de Gamboa (2007 [1572]:180) all provide similar descriptions of the battle with the Cayambes and the rescue of Huayna Capac.

493 Also see Cabello Valboa (1951 [1586]:371).

be relied on or feared as potential rebels. To secure the land, he removed and trans-planted them to other [areas] with the same climate and qualities, making them *mitimaes*, as had always been done in all the regions that he had conquered. When [Huayna Capac] returned to Cuzco, he included those that he could within his tri-umphant [celebration], as above all else, he wanted to surpass all of his predecessors and be the most magnificent Inca. So, he arranged and ordered everything, accord-ing to the information that his governors gave him.[494]

[F.69R] CHAPTER 34

The mutiny that arose in Tomebamba by Michi and other orejones, captains, and how Huayna Capac ended it

After Huayna Capac organized the newly conquered provinces that were described in the previous chapter, he relaxed and rejoiced with his people in Tomebamba. Meanwhile, he had neglected to provide the necessities for the war and conquests, as well as to help those [that] he had left behind at the Caranqui fortress, which was his greatest concern at that time. There was much animosity between the Inca and the *orejones*, who had abandoned him when he fell during the battle of the [Caranqui] fortress. If the enemy had known [of this] that day, the war would have ended with his death at their hands. Because of this, [Huayna Capac] had ill will [against the *orejones*] and showed it by not bestowing them with the same benefits he provided at his parties and banquets, nor ensuring that they were given their ordinary rations as before; [originally,] they were given [rations] every ten days, but this was [changed] to monthly. This caused the *orejones* to experience great needs and misery, to suffer great need and misery, while all of Huayna Capac's celebrations and festivals were attended only by the Yanayacus of Cuzco, those of Jaquijahuana, whom he showed great affection and love to. He granted them great favors and gifts, giving them preference in everything, and declared them his brothers and compan-ions. He also [promised] to enrich them with the spoils of war and expressed his gratitude for saving his life because, despite the danger and fatalities, they had saved him from the hands and control of his enemies.[495]

These things were seen by the *orejones*, whose need for food and other things grew daily. Therefore, the captains Michi, Huayca Mata, and Ancascalla met in council,

---

494   Folio 68v is blank.
495   Most of the above information can also be found in Cabello Valboa (1951 [1586]:371–372) although with slightly different details.

along with the most valuable and righteous *orejones*. Michi, their general, then stood and said to them: "You all know and understand the little concern and wealth that Huayna Capac, our lord Inca, gives us and the contempt and ill will he has shown us day after day. We know the hardships we have endured [and] there is no other solution left but the one that I have thought of, which brings general and individual benefits. I ask for everyone's unanimous [support] and agreement to help me with all their strength. I have decided that we [should] return to Cuzco, our natural land, from which we left and [where we] have our *chacras*, women, and children and where we can live working with our hands without [having to] wait for the Inca to provide us the necessary food. No one will harm us, knowing that we were forced [to return] out of hunger and not because we lack obedience to our lord. To better achieve this goal, we will take the figure of the Sun with us, for we came from Cuzco under its guard and defense. All this *[f.69v]* must be done tomorrow at sunrise, and we need to be ready with our weapons, *ato*,[496] and whatever else is necessary for our journey in the plaza of Huachao Huaire Pampa.[497] Once together, the captains and I will enter the Coricancha and take the figure of the Sun, and with it, we will begin and continue our journey to Cuzco." Upon hearing [this] from the captains and the other *orejones*, they all approved and confirmed [the plan] by common consent. They thanked their general for the well-conceived plan he had developed, and that they were satisfied with and agreed to do even if it cost them their lives.[498] They agreed that they would come together at sunrise to put their plan into action.

The sun had hardly shown itself in the east when the entire army of the *orejones* gathered and met up in the place selected the day before. At this time, Huayna Capac learned of their gathering, and astonished by the news, he asked them what was happening and why they had gathered so early in the morning. The *orejones* replied that he would find out later. When Huayna Capac heard this, he asked them what war they were preparing to go to, as they had left for the *pampa* in formation. General Michi had the messenger stopped, and when Huayna Capac saw that he did not return, he decided to send another important lord, to whom the captains replied together: "Our lord is already fed up with our anger and displeasure. We want to return to our homes and lands because hunger and necessity compels us to do so." On saying these words, Michi and the other most important and brave *orejones* entered the House of the Sun. Michi grabbed the figure of the Sun and took it outside. Seeing this, the *orejones*, which were on guard, were very pleased. At that

---

496   Herd or cargo bundle.

497   Cabello Valboa (1951 [1586]:372) refers to this plaza as Guacha Opari Pampa.

498   Most of the above information can also be found in Cabello Valboa (1951 [1586]:371–372) although with slightly different details. Sarmiento de Gamboa (2007 [1572]:181) dedicates only two sentences to the revolt of the *orejones*, while Cobo does not describe it at all.

moment Huayna Capac arrived, and he angrily asked Michi: "What is happening here?" To which Michi replied, "Enough, Lord. The annoyances and displeasure that we have given you are reason enough. As we are of no use here, we [will] return to our lands and we want to take the Sun, our father, with us." Having said this, [Michi] left [the Coricancha] and the Inca. When the people of Collasuyu heard this news, they were very pleased as it seemed they would return to their lands. Upon hearing Michi's request, Huayna Capac had no choice but to let him go and Michi began to set off through the *pampa*, with the figure of the Sun, toward the army of the *orejones*.

On seeing this, Huayna Capac [realized] that the *orejones* had reason to mutiny, as they were starving. He [knew] that it would be difficult to prevent them from leaving by force, and that depending on his decision, deaths and scandals could occur. [Accordingly, Huayna Capac] decided it would be prudent to take them by soft means, and he ordered that the image of his mother, together with all the *huacas* that were in Tomebamba, go out on the road to hinder [Michi]. So, they were carried out on the shoulders of the most important individuals of the council of Huayna Capac, and a very important Cañari woman said to Michi: "Where are you going, son, [dressed] in that way? Wait only today, and you will wear *[f.70r]* ojotas for the road and the clothes that I have woven, and you will go slowly." Hearing these reasons, Michi and the other captains gave in to her [and] returned with the figure of the Sun to Mullucancha. There, in the name of the figure of Mama Ocllo, [the *orejones*] with great urgency began to beg [Michi] not to leave, despite that the other *orejones* who were outside were prepared to leave and urged him to start his trip. But he remained there being entertained until it was noon.

Then Huayna Capac entered Mullucancha, where Michi was. [The Inca] spoke to him with loving words, and they remained there that day against the will of the *orejones*. That night, Huayna Capac ordered a huge quantity of corn, cattle, food, [and] clothing of *cumbi*, *ahuasca*, [and] cotton amongst a thousand other kinds be placed in the plaza. At dawn, he publicly proclaimed that only the *orejones* of his army could take the items, [and that] they could take more home as he had ordered all these things placed in the plaza for them alone. Hearing this announcement, the *orejones* quickly began to fight over and collect clothes and food, forgetting about their departure due to the abundance of presents and gifts. Once they collected everything they could, they went to their homes. Huayna Capac then gave principal women from the Cañari to General Michi and the other captains, honoring and favoring them greatly, and enriched them with gifts. In this way, he was able to break their grievances, calm and appease them. From that time forward, he remained cordial and affable in all matters as he had been before. [The *orejones*] decided to remain in Tomebamba, with no thoughts of returning to Cuzco, as they were treated [kindly].[499] It is possible to attain and accomplish so much through gentle methods with moderation and prudence, that it allows for the resolution of tasks that seem impossible to men. In all this, Huayna Capac acted as a wise and prudent ruler.[500]

[F.71R] CHAPTER 35

How Auqui Tupa, Huayna Capac's brother, died attacking the Caranqui fortress, and [how] later [Huayna Capac] took it himself

After the mutiny had subsided, the people and army requested by Huayna Capac from Collao began to arrive in Tomebamba. They paraded, and the Inca was[501] very pleased and greatly satisfied to see them. At this [time], news arrived at Tomebamba that the Cayambes had left the fortress where they were gathered and had attacked those whom the Inca had left to guard the passes, [causing] his people to scatter and many were killed. Huayna Capac was furious when he heard of the damage caused to his people in his absence. To remedy this defeat, he then sent his brother, Auqui Tupa, with an excellent army with many captains, disciplined and coura-geous men, and the garrison that was in Huchalla Pucara. With all these people, [Auqui Tupa] was to take revenge on the Cayambes for the damage they caused and to do whatever it took to take the fortress.

Eager to lead this company, Auqui Tupa left Tomebamba with this army of all nations.[502] Following Huayna Capac's order, he arrived at the Caranqui fortress and besieged it from all sides, leading some battles with much spirit, resulting in the deaths of many people on both sides. In the final [battle], the *orejones* were cho-sen over the other nations [to lead the charge], and by a sheer force of arms, they took [the first] four lines of defense of the fortress. However, during their attempt to take the last one, the good captain Auqui Tupa and the *orejones* perished. So many people [died] on both sides that the bodies were piled on top of each other in infinite numbers. As they fought with deadly rage, when all spears and arrows had been used, they fought hand to hand. At this point, upon seeing that their

---

499   Much of the above information can be found in Cabello Valboa (1951 [1586]:372, 373–374, 376) although with slightly different details.
500   Folio 70v is blank.
501   An error has been corrected (Murúa 2008 [1616]:71r).
502   Cabello Valboa (1951 [1586]:376–377), Sarmiento de Gamboa (2007 [1572]:181), and Cobo (1979 [1653]:158) provide similar descriptions of the attack on the Caranqui fortress, the death of Auqui Tupa, and the loss of life at the river.

Captain-General was dead, the Inca army lost courage and began to retreat in an orderly manner. The common people retreated first [and] reached a river swollen by the rains of the night before. Filled with illogical fear, they rushed into it, without noticing the dangerous current. Many were swept away and those who were wounded drowned on the banks, staining the river [red] with blood. Consequently, Huayna Capac's army suffered great losses, including those who perished in the fortress, [were killed] during the retreat, and drowned in the river.

Those who were able to cross the river *[f.71v]* stopped on the other side, and diligently dispatched messengers to their lord Huayna Capac, informing him of everything that had happened in the battle of the fortress, the death of his brother Auqui Tupa, and the numerous soldiers who had died at the hands of the enemy in the fortress, during the retreat, and those who had drown in the river. [They also reported] that they had remained, strengthening their position so that the Cayambes could not leave again, [and that] they awaited instructions on what to do: whether to wait there for new forces or to withdraw altogether.[503]

Huayna Capac received this news with immense sadness. There are no words that can express the special feeling he felt for the death of his brother, Auqui Tupa, for whom he cried, along with the rest of his entire army. [Huayna Capac] burned with the desire for revenge, and he decided to finish everything in one go and to personally conclude the conquest [by] ravaging the fortress of Caranqui, slaying all who were within it. Thus, with the rest of the army and power he had, [Huayna Capac] left Tomebamba, dividing his people as follows: Michi should secretly go with the *orejones* of Cuzco to one side of the fortress, while the nations of Chinchaysuyu [were sent] to the other side. They were instructed to [march] for five days away from the fortress, giving the impression [that they] were going to other provinces, thus tricking the enemy spies who [Huayna Capac] assumed they had. With the spies fooled, each [captain] was to attack the fortress again with great eagerness and diligence, burning and ravaging everything in their path, not allowing the enemy to fortify themselves, and thus winning [the battle]. After giving this order, Huayna Capac stayed with the rest of his army, which included a vast number of people, and he personally approached the fortress of Caranqui to lead the attack. When he arrived, he attacked with all his forces, which was met with fierce resistance and resulted in [many] deaths on both sides.

He continued [the attack] for several days until he believed that it was time for the army's station behind [the fortress] to arrive. Thus, he ordered an assault on the fortress with part of the army, and at the height of the [battle], he signaled for his [men] to withdraw, appearing to be frightened by some event. They did so

---

503   Betanzos (1996 [1557]:182) suggest that Atahualpa was involved in this failed assault.

in a disorderly way and displaying great fear. The Cayambes saw the sudden and swift retreat of the Inca's army. Unaware of the impending destruction that was about to befall them, failing to recognize the danger, believing it to be like the preceding battle, they began to leave the fortress in a chaotic throng in pursuit of their enemies. *[f.72r]* They shouted insults at them, calling them cowards, and they began to fight with them, killing and wounding some. But, in their carelessness, they did not anticipate the damage and destruction that would come from behind. The Inca's army, led by Michi, and those of Chinchaysuyu on a different side, began to appear at the top of the fortress, well organized and in battle formation. They charged the fortress, expecting to find little resistance, as indeed there was none, because most and the best Cayambes soldiers were locked in battle outside the fortress with [Huayna Capac's] forces. Thus, they easily entered [the fortress], and they began to set fire to the houses and estates of the Cayambes, killing and injuring those within the fortress, who, realizing and seeing the situation, attempted in vain to defend themselves.

The Cayambes, understanding what was occurring from the noise and clamor, turned their heads to see the fortress taken and flames and fire above it. With their houses burning, they began to weaken and lose heart, as usually happens when confronted with the unexpected. Though they wanted to return to the fortress, they were attacked by the Inca, leaving them with no choice but to flee to a large lake that was nearby, hoping to hide in its swamps until nightfall and escape in the darkness. So, they entered the reeds that were on one side of the lake. But Huayna Capac followed swiftly, ensuring no one escaped him, and encircled the entire lake with the best soldiers that he had had with him. The Cayambes were cruelly slaughtered, and so much blood was spilled that the water turned red, and since then, the lake has been known as the Yahuarcocha, which means "Lake of Blood." There were many large willows in the center of the lake, and many Cayambes climbed them in an effort to escape, but ultimately, they were either killed or imprisoned by Huayna Capac's people, and among them was Canto, a very important Cayambes *cacique* who was pelted with stones. That night, Pinto,[504] another *cacique*, escaped with a thousand Indians in the confusion of the battle.[505]

---

504 Guaman Poma de Ayala (2004 [1615]:87) mentions that Huayna Capac defeated a lord named Apu Pinto.

505 Cabello Valboa (1951 [1586]:378, 381–382), Cobo (1979 [1653]:158–159), and Sarmiento de Gamboa (2007 [1572]:181–182) provide similar descriptions of Huayna Capac's attack on the fort and the killing of the Cayambes in Yahuarcocha. Folio 72v is blank.

How Huayna Capac captured Pinto, [the] Cayambe cacique, *and sent a captain against the Chiriguano*

Huayna Capac was very sorry that Pinto, the *cacique* of the Cayambe, had slipped through his fingers. As he was renowned for his courage, bravery, and strong spirit, it seemed to [Huayna Capac] that the war could not be concluded until he was captured. [Huayna Capac] dispatched a squad of skilled soldiers to apprehend him and his followers by any means necessary. The troops began to gain on Pinto until, realizing he was being pursued, he entered a forested mountain. [Pinto] created many difficulties for the Inca soldiers, as he wandered from place to place with a clear destination, inflicting great damage upon the conquered towns. He killed and robbed their inhabitants, and destroyed their crops, until Huayna Capac decided to personally pursue [him] with his army. When [the Inca] arrived at where [Pinto] was, he blocked off all possible escape routes through the mountains, leaving no route through which he could escape or leave. Being on the brink of starvation, Pinto was forced to surrender to the authority of Huayna Capac.

Pinto was very brave, courageous, and spirited, so much so that, even when he was imprisoned under the power of the Inca, and shown kindness and given gifts, even with the gifts and kindness they gave him, they never saw him smile or look content. As a result, he died of anger and sadness. After his death, Huayna Capac commanded that he be skinned and his leather used to make a drum to perform the *taqui* for the Sun in Cuzco, and so it was sent there.[506]

Having concluded all the above, Huayna Capac ordered that the most important, finest looking, and most outstanding prisoners, both men and women, be selected according to their ages and to be sent to Cuzco. They were to be kept there and then used, according to their ancient customs, during his triumphal entrance.

On seeing this order, and that the most important and lustrous of them were being chosen, the common people assumed they were being selected to be killed with the most important individuals being selected so that they would not rebel. Consequently, they made weapons as best they could and brought out others they had hidden, intending to start a new war and protect their people. When Huayna Capac viewed this, he became extremely outraged and commanded his army to encircle them and tear them apart. Among these were many of those who had been chosen for the triumph, and thus those who would not have died had they known what

---

506   Sarmiento de Gamboa (2007 [1572]:182–183) tells of the same events concerning Pinto's capture and death but with slightly different details. Also see Cabello Valboa (1951 [1586]:383).

Huayna Capac intended to do with their lives—which was for them to be kept and settled in other lands as *mitimaes* to keep them from rebelling, as was their ancient custom—were killed.[507] *[f.73v]* With this, the conquest of the Cayambes was concluded; it had lasted so long, taught the Inca so much, and cost the lives of so many of his people, including his own brothers, relatives, and other important captains.

At the end [of the war], Huayna Capac returned to Tomebamba with his army, first leaving a garrison of good soldiers in the fortress for the security of the land and to prevent enemies fleeing to other provinces from rebelling and stirring up the region, which was now at peace.

When Huayna Capac arrived at Tomebamba, news had arrived from Cuzco that the Chiriguano had left their lands in large numbers and entered those of the Inca, causing incredible damage and destruction, killing the people who were garrisoned in the fortress of Cuzcotuyo[508] and many of the people of that area. They did not cease the destruction until they had reached Chuquisaca, which is inland. This news deeply angered Huayna Capac, and he was determined to take revenge on them. Thus, he ordered a renowned captain, named Yasca, who was knowledgeable of the land and its people, to assemble fresh people and soldiers in Cuzco. He was to go to the borderlands with as large of an army as possible, where he could take all the necessary resources from the populations who had fled in fear of the enemies, as well as the killing of the natives and soldiers that [Huayna Capac] had left there. [Yasca was to] defeat the insolent Chiriguano, to ensure they would never again dare leave their own region.[509]

Yasca, the aforementioned captain, then left with great urgency for Cuzco, and at the command of Huayna Capac, he took with him [certain] *huacas*, [including] Catiquilla,[510] the *huaca* of Cajamarca, along with its people who had been at war in that province and in Huamachuco, and the *huaca* Curichaculla of the Chachapoyas, and its people, and the *huaca*[s] Tumayrica and Chinchaycocha with the people of Tarma and Atavalo. They came together and walked to Cuzco, where the governors

507   Sarmiento de Gamboa (2007 [1572]:182) mentions the Cayambes' misunderstanding regarding the selection of individuals to be sent to Cuzco.

508   This fort is mentioned by Sarmiento de Gamboa (2007 [1572]:183) and in the *Probanza de los Incas* (Rowe 1985). We have used the spelling provided by Sarmiento de Gamboa, instead of Murúa's "Usco Turo."

509   Cabello Valboa (1951 [1586]:383) and Sarmiento de Gamboa (2007 [1572]:183) also describe Huayna Capac declaring war on the Chiriguano and that various groups took their *huacas* to battle.

510   For additional information on this *huaca*, see Topic, Topic, and Melly Cava (2002).

Apu Hilaquita and Auqui Tupa Inca[511] welcomed them.[512] They then ordered that everything necessary for the journey to be prepared, both for the soldiers from Cuzco and from other parts, including food, *ojotas*, and weapons. Leaving Cuzco, Yasca gathered a large group of people from the Collao province and marched them to the Chiriguano. When he arrived at the Chiriguano a laborious and difficult war ensued, yet he was skillful enough to defeat them in some encounters and harass them in such a way that they had to retreat to their own lands and mountains, where they usually lived. [As a result] they left the towns that were *[f.74r]* occupied by the Inca. Captain Yasca seized some Chiriguano during this war, which he later sent to Quito for Huayna Capac to see, as he had never seen [a Chiriguano] before. After repairing and repopulating the destroyed lands, fortifying the necessary posts to prevent any further damage, [and] leaving garrisons in the forts, just as there had been before, [Yasca] and the rest of the army returned to Cuzco with great joy with the successful conclusion of the journey. They had been very worried, as the [Chiriguano] were known in the kingdom for their bravery, spirit, and strength. When [Yasca] arrived in Cuzco, in accordance with Huayna Capac's instructions, he allowed all the people of the provinces that had accompanied him on the journey to return to their natural lands. They were pleased since they were exhausted from the long roads they had walked and [the] dangerous battles, and they returned with their *huacas*, as described above.[513]

511   Murúa (2008 [1616]:71r–71v) states in the previous chapter that Auqui Tupa was killed while fighting in the north.

512   The names included in this section have been slightly rewritten based on information provided by Cabello Valboa (1951 [1586]:397) and Sarmiento de Gamboa (2007 [1572]:183).

513   Similar information is found in Cabello Valboa (1951 [1586]:397). A slightly shorter version of the Chiriguano war and their defeat by Yasca is told by Sarmiento de Gamboa (2007 [1572]:183). Also, folio 74v is blank.

How Huayna Capac became in grave danger while continuing his conquests and of his death

After Huayna Capac had dispatched Captain Yasca to fight the Chiriguano, as has been described, he remained in Tomebamba to organize it and to inspect all the surrounding areas. As he continued his conquests, he arrived at Ancasmayo, the final boundary and limit of his lordship and kingdoms. There, in a great display for future [generations] and as an illustration of his power and great showmanship, he marked the boundary with some stakes of fine gold in imitation of Alexander the Great, who, at the request of his people in India, built markers to designate the end of his conquest and to serve as reminders for centuries to come.[514]

When Huayna Capac completed that task, he and his army turned downstream toward the ocean, in search of new peoples and nations to add to his empire. He conquered the Curua, Ninan, and people from the [island of] Puná.[515] As Huayna Capac and his army ventured further away from the ocean, they faced large deserts with no access to food or water, leaving them exhausted and disheartened. And [having] established an encampment one morning at dawn, all his army was [suddenly] surrounded by an infinite number of people they did not recognize or even know what province they belonged to. As the Inca army and soldiers were exhausted, listless from the travel, and taken by surprise by such a sudden peril, of finding themselves surrounded by the enemy, they started to retreat with fear and apprehension of death. [They] worked their way back to where Huayna Capac was in his litter. [He] was surprised at what he saw and could not imagine who had put them in such a predicament.

Finding themselves in this [situation], the weak and cowardly people were determined to save themselves by fleeing when they could, or at the first lucky chance, as they saw no solution to the danger before their eyes. But at this time, the Indians say that an Inca boy, dressed in a black shirt, came to Huayna Capac, and said: "Do not be afraid, Lord, these are the people we have traveled so far to conquer. Order us to unload our *atos*, prepare our weapons, and go into battle

---

514   Cabello Valboa (1951 [1586]:384) and Sarmiento de Gamboa (2007 [1572]:184) mention Ancasmayo and the boundaries of the Inca Empire.

515   Cabello Valboa (1951:385–386) provides a much more detailed description of this battle and its aftermath, some of which echoes information provided by Murúa. Sarmiento de Gamboa (2007 [1572]:184) skips over this conquest, while Cobo (1979 [1653]:159) may make a brief reference to it.

with great courage, showing that we are not[516] afraid of them. We will certainly defeat and slay them and take their spoils and their farms." Once the Inca boy spoke these words, the captains Michi, Chalco Mayta,[517] and others accompanying the Inca who were to provide all that was *[f.75v]* necessary in dangerous situations, unanimously agreed with the boy's advice and counsel, and resolved not to stop, but to fight with courage and bravery. So, the Inca instructed them to do so. They offloaded their *atos*, which were carrying [their cargo], onto the ground. They equipped themselves with their accustomed weapons and, with new energy and courage, which they gained from a speech given by Huayna Capac, they set out to face the enemy. They marched in good formation and, with the promise given to them by Huayna Capac, that each one could have the spoils that he earned [in battle]. So, they attacked the enemy with great enthusiasm and audacity. [The enemy] was put in such a difficult situation, that they were quickly forced to withdraw, abandoning their siege on the Inca. Seeing that they were retreating in confusion and disorder, [the Inca's soldiers] were encouraged to press their victory with more boldness and ferocity, causing an incredible slaughter. Finally, unable to suffer the fury of Huayna Capac's forces, they fled, broken and frightened, to their village, which was not far away. The soldiers of the Inca quickly overcame them before they could find a place or have time to reorganize. So, their entire army charged the village where that nation lived, which was by the sea.[518] They killed all those who defended themselves without sparing anyone, except those who ran away and those who, seeing themselves defeated, surrendered their weapons and pleaded for mercy from the victors.

Innumerable riches were collected in the plundering and sacking of this town, including very large and fine emeralds, one the most precious turquoise[519] that the Inca had ever seen, and a great quantity of *mullu*, which is made of seashell and was held in higher appreciation and esteem than gold by those people. They also found in the sacking, a number of *llautus* and Cuzco earplugs as well as very fine *cumbi* clothing, which the lords of that land told Huayna Capac had been given to them by Tupa Inca Yupanqui, when he had passed through there in his conquests.[520] Joyful and victorious, the soldiers of the Inca held large celebrations, seeing

516   The word "not" has been inserted into the manuscript (Murúa 2008 [1616]:75r).

517   Guaman Poma de Ayala (2004 [1615]:162 [164]) also mentions Chalco Mayta.

518   Sarmiento de Gamboa (2007 [1572]:184) suggests that this event occurred near the town of Coaques in western Ecuador, although he provides a less detailed description of the battle and the subsequent looting of the town. Cabello Valboa (1951 [1586]) skips over the battle and instead focuses on the explorations of Columbus.

519   A spelling error has been corrected (Murúa 2008 [1616]:75v).

520   Sarmiento de Gamboa (2007 [1572]:184) does not mention the recovery of the gifts left by Tupa Inca Yupanqui.

themselves free from imminent danger and enriched by the spoils of their enemies, something that they not expected when the day began.

After this event, Huayna Capac, who was of great courage and magnanimity, did not want the young Inca—who had encouraged him during a time of confusion and trouble, and who had said that the people were the ones whose land they were looking for, and that they would give in and that [the Inca's army] would achieve victory—to be left without the prize and reward deserved by such profitable advice to encourage others in such circumstances. Despite their best efforts, looking for him in all the units of the Inca, [those of the] *orejones* of Cuzco, and throughout the rest *[f.76r]* of the army, they were unable to find him; no one had seen or known him before. Therefore, all the captains and advisors of Huayna Capac concluded that he could be no other than a messenger of Huanacauri,[521] his principal *huaca*, which was held in common veneration. That being so, they should thank [Huanacauri] for the success and for the overwhelming victory they achieved.[522]

While Huayna Capac was there, ambassadors arrived from the Lord of the Island of Puná. They brought him gifts of great honor and value, including very fine emeralds, *mullu*, and very fine and delicate cotton clothing. They said that their lord humbly begged [Huayna Capac] to accept him and these gifts and presents as his own, as [well as] the island's subjection, as was due. And that he should go to see [the island] and what it offered. When Huayna Capac saw that the lord [of the island] offered himself to him so willingly, he agreed to do what was requested. He accepted the gifts and treated the messengers with great humility and courtesy. He then sent them back with additional gifts for their lord, as well as gold, silver, *cumbi* cloth from Cuzco, and other precious items.[523]

After this, Huayna Capac left [for the island] with two thousand chosen soldiers, leaving leaving [*sic*] the rest of his army [on the mainland]. When he arrived at the island, he was given a very solemn welcome by the Lord of [the island] and he rested there greatly contented. He was [especially] delighted to see the pleasantness and fertility of the island, so he had a road made by hand from the mainland to it since the distance was not very long. After resting and rejoicing with his people[524] there, he left for Huancavilca, where he had left the rest of the army. While he was there, he learned the sad and mournful news that there was a pestilence in Cuzco, and that

---

521   A spelling error has been corrected (Murúa 2008 [1616]:76r).
522   Sarmiento de Gamboa (2007 [1572]:184) does not mention the role of Huanacauri in this victory.
523   Sarmiento de Gamboa (2007 [1572]:184) provides a very brief description of Huayna Capac's encounter with the Lord of Puná. Cabello Valboa (1951 [1586]:392–393) and Cobo (1979 [1653]:159) provide much fuller accounts.
524   A possible mistake may have been corrected in the manuscript (Murúa 2008 [1616]:76r).

his brother, Auqui Tupa Inca, his uncle, Apu Hilaquita, his sister, Mama Coca, and several other lords of his lineage were dead.[525]

When Huayna Capac learned this, he was filled with grief and sorrow, and to bring some order to his lands, he sent messengers to Cuzco and then he left with his army for Tomebamba. Some say he died of fever upon arriving in Quito, while others say that there was a great plague of smallpox in a town called Pisco and he locked himself in some underground buildings to escape the disease. Regardless, wherever he was, death found him, and he could not escape it. When he died, many thousands of common people [also] perished due to smallpox as it spread among them.[526]

Huayna Capac was the most powerful Lord of his ancestors, extending his dominion the most, conquering the largest number of people, and subjecting and placing them under his obedience the longest. He was also the wealthiest in terms of silver and gold, so much so that when his son, Tupa Cusi Hualpa, was born, he ordered an incredibly valuable and heavy gold chain to be made as a grand gesture.[527] Many Indians could not lift it from the ground, and in memory of this remarkable chain he named his son Huascar Inca, *[f.76v]* which means "Lord and King Rope."

Some old and elderly people say that this wondrous chain was thrown in a large lake that is in Huaypo,[528] three leagues from this city of Cuzco,[529] when the Spaniards arrived. Others say that [it was thrown] into the lake near the town and *tambo* of Urcos, on the royal road to Potosí, six leagues from this city [i.e., Cuzco]. When this courageous Inca died, more than a thousand people whom he had loved most in his life and shown the most fondness for, including servants, officers, and women, were killed for his burial and funeral rite, as was always the ancient custom of the Incas.[530]

Huayna Capac built [many] important and famous buildings in Cuzco, and elsewhere roads, highways, and fountains, and baths in Lares,[531] twelve leagues from

525 Cabello Valboa (1951 [1586]:393) and Sarmiento de Gamboa (2007 [1572]:184) both note that Huayna Capac learned of a pestilence in Cuzco while he was in Huancavelica, and these authors provide the same list of relatives who perished in the epidemic.

526 Cobo (1979 [1653]:161) provides a very different account of Huayna Capac's death, while Cabello Valboa (1951 [1586]:393) offers a similar description. On the other hand, Sarmiento de Gamboa (2007 [1572]:185) focuses more on the issue of the succession at the time of Huayna Capac's death. Pizarro (1921 [1571]:197, 199) suggests that Huayna Capac died of smallpox about ten years before the Spaniards arrived.

527 Cobo (1979 [1653]:163) mentions this chain.

528 Modern Lake Huaypo.

529 This reference to Cuzco suggests that this part of the manuscript was written in that city.

530 Some other writers mention that 1,000 individuals were killed when Huayna Capac died (e.g., Acosta 2002 [1590]:365). Xerez (1985 [1534]) suggests that Huayna Capac died in 1524.

531 The town of Lares is renowned for its hot springs.

Cuzco. He was revered and respected by his [people] as something divine. He harshly punished the crimes of theft and robbery, [and] strove to be extremely vigilant so that his vassals would not rebel. He was frank and magnanimous with the soldiers that distinguished themselves in battles. During his rule, the *acllas*, who as we have told and will tell, were females Indians selected from across the entire kingdom, grew old, as he did not want to give anyone permission to distribute them; because he personally gave them to reward and gratify the soldiers who had excelled in a conquest or in capturing fortresses. By his order and command, the Indians constructed two roads: one in the mountains, smoothing out the ravines, and the other on the coast. The remains and vestiges of [these roads] can still be seen today, and they are grand demonstrations of the great power, grandeur, and majesty of the Incas, [the] Lords of these kingdoms, and how they were obeyed and respected, and how quickly their orders were fulfilled everywhere. This Inca, Huayna Capac, is attributed with commanding that the language of Chinchaysuyu, now commonly known called General Quechua or Cuzco [Quechua], be spoken across the kingdom, since his mother was [a] *yunga* and was born in Chincha. Although it is more likely that his mother was Mama Ocllo, the wife of his father, Tupa Inca Yupanqui, and that the order that the language of Chinchaysuyu should be used as the general language was because [Huayna Capac] dearly loved [another] woman, who was from Chincha.[532]

What he ordered in his last will and testament and [how the] heir to all his kingdoms was installed will be told in chapter 39, but now Rahua Ocllo, his wife, needs to be discussed.[533]

[F.77V] CHAPTER 38

The great Coya, Rahua Ocllo, [the] wife of Huayna Capac, and the remarkable thing that happened in the town of Yauqui Supa

To continue discussing the Coyas and Queens consecutively with their husbands, I will describe Rahua Ocllo, [the] wife of Huayna Capac, in this chapter. We will also discuss her in the life and events of her son Huascar Inca, as she died during

---

532   The mummy of Huayna Capac was later discovered by Polo de Ondegardo and sent to Lima (Bauer and Coello Rodríguez 2007).

533   Cobo (1979 [1653]:161) notes that Huayna Capac's first wife, Mama Cusi Rimay Ocllo, died early in life, leaving their son Ninan Cuyuchi. He also notes that Huayna Capac fathered a second son with Rahua Ocllo and another son with Tocto Ocllo. Also, folio 77r is blank.

[the life] of Huascar Inca, as will be told. This great Coya was the sister and second legitimate wife of Huayna Capac, as was described above, and she was also known as Pilco Huaco.

She was of great majesty and discretion and above all, [she was] ~~charitable~~[534] very pious and very merciful to the poor, to whom she always gave many alms. Along with this, she ordered her *chacras* be worked and had an abundance of agricultural fields, and she had many storehouses and deposits, so that she had much to distribute. She rarely left her royal palace, but when she did, it was with great applause and nobility, accompanied by an innumerable number of servants and *ñustas* who served her. When she went to pray in her chapel, she would have the entire way from her home to the [Temple of the] Sun decorated with many pieces of *li[m]pi*.[535] The ground was covered with golden straws, and [there were] many feathered arches with many different types of birds wherever she walked. When she returned from her stay, she secluded herself and did not see the Inca for four days and nights, nor did she enjoy any kind of pleasure.

Her palace was superbly decorated with every imaginable thing. [Rahua Ocllo] had a son, Huascar Inca, [the] universal heir of these kingdoms, and a daughter, Mama Huarcay, who was known as: Chuqui Llanto,[536] or Chuqui Huipa, [who became the] wife of Huascar Inca.

Something happened during the time of Inca Huayna Capac and his wife, Rahua Ocllo, an event worth remembering for those living today who love and adore the poor who represent Christ our redeemer, who from being rich and powerful became poor and a beggar. I want to mention it, even if it means suspending the thread of this history. The old people say that on the road to Omasuyu, in the province of the Canas and Canchis, in a town called Yanqui Supa, that is next to a large lake, there was a town of Canas in the same place where the lake is [today].[537] *[f.78r]* As the native townspeople were joyfully celebrating in a party and drinking, a poorly dressed man came to them, clearly in need and misery, asking for alms. Seeing the beggar, [and] instead of helping him and feeding him, they threw him out, mocking, scorning him. Forgetting what the natural law teaches, they ordered him to leave the village at once or if not, they would kill him. The poor man, hearing such harsh and offensive words, and enduring the inhuman manner in which they had

---

534   The word "~~caritative~~" (Murúa 2008 [1616]:77v) is crossed out and replaced with "piadosa" by Remón (Adorno 2008:104).

535   Cinnabar.

536   Guaman Poma de Ayala (2004 [1615]:88, 108, 111) mentions Chuqui Llanto as Huascar's wife and their daughter Rahua Ocllo.

537   Guaman Poma de Ayala (2004 [1615]) also mentions, albeit in far more general terms, catastrophes that struck towns that turn away beggars.

Figure 38.1. The figure reads: "Mama Rahua Ocllo Coya." The figure was originally labeled "Rahua Ocllo Coya." The word "Mama" was added later (Murúa 2008 [1616]:79r). This illustration has been removed from the *History and Genealogy of the Inca Kings of Peru* (Murúa 1590 [2004]) and has been inserted into the *General History of Peru* (Murúa 2008 [1616]). Note that this Coya, unlike all the other Coyas and Incas of the manuscript, stands outside on a grassy mound rather than inside on a tiled floor (Ossio 2008a:88). The backside of this sheet contains chapter 29 from the *History and Genealogy of the Inca Kings of Peru* (Murúa 1590 [2004]) (courtesy of The Getty Museum, Los Angeles: Ms. Ludwig XIII 16 [83.MP.159], f.79r).

sent him away, left the village immediately. [Soon] after, the strength of divine justice came upon them, and the entire [village] was flooded, and no one escaped alive from any of the houses.

They say the lake now exists was created [by this flood], a manifestation of the dwellers' and natives' malice, silently shouting and making the justice of God known. Those who behold it and recall the event, or who know it, must fill their bowels with mercy, giving food to the poor and covering their nakedness, so that the merciful God may help us in our needs and liberate us from our persecutors.

The old people say that seventy years ago, when the Spanish arrived in this land, a large, square, carved stone, up to ten palms [high], emerged from the lake. On that [one face of the stone] was carved a poorly dressed man, and fish were carved on the two sides.[538] According to these Indians, this was the beggar who asked for alms from the people of the flooded village. Let us give praise and glory to the Supreme Artist and Creator of all visible and invisible things, who diligently and justly rewards the good and those who, in His name, protect and give aid to the good and the[539] poor. He teaches us, with clear and appropriate punishments, how much He detests those who reject and mock those who, in His name, ask for help and protection.

This is what she looked like.[540]

[F.80R] CHAPTER 39

What Huayna Capac ordered in his will, and how Tupa Cusi Hualpa, also known as Huascar Inca, was named as Inca

Beginning with the famous Assyrian monarchy, which was the first, the most illustrious, terrible, and feared in the world, none have endured longer than that of the Romans. However, disunity ended and consumed Rome, which had so many nations, kingdoms, and cities under her hand. It was trampled, taken, and sacked by those she had dominated. In the end, nothing in nature remains untouched by time, accidents, or events. The Indian monarchy rose in these kingdoms from Manco Capac, the first founder of the monarchy, with such speed and rapidity that there was no province in it that was not subject to the rule of its king. I do not believe

538 Based on this description, it seems that a stone related to what is now known as the Yaya-Mama Religious Tradition (Chávez and Chávez 1975) was found near the lake.
539 The word "que" has been removed from the manuscript (Murúa 2008 [1616]:78r).
540 This final sentence was added by Murúa (Adorno 2008:101). Folio 78v is blank.

that the Roman [monarchy] was greater in wealth and size, for all of its empire and kingdom, all of its power and majesty, all of its riches and power declined and died because of its division, affirming clearly what the Savior said that all divided kingdoms and rulers would be laid to waste, and their cities and houses would be destroyed and leveled by the earth,[541] as experience shows and teaches us in the monarchy that we are discussing. The divisions, discords, and civil wars between Huascar Inca, Lord of these kingdoms, and his brother, Atahualpa, were the main and sole cause of the downfall of the monarchy, their lineage, and their generation. Both died miserably and [their empire] was subsumed by the Spanish monarchy, under whose dominion it remains today. The natives [now] live under different lords, with new laws, customs, and rites and ceremonies. Nevertheless, everything has changed for the better for so many, and so many souls have been saved throughout this new monarchy and lordship that would have been condemned for being under the obedience and subjection of their former lords.[542]

While Huayna Capac was ill with the disease[543] from which he eventually died, he named his beloved son Ninan Cuyuchi as his successor.[544] [However, Ninan Cuyuchi] was with Huayna Capac, and was himself taken by his father's illness. Shortly after [Ninan Cuyuchi's] death,[545] the succession of the kingdom passed to Tupa Cusi Hualpa, also called Huascar Inca,[546] who was the legitimate son of Huayna Capac and his second legitimate wife, Rahua Ocllo.[547]

---

541   Book of Matthew (12:25): "Jesus knew their thoughts and said to them, 'Every kingdom divided against itself will be ruined, and every city or household divided against itself will not stand.'"

542   In the above treatise, Murúa departs from the historical guide he was using to provide what he deemed an appropriate introduction for the chapter.

543   Betanzos (1996 [1557]:183) provides perhaps the most detailed description of Huayna Capac's illness: "He fell ill and the illness took his reason and understanding and gave him a skin irritation like leprosy that greatly weakened him."

544   Cabello Valboa (1951 [1586]:394) and Cobo (1979 [1653]:161) also mention of the death of Ninan Cuyuchi. Sarmiento de Gamboa (2007 [1572]:185) records a slightly different story of Ninan Cuyuchi's death. Betanzos (1996 [1557]:183–184) mentions Ninan Cuyuchi but suggests that he was barely a month old at the time of Huayna Capac's death and thus was unsuitable to be Inca. Betanzos also writes that Atahualpa was initially selected but turned the kingship down, leading to it being offered to Huascar. Also see Santa Cruz Pachacuti Yamqui Salcamaygua (1993 [1613]).

545   Betanzos (1996 [1557]:184) also suggests that Ninan Cuyuchi died around the same time as Huayna Capac and of the same illness.

546   Betanzos (1996 [1557]:190) confirms that Huascar was also known as Tupa Cusi Hualpa. Guaman Poma de Ayala (2004 [1615]:9, 114) also uses the name Tupa Cusi Hualpa Huascar Inca.

547   Cabello Valboa (1951 [1586]:394) also provides information on Huascar Inca being the son of Huayna Capac and Rahua Ocllo.

When Huayna Capac died, he told his beneficiaries *[f.8ov]*—Colla Topa, Latunqui, Adcayqui, Ataurimache, Cusi Tupa Yupanqui, Huachao Chico, and Tupac Yupanqui[548]—everything that needed to be done after his death, since Michi, the captain of the *orejones*, had already died. To ensure that his wishes were followed, he gave them a long stick, with colored signs on it, like a staff.[549] He [also] created a *quipu* and gave the orders to enter Cuzco triumphantly with his body and all the items to be brought from Tomebamba and [instructions] for governing all the conquered provinces with garrisons and guards. And with this, he died.[550]

When Huayna Capac died, his relatives and captains embalmed his body in complete silence, without crying or showing any sign of grief, so that the natives of the region would not take note and rebel.[551] They carried him into Tomebamba with the same solemnity, where they gave governing instructions to the governors and garrisons of soldiers who remained in the provinces. In Tomebamba [they named] Aqui Hualtopa,[552] a native of Cuzco, as the leader and superior to all. They then departed Tomebamba and made their way, taking with them the figure of the Sun and the other *huacas* they had brought from Cuzco when they began the conquest.[553] Likewise, all the nations who had joined the war brought their own [*huacas*] that they had with them, as well as the captive, important, and common, individuals from all the conquered provinces who had been selected for the triumph in Cuzco. In addition, they [brought] all the spoils and riches of gold and silver, emeralds, *mullu*,[554] clothes, and weapons. They left all the riches that belonged to Huayna Capac in the house of Mullucancha in Tomebamba since he placed them there when he built those famous buildings.

---

548 Murúa spells these names in different ways. We have followed the spelling provided in Sarmiento de Gamboa.
549 No other writers mention this kind of mnemonic device.
550 Cabello Valboa (1951 [1586]:393) provides similar information. However, some names are spelled so differently that it is challenging to ascertain if they refer to the same individuals. Cobo (1979 [1653]:163–164) notes that some people believed that Huayna Capac divided the kingdom into two parts at the time of his death, while others believed that this was later done by Atahualpa.
551 Betanzos (1996 [1557]:185) describes the embalming process: "When he died, the nobles who were with him had him opened and took out all his entrails, preparing him so that no damage would be done to him and without breaking any bone. They prepared and dried him in the sun and the air. After he was dried and cured, they dressed him in costly clothes and placed him on an ornate litter well adorned with feathers and gold."
552 Guaman Poma de Ayala (2004 [1615]:154) notes that Aqui Hualtopa died while on conquest in the north.
553 Cabello Valboa (1951 [1586]:394) provides similar information concerning the embalming of Huayna Capac.
554 The word "mullu" is underlined (Murúa 2008 [1616]:8ov).

The most important lords and *curacas* of that land accompanied the body of Huayna Capac to Cuzco, as a sign of his majesty and greatness. Of his children, only Atahualpa remained in Tomebamba refusing to return to Cuzco. At the departure, [Atahualpa] gave a long and heartfelt speech to the captains and lords who were [traveling] with the body of his father, which evoked great pity and sadness. [Atahualpa] concluded [by saying] that it was his wish and last will, to die and end his life where his father, Huayna Capac, had died.[555]

It was never believed that Atahualpa was staying with the evil intent to rebel against his brother, Huascar Inca. He showed no signs of this in his words or actions until he was provoked by the troublemakers[556] and his brother. At least, if his remaining behind was with sinister intentions, no one imagined it. [Atahualpa] was a brave man of great courage, effort, intelligence, and wise understanding of situations, and above all, he was liberal and frank with his [people], which would have been sufficient to achieve the lordship and greatness if fortune had not changed for him, as we shall see.

After Huayna Capac died in Quito, the main captains left for Cuzco in great haste, with messengers spreading the news of their lord's and Ninan Cuyuchi's deaths to Tupa Cusi Hualpa, also called Huascar Inca, *[f.81r]* as previously mentioned. When the news arrived in Cuzco, sadness and sorrow replaced the happiness and joy that they had expected with the return and triumph of Huayna Capac. As a result, the people of the city began to weep with the sober ceremonies that they customarily held for the Incas, their kings and lords. The same [news] was publicly proclaimed throughout the kingdom, in all places and provinces. The news of his death traveled across the kingdom, and everyone mourned and lamented for him because he was [both] feared and respected by all.[557]

They coronated Tupa Cusi Hualpa, also called Huascar Inca, with great solemnity, joy, and majesty as Inca and lord in Cuzco. [At that time,] Apu Chalco Yupanqui, the grandson of Viracocha Inca, was the high priest of the Sun. After the coronation ceremonies and the related festivities, they appointed his father's brothers, Titu Atauchi and Tupa Atau, as royal advisors, allowing [Huascar Inca] to begin his reign with the hope he would be accepted and loved by his vassals as king.[558]

Once all this had concluded, [Huascar Inca] sent messengers to the captains and chiefs who had accompanied his father's body, along with the army and spoils for

---

555   Cabello Valboa (1951 [1586]:394) provides similar information. Sarmiento de Gamboa (2007 [1572]:186) offers a much longer explanation.

556   Murúa is referring to Ulco Calla and other Cañaris.

557   Cabello Valboa (1951 [1586]:394) provides similar information concerning the news of Huayna Capac's death.

558   Cabello Valboa (1951 [1586]:395) provides similar information on Titu Atauchi and Tupa Atau being advisers to Huascar Inca.

the triumph. [He instructed them] to come to Cuzco one by one, as he was waiting for them, and that they should remain well organized and vigilant. [Huascar Inca] appointed Inca Roca, Nano, Urco Huaranca, and Tizo Conde Mayta as his advisors. Since [Huascar Inca] saw [the empire] at peace and himself obeyed as the great ruler of [many] lands and many thousands of people, he eagerly, frankly, and liberally sought to become closer to all his personal and favored individuals, as well as to all the important people who had supported his father during his lifetime. He gave [gifts] including gold, silver, clothes, and women, many of which had been reserved from the time of his father.[559] He gave servants and lands, and through these, he won the goodwill of his captains and soldiers of his guard, and everyone was content and happy. He then left Cuzco and went to build buildings for his relaxation where he had been born, which is next to Lake Mohina.[560] He [also] had the houses of Amarucancha[561] and Colcampata[562] constructed for his home and palace, where his nephew, Don Carlos Inca, later lived.[563]

[F.82R] CHAPTER 40

The cruelties that Huascar Inca committed against his brothers and those who came to Cuzco with his father's body

How many traitors do we see perched on the top of the wheel of fortune, yet due to the betrayals they initiated and justified, deserved to be at the bottom and cast out of society? How many innocent [people have, conversely] followed the path of truth and purity only to be punished, or even worse, counted among the evil? All of this is caused by flattery; the mask of an infinite number of vices with which they cover up and disguise themselves. It has a seat and throne in the seats and chairs of the great monarchs of the world, and it commands and controls everything. [Therefore, flattery] did not want to stop having her ambassadors representing her

---

559 Sarmiento de Gamboa (2007 [1572]:186, 187) mentions these gifts.
560 Sarmiento de Gamboa (2007 [1572]:186, 187) calls these buildings Huascarquiguar. Betanzos (1996 [1557]:176) also mentions this location. These buildings are widely believed to be the ruins now called Cañaracay on the shore of Lake Huacarpay near Lucre.
561 This building was given to Hernando de Soto after the fall of Cuzco. It was later acquired by Hernando Pizarro and still later by the Jesuits (Bauer 2004:124–125).
562 Colcampata became the palace of the Incas after the city of Cuzco was taken over by Francisco Pizarro. It is mentioned again by Murúa in book 3, chapter 10 of his chronicle.
563 Cabello Valboa (1951 [1586]:395) and Sarmiento de Gamboa (2007 [1572]:187) provide similar information on the houses of Huascar Inca. Also, folio 81v is blank.

in the court of Huascar Inca, [the] king and lord of so many provinces, as will be seen.[564]

Knowing that his father's body was arriving with the army, Huascar Inca sent messengers to his mother, Coya Rahua Ocllo, who was traveling with [Huayna Capac] to keep him company. They informed her to come ahead of the rest, so she could [join Huascar Inca in] thanking the Creator and the Sun, his father, for his ascension to the rulership and kingdom, and to make her [offer] sacrifices with him. When Rahua Ocllo was close to [Cuzco], Cononuno and [Huascar Inca's] other brothers from his father's [side] asked Huascar Inca for his permission [to travel], saying they wanted to receive [Huayna Capac's] wife and [Huascar's] mother, Rahua Ocllo, and accompany her to Cuzco. Huascar Inca gladly granted [their request], so they left Cuzco with a large entourage. When they arrived in Vicos Calla, they stopped to rest and drink according to their custom. While they were drinking, Chuquis Guaman started a conversation. It is unclear whether he had real intentions to commit what he later tried, or if he was [merely] testing the convictions and wills of the other brothers, to determine if they were firmly in the service of, and obedient to, Huascar Inca. But whatever was in his heart, [his actions] were indicative of a treacherous and deceitful nature. [Chuquis Guaman] suggested that it would be advantageous to kill Huascar Inca, their brother and lord, and to crown Cusi Atauchi as king, as he was their brother and was closer and more affable with them and more experienced.

When the other brothers heard this, they were at initially shocked and appalled by such talk. But the traitor was so adept at manipulating them with his words, and they were so gullible, that they believed his false intentions and submitted to his demands [f.82v]. They agreed that after they found Rahua Ocllo, the mother of Huascar Inca, whom they were going to receive, they would kill her and [then] return as quickly as possible to Cuzco do the same to Huascar Inca, crowning Cusi Atauchi as king, just as Chuquis Guaman had proposed. Having reached this agreement and treacherous pact, they continued on their journey, planning how to carry out the execution.

The treacherous and deceitful Chuquis Guaman, who had already ensnared his brothers, making them part of the plot that he had duplicitously and deceitfully planned for trapping them through the conversation he held before arriving at Siclla Pampa, left with some excuse, saying that he would return later from Cuzco. When he arrived [in Cuzco], he secretly went to his brother Titu Atauchi, who was Huascar Inca's second in command. In a convincing lie, with secrecy and acting in

---

564   Murúa appears to add his own introduction before returning to the materials that he was perhaps copying.

distress due to this treason, he revealed to [Titu Atauchi] everything that had been discussed and agreed upon among the other brothers; and what they had agreed to do after killing Rahua Ocllo and returning to Cuzco. [Chuquis Guaman] begged [Titu Atauchi] to reveal this traitorous plot to his brother Huascar, before [the brothers] could attempt it. So, Titu Atauchi, accompanied by the traitor, [Chuquis Guaman], left his house and they went to where Huascar was, who knew nothing of these events. [There], they told him everything that the traitor [Chuquis Guaman] knew about the brothers' plot.

On hearing the news, Huascar, on the advice of Titu Atauchi and the traitor [Chuquis Guaman], dispatched the captain of his guard to cut the throats of Cononuno and his other brothers wherever he found them. The captain of the guard set off with all possible speed, and he easily found them as they were not aware of the danger and did not understand [the captain's] intentions, although they were suspicious of the delayed return of the traitor Chusqui[565] Guaman. Before they understood why he was there, [the captain] killed them.

Cusi Atauchi, whom the other brothers wanted to name as king, had stayed in Cuzco, well out of the plans and conversations of the others. As he had never tried or considered [rebelling], he went about his daily activities without any concern and he went to see his brother, Huascar Inca, at his house. On arriving, the main guard at the door suddenly attacked and killed him due to an expressed order from Huascar Inca, that wherever [Cusi Atauchi] was seen, he should be killed. With [Cusi Atauchi] dead, Huascar Inca was secured against the suspicion that he had of his brother, and Chuquis Guaman, the traitor who had carefully plotted the betrayal, obtained [Huascar's] favor, like the other flatterers of the world. However, the revenge of this betrayal would occur only a few years later with the Chachapoyas, as will be seen later.[566]

After a few days, news arrived that the captains accompanying the body of [Huascar's] father, as well as the spoils and other riches they were bringing [to Cuzco] for the triumph, were close. When Huascar learned that they had arrived at Punchau Puquio, which is near Curahuasi, he sent the order that his father's body should stay there, and that Colla Topa, Latunqui, and Cuacusi Hualpa should first come to Cuzco, not all together, but one by one, as he wanted to be informed in person [f.83r] by each of them about his father's death: how he died, the things that he had ordered in his will, the plans he had given for the triumph in Cuzco, and other things concerning their journey and the army. These captains obeyed their master's orders, without suspicions [of the accusations] against them, as they

---

565   The spelling of the name "Chusqui" has been corrected (Murúa 2008 [1616]:82v).
566   The death of Chuquis Guaman is described in chapter 44.

had been saved from [Chuquis Guaman's] treasonous [acts] and uprising. When Huascar learned they were nearing Cuzco, he dispatched people to kill them wherever they were found before reaching him, and to torture them first, asking why they left his brother, Atahualpa, in Tomebamba against his orders. When the captain of this group arrived at the slope of Vilcaconga, on the descent to Limatambo, with this cruel order, [he found] Colla Topa,[567] unaware and oblivious of his misfortune. After capturing and cruelly torturing him, they finally killed him. Continuing with great thoroughness, they captured Latunqui and subjected him to the same [treatment] as they had with Colla Topa, and then they [killed] Cuacusi Hualpa, before any of them had learned what had happened to the others along the way. Once this was completed, [the captain] returned to Cuzco.

The army and the other individuals who were still arriving with the other captains and principals received this disheartening news with concern and confusion. They could not comprehend why the Inca had ordered so many cruelties on such important people who had faithfully served his father, Huayna Capac, in his wars and conquests and who had never attempted anything against Huascar Inca. They were close to rebelling and returning to Quito, uncertain if [Huascar Inca] intended to do the same to the rest of the army as he had done to the principal captains. However, some of the captains, who were fond of Huascar Inca, appeased them with soothing words, removing the mistrust and fear that they felt in their hearts because of the deaths [of the captains]. Nevertheless, many people from different provinces fled the encampment that night when all was quiet and calm, retreating toward Quito to report the news of what had happened to Atahualpa, who had remained there. We shall leave them there and describe the triumphant arrival of Huayna Capac's body in Cuzco.

[f.83v] How the Inca Kings went about[568]

Figure 40.1. *(facing page)* A drawing by Guaman Poma de Ayala from Murúa's *History and Genealogy of the Inca Kings of Peru* has been inserted into the *General History of Peru.* "Huascar Inca," written by Murúa (Adorno 2008:101), is written across the top of the page. Guaman Poma de Ayala has written on the ends of the four poles of the litter the names Chinchaysuyu, Antisuyu, Collasuyu and Callavaja (rather than Cuntisuyu, as would be expected). Under the litter he has written: "There are two Tampos Indians on the sides

567   A spelling mistake appears to have been corrected (Murúa 2008 [1616]:83r).
568   Written by Murúa (Adorno 2008:101).

playing two flutes they call *chiuca*, and in front are guards and behind [are] Indians with food and drink and ornaments for the king." The term "tambos" refers to the people from the town of Ollantaytambo. The opposite side of this folio contains the cover page of book 3 from Murúa's *History and Genealogy of the Inca Kings of Peru*. The cover page was pasted over to hide the text. For a detailed discussion on the migration of pages from Murúa's 1590 manuscript to his 1616 manuscript, see Adorno and Boserup (2008) (courtesy of The Getty Museum: Ms. Ludwig XIII 16 [83.MP.159], f.84).

[F.85R] CHAPTER 41

The solemn triumph with which the army of Huayna Capac entered Cuzco

I wanted to pause and describe the very solemn triumph of Huayna Capac's army so that it will be understood that these nations, considered by all as barbarians, celebrated their victories through rejoicing and military festivities. [These included] showing and displaying the courage of their soldiers, the weapons that they had taken from their enemies, the spoils that they seized, the people they had captured in battles, as well as their superior lineage and chivalrous spirits.[569] These [exhibitions] were followed by sacrifices to the Creator, the Sun, and the other *huacas* and shrines that they had. There were also great dances, parties, and songs, all with abundant food and drink, for without these things, no feast, party, or celebration is considered accomplished and perfect, but instead sad and disappointing. For the triumph, they brought a bundle and a carved figure of Huayna Capac, who arrived in a lavish litter, built like a stage and throne. He stood there, armed with his usual battle weapons, and wearing his war garments.[570] This figure, and the entire triumphal army, entered Cuzco in an orderly and military formation, as follows:

First of all, to honor and celebrate the triumph and arrival of his father, Huascar Inca ordered that all the streets of Cuzco, the terraces around it, and all the facades facing Cuzco, be fitted and covered with fine, colorful cloth and the houses and towers of Cuzco to be covered with their richest and eye-catching *cumbi* cloth with gold and silver embroidery.

An infinite number of inhabitants from Cuzco, both men and women, and [people] from all the provinces of the region, who had gathered to witness the triumph, filled the city. So, the [troops] began to descend the slope of Yauira,[571] as they believed this was the best way to make their [grand] entrance and for the troops to further display their rank and courage. They passed through Picchu[572] and then Sahuamarca, and from there they marched in good formation to the famous Temple of the Sun.

---

569 Betanzos (1996 [1557]:190) provides a description of the return of Huayna Capac to Cuzco.

570 Guaman Poma de Ayala (2004 [1615]) provides an illustration of Huayna Capac in this position.

571 Apu Yauira is a large standing stone on the slope of Picchu. It was included on the Cuzco Ceque System (Bauer 1998:70–71) and is mentioned by Albornoz (1984 [1582]:204), Betanzos (1996 [1557]:62), Cieza de León (1976 [1553–1554]:35), Molina (2011 [ca. 1575]:59, 61, 61), and Sarmiento de Gamboa (2007 [1572]:119, 196, 232).

572 Picchu was located just outside of Cuzco and was owned by the Jesuits soon after the conquest. It was also a place within the Cuzco Ceque System (Bauer 1998:70).

The vanguard entered reenacting the battles exactly as they had occurred. They were divided into three companies, with the *orejones* of Cuzco behind them singing songs[573] of delight. They were pompously dressed in their finest decorations, carrying their weapons with the heads of some of the important people that they had killed hanging from their spears, along with the most precious spoils that they had won in the war. Others had gold and silver disks hanging from the tips of their spears, and some [had] shirts made of gold and silver.

It took the people of Hurin Cuzco an entire day to enter. They included more than a hundred regiments, and before and after each regi [*f.85v*] ment the defeated walked with their heads down, as the *orejones* forbade them to look at the sky, declaring that the [prisoners'] pitiful, sad, and distressed faces should not cause the Creator pain and sorrow. [This also] prevented them from asking for revenge on those who had won and made them march in the triumph.

[The prisoners] wore red shirts that extended down to their feet, and their heads were uncovered, with no *llautus* or other headbands. Their hands were across their chests like prisoners. They walked very slowly in rank, to the House of the Sun, which stood on a gold platform in the plaza.[574] In [the plaza], there were many [other] benches, some made of gold, and others of silver, [with] feather arrangements of different colors and sheens that made a wondrous sight. The clothes of the Sun matched the coverings of the benches, and there they knelt on the ground worshipping [the Sun]. The soldiers slowly passed by in formation, and the captives remained seated in the plaza according to their rank. The soldiers would also bow and adore the Inca, who was also there, and after bowing, they would sit according to their rank. The most important citizens of Cuzco resplendent in their finery surrounded the plaza to witness the triumph. The entrance of the Hurin Cuzco lasted until nightfall. Then the Inca went to his palace with a great assemblage of his most trusted *orejones* and important kinsmen. The *orejones* of the Hurin Cuzco division, along with the other soldiers from outside Cuzco who had entered with them that day, spent the night there, as Huascar Inca had ordered. The captives remained that night in the plaza, guarded by many soldiers.

Early the next day, the statue of the Sun with its platform, along with the figures of [Chuqui Ylla] Yllapa Inca [and] Pacha Yachachi,[575] were brought out to the plaza,

---

573   A spelling error has been corrected (Murúa 2008 [1616]:85r).

574   Pedro Pizarro (1921 [1571]:212, 254–255) writes that Quisquis sent this bench to Cajamarca. He also writes: "For the Sun, they had placed a bench in the center of the plaza, all garnished with mantles of feathers, very colorful and very delicate" (253). This bench was claimed by Francisco Pizarro as his personal reward for the capture of Atahualpa.

575   Molina (2011 [ca. 1575]:15) also uses the term "Pacha Yachachic" in references to the creator God.

arranged like the day before. Whenever they went out to the plaza or anywhere else, they did the same. So, the Hanan Cuzco group started to enter the plaza in great order and formation, like the day before, making a beautiful display that the residents of Cuzco and the other people who had come to [the plaza] admired. They had the richest and most precious spoils and wore the best and most valuable clothes of the soldiers and captains. Their *[f.86r]* entrance and triumph were more colorful and spectacular as those of Hanan Cuzco were always better and held in a higher regard. Adcayqui, Ataurimache, Cahuamana, Conchi Chapa, and Huaipar entered first. There were more than a hundred regiments, and just like the day before, it took them until nightfall to enter. After they had paid homage to the statue of the Sun and paid reverence to Huascar Inca, they gathered to rest as they had done the day before, leaving the captives in the plaza guarded by soldiers.

The next morning, the leading *orejones* of the two[576] divisions of Hanan Cuzco and Hurin Cuzco held a council meeting and agreed that the Sun, their father, would give the triumph to Huascar Inca and he would enter triumphally with the remaining spoils, riches, prisoners, and with the statue and body of his father, which had been brought from Quito. Some say that Huascar Inca asked the Sun for [this triumph] out of greed, and it was granted, so he sent sacrifices to the body of his father, Huayna Capac, proclaiming himself to be his right arm, since he was his son and successor, and he wanted to have the triumph in his honor. [Huascar Inca] ordered the preparations that were needed for such an honorable and famous triumph. He ordered the streets be decorated with new, elaborate, and exquisite cloths, with an abundance of worked gold, silver, and feathers unlike any seen before.[577]

[F.87R] CHAPTER 42

How Huascar Inca triumphed in the name of his father, Huayna[578] Capac, and the parties he later held

Once the Incas had prepared the best way for Huascar Inca to commemorate the triumph that would be held and celebrated in the name of his father, Huayna Capac, with great majesty, Huascar departed from Cuzco, accompanied by the most arrogant and ostentatious entourage of family members, brothers, nephews, important *curacas* from the provinces, servants, and close friends that any prior Inca had ever

576   The word "two" has been inserted into the manuscript (Murúa 2008 [1616]:86r).
577   Folio 86v is blank.
578   A spelling error has been corrected (Murúa 2008 [1616]:87r).

chosen to take part in the triumph for his father. He included all the Lords of the provinces, who arrived in formation with those who reenacted the battles of their squadrons. Between the squadrons [were] the defeated, dressed as described. Over their own shirts, they wore red [shirts], with their arms inside, since they were prisoners. They went to the plaza of the Coricancha to pay homage to the Sun, along with the other figures that were with him. The defeated captives were left in the plaza, and [then Huascar] returned home.

The figure of Huayna Capac entered the plaza [of the Coricancha] that day on a litter. In front of him were all those that Huayna Capac had captured because of his bravery. He had the head of a provincial lord in his hand and was surrounded by his most favored and privileged [soldiers] who had fought in the heat of the battles and had shown themselves to be the most courageous. He was [also] surrounded by an infinite number of people with the musical instruments that they use. Following the litters came all the soldiers who had survived the wars, and those who had distinguished themselves in combat, along with many captives who had shown great courage in war.

The next day, the rest of the common soldiers entered Cuzco with what was left of the spoils. They came laden with gold, silver, *ahuasca* cloth, *cumbi*, cotton, featherworks, weapons of all kinds, clothing, *llautus*, *ojotas*, and, finally, all the finest and most costly items that they had acquired and won through force of arms in the conquered provinces. Their display of plunder entering the city lasted from dawn until sunset.

[f.87v] The next morning, the embalmed body of Huayna Capac entered, as he had come from Quito, on the shoulders of the most important *orejones*, fabulously dressed and armed, as they used to carry him when he was alive. They entered above the fortress triumphantly, accompanied by a great many captives, including the richest and most important, [as well as] the wife and children of Pinto, the Lord of the Cayambes, who we have already said died of rage and anger. Many lords and people left Cuzco just to accompany the body of Huayna Capac and to enter with him in the triumph. They sang sad and melancholy songs, recounting Huayna Capac's heroic deeds and praying to the Creator for him. There were also a vast number of women and maidens accompanying him, who had served and been favored by him, who were given to him as gifts, singing sadly; their cries caused pain and tears to those who heard them in the streets.

In this way and very slowly, [Huayna Capac] arrived at the House of the Sun, from which he was taken to his house in that city. Then, in the presence of Huascar Inca, all the most important *orejones*, who had come from the war and had been the most outstanding, took the figures of the Sun, the Creator, and Thunder on their shoulders. Very slowly, with all the majesty in the world, the soldiers of the army started to play all the instruments that they used in war, along with other songs, while they screamed and shouted. They walked over the defeated, treading on them according to their ranks, as they lay on the ground. After this, Huascar Inca also walked upon the defeated. After him, pairs of *orejones* walked over the defeated, stepping on them while carrying the embalmed body of a prominent lord who had died in the war and conquests. Then, some of the important women whose husbands had gone to war with Huayna Capac walked over the defeated, stepping on them as a sign of mockery and contempt.

When this [event] was over, the triumph was finished. They took and placed the captives in the prisons of Sanca Cancha[579] and Puma Sanca, where they were kept overnight. The next day, they took them out of the prisons and gave them, by order of Huascar Inca, clothes like they used [*f.88r*] to wear, food, and drink.[580] They were distributed among the captains and the most important and selected people, so that they could keep them and give them whatever they needed until they were assigned as *mitimaes*. Those who were granted permission to return to their lands were allowed to leave.

When Huascar Inca had completed everything related to the triumph of his father, Huayna Capac, he agreed to have a solemn celebration to reward and rejoice with the soldiers who had been outstanding. So, each nation and province held [their own] separate celebration on different days, where there were parties and dances, challenges, competitions, and other activities. When they finished, Huascar Inca generously rewarded the captains and soldiers [with] gold, silver, clothes, fine *cumbi* and *ahuasca* cloth, cotton, lands, servants, and women, thanking everyone in general and in particular, according to their value and merit. With these [gifts] [Huascar Inca] won the will and love of the soldiers.

After that, [Huascar Inca] ordered everything necessary for another mourning rite that he wanted to hold for his father, Huayna Capac. This was done in Cuzco and throughout the land, with a range of emotions, crying, and infinite signs of sadness. The last wake was in Yucay, where Huascar himself attended in person. When it ended, he gave many of the *aclla* women that his father had left to the important individuals who had assisted in his service, and he returned to Cuzco.

[*f.88v*] How the Coyas and Queens of the Inca went about.

---

579   There are various references to the prison of Sanca or Sanca Cancha (Albornoz 1984 [1582]:204; Betanzos 1996 [1557]:89; Cabello Valboa 1951 [1586]:353; Guaman Poma de Ayala 2004 [1615]:302–303 [304–305]; and Loarte 1882 [1572]:234). The prison was also on the Cuzco Ceque System (Bauer 1998:66).

580   Betanzos (1996 [1557]:190) mentions that the prisoners who survived were then honored and used as *mitimaes* in Yucay.

Figure 42.1. The title reads "Chuqui Llanto, wife of Huascar Inca," written by Guaman Poma de Ayala. "Coya and Queen" as well as "the young hunchback" are also written on the figure. This illustration, drawn by Guaman Poma de Ayala, was removed from the *History and Genealogy of the Inca Kings of Peru* (Murúa 1590) and inserted into the *General History of Peru* (Murúa 2008 [1616]:89r) as a way to illustrate Chuqui Llanto. There are also some similarities between this drawing and that of Chuqui Llanto in Guaman Poma de Ayala (2004 [1615]:142). On the opposite side, which had been pasted over with another sheet of paper, is chapter 9 of the *History and Genealogy of the Inca Kings of Peru* (Murúa 2004 [1590]) (courtesy of The J. Paul Getty Museum, Los Angeles, Ms. Ludwig XIII [83.MP.159], f.89r).

[*F.90R*] CHAPTER 43

How Huascar Inca married his sister, Chuqui Huipa, and
the great marriage celebrations that were held

With Huascar Inca's lordship established in all of these kingdoms and the mourning that he ordered for his father completed, his Captain-General, Inca Roca, decided that he should take a legitimate wife to ensure the succession of the state would continue through their legitimate children, because although the Incas had an infinite number of women, only the offspring born to the Coya and queen held the right to the kingdom and its succession. They were respected and feared the most; the others were considered bastards. Having discussed this, they called the priests of the Sun and other important people, brothers, relatives, and *orejones* to know which of [Huascar's] sisters he should take as his legitimate wife. After much deliberation, they all said and agreed that [Huascar Inca] should marry his full sister, Chuqui Huipa.[581]

They summoned Rahua Ocllo, the wife of Huayna Capac and the mother of Huascar Inca and Chuqui Huipa, to inform her they had chosen Huascar Inca's full sister, Chuqui Huipa, to be his wife. Upon hearing the rationale for this arrangement and seeing the desire of her son, advisers, and captains, Rahua Ocllo [adamantly refused]. It is not known why she did this; it could have been due to the cruelties she had seen [Huascar Inca] inflict on his brothers and relatives, or because he had not shown her the reverence and respect that she desired, or perhaps it was for some other reason. [Rahua Ocllo] emphatically denied his request, saying that she did not want to give [Huascar Inca] his sister as a wife. When he heard such a blunt and unpleasant response, Huascar Inca became extremely angry. Filled with fury and contempt, he rose from where he was sitting and spoke harshly and unjustly to his mother, treating her with distain and contempt. When she heard him, she [too] became incensed. She stood up and left for her home, leaving her son and his advisers seething with anger.

[Although] Huascar Inca's counselors saw Rahua Ocllo's determination, they decided that even if his mother did not want it, Huascar should demand the Sun, his father, to give his sister Chuqui Huipa as a wife, accompanied with sacrifices, expensive gifts, and other offerings that he would bring to the Sun. Furthermore, he should present numerous and very expensive gifts to the body of Tupa Inca Yupanqui, his grandfather, and the father of Rahua Ocllo, his mother. Having decided this, Huascar Inca, followed his advisors' instructions and guidance. He

---

581   Betanzos (1996 [1557]:182) states that Chuqui Huipa was the full sister of Huascar Inca, and that she was born during Huayna Capac's conquest of the Cañaris.

first went *[f.90v]* to the body of Tupa Inca Yupanqui with impressive presents, to ask for Chuqui Huipa, his granddaughter, as his wife. Adcayqui, Ataurimache, [Otorongo] Achachi, and Manco, who were representing the body of Tupa Inca Yupanqui, received [the gifts] and accepted them in his name. They also granted [Chuqui Huipa] as [Huascar's] wife. From there, Huascar went to the Temple of the Sun with great sacrifices and offerings, and asked her father, [the Sun], that Chuqui Huipa, his sister, be given to him as a legitimate wife. All the priests of the Sun received the gifts, and they agreed in the name [of the Sun], to give her to him as a wife. [Furthermore] as Huascar wanted the marriage to occur with the approval and goodwill of Rahua Ocllo, her mother, who was angry, they brought her lavish gifts of gold, silver, clothing, and servants to win her favor and make her happy. Then, all the priests, brothers, and counselors of Huascar again solemnly swore that [Chuqui Huipa] would be the legitimate wife of Huascar. To celebrate this oath, new parties and celebrations were held in Cuzco with performances and dances. It was also ordered that for all that month, fires would burn on all the towers and houses of the city, and that all the styles of music from the [different] nations that were there would be played. These orders were carried out immediately.

After the body of Tupa Inca Yupanqui, the Sun, and Rahua Ocllo granted Chuqui Huipa as a wife to Huascar Inca, it was agreed that the marriage should take place, and for greater majesty, grandeur, and ostentation it was agreed that the Sun and the body of Tupa Inca Yupanqui should go to the wedding, and that they would represent Huayna Capac, the father of the bride, since they had given [Chuqui Huipa] to [Huascar Inca] as a wife. Also, Huascar Inca should come out with the image of the Thunder, as they were the ones who would host the celebration for the Sun and Tupa Inca Yupanqui. To further celebrate [the wedding], they ordered that the house of Tupa Inca Yupanqui and that of Huayna Capac be adorned with worked silver and gold, and [the] four towers and the walls [of the city] were draped with fine cloth.

The representatives of Tupa Inca Yupanqui, Huayna Capac, and the priests of the Sun, ordered that the houses of Huascar Inca and the bride be decorated with equally fine gold works and cloth decorations. Also, the roofs of the houses of all the dead Incas should be covered with featherworks and their walls should be covered with fine *cumbi* and cotton cloth, and the towers of the plaza were to be decorated similarly, and music, songs, and dances would be heard in them day and night, as long as the festivities and celebrations lasted.

On the day of the wedding, Huascar Inca left his house accompanied by the image of the Sun, the bodies of Tupa Inca Yupanqui and Huayna Capac, [the image of] Chuqui Ylla [Yllapa], all the priests, [along with Huascar's] brothers, relatives, counselors, *orejones*, [the] captains of his army, and a huge crowd with various things that had never been seen before. [They all] went to the house of Rahua Ocllo, which was richly adorned with tapestry. There, they gave and delivered Chuqui Huipa, his sister, to Huascar Inca with all the solemnity and the ceremonies used during such marriages. They were there from the morning until vespers, and then they took her out with great music and singing *[f.91r]* to take Huascar's house. Everywhere she went with her husband, the way was strewed with gold and silver powder, and an infinite number of *chaquiras* and feathers. This and what later followed have never been seen before at any monarch's celebration or wedding in the world since the first man until now by any author, or at least it has never been written about it. They went from the Casana to the Amarucancha, which were the houses and dwellings of Huascar Inca. Everything that remained from that day was used for singing, dancing, and rejoicing until the night.

The next day, for greater splendor and grandeur, all the nations in Cuzco gathered to celebrate their lady, and these [festivities] lasted for more than a month. Huascar Inca, in an effort to demonstrate prestige and ensure that their marriage would be remembered forever, ordered that all the types of corn and various vegetables that they eat be crafted in gold and silver. In addition [he ordered that] all the [different] types of birds, [including]: pigeons, herons, *guacamayos*, parrots, falcons, finches, thrushes, eagles, hawks, and condors as well as all the different kinds of fish from the sea and the lakes that they knew, and firewood, both whole and split, and all the different kinds of land animals that they have, should be made of gold, silver, feathers, and *mullu*. Huascar's servants placed these [objects] on the tables as if they were things for the participants of the parties to eat.

They also brought an infinite number of live animals—including bears, tigers, lions, jaguars, ounces, monkeys, deer, *vicuñas*, *vizcachas*, and camelids—which were dressed in clothes of different colors, giving the appearance that they had been born this way. These animals had been raised for such a purpose. Furthermore, all the pitchers, *aquillas*, and other vessels and dishes were made of gold and silver.

There was such a vast multitude of people and things at these wedding [celebrations], and without calculating or accounting for the drinking that deprived them of [good] judgment, without knowledge of the true God, many left with valuable pieces of gold and silver, which were never accounted for, or even missed, in the confusion. In this way, the most magnificent and stately parties that any Inca, or as I noted above, any lord or prince in the world, had ever held or organized concluded and ended. [This was] because although some might have surpassed this one in objects, splendor, or pomp, none of them [exceeded it] in the abundance of gold or infinity of silver. It was such that [these precious objects] were offered to the guests as if they were edible delicacies.[582]

---

582   Folio 91v is blank.

[92R] CHAPTER 44

The journey that Huascar Inca ordered undertaken to the Chachapoyas and [the] death of his brother Chuquis Guaman

It is certainly true that no one is happy with their fate, and that the hunger and desire for gold and silver, as well as the ambition of kingdoms and dominions, increases every day like the sickness hydrops; expanding and growing without ever being satisfied. Huascar Inca provides a very clear example of this.[583]

Immediately after the unprecedented celebrations of his coronation and marriage had ended, the first thing he tried to do, without giving the captains who had served his father in the war a chance to rest, was to expand and enlarge his state. [This is] because among the Inca, it is considered to be shameful if after [an Inca] gains power they do not conduct deeds and conquer new lands and nations.

So, Huascar decided, along with his counselors, to enter the area of the Chachapoyas. For this, he ordered that all the provinces of his kingdom should prepare new soldiers and form two [separate] armies: [one including] the bravest and the most courageous to be found [outside of Cuzco, and the other] the best and the most daring *orejones*. After meeting with the people who came from outside Cuzco, [Huascar Inca] declared that he did not wish to go to war in person, but he wanted to do it through his captains. So, he named the traitor Chuquis Guaman as his Captain-General, who, as already mentioned, was to soon pay for his treachery, and Titu Atauchi, his brother. He also ordered that Untu, the governor of the Chachapoyas, accompany them.

Once everything was ready for the departure, an inspection was made of the troops with Huascar Inca present. The two brothers slowly left Cuzco, not wanting to tire their people early with long days. They arrived at Levanto and, from there, they entered the province of Pumacocha, conquering part of it.[584] Then, they continued with the intention of arresting the main lord of the entire province, who, knowing the plans of the Inca captains, withdrew to a place and fortress called Pumacocha, with the bravest people with whom he had the most confidence. There, he [was able to] strengthen and improve the fort's defenses as best he knew and could, using the resources available. When Chuquis Guaman discovered where [the lord] had barricaded himself, he marched his entire army toward him, and when he arrived at [f.92v] Pumacocha, he surrounded him, placing guards and spies, so that he would not escape. Believing that if he could not capture him by force of arms, he would surrender from hunger.

583 Here Murúa interrupts the historical narrative to intercede with some spiritual thoughts.
584 Betanzos (1996 [1557]:172, 237) briefly mentions Levanto and the conquest of the Chachapoyas.

After being surrounded for several days, realizing that the siege would continue for some time until his enemy starved him out, [the Lord of Pumacocha] understood that this was his downfall. Unable to get any support due to the many guards and the overpowering force of the Inca's great army, the Lord of Pumacocha decided to free himself through cleverness and trickery, as the strength [of the enemy] surpassed him. He dispatched messengers to Chuquis Guaman and Titu Atauchi, with much humility, expressing that he fully understood that it was impossible to defend himself against an invincible army. He offered to surrender the fortress and all his land, and to be subject to Huascar Inca, recognizing him as king and lord forever. [Moreover], he would command that the rest of his land, which had not [yet] come under [Huascar's] power and obedience, do the same, with the condition that they would not steal, destroy the land, or kill the people, as he wished to peacefully surrender and end the fighting.

After hearing from the embassy, Chuquis Guaman and Titu Atauchi treated the ambassadors of the Lord of Pumacocha with much courtesy and humanity. They thanked [the ambassadors] for their good intentions and for the good decisions and agreements they offered, and, in the name of Huascar Inca, their lord, they accepted the offer of the fortress and all their other lands. [Chuquis Guaman and Titu Atauchi] promised that the Lord of Pumacocha and all his vassals would be treated with respect and honor by the Inca and by his captains, and that nothing of theirs would ever be taken away now, or in the future ever, but, instead, their [wealth] would be increased and new favors granted daily. After the discussions were completed, [the captains] gave the ambassadors many gifts, food, and drink, as well as numerous kinds of fine clothes, before being dismissed.

Chuquis Guaman and Titu Atauchi were very pleased with the great success that appeared to have come their way in the conquest. [Chuquis Guaman] accepted that he would return to Cuzco, rich and triumphant and that he would be greatly appreciated by the Inca for having successfully completed his mission. To enter the fortress of Pumacocha and to take possession of it, as agreed, [Chuquis Guaman] ordered three thousand armed *orejones*, Charcas, and individuals from other nations—the most notable of the entire army—to accompany him while the rest of the army remained encamped [*f.93r*] on the other side of a nearby river.

To better conceal his planned treachery and to better fool the captains of Huascar, the Lord of Pumacocha sent them valuable gifts of very colorful and beautiful feathers and birds. Upon receiving [these gifts], Chuquis Guaman sent them to his lord, Huascar Inca, with messengers telling him that he had already conquered that province and that [the Lord of Pumacocha] had given [Huascar Inca] his obedience and that everyone recognized him as a lord; not knowing the deception that would be revealed.

After dispatching the messengers to the Inca, Chuquis Guaman left his camp, leaving his brother, Titu Atauchi, there. He traveled with three thousand *orejones* Indians and [soldiers] from other provinces, who were prepared to accompany him. As they reached a small hill near the fortress, they began to climb it. While en route, the Lord of Pumacocha again sent him many gifts and presents of things from his land to increase their confidence. When Chuquis Guaman arrived at the entrance of the fortress, the Lord of Pumacocha came out to meet them, and with a pleasant face and with great signs of goodwill, he bowed to all the chiefs of [Chuquis Guaman]. He offered them obedience in the name of their lord, Huascar, offering themselves as subjects and giving them the fortress and all his land, as promised. They then sat down in the *pampa* and held a solemn celebration for those who had arrived with Chuquis Guaman, providing them with plenty of food and drink.

The following morning, without giving any sign of his devious and deceitful heart that would raise neither the suspicion of Chuquis Guaman nor that of his [people], the Lord of Pumacocha offered [Chuquis Guaman] and his people the chance to rest in the fortress so that they could see with their own eyes the vassals and the new people who would pledge obedience to his brother and lord, Huascar Inca. Chuquis Guaman happily and eagerly accepted this request, so a large number the Pumacocha Indians entered gathered in the plaza of the fortress, which was very large, to hold a feast for Chuquis Guaman. They all came carrying secret weapons so that none of the Inca Indians could see them.

They then began to celebrate their feast with performances, dances, and great presentations of joy and happiness. To further please them to show them [his] love, Chuquis Guaman gave them many gifts from Cuzco that were not available in that province. Thus, [Chuquis Guaman's troops] were at ease from the morning until well past [f.93v] noon, with the Chachapoyas hurriedly toasting the *orejones* and the other soldiers of the Incas. The [soldiers] were continuously consuming the glasses of drink, faster than they were being served, until the [alcohol] went to their heads and legs, indicating that [the Chachapoyas] had already taken control of the highest and lowest parts of the soldiers' bodies.

Then the Chachapoyas, who had been [drinking] moderately and were aware of the plan, seized them by the hair and closed the doors of the fortress. Then more people of the Lord of Pumacocha suddenly appeared, and attacked the *orejones* and the others with furious energy. Among the first to be killed was the traitorous Chuquis Guaman. With this, his life and betrayals ended, and he never enjoyed the triumph he hoped for, and along with him, Untu also died, as he was among those who had entered [the fort]. The slaughter and desire to [kill] were so great that none of Inca's men escaped, and only a thousand Indians of the three thousand who had entered the fortress [survived]. Those who managed to escape were helped more by luck than their own industry or diligence. After the massacre, the Chachapoyas bathed themselves in the blood of Chuquis Guaman, smearing their faces with it and with that of their enemies. Then, joyfully and rejoicing, they again began to feast and dance.

The thousand warriors that escaped the hands of the Chachapoyas arrived to warn the encampment where Titu Atauchi and the army had remained. The news caused great confusion and chaos, [as they] did not know where to flee in such circumstances, fearing that their enemies would soon attack them, and knowing that if [the enemy] did advance and attacked the encampment, they would without a doubt, be defeated and suffer extraordinary destruction. However, [the Chachapoyas] did not think of this, and they did not leave the fortress as they should have. Nevertheless, Titu Atauchi and [the] other captains, scared and worried by this unthinkable event, decided the only thing they could do was retreat to Levanto in the best order they could, where they could recover. [Meanwhile] as signs of their courage, or better said, of their betrayal, the Chachapoyas took the heads of Chuquis Guaman and other important individuals who had died and put them at the doors of their houses as trophies.[585]

The revenge of the death of Chuquis Guaman, and how messengers from his brother, Atahualpa, reached Huascar Inca

Titu Atauchi and the other captains confirmed Chuquis Guaman's death when they saw his head displayed in public, despite having suspected that he had been captured. Having retreated, as noted, they sent messengers to inform the Inca of the death of his brother and of all the [other] events, including the Pumacocha peoples' betrayal, the capture of [Chuquis Guaman], and his death. At the advice of Tambusca Mayta, captain of the Hurin Cuzco people, and Ticsi, captain of Hanan Cuzco, they also sent a drawing of the region, showing where the fortress was located and the lands around it. When the messengers arrived in Cuzco, they gave Huascar Inca the completely unexpected news of the death of his brother, Chuquis Guaman. There are no words to express the sorrow he felt and the tears that he shed in private. Due to his past betrayal, [Chuquis Guaman] was very much in Huascar's good graces and he greatly appreciated him. [Huascar Inca] wanted to go himself to avenge this great betrayal, but Inca Roca, the eldest priest, and the others restrained

---

585   Folios 94r and 94v are blank.

him, explaining the risk he might take from the enemies' assaults. Together, they agreed that he could help his people and conclude the conquest by destroying the land [of Pumacocha].

[Huascar Inca] again commissioned Titu Atauchi and Mayta Yupanqui, the uncle of Huayna Capac, with a new army of very brave soldiers from all nations. He also commanded, based on the drawings that he had seen, the way and manner they had to attack the fortress of Pumacocha. The Indians who were from rough and rugged lands should enter the fortress through the mountains, while the others [should enter] on the side that was flat, and the *orejones* by way of the royal road that passed in front of it. The new army left Cuzco and, when they reached Levanto, where Titu Atauchi and the others had retreated, they joined together. When they saw that there was a new command and a better plan had been established to take the fortress, they left [Levanto] more carefully and demurely than the last time, with the army in good formation.

[f.95v] When they arrived at the fortress of Pumacocha, they surrounded it, destroying all the land around it and burning many of the nearby mountains, through which reinforcements might suddenly arrive. They fought for a month, and at the end, they furiously attacked from all fronts. One [group] entered the fortress, mercilessly destroying those who were there and satisfying their desire to avenge the death of Chuquis Guaman and those who had died with him. The Tomebambas, Quihuares, Huaros, and Chupacas carried the victory in the capture and taking [of the fort]. Having imprisoned a great multitude of the Chachapoyas, Titu Atauchi conducted a meticulous inquisition of those who had been in the fortress when Chuquis Guaman was killed and all who had aided this treason were cut to pieces. To memorialize this punishment, he devastated and destroyed their lands and populations. He spared some good-looking people for the triumph with whom he would enter Cuzco, and he left those who had not been found to be involved with the death of Chuquis Guaman in the fortress to settle [Pumacocha] and other lands. After pacifying and organizing [the region] according to his practices, and leaving a garrison of soldiers, he returned with the victorious and triumphant army to Cuzco. Following the orders of Huascar Inca, [Titu Atauchi] brought the sons of the Lord of Pumacocha for the triumph, just as Huascar had ordered, because after [Titu Atauchi] captured their father, he ordered him to be quartered, and he put [his remains] along the roads of their own land to further frighten his vassals to ensure so that they would not attempt to rebel again.

When Huascar Inca knew that they had arrived near Cuzco, he went out, accompanied by all his brothers and relatives, and they entered with the victorious army and triumphed over the solemnly defeated captives. This was immensely [important], as it was the first victory that his captains had achieved in his name. He gave gifts to all those who had excelled in the army, [such as], cattle, different kinds of clothes, servants, and women. He also ordered joyous festivities in Cuzco to celebrate and commemorate the victory.

While Huascar Inca was in the midst of his celebrations and parties, messengers came to him from Quito, sent by his brother, Atahualpa, *[f.96]* to congratulate him on his assumption to the kingdom and on being Inca and lord. Atahualpa also told him that he was in [the northern] provinces [to help] him, and he begged [Huascar Inca], as his obedient brother, to give him the governance of [the northern provinces]. In this way, he could guard them, defend them from his enemies, and rule them in Huascar's name. [Atahualpa also said] that the Creator should take [Huascar Inca] by the hand and that the Earth should obey him as he was the sole lord of it, and that the Sun, his father, should give him infinite kingdoms and dominions, to possess and rule in peace and humanity forever, and that he should grow old in them and leave his children as his heirs, and that he should enlarge the kingdom of his father, increasing it as his ancestors had done, and be respected and feared by his enemies as were his Inca ancestors.[586]

When Huascar Inca heard of the embassy's arrival, he was very pleased, as he was amidst the pleasures of the triumph. He honored the messengers from his brother, Atahualpa, and gave them gifts. The messengers [also] brought many presents and expensive gifts for Rahua Ocllo, Huascar Inca's mother, and his wife, Chuqui Huipa. Rahua Ocllo happily accepted them. However, when Huascar Inca learned that [the messengers] had brought his mother and wife gifts, he became suspicious. A few days later, he angrily summoned Atahualpa's messengers, and told them with little courtesy or kindness: "Tell my brother that he has stayed in [the north] and has been there since the death of my father and that he takes care to govern it by treating the natives and the garrison soldiers kindly so that no complaints arise about him. I will send my [own] messengers to Quito and through them, I will tell [Atahualpa] what to do there." With this, he sent them away.

The messengers returned to Quito, where Atahualpa was, and reported to him all that his brother had told them. Upon hearing this, [Atahualpa] did not suspect any ill will or lack of love from his brother. He was very pleased and believed that he was in his good graces, and after bidding farewell to the messengers, he went to Tomebamba and there he had some very sumptuous palaces made with much labor and expense for his brother Huascar. Under this delusion, he also had others made and built for himself of no lesser importance or majesty. These became the sources of the differences and rivalries between the two brothers, as will be described later.[587]

---

586   This final sentence, while unique, takes the form of many of the poems recorded by Molina (2011 [ca. 1575]:41–49).

587   Folio 96v blank.

[F.97R] CHAPTER 46

How the differences between Huascar Inca and his brother Atahualpa began

To make [matters worse], his suspicion and ill will toward his brother Atahualpa were confirmed when messengers arrived from the governor of Tomebamba and the head *cacique* of the Cañari, named Ullco Colla. They reported that Atahualpa had constructed grand palaces for [Huascar Inca] and built even more lavish and splendid ones for himself. He was also treating and serving himself as if he were the Inca and lord, with much majesty and approval, and was held with high esteem in those provinces. When Huascar Inca heard this news, being ill willed and with infinite anger, he once again began to investigate why Atahualpa had remained in Quito. He had a heated agreement with his mother about it, as she had not revealed to him some of the events that had occurred [in Quito] before her departure.

Within eight days, messengers sent by Atahualpa from Quito arrived while Huascar Inca was in Calca.[588] They brought numerous luxurious items for him to see, including the layout and a model of the palaces [Atahualpa] had made for him and great quantities of fancy garments decorated with stone and elaborate featherwork. However, Huascar Inca viewed them with disdain and contempt, saying to the messengers: "Why does my brother send these things to me? Does he think there are no such [items] here and I need them? I have much better ones than these. Moreover, the artisans who made them and who are with him there *[f.97v]* are mine and not his." Then, Inca Roca, his adviser, told [Huascar Inca] that what he said was true and correct in every way. Huascar Inca, [being] angry and upset, then had all the clothes thrown into a fire that they were using, because it was morning, and everything was burned with nothing escaping the fury of the fire. When Huascar returned to his brother's ambassadors, he insulted them and showed no regard for the respect that is always kept for such [representatives], even among most barbarians. He killed some of them and from their skins he made drums for his *taquis*.[589]

Chuqui Huipa, Huascar's sister and wife, was deeply saddened by the events that had transpired because she loved her brother, Atahualpa, very much. She secretly sent for the surviving messengers and asked them about her brother, and she told them of her unhappy life with her husband, Huascar, and the fight he had had with her mother, and how he had shouted at her. Hearing these things, the messengers,

---

588   Betanzos (1996 [1557]:194) also associates Huascar with Calca.

589   Betanzos (1996 [1557]:192–193) also mentions that Atahualpa sent Huascar elegant clothes as a gift, that were then rejected, and that the skin of the messenger was used to make a drum.

fearful of meeting the same fate as their companions, tried to return to Quito and distance themselves from Huascar Inca, who was so angry with their lord Atahualpa. When they asked [Huascar Inca] for permission to return from [Quito], Huascar Inca granted it and said they should depart quickly and that when they arrived, they should tell his brother Atahualpa that he should leave and come to Cuzco. [He should] leave everything well organized and guarded and the frontiers in good order and that he should not wait to be summoned a second time.

After these messengers left Cuzco, they rushed on their long journey out of fear. When they arrived at Tomebamba, where Atahualpa was, they told him everything his brother, Huascar Inca, had said with great contempt and disdain [and] how he burned all the fancy clothes they had presented in [Atahualpa's] name. Furthermore, [they reported] how he killed some of them, making drums of their skins, and even what his sister, Chuqui Huipa, had told them. Lastly, they informed [Atahualpa] that his brother had ordered him to get ready and come to Cuzco immediately, as it was his wish.

Atahualpa received this news with immense sadness and confusion, now understanding and fearing his brother's indignation *[f.98r]* if he went to Cuzco. [Huascar Inca] had killed others who were there with little cause or suspicion, like the many captains who had served his father, Huayna Capac, in the war. Seeing him in confusion,[590] Ullco Colla, [the] *cacique* of the Cañari, and [Captain] Atoc[591] asked him: "Why are you so sad and unhappy? Become Inca and lord! You are a son of Huayna Capac as much as your brother, Huascar, and you deserved [to rule] more than him because of your character since he spends all his time in vices and drunkenness." Although Atahualpa might have felt pleasure in his heart[592] at these words if he had the desire to rebel against his brother, he gave no response in order to conceal his [feeling].

[Atahualpa] did not want the people and soldiers who were with him to witness his melancholy and sadness, as this would make them worried. So, the next day, he ordered grand feasts and celebrations to keep them joyful and happy. He also summoned the messengers who had returned from Cuzco to learn everything that had happened to them with Huascar and what he had told them and about his sister Chuqui Huipa, and what was in Cuzco, and the state of his brother's ruler, captains, and advisors.

A few days later, in defiance of his brother's orders, [Atahualpa] left [Tomebamba] to return to Quito, taking by his own authority the elaborate litters that his father,

---

590   A spelling mistake has been corrected (Murúa 2008 [1616]:98r).

591   Betanzos (1996 [1557]:201, 207) also mentions Atoc but in very different terms. Also see Sarmiento de Gamboa (2007 [1572]:189).

592   A spelling mistake has been corrected (Murúa 2008 [1616]:98r).

Huayna Capac, had left in Tomebamba, as well as the finest and most precious clothes which had been made for his father from the storehouses. This is because wherever the Inca went, all the garments he wore in that area were customarily kept as relics forever. Atahualpa took out and put on the [clothes] kept in Tomebamba, which could only be done with the Inca's permission, and he left for Quito with great approval and a large following.

When Ullco Colla and Atoc, who were the ones who had given [Atahualpa] advice with the vile intention of turning the two brothers against each other, saw that he had departed for Quito, they dispatched messengers to Huascar Inca to tell inform him how Atahualpa had taken the litter, clothes, and accessories of his father that were stored the warehouses and how he had put them on and was leaving with great majesty toward Quito. [They suggested] that he seemed to be rebelling, as he had not [f.98v] followed [Huascar's] command, that he must not return to Quito.

When Huascar Inca heard this news, his hatred for the captains who had come from Quito with the body of his father intensified, as they had left his brother there. So, he summoned all his council to address this matter, inquiring about what he should do with his brother in this situation, since [Atahualpa] had disregarded his orders and had gone to Quito instead of coming [to Cuzco] at his command. Everyone agreed that [Huascar Inca] should immediately order his brother's arrest, without him being aware, so that there would be no more trouble and he would be caught off guard. Although they all agreed that [Atahualpa] should be imprisoned, they disagreed on how this should be done. Some said that it should be done differently and that the army should be sent to bring him to the prison in case he defended himself. Huascar Inca favored this opinion, and he sent the captain Atoc along with people from Cuzco and commanded that the entire Cañari army, and their *cacique* Ullco Colla, should go from Tomebamba [to Quito]. So, Atoc set out with the people of Cuzco, and after a long journey, he arrived at Tomebamba, where he joined with many Cañari and Tomebambas. He then departed with them for Quito to seize Atahualpa if he were to defend himself.[593]

---

593   Folio 99r is blank.

[*F.99V*] CHAPTER 47

How Atahualpa prepared to defend himself, knowing
that his brother had ordered his capture

After Atoc arrived in Tomebamba with the people from Cuzco, Atahualpa was warned by spies and friends, who told him to leave, warning[594] him why [Atoc] had come. [Atahualpa] was very distressed and fearful that if they caught him, he would be killed. He called Chalcuchima[595] and Quisquis, the leaders of his council, and trying what seemed to him to be expedient, he ordered all the nations around Quito and all the *mitimaes* placed there by his grandfather, Tupa Inca Yupanqui, to gather. Once they were assembled, he stood up, tears streaming down his face. He first spoke to the *mitimaes*, saying: "You know, my brothers, that my father and grandfather sent you here to guard and protect this land, and that I, loving you with all my heart, stayed with you to help and defend you. Now, for some unknown reason, my brother hates us, and he has not received any service or present that I have sent with kindness; rather he has dismissed them, considering them of little worth. He also shamefully dismissed and affronted my messengers, despite our loyalty as vassals, just because he wanted to. You know that if I am caught, you will share in my punishment, as I remain amongst you, and you have shown me kindness. I now ask that you help me with your people, and all your might, since you know that, like my brother Huascar Inca, I am a son of Huayna Capac, and I have the courage to defend myself and to fight until death against all those in the world who wrongfully seek to harm me."

Hearing this, Chalcuchima, Quisquis, and other captains of the *mitimaes* stood up and told him that what he proposed was right because[596] his brother had badly treated those who had loyally served his father and who, at the cost of their own blood, had conquered so many provinces. Furthermore, [Huascar had] killed many of those who had gone [to Cuzco] to accompany his father's body, and still not being content, he now sent warriors to seize them as if they were outsiders or strangers, who failed in their duties and were rebelling and disobeying his orders. [They continued, asserting], "We are not women, but men who know how to, and will, employ weapons and will defend ourselves by force of arms against the entire world, for our lord [Huascar Inca] unreasonably pushes us towards war, which he himself demands and asks of his vassals. So, we are well-versed in battle and have honed our strength and courage in the wars your father fought. It is only right that we should defend ourselves against [Huascar Inca], being men of great courage to do so."

---

594   A spelling mistake has been corrected (Murúa 2008 [1616]:99v).
595   Guaman Poma de Ayala (2004 [1615]:161 [163]) provides a drawing of Chalcuchima.
596   A textual error has been corrected (Murúa 2008 [1616]:99r).

When Atahualpa heard these declarations, he stood up and thanked them with much compassion and appreciation. On seeing their swift willingness to serve him according to his will and desire, he said to them: "My brothers, you who are prepared with everything and in every way to follow me, from today forward carry your weapons in your hands and be prepared as if you were on the enemies' border." Having heard this, the *mitimaes* returned and sat down, deeply admiring Atahualpa.

After speaking to them, [Atahualpa] asked the natives of the land and provinces around Quito, who were seated according to their *ayllus* and who had been listening to the explanations given to the *mitimaes*, to come before him. He said: "You know, my brothers, what I have done and said to the *mitimaes*; now I want to tell you what I feel in my heart. You will remember how my father conquered you and destroyed you by war and how your fathers and brothers were taken captive from this land and imprisoned in Cuzco to be triumphed over for his honor and greatness. Furthermore, you know that I am a son and heir [of Huayna Capac], and that I have been loyal and obedient to my brother, Huascar Inca, and have not broken any of his orders. [Yet he] has treated me and treats me as an enemy and has now begun an unjust and illogical war against me. Because you have given me your service, I believe that he will now overwhelm and steal from you, like the first [time]. You have yet to recover from the prior destruction or return to your original state. [Nevertheless], I am determined to defend myself with my weapons in my hands until I die, and I will not allow any wrong to be done to you. Look, my brothers, think about what you are going to do. *[f.100v]* You know and have seen how I have provided for you in these circumstances, and that I have done nothing to harm you nor allowed anyone else to. [You have received] nothing but good treatment. Even if it were only for revenge, you should remember how many of you my father killed in Yahuarcocha and elsewhere and comply with what I request of you."

He told them the above reasons because when they understood what had happened with the *mitimaes*, they had asked him: "How can you surpass your brother, the Inca, who is so powerful and has so many soldiers?" But as he reminded them of the labors and destructions that had occurred to them in the [previous] wars and conquests, and of the deaths of their own [people], they declared in a single voice that they would follow his will. They also [said] that they were all in agreement and that he should decide what he was going to do, for they had their weapons ready to support him.

Atahualpa was very pleased with the natives' answer. [To show] his pleasure and goodwill, and to further demonstrate his resolution and determination, he ordered a great quantity of clothes of all kinds, silver, gold, and other esteemed and valued items taken out of his father's storehouses and, as a gesture of generosity, love, and magnificence, he distributed them to everyone according to their status and merits.

This made everyone extremely happy and content with Atahualpa's spirit, and they secretly took up arms.[597]

The two battles [that took place] between the troops of Huascar Inca and Atahualpa

When Atahualpa had arranged the necessary things for his defense and gathered weapons, he wanted to know the plans of Atoc, his brother's captain, who was coming to arrest him.[598] So, he sent a messenger to ask why [Atoc] had come and why he was arriving with armed people into this province, and if his brother wanted to enter the region, and [if so,] where, because all the provinces were peaceful and quiet, just as his father, Huayna Capac, had left them, with no changes to the provincial governments in any way. When Atoc, who was already near Quito, heard this message, he replied, "Tell Atahualpa, that I do not come to conquer but to seize and kill him, as he has made himself Inca without being so, and he is not legitimate. Where did he hear that Inca lords come from foreign lands, since the legitimate Incas are traditionally selected and vested specifically by the hands of the priests and the Sun, and they receive the oath of all the provinces, being revered before the Sun? And more importantly, Atahualpa had started certain customs which contradicted everything prior Incas had kept. This being the case, he had determined that there was no reason for [Atahualpa] to ask him if he came in search of a fight or conquest. So, tell him this."

Having heard this bold answer, Atahualpa's messengers returned to their lord in Quito, who, on hearing [this reply and] seeing Atoc's resolute determination, [Atahualpa] declared: "He is truly coming for us and there is no reason for us to die acting and looking like cowardly women." So, [Atahualpa] ordered all his people to

---

597   Folio 101r is blank.
598   Betanzos (1996 [1557]:197–198, 207) suggests that the leaders of Huascar's army at this time were Cusi Yupanqui, brother of Cusi Rimay Ocllo, and a captain named Hango. Betanzos also suggests that the battle took place near a town called Mochacaxa, that the fallen soldiers were placed at the summit of the mountain Ambato, and that both Hango and Atoc were killed in the battle. Betanzos further states that following the battle, Cusi Yupanqui changed sides and began to fight for Atahualpa and that his sister, Cusi Rimay Ocllo, who was only ten at that time, was brought north as she was betrothed to Atahualpa. She was later known as Angelina and was living in Cuzco and married to Betanzos when he was writing his chronicle.

take up arms, displaying a very impressive army. To begin the war against Atoc, he sent a captain ahead of him.

When Atoc left Cuzco, he took with him the image of the Sun, by order of Huascar Inca. They believed that when Atahualpa saw it, he would surrender, but they were mistaken. When Atoc met the captain sent by Atahualpa, they began to fight. [The battle] was even and hard-fought, and many of Atahualpa's soldiers were killed. [In the end] they were defeated by Atoc, the captain of Huascar Inca. Those who escaped from the battle retreated to Quito, and told Atahualpa the news, causing him great sorrow. When those who were with him heard [the news], they fainted in fear. Many wanted to abandon [Atahualpa] and flee, believing this was a disastrous start to their cause and their expectations of him. However, Atahualpa, who was courageous and kindhearted, encouraged them again, reminding them of the misery and misfortune that awaited them if they surrendered to the hands of their enemies, which were [already] drenched with their blood, and that they had to go out with new bravery and courage to avenge their relatives and friends who had died in the battle.

Having ordered all that was necessary, [Atahualpa] did not wish to entrust the second encounter, on which all his faith and fortune hung, to any of his captains, but rather take it upon himself, accompanied by all his followers. So, he left Quito to fight Atoc and he found him at Mullu Ambato, where they fought with great determination. [The battle] was so hard fought and locked that it lasted from morning until vespers, with neither side gaining an advantage over the other, and an infinite number of courageous men died on both sides. In the end, Atoc was defeated and captured by Atahualpa, and those who fled the battle arrived at Tomebamba to report the news of this disastrous event.[599]

Having won the battle and gathered the spoils, Atahualpa returned to Quito triumphant and joyful, with the prisoners. With this victory, he strengthened the support from all the nations of the Quito area, who had already decided to obey him with even greater spirit and determination than they had earlier. [Atahualpa] then wanted Atoc to tell him [all he knew] about Cuzco, including the organization of Cuzco during the war and other things, including secrets that would be advantageous for him to know. At first, Atoc refused, not wanting to answer anything that was asked. But in the end, Atahualpa had him cruelly tortured, until he confessed everything there was to know about Cuzco. Having learned all the information that he wanted, in the end, [Atahualpa] ordered him to be killed, and he did the same to Ullco Colla, the *cacique* of the Cañari, [who had been] also imprisoned during the battle. [Atahualpa] ordered [Ullco Colla] to be shot with arrows, for he had been

---

599   Cobo (1979 [1653]:165) briefly mentions the death of Atoc.

the main source of the discontent between him and his brother, Huascar Inca, and the one who *[f.102v]* had fomented arguments and discords between them, having been the first to suggest Atahualpa to become the Inca because he could do so.

When this was over, Atahualpa remained in Quito to rest, relaxing with his own [people], with no intention of making war on his brother, or of disturbing his lands. He granted permission to all those who wanted to return to Cuzco to do so, and they left as they had requested, without any guards being placed along their route.

Earlier, the differences between him and his brother weighed on him.

[Aqui] Hualtopa, the governor of Tomebamba, sent messengers to Huascar Inca letting him know how his captain, Atoc, had been defeated, imprisoned, and killed, with much of his army destroyed. Although this news caused incredible pain and sorrow in Huascar's heart, he hid his true emotions, not wanting to show it, so he laughed and smiled in front [of others], saying: "Let my brother rest and eat now; for his time to be punished by me will soon come, and he will witness it."

A few days after receiving this news, he decided to send captains and people to arrest and kill his brother. They were to go silently, as they say, not making a noise or sound, so that [Atahualpa] would become more careless.

At this time, Atahualpa decided in Quito to divide the kingdom, planning to take half [for himself]. He reached an agreement with the captains of his council, determining that [the area] from Yanamayo, which is two days from Cajamarca to Pasto and everything in between, would be his alone, and that he would rule the nations that fell in this district; and that [everything] from Yanamayo to Chile would be that of his brother Huascar. After approving this distribution with all his [council], [Atahualpa] made solemn sacrifices to the Sun to bless his new kingdom, and with this, he revealed his true intentions for why he stayed in Quito after his father, Huayna Capac, died. With this, he finally laid bare the deceit he had kept since Quito, when his father, Huayna Capac, died, [which] was he would not rebel [against Huascar]. As we have seen, he had disguised his intent to not recognize his brother, Huascar Inca, as king and lord with tricks and excuses. But only God can truly know what is hidden in the hearts of men.[600]

---

600   Folio 103r is blank.

[*F.103V*] CHAPTER 49

How Huascar learned that his brother had divided the kingdom and [how] he sent Huanca Auqui against him, and of the battles that took place

Huascar Inca was filled with grief and anger when the news reached him concerning Atahualpa's intention to divide his father's, Huayna Capac's, kingdoms and estates and how he had openly rebelled, not wanting to be recognize as his lord, and that there was no other remedy but to subject him by force. He knew how laborious a war would be, even more, a civil war, and the destruction it would bring to his people and the many that would be lost. Above all, [Huascar Inca] knew his brother had been trained in his father's wars and conquests. Furthermore, [Atahualpa] was a man of good spirit and [generous] heart and was frank and liberal with his [people], which was why he was loved by all. Moreover, the armies in Quito, who had fought, labored, and battled for his father, would follow his brother. So, he believed there was no more time for secrecy and he could delay no longer, as [Atahualpa] could get stronger and better equipped.

[Huascar Inca] dispatched a powerful army from many nations, with his brother Huanca Auqui,[601] as general. Huapanti,[602] Huaca Mayta, and the other most powerful captains that he had and trusted the most were also included. To honor Huanca Auqui even more, [Huascar Inca] provided him with several litters to carry him, which pleased him greatly. The other [captains] were praised with words and deeds and given much gold, silver, fine clothes, and other precious gifts, which pleased them all so much that they willingly expressed their desire to serve Huascar on all occasions. After setting out on their journey, they arrived in Tomebamba, where the army encamped to rest and recruit people from that province so that they could begin the war with the greatest number of people.

But Huanca Auqui wanted first to tempt Atahualpa with good intentions, so he sent special messengers from Tomebamba to ask why he was rebelling. [*f.104r*] Atahualpa answered, saying that [Huanca Auqui] already knew [the answer] and that he had seen that he was safe and in peace in Quito, without having done or said anything that could offend or disserve Huascar, his brother, nor had there been any

---

601   Betanzos (1996 [1557]:207) notes that Huanca Auqui was given charge of Huascar's army and sent north to fight. Cobo (1979 [1653]:165–166) also briefly mentions Huanca Auqui and his string of defeats.

602   Betanzos (1996 [1557]:207, 208) mentions Huapanti but suggests that he had gone north to fight Atahualpa with Atoc's and then went into hiding. Guaman Poma de Ayala (2004 [1615]:162 [164]) also briefly mentions Huapanti.

thought of rebellion on his part. [Yet] Huascar Inca had sent [Atoc] with an army to arrest him as if he were a rebel, and to protect his life and the lives of those who were with him, [Atahualpa] had fought back. He stated that Huascar, his brother, had killed Cononuno and others of his brothers, without a cause or reason, with a cruelty never seen before and an insatiable thirst for their blood. Also, he had done the same to many of the captains who had accompanied the body of his father from Quito, despite their never having attempted anything against him and their loyal services to his father in the war. [Atahualpa] told [Huanca Auqui] to look at the pride and arrogance of [Huasca Inca] and the contempt with which he treated them; and that someday he would do the same to Huanca Auqui, disregarding that he was his same blood and had followed his orders.

When Huanca Auqui heard these reasons, it is said that he felt sorry for his brother, Atahualpa, understanding the bad events he was referring to, and he also cried, remembering the death of his other brothers. But, after gathering the captains of the army to advise him, he declared to them: "[Atahualpa] is not going to surrender easily, so we will need to fight him, since our lord, Huascar Inca, sent us here for that purpose."

Others say that Huanca Auqui, moved by his brother Atahualpa's reasons and the misery he would suffer if he were defeated, made a secret [agreement] with him. So, Huanca Auqui ordered his captains to fight in Tomebamba itself and commanded those placed in squads do so with good organization and order. However, his captains became suspicious of Huanca Auqui's lack of enthusiasm, hesitations, and lukewarm commitment to battle, believing without a doubt that his [war preparations] were in concert with Atahualpa's instructions. Nevertheless, they prepared for war as best they could.

Atahualpa, seeing that the battle was unavoidable, sought to rally his [troops] in a speech, by reminding them of the humiliation of defeat, the hardships of being under their enemies' control should they survive, the glory and honor of the victory, and the riches that they would enjoy when stripping their opponents. He then ordered them to organize themselves and he personally visited each squad, who had crossed the Tomebamba River, [f.104v] showing himself to the enemy. Huanca Auqui divided his people into in ten divisions and entered the battle. He began on top of the bridge called Rumichaca, and with great effort and courage from both sides, thousands of [soldiers] who were fighting continued to be killed. [The battle] lasted all day with incredible determination, without one side being able to defeat the other. [Only] the night could split them since they were tired of fighting and killing each other.

The next morning, they returned to the battle anew with greater bravery and courage than the day before. In the battle, Atahualpa's [army suffered] more deaths than that of Huanca Auqui's. Huanca Auqui and his captains commanded the army so skillfully that they broke and defeated Atahualpa before midday. Despite this he was not discouraged, retreating in good order with the rest of his people to a hill called Mollo Tuyru. There, with great enthusiasm, he fortified himself, so that he could defend himself if he were attacked.

Huanca Auqui, very pleased with the victory, attacked his brother and ordered the hill to be surrounded so [Atahualpa] could not escape. Fearing that [Atahualpa] would escape during the night, and without waiting for all of his people, many of whom were scattered about, enjoying the spoils of the dead on the battle[field] and still in disorder from the victory, believing that the war was already over, Huanca Auqui renewed the attack with only the part of the army that was with him, too soon and without order. Some say that he had agreed with Atahualpa not to oversee his soldiers as well as he could or should. Atahualpa, experienced in war, understood the situation and the confusion of his enemies' attack. On seeing their disorderly advance, [Atahualpa] encouraged his own [people], and they charged those who were climbing the hill with striking courage, with him leading [the attack]. They easily pushed the enemy back and made them flee downhill.

Seeing the army of General Huanca Auqui decimated, the remaining [soldiers] lost their courage and broke ranks, slowly retreating to Tomebamba. Ambitious and wanting take advantage of the good opportunity Atahualpa attacked, mercilessly killing and wounding them, and in the end, he defeated them at the abovementioned river, where Huascar's troops had stopped. There he killed and drowned an infinite number of people who, between the speed of the enemies who charged them, the general confusion, and lack of good order, failed in crossing the river or finding a ford. That day [the river turned] the color of blood spilled on both [sides] during the battles of the previous day and during Atahualpa's marvelously executed counterattack.[603]

[F.105V] CHAPTER 50

How Huanca Auqui, having lost another battle, retreated to Cusipampa and conquered the Pacamoros

Huanca Auqui sadly withdrew from the battle that had begun so prosperously and finished and ended [so poorly], all caused by the lack of order with which he had attacked Atahualpa on the hill to Tomebamba. Had he led [the attack] with his entire army in good order, without a doubt, he would have thwarted his brother and

603   Folio 105r is blank.

captured him, [and] thus ending the war, and preventing the destruction, deaths, misfortunes, and miseries that occurred afterward to Huascar and his people, as well as to Huanca Auqui himself. So, it can be truthfully said that the mistake of that day, and [Huanca Auqui's] lack of respect for his opponent, were the cause of his ruin, and the beginning of Atahualpa's rise to greatness, who was so pleased by the unexpected outcome that he placed even more trust on his good luck and fate.

[Atahualpa] found that Fortune was his friend and in his favor, and saw that his brother, Huanca Auqui, had retreated to the town of Tomebamba, and he was fortifying there, blocking off the streets. As a vigilant captain, [Atahualpa] did not want to give [Huanca Auqui] time to reorganize, so before [this could occur], he again ordered his army, which, with the recent and unexpected victory, was now encouraged and had gained new strength, to attack Huanca Auqui. They easily defeated him. [Huanca Auqui], knowing [this was] his downfall, fled from Tomebamba with the remains his army. He quickly collected up all the precious items that his father, Huayna Capac, had stored there, including Mama Ocllo's placenta, contained in a bundle called Tomebamba Pachamama. When the Cañari of Tomebamba presented the bundle to him, they said, "This will please Huascar Inca, our lord, and he will reward us for it." Huanca Auqui then left, retreating slowly, with his followers until they reached the Cusipampa Valley, where he fortified and remained for three years.

Atahualpa, upon seeing his brother and his enemy retreat, entered Tomebamba with his army, taking possession and fortifying it with great care. Since he was very angry with the Cañari, for turning on him with his brother, he began to inflict *[f.106r]* terrible punishments on them, saying, "Your *caciques* were the first to start [the] uprising with evil intentions, and they moved on me and cause me to rebel. Now they have taken my brother's side, so they will all pay for this." There was such cruelty that even the bellies of pregnant women were cut open, and the living children were taken out and killed. Knowing that it was impossible to secretly escape, many of the Cañari hid in caves, mountains, and other concealed places, [then] fleeing to Cusipampa where Huanca Auqui had retreated.

Old people commonly say, that the Cañari nation has always been traitorous, troublemakers, liars, and gossipers, and that because of the many rumors, with and without foundation, that they told Huascar Inca about Atahualpa, he ordered them to be killed and destroyed as we have described above. Even today, they still hold this same trait, and it is not uncommon in revolts and conflicts for them to change sides, based solely on who is winning.

Atahualpa, after having executed his rage, concluded his punishment and quenched his thirst with the blood of the Cañari, returned to Quito in great triumph and majesty, leaving guards at Tomebamba and all the frontiers. Atahualpa reaffirmed the loyalty of those provinces, with both benefits and punishments. Arriving in Quito, and [after] resting for some days, he entered the area of the Quijos and Yumbos with considerable power and strength. While the harshness of the region made the conquest difficult, he subjected and dominated them.

Thinking only of keeping the provinces around Quito, including Tomebamba, Huancavilca, and other nearby nations, [Atahualpa] spoke with his captains and advisers, saying that he did not want disagreements or wars with his brother, but rather, he wanted to have him as a friend and live in peace and harmony with him. So, he prepared to send some of the people that he had taken captive from the Quijos and Yumbos as presents, along with other items. However, his [plans] were disturbed by what we shall see later.

[f.106v] While Huanca Auqui was in Cusipampa, saddened by his disastrous fortune, he dispatched messengers to his brother Huascar Inca, warning him of his misfortunes with Atahualpa, the numerous people he had lost in battles, and his retreat to Cusipampa, where he had constructed many forts and buildings so he would be prepared and fortified, if Atahualpa attacked him. Hearing this, Huascar Inca felt incredible sorrow, cursing his luck, and blaming all the ill-fated events on those who had left Atahualpa in Quito when they came with the body of his father.

At this time, Huanca Auqui, [seeking] to restore past losses and to repair his damaged reputation from the war, led a conquest into the [area] of the Pacamoros and took even more. Encouraged by the news of his brother Atahualpa's incursion into the Quijos and Yumbos, [Huanca Auqui] said to his captains: "Let us make another entry and be no less than my brother, for we have such good people in our company." Thus, he continued the conquest and won two [more] villages and captured many prisoners. [Huanca Auqui] selected the best and most important among those he captured and sent them to Cuzco as gifts, hoping to provide some pleasure to his brother, Huascar Inca, who he knew was angry with him, due to the poor dealings he had had with Atahualpa. [Huascar Inca] could also receive information from the [prisoners] and learn details about their land.

As the people of the region saw the destruction of their neighbors and that the Inca army was entering their lands, they held a general meeting and unanimously agreed to unite to turn on Huanca Auqui, destroy him, and expel him from their territory. Having reached this agreement, they gathered in complete silence near where Huanca Auqui was lodged and then they suddenly attacked him. The sudden uproar caught them [by surprise], and they scattered with many being killed. Huanca Auqui had to flee, taking the prisoners who were to be sent to Cuzco, but [the enemy] followed them with great determination for an entire night and day. Without resting or giving them time to restore themselves [f.107r] anywhere, they hurt and killed them, as they knew that rough and rugged land better than those of

Huanca Auqui. They were able to safely continue their infinite slaughter until the Paltas, where they [finally] left them.

Barely escaping, Huanca Auqui cursed his luck, which was so against him in everything he intended and tried to do. He was there for some days until the Pacamoros, not satisfied with the outcome, dared to leave their land and come in search of the Inca army, which was camped in Cusipampa. One night, they attacked Huanca Auqui's encampment and killed several people. [In response], the army took up arms, and using forethought and swiftness, Huanca Auqui ordered his forces to disperse the Pacamoros, making them retreat. They [then] pursued them to punish them for their audacity. They were so successful in their attack that they killed most of them, with only a few escaping. Furious at the damage that they had caused when they first attacked him, Huanca Auqui immediately decided to enter [their territory] with his entire army and end the conquest.[604]

[F.108R] CHAPTER 51

The embassy that Huascar Inca sent to Huanca Auqui, and the battles he had with the people of Atahualpa, and his final retreat

While Huanca Auqui was developing these plans and was getting ready to start the journey and conquest of the Pacamoros, [two] messengers, Huapanti and Huaca Mayta, arrived from his brother Huascar Inca. They brought *acsos* and *llicllas* for [Huanca Auqui's men] to wear, as well as mirrors and *mantur* to shave with, scorning them as if they were women. [Huascar Inca] sent [these items] to express his regret for entrusting them with that task, thinking and believing that they would conduct themselves as men of honor. But they had done just the opposite, worse than if they were women. Where were the words and oaths of honor that they had given and promised before the Sun, their father? Everything had ended poorly, and they were no longer worthy or deserving of taking up arms or putting on the garments or clothes of brave soldiers, but instead [they should] dress in *acsos* and *llicllas*, like women, since they and the many people they had taken with them had done so poorly. There was no doubt that they had allied and joined with Atahualpa, because they were always sending each other messengers and presents. So, when they came to Cuzco to give an account of their battles and encounters to the Sun, they [should] come dressed in women's clothes as they had performed worse than women.[605]

604 Folio 107v is blank.
605 Cabello Valboa (1951 [1586]:441–442) and Sarmiento de Gamboa (2007 [1572]:189) offer

When Huanca Auqui heard the vile and offensive message from Huascar, with its many disdainful and outrageous accusations, he held a council with his captains to discuss [how] to attack Atahualpa's captains again, who were in Tomebamba, to try to reverse their past failures and losses. Everyone agreed, and they quickly left Cusipampa in good order so [Atahualpa] would have no knowledge of him coming. [When Huanca Auqui] arrived at Tomebamba he attacked and gave battle, scattering all of Atahualpa's people.[606] *[f.108v]* He killed many of them, and the few who escaped went to Quito to inform Atahualpa of this news.

When Atahualpa heard what happened, he felt great sorrow in his heart, and as he was being challenged, he decided to continue the war without a pause until its end. He declared: "How is it possible that after I stopped destroying my brother, Huanca Auqui, and left him in peace when I defeated him in Tomebamba, and after I placed my landmarks in Cusipampa, hoping to live quietly and not wanting to displease my brother, Huascar Inca, or bother or make war on his vassals, now he wants to make a mockery of me? However, this being the case, I determined to resolve this dispute and fight him, and as you will see, I will continue until one of us has obtained and is content with the lordship."[607]

Later, he sent a messenger to Huanca Auqui, asking him, to his shame, if he had put on the *acsos* and *lliccllas* that Huascar Inca had sent him in payment for the many battles that he had won. And if he had not put them on, he should do so and return to Cuzco with them to enter in triumph.

After sending the messenger, [Atahualpa] ordered the most powerful army, with the largest number of men, that he had ever created to be assembled.[608] He appointed Quisquis as general, having served his father, Huayna Capac, in all of [his] wars and conquests, and Chalcuchima as his lieutenant, or Field Marshal, as it now is called, as he was a cruel, cunning, and ingenious Indian with great tricks of war.[609] As captains, he named Yura Hualpa, a native of the Chilque, [and] Rumiñavi,[610] a native of Quilliscachi, which is subject to Corca three leagues [southwest] of Cuzco, and Tumayrima and Ucumari and many others. After reviewing the army, which

similar information. Guaman Poma de Ayala (2004 [1615]:117) also describes women's clothing being sent to shame Huanca Auqui.

606 Cabello Valboa (1951 [1586]:441–1442) and Sarmiento de Gamboa (2007 [1572]:189) present similar information.

607 Cabello Valboa (1951 [1586]:442) presents similar information.

608 Cabello Valboa (1951 [1586]:441) presents similar information.

609 This is a reference to the final victory of Atahualpa's forces over those of Huascar's, which involved a ruse.

610 Rumiñavi later played a significant role in fighting against the Spaniards in Ecuador. He was the last of Atahualpa's captains to be captured and killed. Guaman Poma de Ayala (2004 [1615]:163 [165]) provides a drawing of him.

was [composed] of all the nations near Quito and the old soldiers that his father, Huayna Capac, had brought there, [Atahualpa] dispatched them, commanding the general to follow Huanca Auqui to Cajamarca, where he was to plant his markers at the Yanamayo River. Quisquis and the army marched to Cusipampa,⁶¹¹ where he found Huanca Auqui, who came out with much determination and courage to fight him. The battle was so evenly matched that an infinite number of people died on both sides. As the strength of Atahualpa's army was large and undoubtedly greater *[f.109r]* than that of Huanca Auqui [the latter] was defeated, and he retreated to the forts that he had built in Cusipampa.⁶¹²

When Huanca Auqui saw the victorious and proud enemy, how poorly he had done, how many people he had lost in the battle, and what little help he could expect from anywhere soon, he agreed to meet that night with the Cañari and Tomebambas who had been settled there as *mitimaes* by his father, Huayna Capac, and his captains. He told them that they could see with their own eyes what few options they had to escape from the hands of their strong enemy, and that it seemed to him if they agreed and approved, that they should flee that night to Cajamarca with all the riches and *huacas* that they had brought from Tomebamba, until they found reinforcements who could help them. They would take refuge in some strong place until Huascar told them what to do next because if they did not retreat, they would be killed. And if they were killed, which was certain, all the wealth they had there would fall into the hands of their enemies, making them more powerful and proud. Hearing what Huanca Auqui proposed, everyone agreed that his fear was justified. Because of the [previous] disastrous outcomes, they had become cowardly, so they agreed to follow [the plan]. That night, in complete silence and not giving any indication that they were fleeing, they began to withdraw, taking the *huacas* and the riches with them. As they passed though the provinces, they reinforced their army by force or order with [new] people.⁶¹³

So, little by little, supporting themselves as best they could, they withdrew toward Cuzco, with Quisquis and his army always on them, never missing a chance to harm or kill stragglers so [Huanca Auqui] could not use them. In this way, they arrived at Cajamarca where Huanca Auqui found a strong force of ten thousand Chachapoya Indians that Huascar Inca, knowing the ruinous state of the army, had sent to help and reinforce him. Huanca Auqui was greatly encouraged by this, and

611   Cabello Valboa (1951 [1586]:435, 441, 444) and Sarmiento de Gamboa (2007 [1572]:189) both mention Cusipampa.
612   Cabello Valboa (1951 [1586]:443) and Sarmiento de Gamboa (2007 [1572]:190) offer similar information. Among the differing details, Sarmiento de Gamboa describes the order and the locations of some of the battles differently.
613   Cabello Valboa (1951 [1586]:444) presents similar information.

his spirits were lifted. He ordered [his troops] to go and meet Quisquis, who was arriving nearby, taking with him the people he had from the Cañari, Tomebambas, and other nations with them, and to fight him in some strong place where they had the advantage.[614] Exhausted, [Huanca Auqui] did not want to go with them, believing that his bad luck would make them lose the battle, so he stayed in Cajamarca to rest a little from the past events.[615]

[F.110R] CHAPTER 52

How Quisquis defeated the Chachapoyas and Huanca Auqui in two other battles

Together, the newly arrived Chachapoyas and the rest of Huanca Auqui's army quickly left Cajamarca and went to meet Quisquis. They found each other in Concha Huayla,[616] which is between Huancabamba and Cajamarca. Early the next day, they successfully brought the battle to [Quisquis], despite being weary from the journey. However, Quisquis and his soldiers were victorious, quickly breaking up and destroying the Chachapoyas and those who had joined them. The death toll was so high that of the ten thousand Chachapoyas involved, no more than three thousand escaped Quisquis. The wounded [Chachapoyas] and those from the other nations who could retreat, ran to where Huanca Auqui was in Cajamarca. Some other Chachapoyas who had survived, and did not want to put themselves in danger again, knowing that things were collapsing for Huanca Auqui, secretly returned to their lands.[617]

Huanca Auqui, experiencing so many blunders and hardships and seeing that the size of Quisquis's army was increasing every day and was becoming more feared with each victory, decided not to wait for him in Cajamarca as he did not have the number nor the means to resist him. So, Huanca Auqui left Cajamarca with what little remained of his army, and after a long journey, he withdrew toward Cuzco, leaving those provinces helpless and subject to the fury of the enemy who was

614   Cabello Valboa (1951 [1586]:448) and Sarmiento de Gamboa (2007 [1572]:190) offer similar information on the reinforcements sent to Huanca Auqui.

615   Folio 109v is blank.

616   Cabello Valboa (1951 [1586]:444–445) and Sarmiento de Gamboa (2007 [1572]:190) presents similar information on the battle of Concha Huayla.

617   Cabello Valboa (1951 [1586]:445) and Sarmiento de Gamboa (2007 [1572]:190) present similar information. However, Murúa offers more details.

close behind. When Huanca Auqui arrived at Pumpu,[618] he found a large army that Huascar Inca had sent from the southern provinces of Collao and other neighboring provinces. Happy with such good help, he and his followers rested and resupplied there. He took advantage of all that was needed in terms of arms and clothing from the storehouses, as his people had suffered many losses and were arriving shattered, naked, and even hungry. So, he waited [in Pumpu] for his enemies, eager to restore the past damage.[619]

Knowing that [Quisquis and his army] were nearing Pumpu, Huanca Auqui went out to [meet] them with good formation *[f.110v]* and confidence, having given his people words of great conviction to encourage them. He waited at the bridge over the Pumpu River to fight, and there [both sides] charged each other with fierce rage. The battle was so fierce that it lasted until the night, with neither side gaining the advantage. The next morning, Huanca Auqui returned with new energy and determination, which encouraged his [troops], knowing they had resisted the enemy, who was so used to winning, the day before. They fought all day, but the night brought no end, only countless deaths. On the third day, they returned to fight, but in despair. Quisquis had grown in strength, his army had doubled since he left Tomebamba, as he had been reinforced with new people in all the provinces that he won. Everyone joined him out of fear of the great and cruel punishments he inflicted on those who did not obey him and because of the governors that Huascar Inca had placed in those provinces. [Quisquis] was so successful, that in the end he scattered the army of the Inca and defeated it, killing a vast number, causing those who escaped to flee in shame.

Huanca Auqui, having seen so much misfortune, disruption, and the destruction of his army, and having been forced to flee and withdraw with his men, did so in great sorrow. He retreated to Jauja,[620] where another sizable group [had] arrived, composed of Soras, Chanka, Lucanas, Aymaraes, Quechuas, Huancas, and Yauyos.[621] Seeing this, he agreed to collect and organize these armies and go out

---

618 Also called Bombon by Murúa and some other early writers. This Inca city is on the shore of Lake Junín. Betanzos (1996 [1557]:208) also describes aid coming from Cuzco: "When Huascar learned this, he sent another captain, named Coriatao, a native of Mayo, who took another thirty thousand men and found Huanca Auqui at the Bombon bridge." However, Betanzos describes the subsequent battle very differently.

619 Murúa provides more details concerning these events than Cabello Valboa (1951 [1586]:448) and Sarmiento de Gamboa (2007 [1572]:190) do. Cobo (1979 [1653]:166) describes the battles of Bombon and Jauja in just one sentence.

620 Betanzos (1996 [1557]:208) also tells of the battle of Jauja but describes it in very different terms.

621 All these groups are from the central Andes, most within what are now the departments of Ayacucho and Apurímac. Sarmiento de Gamboa (2007 [1572]:190) mentions only four

to try his luck again, challenging Quisquis, who was already advancing upon him with great ferocity. He organized everything [and] traveled two leagues from Jauja to Huánuco in the Yanamarca Valley, where he met his enemies. He charged them into battle, demonstrating that his courage had not been diminished by past disasters and successes. Both sides started fighting with great determination and bravery, [with a] huge number being killed, and the battle continued almost the entire day.[622]

As Huanca Auqui had already had bad luck and powerful enemies, he was eventually defeated by Quisquis and Chalcuchima, with such a pitiful destruction of his [army] that it cannot be counted. The slaughter was such, that until today, the entire valley is [still] full of the bones of those who died there. Huanca Auqui was unlucky *[f.111r]* enough to be defeated, yet he was fortunate enough to escape from the hands of his enemy, and with a few people, he withdrew in disarray to Paucaray.[623] He rested there for a few days. His opponents were unable to pursue him, as they were exhausted and had to tend to their wounded and regroup, having suffered numerous casualties in the battle.

While Huanca Auqui was in Paucaray, not knowing what to do with such misfortune, a troop of *orejones*[624] arrived with a captain named Mayta Yupanqui,[625] who told Huanca Auqui on behalf of his brother, Huascar Inca, that it was impossible, given how [bad] things were, and his dismal performance in the war that included losing so many battles and people as well as by retreating leaving the provinces in ruin; that [all] of this had to have been done in concert with his brother Atahualpa, and his general Quisquis, since so many things had occurred between them and so many of the very best people had been killed in the battles. To which Huanca Auqui, feeling that his loyalty was questioned and doubted, replied that it was not true that there was an agreement or alliance between him and Quisquis to prevent him from fulfilling his obligations, and that he had done all he could, that he had done everything in his power to direct the battles in the best way he knew, to overcome his enemies, and that if he had been defeated, [it was] not due to his efforts, but to the will of the Creator, who had allowed that to happen.[626]

---

of these groups, while Cabello Valboa (1951 [1586]:448) is even more general.

622   Cabello Valboa (1951 [1586]:449) and Sarmiento de Gamboa (2007 [1572]:190) offer similar information on this battle.

623   Betanzos (1996 [1557]:20, 30) also mentions Paucaray but in relation to the Chanka.

624   The *orejones* would have been from the Cuzco region.

625   Cobo (1979 [1653]:172) notes that Mayta Yupanqui was a son of Huayna Capac and was later killed on orders of Atahualpa. Pizarro (1921 [1571]:191) mentions that a Mayta Yupanqui was in Cajamarca when Atahualpa was captured.

626   Sarmiento de Gamboa (2007 [1572]:190) provides similar information concerning Huanca Auqui.

They then say that Huanca Auqui, filled with anger and rage over what Huascar had sent [the captain] to say, was resolute and determined to go over to his brother, Atahualpa, and to join with him in revenge for the accusations made against him. However, the captains who had been with [Huanca Auqui] from the beginning in Cuzco and had participated in all the battles persuaded him not to do so, as that would confirm the suspicions that the rumormongers and gossips had told Huascar about him. Furthermore, if Huascar learned that Huanca Auqui switched to Quisquis's side he would kill his children, relatives, and friends who were *[f.111v]* with him and those who were in Cuzco. Consequently, he changed his mind, but he was no better off since he later died along with Huascar, by order of Atahualpa when they were taken prisoner, as we shall see.

Huanca Auqui then told Mayta Yupanqui, the captain of the *orejones*, to go and meet Quisquis, so that he could see the strength, courage, and size of his army. The *orejones* bravely advanced to meet Quisquis at the Ancoyaco[627] bridge, where they had a bloody battle. [The *orejones*] stopped [Quisquis's] army from crossing the wide river. For more than a month, Atahualpa's army was on one side and the *orejones* on the other. This being the case, and as Huascar sent no additional reinforcements and none of his captains were there to help, Quisquis eventually attacked [the *orejones*] with such boldness that he scared and scattered them.[628] They crossed the river and chased Huanca Auqui, who was retreating toward Vilcas[huaman] and waiting for instructions from Huascar Inca.[629]

[F.112V] CHAPTER 53

How Huascar Inca, having offered great sacrifices, personally went out to defend his domains and defeated Quisquis in a battle

There are no words to describe the pain and sorrow that Huascar Inca felt when the news of so many sad and disastrous events reached him in Cuzco. Knowing that all of his efforts and plans had gone awry, he decided to fast and go to his *huacas* to make innumerable sacrifices and offerings to them. After consulting with the priests about this, he left Cuzco and went to Huanacauri to conduct a fast. He was there for several days, contemplating with his closest and dearest [relatives], and placating

---

627   Now called the Izcuchaca over the Mantaro River.
628   Sarmiento de Gamboa (2007 [1572]:190) provides similar information on the battle of the Ancoyaco bridge. Later, Migual Estete (1872 [1534]:91), shown the location of the battle by Quisquis, stated that the fighting lasted two or three days.
629   Folio 112r is blank.

the Creator by sacrificing thousands of different types of animals to the *huacas* of Cuzco, according to their rites and ceremonies. Seeing that he had received negative answers from all the demons that had spoken to him and that [these answers] did not align with his intentions and plans, [and] not knowing what to do, he agreed to call a general meeting of the sorcerers once again. He then sent [someone] to consult other *huacas* that could speak and to ask them what he should do as he was surrounded by so much misfortune and misery. Yet none [of the *huacas*] offered him a remedy or an answer that satisfied his desires.[630]

[When Huascar] asked the soothsayers and sorcerers to tell him how he would fare in the war, appease, and avoid endangering him with the truth, they replied that he would do well, and all would occur according to his wishes in the war, and that he would vanquish his foes with a resounding victory in the war. God[631] permitted all of this for His sake, as it was time for His Holy Gospel to be promulgated in these remote regions, thus bringing an end to Lucifer's rule and monarchy that he held so tightly and imprisoned under his hand in these kingdoms.[632]

[*f.113r*] Huascar Inca was satisfied with the sorcerers' promise and answer, so he left Cuzco, accompanied by many brothers, relatives, and close friends, and went to Sacsahuana.[633] There, he gathered the most powerful army of all nations [from Cuzco] to Chile, who came with great effort. He reviewed [the troops] and provided weapons and clothes to those who lacked what was needed. He also encouraged them by praising their efforts and courage, telling them that he had placed his hopes in them to defeat all of their enemies at once; that [their enemies] had unjustly and without reason rebelled against him and had denied the obedience due to him as their natural lord. So that they would [fight] like good soldiers, he offered and promised to honor and reward them all according to their courage and how they fought. Once this was done, [Huascar] set out on the road to Cotabambas[634] to meet Quisquis and Chalcuchima.[635]

---

630 Cabello Valboa (1951 [1586]:453) presents similar information on Huascar's meetings with the *huacas*.

631 The word "God" has been added to the text (Murúa 2008 [1616]:112v).

632 Cabello Valboa (1951 [1586]:453) presents similar information on Huascar's meeting with the soothsayers.

633 This could be a reference to Jaquijhuana; however, it is more likely related to Sacsayhuaman.

634 The more traditional route for Atahualpa's army to arrive in Cuzco was to cross the Apurímac River near the town of Curahuasi. However, in this telling, Atahualpa's army marched south and crossed the Apurímac River near Cotabambas at the Hualpachaca Bridge.

635 Betanzos (1996 [1557]:222–230) provides a detailed description of the fighting between the two armies near Cotabambas.

To be better organized, he ordered the people of Collasuyu, Cuntisuyu, Chuis, Charcas, and Chile[636] to be distributed above Cotabambas, toward Omasuyus,[637] and to try by all possible means to drive their enemies until the Cotabambas River. Huanca Auqui, Huapanti, and Pacamayta[638] went together, along with the people that they brought who had survived the previous battles, further downriver which is toward the Apurímac Bridge[639] to attack the enemy from the other side. In this way, [Huanca Auqui] planned to climb the Cotabambas hill to enter the battle, with the intention of trapping [Quisquis and Chalcuchima] between them so that they could be more easily destroyed.[640]

The Chumbivilcas, Chuis, Charcas, Chile, and other nations that had been ordered to drive the enemy toward the Cotabambas River, where Huanca Auqui was to go, found with little effort, a large army at Tauaray,[641] which Quisquis and Chalcuchima had ordered to enter Cuzco by way of Chumbivilcas. The captain of Huascar Inca's army, whose name was Arampa[642] Yupanqui, saw them and enthusiastically encouraged his people, telling them to fight like brave soldiers [and] that, once [this force was] defeated, the others would be easy to overcome and control. It is said that a battle occurred in Tauaray, behind Omasuyus. *[f.113v]* It was very cruel and bloody, and Arampa Yupanqui defeated Atahualpa's army, resulting in the death of more than ten thousand Indians, including their captain, Tumayrima, and very few of Huascar's men were killed. Arampa Yupanqui was very pleased with the victory and ordered Atahualpa's captains and other prisoners to be beheaded, inflicting severe punishments.[643]

---

636   Cabello Valboa (1951 [1586]:452) and Sarmiento de Gamboa (2007 [1572]:193) mention these same groups.

637   There is an area of Bolivia, near Lake Titicaca, called Omasuyu but this refers to a region of the same name south of Cotabambas.

638   Sarmiento de Gamboa (2007 [1572]:193) mentions these same leaders.

639   This is the bridge across the Apurímac below Curahuasi on the central road to Cuzco. It was one of the largest bridges of the Inca Empire (Bauer 2006).

640   Sarmiento de Gamboa (2007 [1572]:193) provides similar information.

641   Betanzos (1996 [1557]:229) states that Huascar was captured at a place called Guanaco Pampa, which belonged to the town of Cotabambas. Sarmiento de Gamboa (2007 [1572]:193) and Titu Cussi Yupangui (2005 [1570]:66) also state that the final battle took place on a plain called Huánuco Pampa. This should not be confused with the better-known Inca provincial center also called Huánuco Pampa in the Department of Huánuco, and it may be related to an area called Huanucpampa near Chinchaypujio. In contrast, Cabello Valboa (1951 [1586]:456), like Murúa, states that the final battle occurred at a place called Tauaray near Cotabambas.

642   Sarmiento de Gamboa (2007 [1572]:193) also mentions Arampa Yupanqui. We have selected to use Sarmiento de Gamboa's spelling, rather than Murúa's (Uampa Yupanqui).

643   Cabello Valboa (1951 [1586]:455–456) and Sarmiento de Gamboa (2007 [1572]:193) offer

Arampa Yupanqui then sent messengers with the news of this most fortunate event to Huascar Inca, who received it with great joy and happiness, forgetting all his previous losses and misfortunes. Laughing, with a face filled with relief and joy, he told his brothers and captains who were present, that since the Collas, Chuis, Charcas, and the other people [from Collasuyu] have had achieved such an illustrious victory, and having beaten the enemies and killed so many of them and their captains, "My brothers, we are more righteous than before, being who we are we have the unavoidable obligation to take the lead of those who remain, as our ancestors did. So, with great courage and bravery, let us go and face Quisquis and Chalcuchima who are approaching us and give them battle, so that they understand that the forces of the Incas are not completely finished, and that the Creator wanted them to come here from Quito, where they fought and won so many battles, they killed so many captains, and committed so many and such innumerable cruelties. Let them finally pay for their wickedness, [just] when they thought to enjoy our wives and daughters and to take our estates. All this done by His hand for His greater glory and honor."[644]

With these thoughts and others, he inspired his captains with even greater courage to fight and to prove themselves worthy of the prizes he had offered them. Titu Atauchi[645] and Tupa Atau, his brothers, as well as Nano and Urco Huaranca, his relatives, and other captains who were with him, then began to organize the army according to their nations, dividing them by their ways and means of fighting, so that they would not be humiliated [in battle]. They placed the squadrons in the field as Quisquis, Chalcuchima, and Ucumari[646] approached with their people, still saddened by their defeat at Tauaray. Huascar Inca went out on his *[f.114r]* litters to observe his soldiers and squadrons in formation. Upon seeing [Huascar Inca], they played an array of military instruments that they usually use in battles, such as horns, flutes, shell[s], and bone[s], which delighted him. They enthusiastically prepared themselves for battle, as Quisquis and Chalcuchima were already sending their squads.[647]

They attacked one another with an unprecedented level of courage and daring. The battle began with chaotic shouting, [with warriors] falling in heaps on both

similar information on this battle. Betanzos (1996 [1557]:222–223) also suggests that Huascar's forces won the first skirmish, but he provides different details and different names for most of the captains.

644   Cabello Valboa (1951 [1586]:456) presents similar information. Sarmiento de Gamboa (2007 [1572]:193) provides a much shorter version of this speech, reducing it to only one sentence.

645   Titu Atauchi is mentioned by Guaman Poma de Ayala (2004 [1615]:114).

646   Ucunari is mentioned by Guaman Poma de Ayala (2004 [1615]:168 [170]).

647   Cabello Valboa (1951 [1586]:457) presents similar information.

sides. The conflict continued with great tenacity until the afternoon without a win-
ner. But Fortune favored Huascar Inca that day, who broke the enemy and ripped
them apart with singular joy. An innumerable amount of people perished on both
sides, though more [died] in Atahualpa's [army]. As his army collapsed, many
retreated to a slope and a hill where there was a large grassland. When Huascar
Inca saw this, he ordered the hill and grassland to be set on fire, and once this was
done, many Indians were burned, and those who escaped by fleeing from the fire
surrendered to Huascar's forces, [but] they were killed without pity, and most of
Atahualpa's army died.[648] Quisquis and Chalcuchima, seeing their loss and dismem-
berment, gathered up the remains of the army and slowly withdrew, showing their
faces to the enemies on the other side of the Cotabambas River.[649]

[F.115R] CHAPTER 54

How Quisquis and Chalcuchima fought Huascar Inca the next day, beating and capturing him

When the famous and celebrated Carthaginian, Hannibal, who was the terror of the
Roman monarchy, won the last and most damaging battle for the Romans, with a
pitiful and never-before-seen destruction, a captain of his told him: "Follow the victory, Hannibal, you will be victorious on the fifth day." Blinded by the good fortune
that had occurred and to the good fortune of the Romans who did not want to be
completely destroyed, he answered: "Let them take the news of the victory to Rome."
To which the captain replied: "Ah, how the gods did not give all the graces to one
[person]! You know how to win, but not [how] to enjoy the fruit of the victory."

The same can be now said of Huascar Inca, who, even though he was able to
defeat the army of his brother Atahualpa by killing them all, failed to follow the victory, and he left the good opportunity that he had by the hair. This was the principal
reason why he lost his freedom, kingdoms, and lordships, as well as of his death,
of that of his wives, children, sisters, relatives, and all those who loved him; all of
whom experienced the severities of the victor's knife. Indeed, it was true what was
said, "The mistakes and errors that are committed in war cannot be corrected," as
we can easily see today.[650]

---

648   Cabello Valboa (1951 [1586]:457) presents similar information. Sarmiento de Gamboa
        (2007 [1572]:193–194) provides a much shorter description of this battle.
649   Folio 114v is blank.
650   Here, it appears that Murúa added a prologue before returning to the historical text he
        was using.

Huascar was very proud and happy that such a marked victory had been achieved, as he [had] wished. Seeing that his enemies were retreating to the other side of the Cotabambas River, [and that] his people were tired by the tenacity of the day-long fight, [and] did not want them to become more exhausted by continuing to advance, he ordered the soldiers to stop, ~~and~~[651] since the next day, they could attack their enemies with new effort and courage, and finish destroying them. Because he was waiting for the return of all his forces and people, whom he had ordered to go with Huanca Auqui and the other captains, *[f.115v]* to attack Quisquis's rear guard in order to strike him from all sides, Huascar Inca believed that this would be an easy task and that it would end in the devastation of his opponents, and that none of them would escape without being killed or captured, which was what he most desired, so [that he could] exact his rage and revengeful appetite on them.[652]

When Quisquis and Chalcuchima withdrew to the other side of the river, they saw the great destruction and damage that had been inflicted on their army, which was far less than that of Huascar's [army]. They wanted to slowly withdraw toward Quito, as they had been badly [defeated]. But seeing that neither Huascar nor his people were following them, they were encouraged and hoped to improve their position, especially when they saw that [their enemy] had let them rest where they had retreated for the night. As industrious men and experts in war, they agreed that before the sun rose the next day, the entire army would be ready to attack the entire army of Huascar Inca, who would be careless in the joy of victory. They knew their own lives were at risk, [so they resolved] to fight bravely. These two captains clearly understood how it would play out: all of [Huascar's army] would be celebrating and dancing joyfully, not expecting that [Quisquis and Chalcuchima] would have enough courage left to attack them.[653]

The following day, before sunrise, they went down in good order and with a great diligence to cross the river, knowing that the entire battle depended on it. They advanced to fight Huascar's [army], who were not expecting a sudden attack. When Huascar and his captains saw this, they began to organize themselves as quickly as they could, crossed the river to meet their enemies who were already advancing. When they reached a half-slope called Chinta Capa,[654] the squadrons met, and their

---

651   The word "and" has been removed from the text (Murúa 2008 [1616]:115r).

652   Cabello Valboa (1951 [1586]:457) and Sarmiento de Gamboa (2007 [1572]:194) offer similar information on Huascar's delay.

653   Cabello Valboa (1951 [1586]:457) and Sarmiento de Gamboa (2007 [1572]:194) offer similar information on the reorganization of Quisquis and Chalcuchima.

654   Cabello Valboa (1951 [1586]:458) writes "Chontacaxas." If this is the correct spelling, it may be related to the community Chonta, located between Limatambo and Chinchaypuquio.

battle began with great courage. Huascar Inca was richly armed with his weapons of gold and silver, which shone ostentatiously, and they carried him in his litters, that encouraged his soldiers. *[f.116r]* The battle was very hard fought and stubborn, and so many died on both sides and the battlefield was littered with piles [of the dead]. At nightfall, Fortune, who had favored Huascar up to that point had, now showed her lack of firmness and instability. Chalcuchima was a skilled soldier with many tricks,[655] and although Huascar's army was twice as big, he broke them and captured Huascar Inca,[656] who had fought bravely and served as an admirable leader. Along with him, his brothers Titu Atauchi and Tupa Atau,[657] as well as many other relatives and captains, were imprisoned.[658]

The capture of Huascar is recounted by some very elderly Indians in this way: They say that at nightfall, he and his soldiers, having fought courageously all day long, were winning the battle. [Huascar Inca then] took the lead in his litter to further rally his people. When Chalcuchima saw him, he knew that his own people were starting to lose the battle, [and] it seemed to him that the only way to turn the tide was to take or kill Huascar. So, he gathered many brave soldiers and attacked Huascar's litter with them. They quickly threw some weapons attached to lead balls, which they use to lasso deer, at those who were carrying the litter, wounding their legs, and knocking Huascar down to the ground and Chalcuchima captured him along with the other Indians.[659]

There was confusion everywhere when the *orejones* and other people saw the commotion and Huascar Inca, their lord, captured. Splitting in different directions, they realized that the only solution was to escape. Defeated, they fled and arrived in Cuzco, where they reported the sad news to Rahua Ocllo, Huascar's mother, and his wife, Chuqui Huipa, and the statue of the Sun. When the news was heard in Cuzco, all was confusion and commotion, and the most pitiful and terrible crying

---

655   This may be a reference to a trick that Chalcuchima played to decimate the final troops of Huascar. See Sarmiento de Gamboa (2007 [1572]:195) and Betanzos (1996 [1557]:228–230).

656   The *History and Genealogy of the Inca Kings of Peru* (Murúa 2004 [1590]:45v) includes a drawing of Huascar and Quisquis fighting.

657   Cobo (1979 [1653]:169) also mentions that these two Inca captains were captured in the final battle, although his description of the battle differs. Betanzos (1996 [1557]:227) also notes the death of Tupa Atau.

658   Cabello Valboa (1951 [1586]:458) provides similar information, while Sarmiento de Gamboa (2007 [1572]:194) provides very different details concerning the beginning of this battle.

659   Cabello Valboa (1951 [1586]:459) provides a similar description of the capture of Huascar and the destruction of his army, while Sarmiento de Gamboa (2007 [1572]:194) offers a very different account.

began that until then had never been heard at the death of an Inca. These screams and cries penetrated the heavens.

When the army that had gone to attack [Atahualpa's] rearguard received the news of the imprisonment of Huascar Inca, they were without leadership and they did not regroup and quickly attack Quisquis and Chalcuchima, who were greatly reduced in number due to the people they had lost in the past battles and in the final one. They could have been easily defeated, especially when they were preoccupied with the joy and distraction *[f.116v]* of victory. Instead, each nation divided and separated, returning to their own land, believing that there was no longer any need to wait for Huascar Inca's fortune [to change], since she was so openly in favor of Atahualpa and his captains.

Quisquis and Chalcuchima, joyous after their completely unexpected victory, gathered the spoils of the defeated, which were very abundant, with their soldiers. Carefully placing their brother Huascar and the other prisoners under guard, they left with the entire army for Cuzco, committing innumerable cruelties to those whom they had defeated along the way. When they arrived at Quiuipay,[660] which is half a league from Cuzco, they made their encampment, and some of Quisquis's soldiers went ahead, even viewing Cuzco from the top of Yauira. There, they heard the cries and shouts of Huascar's women and those of the other prisoners and all the common people in Cuzco, believing [that] Huascar and his brothers were dead.[661]

Hearing this, Chalcuchima sent a messenger to Huascar's mother, Rahua Ocllo, as well as to his wife and the other chiefs, saying that they should all come and not be afraid, for they were not to blame for the wars that had been caused by the disagreements between the two brothers, and that they did not deserve any punishment or harm. Furthermore, they should be calm and stop crying, as Huascar Inca, their lord, and the other prisoners were alive and well.[662]

---

660   This place is also mentioned by Cabello Valboa (1951 [1586]:459) and many others. Sarmiento de Gamboa (2007 [1572]:196) writes "Quiuipay." Cobo (1979 [1653]:167) writes "Quipaypampa" and states that it is about a league from the city. He also suggests that this was the location of the last battle of the civil war. Betanzos (1996 [1557]:244) writes "Quicpai." Fernández de Palencia (1963 [1571]:82) writes "Quipaipan," and Garcilaso de la Vega (1966 [1609]:619) takes exception to Fernández's spelling and provides a more complete description of this place: "The name of the battlefield which he [Fernández] gives is a corruption: it should be Quepaipa, and has the genitive meaning of 'out of my trumpet,' as though that was the place where Atahualpa's trumpet sounded loudest, according to the Indian phrase. I have been in this place two or three times with other boys who were fellow pupils of mine." Despite all these references, its location remains unknown.

661   Cabello Valboa (1951 [1586]:459) and Sarmiento de Gamboa (2007 [1572]:196) provide similar descriptions of the cries heard from Apu Yauira.

662   Cabello Valboa (1951 [1586]:459–460) and Sarmiento de Gamboa (2007 [1572]:196) offer similar descriptions of the information sent to Rahua Ocllo and the others.

After Chalcuchima had somewhat calmed them, he sent another messenger to only the *orejones*, telling them all, without missing anyone, to leave Cuzco and come to give obedience to the figure of Atahualpa Inca, their lord, whom he had brought with him and to recognize [Atahualpa] as Inca and king, adoring his figure, which they called Ticsi Capac, meaning "Lord of all the Universe."[663] Through these actions, they would avoid the damages and destruction that could come upon them and the city for rebelling and disobeying orders, since they had no defense nor were not enough to defend themselves.[664]

[F.117V] CHAPTER 55

How Huanca Auqui and the other orejones *gave obedience to the figure of Atahualpa*

On hearing such stressful news, Huanca Auqui, who was in Cuzco, and the other *orejones* and captains who had escaped from the hands of the enemy, gathered in council to discuss what they could accept. For three days, they consulted and discussed whether it would be best to obey the command of Chalcuchima and give obedience to the figure of Atahualpa as they were told, or to leave together and fight their enemies, risking death or victory. In the end, as they were so few and so discouraged and broken by the many misfortunes and defeats, they agreed to do what they were told and to follow their sad fate, giving obedience to the figure of Atahualpa and his captains, who were waiting for their final decision. Having agreed, they put on the most cheerful faces that they could, arranging themselves in *ayllus*[665] according to their rank, and left with sorrowful and sad hearts.

All those who had been captured in the battle where Huascar Inca was imprisoned wore a tassel, as a sign that they had been forgiven by Atahualpa's captains for the crime of having fought against him. When they arrived at the Quiuipay plain, they sat down on the ground according to their rank, bowing [and] making a sign of reverence or *mocha*, as they say, as a sign of obedience to the figure of Atahualpa, who was there.[666] Once this ceremony was over and everyone was

---

663   Cabello Valboa (1951 [1586]:459) and Sarmiento de Gamboa (2007 [1572]:196) offer similar information on Chalcuchima's orders.

664   Folio 117r is blank.

665   This word is underlined (Murúa 2008 [1616]:117v).

666   Betanzos (1996 [1557]:203) provides a description of this statue: "Finding himself lord, he ordered that a statue be prepared of his own nail clippings and hair, which was a representation of his person. He ordered that this statue be called Incap Guauquin, which means

seated, the soldiers of Atahualpa, who had been arranged, positioned, and armed for war for what they were to do, surrounded them, on the orders of Quisquis and Chalcuchima, so that no one could escape or flee once they saw what was to come.⁶⁶⁷

When they had them surrounded, they placed Huanca Auqui, who was the most important, in the middle of the *orejones* along with Huapanti and Paucar Usno. These three received more scrutiny due of the battles they had fought in Tomebamba. To fulfill the mandate of Atahualpa, who, as we said, *[f.118r]* had ordered them be taken prisoner, they also seized Apu Chalco Yupanqui⁶⁶⁸ and Rupaca, the most respected and principal priests of the Sun, asking, why they had given the crown of lord and Inca to Huascar [by] giving him the tassel of authority?⁶⁶⁹

After these imprisonments, Quisquis rose his seat and turned to the people of Cuzco who had come to give obedience. Speaking to Huanca Auqui and to those who had been imprisoned with him, Quisquis told them the following: "You know how you fought me in so many battles in Tomebamba and elsewhere and stopped my advance with great resistance. You also know that Huascar Inca was not the legitimate heir of Huayna Capac, our lord, because when [Huayna Capac] died in Quito, he left Ninan Cuyuchi as his successor, who [also] died. Even if this had not occurred, it is well known to everyone that there were other sons of Huayna Capac who were more deserving of the lordship and kingdom than Huascar Inca, such as Tilca Yupanqui⁶⁷⁰ and others. Nevertheless, you chose to crown Huascar Inca, putting the tassel on his head, mocked, belittled, and scorned Atahualpa, my lord, who the Sun, his father, holds in his hand and whom the Earth sustains and protects and who has now defeated you and has you under his power and control." And listing a thousand other kinds of blessings, he continued saying: "And you also know because of the things that I have recounted, that you are worthy of, and deserve, being killed with unheard of cruelty, so that others might take note of this punishment from

the brother of the Inca. Once the statue was completed, he had it placed on a litter and charged one of his servants named Chima with guarding and watching over it. Giving this statue many other young men as servants, he ordered that it be taken and carried on its litter by the messengers to where his captains Chalcuchima and Quisquis were so that the peoples of the subjugated provinces could render obedience to that statue in place of this person. Thus, this statue was carried and given to the captains, who received it and were very pleased with it. They performed many and great sacrifices and served and respected this statue as if the very person of Atahualpa were there."

667 Sarmiento de Gamboa (2007 [1572]:196) provides similar information on this meeting.
668 Apu Chalco Yupanqui was later killed along with Huascar on orders of Atahualpa.
669 Cabello Valboa (1951 [1586]:460) and Sarmiento de Gamboa (2007 [1572]:196) offer similar information.
670 A brother of Pachacuti Inca Yupanqui was named also Tilca Yupanqui; however, he is thought to have been killed much earlier.

now on. However, out of pity and mercy, so that you may not complain or consider me inhumane or your enemy, I have, in the name of Atahualpa, my lord, forgiven you, provided you always remain stoutly obedient and faithful vassals, recognizing him as lord and Inca. But so that you will not go unpunished or sanctioned, it is just that you should receive the punishment which you greatly deserve, and we will always remember." Turning to his people, he commanded that they be beaten on their backs with truncheons and *champis*. Each one [received] ten blows, more or less, according to their culpability. *[f.118v]* He then ordered that many of the guiltiest be immediately killed, striking fear and dread in the [hearts] of the survivors, thinking that everyone might be killed.[671]

When the above was finished, he ordered all the *orejones* that were present and the rest of the defeated nations to kneel down with much humility and to turn their faces toward Quito, as a sign of subjection, [and while] plucking their eyebrows and eyelashes to bow to Atahualpa, their lord, and offer them as a gift and a present.[672] Upon hearing this, the unfortunate *orejones*, seeing no other [chance of] a minor punishment, only the possibility of being killed, prostrated themselves on the ground with deep humility and fulfilled what was commanded. They cried out in fear: "Long live Atahualpa, our lord, and Inca! May his father, the Sun, increase his life and favor him, and [may he] hold his enemies in his hand and triumph over them, making him lord of all, to the ends of the world!"[673]

Within the group of the defeated was Rahua Ocllo, [the] mother of Huascar Inca and [the] wife of Huayna Capac, along with Chuqui Huipa, the wife of Huascar Inca. [They felt] an indescribable sadness and pain, seeing the unforgettable spectacle of the dead before them and hearing the speeches accompanied by such ceremonies. [They] contemplated their wretched fate and misfortune, which had reduced them from such a high state to such a humble and sorrowful stupor. When Quisquis and Chalcuchima saw them, they were not satisfied with the sorrows they presented nor the words they had said about Huascar in their presence. Quisquis confronted them with disgraceful and dishonorable words, saying that Rahua Ocllo had given birth to Huascar while she was the mistress of Huayna Capac, so how could she be his Coya and queen, and [how could] her son become Inca and lord since she was [not] his legitimate wife, nor the principal [wife] among his women? After these [words], he added other reasons of scorn and insult against

671   Cabello Valboa (1951 [1586]:461) and Sarmiento de Gamboa (2007 [1572]:196) offer similar information on the punishments ordered by Quisquis.
672   Betanzos (1996 [1557]:269) also refers to the ritual of offering eyelashes and eyebrows.
673   While worded differently, the tone of this prayer is like those recorded by Molina (2011 [ca. 1575]:42–49). Cabello Valboa (1951 [1586]:461) and Sarmiento de Gamboa (2007 [1572]:196) offer similar descriptions of Quisquis's dealings with the *orejones*.

her and against Chuqui Huipa.[674] All this was to cause them more pain and to break their hearts, which, already afflicted with misfortune, neither could nor knew how to respond to the many unjust things they were told.[675]

How Quisquis ordered Huascar Inca to be taken out in public and what happened to him and the cruelties [that Quisquis] started to do

Nothing remained to be done to further break the hearts of Rahua Ocllo, Chuqui Huipa, and the other *orejones* who were imprisoned, than what Quisquis had done to humiliate, hurt and scorn them. So Quisquis [then] went to those who oversaw Huascar Inca and the other prisoners and ordered them to be brought out in public as they were, bound in ropes. So, this was done.

Huascar Inca was brought out tightly bound on a bed of *ichu*[676] rope, along with his brothers, Titu Atauchi and Tupa Atau, his senior adviser, and Inca Roca. As they emerged from the house where they were imprisoned, Quisquis's entire army started shouting, mocking, scorning, and taunting them. As they passed through the middle of the *orejones* that were sitting and surrounded by the army, they said: "Behold your lord, who said that in battle he would become fire and water to destroy and finish his enemies and [that] he would deliver them punishments never seen before."

When the *orejones* saw and heard this, they bowed their heads in sorrow, feeling an emotion so great in their hearts that it cannot be expressed, and suffered this affront and punishment with an inner weeping of their souls. Then Quisquis sat down [and] sent for Titu Atauchi and Tupa Atau,[677] brothers of Huascar, and Inca Roca, his counselor, as well as the other important prisoners. Huascar Inca was taken down from the bed of ropes where he was tied, and then [Quisquis] called for Rahua Ocllo, Huascar's mother, Chuqui Huipa, his wife, Huanca Auqui, and other captains, as well as the priests who had given the tassel to Huascar Inca, so that they could retract it in the presence of all. Quisquis asked Huascar Inca in

---

674 Cabello Valboa (1951 [1586]:461) and Sarmiento de Gamboa (2007 [1572]:197) offer similar descriptions of the treatment of Rahua Ocllo and Chuqui Huipa.

675 Folio 119r is blank.

676 This word is underlined (Murúa 2008 [1616]:119v).

677 Cabello Valboa (1951 [1586]:461) mentions Titu Atauchi; however, he does not mention Tupa Atau.

pure contempt: "Who made you lord and Inca when there were other children of Huayna Capac who were more deserving and worthier than you?" Hearing this question, Rahua Ocllo, turned to her son before he could answer a word and said: "Son, you deserve to be told this; in the end, all this toil is sent by the hand of the Creator because of the *[f.120r]* cruelties you have committed to your vassals, and the deaths you caused to your brothers and relatives without[678] any reason, having not done anything offensive."[679]

Huascar Inca answered his mother, saying: "Mother, leave us as we are men. What you spoke of has already been done and there is no solution now." He then turned turning to [Apu] Chalco Yupanqui, the elder priest of the Sun, and said: "You [should] speak and answer Quisquis's question, for you were there and know [the answer]." [Apu] Chalco Yupanqui replied to Quisquis: "What you ask me is true; I raised Huascar Inca before the Sun as lord, following the command of his father, Huayna Capac, who left him and ordered in his will, and because [of that] it was his right to be Inca, as he is the son of [a] Coya; having Rahua Ocllo as his mother, the legitimate wife of Huayna Capac."

Hearing these words Chalcuchima, who was present, rose with great anger and rage and shouted: "You lie! You are a deceiver, and I rightly think this of you. Everything you say is a lie. Huayna Capac did not send such [a message] when he died." Turning to Rahua Ocllo, Chalcuchima said: "If it is true, pound your son and beat him, and confront him." He spoke these words with contempt, and on hearing them Huascar Inca wept tears of blood from his heart and said in a loud voice: "Quisquis and Chalcuchima, stop your questioning. It is not for you to find out what you are asking, since you are only the subordinates of my brother Atahualpa, and this matter and argument is not between the *Hanan Cuzcos and Hurin Cuzcos*,[680] but between my brother and me, as we are both sons of Huayna Capac. I was lawfully and rightfully appointed Inca and Lord, as you well know. I will speak with my brother, and we will go to an agreement about this. You have little to learn from this or anything else." Hearing this, Quisquis was very upset by the ease with which Huascar Inca, his captive, had spoken to him. Almost losing control, he ordered [Huascar Inca] be returned to the prison with the other prisoners, and that they be carefully guarded so that they could not escape.

He then stood up together with Chalcuchima and said to the *orejones*, "Now that you are pardoned, go to Cuzco and spread the word everywhere, so those *[f.121r]*

678   A spelling error has been corrected (Murúa 2008 [1616]:120r).
679   Cabello Valboa (1951 [1586]:461) and Sarmiento de Gamboa (2007 [572]:197) offer similar information concerning this confrontation.
680   A spelling mistake has been corrected (Adorno 2008:102). Also, these words are underlined (Murúa 2008 [1616]:120r).

who have fled to the mountains, and those who have hidden, to lose their fear and come out in public, because all are forgiven." They spoke these words with care and deception, to calm, and then to catch and execute those whom they wanted.[681]

After Quisquis and Chalcuchima had spoken, the *orejones*, heartbroken and aggrieved, returned to Cuzco with immense sadness, saying: "Oh Creator, who gave being to the Incas, where are you now? How did you allow so many disasters and misfortunes to occur to them in the past and in the present? Why did you praise them and give them so much power for so little time?"[682] As they said these words, they shook their blankets toward where the opposing army was, intending it as a curse [a sign] of the misfortune that would come upon them. When they arrived in Cuzco, together with Rahua Ocllo, Huascar's mother, and Chuqui Huipa, his wife, went to their homes. There, their cries and shouts began again, for they had seen how the sad Huascar Inca remained in prison, and they feared he would be killed like the others who had died that day.[683]

The next morning, Quisquis and Chalcuchima, wanting to be more feared and to have their names resound throughout all the provinces of the kingdom due of the punishments that they inflicted, ordered all the Chachapoya and Cañari Indians who had been taken prisoner in battles, along with all the *caciques*, captains, and leaders who were detained in prison, be killed. This took place later with an unprecedented level of cruelty in a horrifying and terrifying spectacle; some were shot with arrows and flaming spears, others were killed by *macanas*, some were cut in half down the middle, some were impaled, and a thousand other kinds of horrible deaths.[684] All this was ordered to be done in this nation because Ullco Colla, the *cacique* of the Cañari, had provoked the two brothers, Atahualpa and Huascar Inca, inciting suspicions between them, possibly in an attempt to make them destroy each other in their wars, however, as previously mentioned, he paid a high [price] for this.[685]

---

681   Cabello Valboa (1951 [1586]:461) and Sarmiento de Gamboa (2007 [1572]:197) offer similar information concerning this confrontation.

682   While unique, the tone of this prayer is like those recorded by Molina (2011 [ca. 1575]:42–49).

683   Cabello Valboa (1951 [1586]:462) and Sarmiento de Gamboa (2007 [1572]:198) offer similar information concerning the end of this meeting.

684   Cabello Valboa (1951 [1586]:462) and Sarmiento de Gamboa (2007 [1572]:198) offer similar information concerning these punishments.

685   Folios 121r and 121v are blank.

[F.122R] CHAPTER 57

How Quisquis ordered, in the presence of Huascar Inca, many of his women killed and the mummy of Tupa Inca Yupanqui burnt

Quisquis was not content with having ordered the cruelties described [above] or having killed as many people as we have seen, or with having insulted the sad Huascar Inca with such offensive words, so the next day he, along with Chalcuchima, ordered all the pregnant women of Huascar, those who had recently given birth, their female servants, and their loved ones, come with their children along with all of Huascar's servants and their [servants], to the Quiuipay Pampa, leaving no one out. The unfortunate women, suspecting the misfortune and disaster that was about to befall them, had to do as they were ordered, so they left Cuzco, their cries rising to the sky, and arrived at Quiuipay, where they were ordered to be seated according to their rank.

Then they brought out Huascar Inca, tightly bound on a bed, as we have already mentioned, and surrounded by guards. To cause him more pain and anguish, Quisquis and Chalcuchima ordered all of his children, women, and servants to be slaughtered in front of him, which was a barbarous and horrendous deed. The soldiers began the slaughter like they were among meek sheep that they were ready to butcher. They killed some eighty sons and daughters of Huascar Inca, something that cannot be mentioned without tears. Among them, they killed a sister and lover of Huascar, Coya Miro, who had a son and a daughter of his, one in her arms and the other on her back. His sister, Chimpo Cisa, also died there.[686]

The sorrow that filled his broken and miserable heart cannot be expressed in words, nor even imagined. With a desperate utterance he turned to Apu Pacha Yachachic Viracocha, the Creator, saying: "O Creator, who gave me a life so brief, let the one who has caused me such pain experience suffering the same that I endure now in his presence and with his *[f.122v]* own eyes may he see the calamity that I see now with my children and loved ones, so that he may understand the distress that I feel in my heart."[687] With this he tried to hide his pain with a strong spirit, averting his gaze, unwilling to witness it.

Some of Huascar Inca's young girls escaped from the cruel and barbaric slaughter because they were neither pregnant nor in labor, pleading with Quisquis and Chalcuchima to spare them for Atahualpa because they were good looking and

---

686   Cabello Valboa (1951 [1586]:462–463) and Sarmiento de Gamboa (2007 [1572]:198) offer similar information. Betanzos (1996 [1557]:244) also describes the killing of Huascar's wives, but his description is closer to Sarmiento's than to Murúa's.

687   Cabello Valboa (1951 [1586]:463) also includes this prayer.

beautiful. Among these were Doña Elvira Chuna, a daughter of Cañar Capac, Doña Beatriz Caruamay Huay, the daughter of the Lord of Chinchaycocha, Doña Juana Tocto and Doña Cathalina Usica, who was the wife of Don Paullu and the mother of Don Carlos Inca. They were very fortunate because, after some time, they were baptized and were on the path of salvation for their souls. All the other women and young girls of Huascar Inca, who were the daughters of poor people, were killed in Chuquipampa[688] in different and horrible ways, cutting open their stomachs and breasts to ensure that there would be no trace of Huascar's lineage that could challenge Atahualpa in the future.[689]

After these deaths, and with Quisquis and Chalcuchima's insatiable appetite for human blood from those innocent [people] who had not offended them still unsatisfied, [Quisquis] turned his anger and rage to those who had been dead for many years. So that everyone would see his insatiable rage and to inflict his fury, [Quisquis] ordered the body of Tupa Inca Yupanqui be taken out and carried to Rocromuco,[690] which is now [a] *chacra* of the Santo Domingo convent, where he had it burnt.[691]

To do this with greater gravity and to instill more fear and terror in the *orejones* and the inhabitants of Cuzco, [Quisquis] had a large army from all nations come out with the body. They were accompanied by an infinite number of *mamaconas*, who were responsible for the deceased's service, as well as many of Tupa Inca Yupanqui's servants. There, [Quisquis] ordered them to be torn to pieces after they had seen the body of their lord burned. The next day, with their rage unabated, [Quisquis] ordered all the children, some of whom were still alive, as well as the grandchildren, descendants and servants who served [Tupa Inca Yupanqui], to go

---

688 This is a large plain within Sacsayhuaman. It was included within the Cuzco Ceque System (Bauer 1998:54).

689 Cobo (1979 [1653]:169, 173–176) and Sarmiento de Gamboa (2007 [1572]:199–200) offer similar information on these four individuals. Cabello Valboa (1951 [1586]:463) provides a similar list, noting that Mama Quizpe Cusi, the sister of Huascar (later called Doña Ines Yupanqui), Mama Usica, the mother of Don Carlos Inca (later named Doña Catalina), and Curi Cuillor also escaped. Elsewhere in his chronicle, Cobo (1979 [1653]:172) notes that of the daughters of Huayna Capac, Ines married Francisco Ampuero, Beatriz Quispe Quipi married Diego Hernández, and two other daughters married Francisco de Villacastín and Hernando de Soto.

690 Rocromuco was a shrine within the Cuzco Ceque System next to the Temple of the Sun (Bauer 1998:126; Rowe 1985:193). It is also mentioned by Cabello Valboa (1951 [1586]:464).

691 This was done because the mummy of Tupa Inca Yupanqui had participated in the marriage arrangements of Huascar. Cabello Valboa (1951 [1586]:464) and Sarmiento de Gamboa (2007 [1572]:199) provide similar information on the burning of Tupa Inca Yupanqui's mummy.

to Chuquipampa, [which is] next to the fortress,[692] saying that they wanted to talk to them and explain why they had killed the *[f.123r] mamaconas* and burnt the body of their lord and, Tupa Inca Yupanqui. Even though they were scared and frightened by so many deaths, they could not do anything else, and eventually, they had to obey the order. Once Quisquis had them [in Chuquipampa], he ordered them to be counted and found that there were almost a thousand grandchildren and great-grandchildren and descendants [of Tupa Inca Yupanqui], as well as a thousand servants. So, he ordered the most [important] servants and descendants to be killed, but many grandchildren and great-grandchildren escaped. Some of those who escaped died during the siege of Cuzco when the Spaniards were surrounded, while others remained alive by fleeing and hiding in the mountains and other places, where they lived in peace.[693]

The reason why Quisquis and Chalcuchima ordered the body of Tupa Inca Yupanqui to be taken out, dragged off, and finally killed[694] and destroyed, along with all the generations related to him, was because he was the father of Rahua Ocllo, the mother of Huascar Inca, and the grandfather of Huascar's father and mother. Thus, they sought to eradicate any trace of Huascar Inca's lineage, which was their motivation for committing the brutal killings and atrocities.

Not content with the things that I have already described, [Quisquis] began again to examine Huascar Inca's council, those who were closest and most favored by him, as well as those who had shown themselves to be on his side and against Atahualpa. When someone was found guilty, [Quisquis] ordered their execution, and those who denied an alleged accusation were tortured to death. As a result, weeping, sobbing, and terrible confusion filled Cuzco and its surroundings for days, and no one trusted anyone else, not even their father or brother. Those who survived waited in fear of being called to death at any moment. No one expected to live longer than what Quisquis and Chalcuchima desired, as they were viewed as cruelly fixated on death, injury, and the destruction of Huascar Inca's lineage.

After this was over, [Quisquis] ordered all the southern provinces, including Chile, Cuntisuyu, and Chinchaysuyu, to *[f.123v]* gather together and immediately recognize Atahualpa as their lord and Inca. This was to solidify and strengthen his authority, which he had not initially considered. However, Fortune showed him the way, [only] then to let him fall harder, as we will see. Having sent these mentioned

---

692   It is worth noting that Tupa Inca Yupanqui had a house behind Sacsayhuaman, so many of these individuals may have been living nearby (Bauer 1998:55).

693   Cabello Valboa (1951 [1586]:464) and Sarmiento de Gamboa (2007 [1572]:199) offer similar information on these killings.

694   It is worth noting that Murúa writes of the "killing" of the mummy of Tupa Inca Yupanqui.

messengers, [Quisquis] dispatched many people to Atahualpa, who brought with them all the dining ware that was in Cuzco as well as all the gold pitchers, pots, *aquillas*, cups used by to Indians drink from, along with the richest objects of silver and gold that were found [in Cuzco], and everything that had great value that belonged to Tupa Inca Yupanqui or Huascar Inca.[695] These items were later found in Cajamarca when the Spaniards captured Atahualpa, along with the highly esteemed[696] and valued gifts that the lords and *curacas* of the provinces had sent him.[697]

[*F.124V*] CHAPTER 58

How after learning of his victory, Atahualpa left for Cuzco and met with the Marquis Don Francisco Pizarro in Cajamarca

The blessed and happy centuries were approaching in which these Antarctic regions, shrouded in the darkness of idolatry, would be illuminated by the fire of the supernatural and divine faith. The lordship and dominion of Lucifer, the Prince of Darkness, who had possessed and enjoyed [the regions] in silence for so many years, would be transformed by Jesus[698] Christ, [the] eternal Word, [the] Son of the supreme Father, [the] Prince of Light and [the] heir of heavenly goods. This was a debt due, promised so many years ago in the Second Psalm, that the Gentiles were to be His inheritance,[699] and that through His ministers, the banner of the Life-giving Cross would be planted and [the banner] of Satan defeated. Multitudes of souls [would be saved] through the rebirth of baptism, which is also the door of the other sacraments, given to the soldiers of the Christian militia to free their bodies and minds from the hard yoke and servitude of the King of Pride. They would receive and hold on to the soft and gentle [rule] of the Emperor of Humility, and many deserving souls would enter the palaces of heavenly treasures they had earned through the passion and blood of Christ. [All this would happen] when the divine and incomprehensible wisdom of God decided to execute what is in His predetermined eternal idea. The trumpets of His priests would be heard in this New World, and the walls of Jericho would fall.[700]

---

695   Cabello Valboa (1951 [1586]:464) provides similar information on the sending of riches from Cuzco to Atahualpa.
696   A word has been corrected (Murúa 2008 [1616]:123v).
697   Folio 124r is blank.
698   A spelling error has been corrected (Murúa 2008 [1616]:124v).
699   Psalm 2:8: "Ask me, and I will make the nations your inheritance, the ends of the earth your possession."
700   In this introduction, Murúa turns from his historical narrative to address the reader.

Every day, Atahualpa was delighted and filled with pride at with the news of the defeat of his enemies and of their kin, along with the great victories his captains had achieved over those of his brother, Huascar Inca; most recently, of the unexpected capture of his own [brother] and how he had been locked prison. Just when the happiest, most prosperous, and peaceful fortune was revealed to him, [with] everything having turned out better than he first thought, or could imagine, or could wish for, *[f.125r]* [as] he already saw himself as the king and absolute Lord of his father's kingdoms and estates, his sad fortune turned upside down, or better stated, [when] the order of the supreme God overthrew his arrogance and pride, and brought about a tragic end for him, as we shall see.[701]

Atahualpa was found in Tomebamba by those of all the provinces who were going to give their obedience. He was lounging and taking pleasure in Tomebamba when Quisquis and Chalcuchima informed him of their fortunate events in the war. They brought him the golden litters in which Inca lords travel, [and he] held great parties and celebrations for everyone who was with him. He decided to go to Cuzco to be crowned and receive the fringe and insignia of Inca and lord, which was the only thing he still lacked to fulfill his desires.[702]

As [Atahualpa] left with a large and well-equipped army from all the nations surrounding Tomebamba and Quito, to increase the splendor, he was told that some people, the likes of which had never been seen before, were in Puerto Viejo. Some of them were riding large rams, which were [actually] horses, and they had beards and were white. They claimed to be messengers from the Pope and the Emperor. Upon hearing this unusual news, which included things never seen or heard of before, Atahualpa gathered all those in his council to ask where those people could have come from. [His council] answered that they must have been messengers sent by Viracocha, and from then on, the name Viracochas was used for the Spaniards. Although others [say that] the name Viracocha was given [to the Spaniards] because they were first seen leaving ships, [so] they were called "foam or fat of the sea," which is what the name Viracocha means.[703] [Atahualpa] did not care for the news, but he agreed to make his trip to Cuzco as planned. He left with great dignity and authority, walking slowly to Cajamarca.[704]

Because of the style of writing, this section is difficult to translate, but the sense is clear: with the arrival of the Spaniards, the doors of salvation opened and Lucifer was defeated.

701   Cabello Valboa (1951 [1586]:465) provides similar information on Atahualpa's reaction to winning the civil war.

702   Cabello Valboa (1951 [1586]:465) provides similar information on Atahualpa's plans to travel to Cuzco.

703   Cobo (1979 [1653]:170) and Sarmiento de Gamboa (2007 [1572]:200) offer similar information on the name of Viracocha.

704   Cabello Valboa (1951 [1586]:465–466) and Sarmiento de Gamboa (2007 [1572]:200) provide similar information on the departure of Atahualpa for Cajamarca.

While traveling, [Atahualpa] sent messengers to Quisquis and Chalcuchima instructing them to send his brother, Huascar Inca, as well as his other brothers who were in prison to him in Cajamarca, so that there he could ask them many things that he had in mind. Quisquis and Chalcuchima immediately did what Atahualpa had commanded, and they sent [Huascar and the other brothers] from Cuzco with many people to carefully guard them so that they could not escape. A month later, Chalcuchima left Cuzco with part of the army and walked toward Cajamarca where Atahualpa was.[705]

[f.135v] While all this was occurring, the Spaniards, led by the Marquis[706] Don Francisco Pizarro, had already disembarked and were slowly walking along the coast toward Trujillo.[707] Upon receiving news that Atahualpa, the lord and king, was in Cajamarca with a very powerful army, they went there. When they arrived, Atahualpa was in the baths of Cono,[708] and the Spaniards took possession of the strong positions that were in Cajamarca. They did not want to take any of the gold and silver objects, which were there, which were plentiful, nor the large number of precious clothes that the Inca always kept storage.[709] They only took the food that they needed from what was there. [When] Caro Atoneo,[710] the Lord of Cajamarca, saw [the Spaniards], he was amazed by their strange size, differences in dress, and beards. He sent word to Atahualpa that the Viracochas had arrived, and that he had never seen people like them before, and that he was afraid to look at them.[711]

The Marquis Don Francisco Pizarro, wanting to gain the friendship of Atahualpa by good means, sent him two messengers, Felipillo and Martín, who were Indian translators they had brought with them.[712] [Pizarro] also sent presents of *chaquira*[713]

---

705   Cabello Valboa (1951 [1586]:465–466) and Sarmiento de Gamboa (2007 [1572]:200) provide similar information on the order to bring Huascar to Cajamarca.

706   The title of Marquis for Pizarro is incorrect at this point in time, as it would come later in his life.

707   Sarmiento de Gamboa (2007 [1572]:201) provides similar information on the movement of Pizarro on the coast.

708   These hot springs are about six kilometers from the center of Cajamarca.

709   Xerez (1985 [1534]:116) provides a detailed description of the storehouses in Cajamarca: "In this town of Caxamalca they found certain houses filled with clothes packed in bales that reached to the ceilings of the houses. They say that it was a depot to supply the army. The Christians took what they wanted, and still the houses remained so full that what was taken seemed not to be missed. The cloth is the best that has been seen in the Indias. The greater part of it is very fine and elegant wool, and the rest is cotton of various colors and rich hues."

710   Cabello Valboa (1951 [1586]:469) writes "Carbacongo."

711   Cabello Valboa (1951 [1586]:469) provides similar information on the arrival of the Spaniards in Cajamarca.

712   Felipillo and Martín were two of three men captured off the coast of Ecuador during Pizarro's second voyage (1528) who were then trained as translators.

713   This word is underlined (Murúa 2008 [1616]:125v).

and other items that were greatly admired and valued by them, which he had brought from Spain. [The translators] said he and his companions had come to that land as messengers from the Pope and the Emperor, to make known the single Almighty God who created the heavens, earth, sun, the stars, and all other visible things.[714] The messengers urged Atahualpa to come to Cajamarca, where Pizarro was waiting for him, so they could meet and calmly discuss what he had to say.[715]

[F.126V] CHAPTER 59

How the Marquis Don Francisco Pizarro met with Atahualpa in the field and captured him

Atahualpa received the messengers of the Marquis Don Francisco Pizarro, Felipillo and Martín, very well and greeted them with great kindness and love. When they told him that the Spaniards were ambassadors of the Creator, he gathered his advisors and asked them what he should do. They all advised him to go, receive, and see the Spaniards. With this [Atahualpa] agreed to go to Cajamarca to see them.[716] He then ordered his army to proclaim that no person accompanying him should carry weapons of any kind because, having learned such wonderful news and having received the messengers of the Creator, weapons were not necessary. He [even] took great care to look in the *chuspas*,[717] which are the little bags that the Indians carry under their left arms, to make sure [that] they did not carry hidden stones or other weapons that could offend the ambassadors.[718]

---

714   Cabello Valboa (1951 [1586]:469–470) provides similar information on Pizarro's message.
715   Folio 126r is blank.
716   Two groups of Spaniards were sent to visit Atahualpa, totaling more than thirty-five horsemen and the translators. The visit is well described in various accounts, as it was the first face-to-face meeting between Atahualpa and the strangers who had just entered the kingdom. The first group was led by Hernando de Soto, and the second was sent as a backup and included Hernando Pizarro. Atahualpa was most impressed with Hernando Pizarro, since he was the brother of Francisco Pizarro. One of the most interesting of the many descriptions of the meeting between the embassy of Pizarro and Atahualpa is provided by Betanzos (1996 [1557]:254–255). It appears to have been provided by an eyewitness who was in Atahualpa's camp, perhaps Angelina Yupanqui (Cusi Rimay Ocllo), a wife of Atahualpa who later married Betanzos. Other excellent descriptions are provided by Hernando Pizarro (1872 [1533]:115–116), Juan Ruiz de Arce (1933 [ca. 1545]), and Diego Trujillo (1948 [1571])—all of whom visited Atahualpa's camp that afternoon.
717   This word is underlined (Murúa 2008 [1616]:126v).
718   Cabello Valboa (1951 [1586]:470) provides similar information about how the men of Atahualpa left without weapons.

After finishing this precaution, which [would prove to be] so unwise, he placed his entire army, which was very large, in formation and left the baths with unmatched majesty and display. He was carried on a litter of the finest gold, which we have already said was brought from Cuzco. The seat was a plank of [gold] with a cushion of very fine wool, adorned with rich stones. He wore his tassel of fine red wool, which was the royal insignia, on his forehead and was surrounded by his most important captains, *caciques*, and Lords of the provinces who had come with him. Some on foot while others [were carried] in litters,[719] which were given as a great favor to the leaders, as up to that point they did not have any.

He slowly walked and arrived at Cajamarca at midday, where the Marquis Don Francisco Pizarro was waiting for him with his men in formation. As [Atahualpa] drew near, Fray Vicente de Valverde, a priest of the Santo Domingo Order, who later became the first universal bishop of all of Peru and who was killed and eaten by the Indians of the Island of Puná, came out to [meet] him.[720]

The priest was carrying a cross and a missal[721] or breviary, and was accompanied by Felipillo, an Indian translator of the Marquis, and some soldiers. Father Fray Vicente explained [to Atahualpa] the purpose and intention of his arrival at this kingdom. He told him that they had come from the Pope and the Emperor to give him [f.127r] news of very important things for the good of his soul and salvation. Mixed within these reasons were others that might seem insolent and out of order at first sight for a king, as [Atahualpa] might first only believe what his barbaric and uneducated understanding could reach, and [he] had never heard of the supernatural, nor [things] that exceeded human capacity, as his understanding was not enlightened by the rays of the divine faith; since to believe lightly is a sign of a lightness of heart.

Although some accounts of what happened during that time have been circulated, not one of them can be considered completely true, as they contradict one another according to the desires of those who tell them. Even among the many who were present and guilty. Therefore, I will not repeat them, only [reporting] that after Father Fray Vicente said to Atahualpa that he was teaching what that book said, he looked at [the book] and tried to listen to it, and when he heard nothing, he became irritated and angry. Realizing how different this speech was from the

---

719   Xerez (1985 [1534]) notes that beside Atahualpa there were two other lords on litters and two others being carried in hammocks. One of litters carried the lord of the coastal Kingdom of Chincha (Pizarro 1921 [1571]:180, 443), and the other was perhaps the Lord of Cajamarca. Both of these lords were killed in the battle along with dozens of Atahualpa's advisors and perhaps as many as 6,000 to 7,000 soldiers.

720   Cabello Valboa (1951 [1586]:470) provides similar information concerning the death of Valverde. Pizarro (1921 [1571]:417) also notes the death of Valverde on the Island of Puná. Murúa again mentions the death of Valverde in book 3, chapter 18 of his chronicle.

721   Cabello Valboa (1951 [1586]:417–418, 428) just lists a missal.

information he had been given and from what he had anticipated and concluded based on his conversation with the messengers, who he thought were from the Creator and Viracocha, [Atahualpa] threw the book on the ground.[722]

Unhappy with not hearing what he had expected, and of being asked for tribute and recognition of [the king of Spain], whom he did not know, [Atahualpa] threw the book on the ground with disdain. With this Father Vicente de Valverde cried out: "Christians, the evangels of God are on the ground!" Don Francisco Pizarro charged with his own [men] and when they arrived Atahualpa's litter, they hit him and knocked him down from it.[723] The Indians saw that their king had fallen on the ground and that the Spaniards were waving their hands and taking advantage of their weapons, especially their harquebuses, which they had never seen or heard before, [and which] seemed [to cause] rays of fire to come down from the sky to burn them. As they had all come without any weapons, as was stated, they all fled, leaving the unfortunate king and lord at the mercy of the Spaniards, who were very pleased with their good luck. Without any loss of life, they captured Atahualpa and brought him to Cajamarca. He was in a room that still stands today, shackled and under guards who carefully watched over him.[724] The sad Atahualpa, who in the morning was so commanding and respected, and held so much power surrounded by the multitude of his army that guarded and respected him, found himself in the afternoon at the mercy of those who treated him without any respect or courtesy. After such a sudden reversal of fortune, he was left with no one to command; this being an example for the great poten [f.127v] tates and monarchs of the world, who reign with pride and arrogance, disregarding the changes in the world of the fate of Inca Kingdom.[725]

When Atahualpa, both courageous and unlucky, was imprisoned, he did not know how to escape because he saw the ferocity and aggressiveness of the people he had presumed to be messengers of the Creator. So, he believed that the most effective solution was to offer a ransom. He said that he would pay a vast sum; [Atahualpa] stood in the room where he was imprisoned, making a line on the wall, saying that he would fill [the room] with gold and silver up to that line, and give it to them if they released him and granted him his freedom. [Atahualpa did

---

722   Sarmiento de Gamboa (2007 [1572]:201) provides only a few sentences on the capture of Atahualpa, telling his readers that it would be described in more detail in the third part of his book. Unfortunately, that section was never completed, or it has been lost.

723   Guaman Poma de Ayala (2004 [1615]:382 [384]) includes a drawing showing the meeting between Pizarro and Atahualpa, which he suggests occurred at the baths rather than in the center of the city.

724   Cabello Valboa (1951 [1586]:470–471) provides similar information.

725   Crossed out by Remón (Adorno 2008:107; Murúa 2004 [1616]:127v).

this] because he already knew [that] the personality and greed of the Spaniards were ravenous, and this was his way to extinguish and satisfy, it if he could. [The other Spaniards], along with the Marquis Don Francisco Pizarro and his brothers, all accepted his [offer]⁷²⁶ ~~as if the prisoner was captured in a legitimate war and as if the war that was held against him was just and [it was] approved of in such a way that they had lawfully defeated him, [being] provoked from injury and bad deeds by him [or he had] denied them food, harm the Spaniards or wanted to kill them. However, as insatiable greed, is the root, source, and origin of all evils, it blinded them and clouded their judgment, so they did not understand how they were proceeding against the rule of justice and fairness. There is no reason to be surprised that it seemed lawful and just to them to ransom a king so unjustly detained and imprisoned against reason and truth.~~⁷²⁷

Once the ransom was agreed upon and [Atahualpa] was promised his freedom if he delivered what he offered, Atahualpa sent [a message to] Quisquis, (either with the approval of the Marquis Don Francisco Pizarro or not), who was in Cuzco with his army, telling his general of his misfortune and ominous fate. [He explained] how he had been imprisoned by the Spaniards, whom he had judged to be ambassadors of the Viracocha, and how he was detained, suffering, and feeling great sorrow, and that [Quisquis] alone could save it. So, with the greatest thoroughness possible, [Quisquis should] collect all the silver and gold he could find, including the dishes he had collected, and all the gold and silver cups, pitchers, and pots that he had collected and kept for himself in Cuzco, because that was what the Spaniards wanted most of everything in the world, so they needed to obtain it.⁷²⁸ Atahualpa warned Quisquis that his life was in danger by the Spaniards if the ransom did not arrive quickly. He also said it would be best if his brother Huascar Inca and the other prisoners were quickly sent to him as well.⁷²⁹

---

726   Cabello Valboa (1951 [1586]:471) provides similar information on Atahualpa making his famous ransom offer.

727   Remón removed this criticism of the Spaniards' actions (Adorno 2008:107; Murúa 2008 [1616]:127v). Also, see Murúa (2008 [1616]:58r) for a similar reflection on evil.

728   Cabello Valboa (1951 [1586]:471) provides similar information on Atahualpa's instructions to Quisquis and the order he sent to Huascar.

729   Folio 128r is blank.

[F.128V] CHAPTER 60

How the Marquis Don Francisco Pizarro sent [soldiers] to Cuzco and Pachacamac and [how] Atahualpa ordered his brother, Huascar Inca, killed

A few days after Atahualpa sent his general Quisquis for the abovementioned ransom, the Marquis Don Francisco Pizarro began inquiring and asking about the secrets of the land so that he could proceed more easily with its discovery and conquest. He gradually learned who Huascar Inca was, and how he was the legitimate son of Huayna Capac, the absolute lord of the entire kingdom, and the differences that had begun years before between Huascar Inca and Atahualpa, and the great wars and battles that had taken place. [He also learned about] the powerful army that Quisquis and Chalcuchima had in Cuzco, and of the extreme cruelties they had committed in Cuzco to the vanquished, including all the children of Huascar Inca, his wives, as well as to other [members] of his lineage and kin. Also, the abominable deaths inflicted on the vanquished, the destruction they had done, and the looting of all the gold and silver treasures and objects of the Incas.[730]

When the Marquis learned of this, he decided to send [Sancho de] Villegas and Martín Bueno[731] to Cuzco, to explore the land, and evaluate its strengths, locations, populations, fertility, and other characteristics to settle it so that they could report back to Spain and the Emperor, our lord with all this information. Most importantly, they were instructed to carefully dismantle and destroy the Temple of the Sun, which was so famous and revered in this kingdom, and to collect all the riches that were in it. These treasures were then to be taken to Cajamarca, which was the primary part[732] of [Pizarro's] objective and desire. Having also heard of another temple celebrated by the Indians that was in Pachacamac, four leagues from the

---

730   Cabello Valboa (1951 [1586]:472) provides similar information on what Pizarro learned about the civil war.

731   Here, Murúa and Cabello Valboa (1951 [1586]:472) are incorrect in naming the first Spaniards to visit Cuzco. They are not alone in this confusion: Pedro Pizarro (1921 [1571]:207), who was in Cajamarca, lists two Spaniards (Martín Bueno and Pedro Martín de Moguer) and an unnamed Inca official. Other writers, such as Agustín de Zárate (1981 [1555]:101), who was also in Cajamarca and who was later copied by Garcilaso de la Vega (1966 [1609]:287), incorrectly suggests that the expedition included Hernando de Soto and Pedro del Barco. Cieza de León (1998 [1553–1554]:224) correctly records the names of all three Spaniards (Martín Bueno, Pedro Martín de Moguer, and Pedro de Zárate) and notes that they were also accompanied by an Inca official. Hernando Pizarro (1872 [1533]:125) suggests that they were also accompanied by a Black slave, who returned from Cuzco early.

732   A spelling error has been corrected (Murúa 2008 [1616]:128v).

City of Kings,[733] [Pizarro] sent Captain [Hernando de] Soto and Pedro del Barco[734] to destroy it and take the riches that were there and bring them to Cajamarca.[735]

After both parties had left, accompanied by people and guides to fulfill their orders, Captain [Hernando de] Soto and Pedro del Barco met Huascar Inca, his mother, his wife, Huanca Auqui, Tupa Atau, and the other imprisoned brothers at Taparaco.[736] They were being taken, well guarded by many people [to Cajamarca], where Atahualpa had ordered them to appear before him *[f.129r]*. Huascar Inca knew what had happened to his brother and how [Atahualpa] was imprisoned under the power of the Viracochas. He was very pleased, thinking that there was a possibility that he would be released from his current captivity and freed from his brother. [He might] even return to his former position and majesty with the help of the Spaniards. With this spirit and desire, he sent for Captain [Hernando de] Soto and Pedro del Barco and told them about his situation. He explained how he had been captured and imprisoned by the captains of his brother, Atahualpa, and the atrocities committed against his sons, daughters, and women. He also [told them] how [a captain] was taking him as prisoner [to Cajamarca] by order [of Atahualpa], and that he feared that they would kill him along with his brothers, mother, and wife on his arrival. [Furthermore, Huascar Inca stated,] that since [Hernando de Soto and Pedro del Barco] were going to Pachacamac in the name of the Marquis Don Francisco Pizarro, they could and should not hesitate to release him from those who were guarding him, return from [Taparaco] and from there take him in Cajamarca to be presented before the Marquis. Also, they should not bother to search for gold, silver, or tableware, as he was willing to provide them with so much of it that they would not desire more because he knew where it was guarded and was willing to share it with them. But Captain [Hernando de] Soto and Pedro del Barco, [filled] with greed and eagerness to reach Pachacamac, where they knew there were great treasures, refused to return with him [to Cajamarca] or remove those who held him as a prisoner. This resulted in the quick and miserable end of Huascar Inca's life.[737]

At this time, the Marquis Pizarro, having learned with greater substance and truth of the issues and affairs between the two brothers, understood with certainty

---

733   Now called Lima. Murúa provides a detailed description of the City of Kings in book 3, chapters 13 and 14 of his chronicle.

734   The Spanish forces, which contained some twenty to twenty-five men, that went to loot Pachacamac, included Hernando Pizarro and Miguel Estete. The latter wrote a detailed report of the journey, which was included within Xerez's narration of the conquest.

735   Cabello Valboa (1951 [1586]:472) provides similar information.

736   Taparaco is in the region of Huánuco. Murúa and Cabello Valboa (1951 [1586]:472) seem to be the only writers to mention this place.

737   Zárate (1981 [1555]:107) presents a similar description of these events, as does Cabello Valboa (1951 [1586]:472–473).

and without a doubt [that] Huascar Inca was the legitimate [successor] of Huayna Capac and the true lord of the entire kingdom, and [that] Atahualpa was a usurper and a bastard, and he ordered that [Atahualpa's] brother, Huascar Inca, be quickly brought to him, as he wanted to learn some things that might benefit both of them.

Upon seeing the great persistence with which the Marquis was requesting to see his brother and the extreme desire with which he was ordering him [to come to Cajamarca], [Atahualpa] thought that if Huascar Inca appeared before the Marquis, he would relate many things that would not benefit him, and [Huascar would] complain about his imprisonment, his state of affairs, [and the] [in]justice[s] and the wrongs done to him by [Atahualpa's] captains in Cuzco, which might result in [Pizarro] setting his brother free and putting him in possession of his kingdom. Furthermore, [Atahualpa thought] that he would lose [his kingdom] and be defeated. To prevent this from happening, *[f.129v]* [Atahualpa] quickly and with great secrecy dispatched messengers[738] to the captain who was bringing [Huascar Inca] as a prisoner with the others, [stating] wherever they found him, he should immediately kill Huascar Inca, his mother, wife, and brothers without delay.[739]

Atahualpa's messengers quickly completed their journey, pressured to bring a permanent end to Huascar's misfortune, bad luck, sorrows, and miseries by killing him. They found him near Andamarca,[740] and conveyed Atahualpa's order to the captain guarding the prisoners, to kill them. Although [the captain] thought what his lord, Atahualpa, ordered him to do was a grave and arduous task, he immediately followed the order, and killed Huascar Inca, [the] true king and Lord of these kingdoms.[741] It is a great dishonor that such a mighty king ended [his life] in this way, in the hands of an executioner who reportedly drowned him.[742] With [the death of

---

738   Betanzos mentions that this messenger was Cusi Yupanqui. However, throughout Betanzos's chronicle, Cusi Yupanqui, the brother of Betanzos's wife, holds an oversized role in the civil war.

739   Cabello Valboa (1951 [1586]:472–473) and Sarmiento de Gamboa (2007 [1572]:202) provide similar information.

740   Also written as Antamarca.

741   Guaman Poma de Ayala (2004 [1615]:115) provides an illustration of Huascar Inca flanked by Quisquis and Chalcuchima at Andamarca.

742   Cabello Valboa (1951 [1586]:471) provides similar information. Sarmiento de Gamboa (2007 [1572]:202) writes that the body of Huascar Inca was cut into pieces and thrown into the Yanamayo River. Cobo (1979 [1653]:170) suggests that the body was burned, but he provides even more detailed information on the location, writing that Huascar was killed "as they were leaving the Tambo of Andamarca, thirty leagues short of Cajamarca and three leagues past a lake called Conchucos." Guaman Poma de Ayala (2004 [1615]:114) and Betanzos (1996 [1557]:268) also state that Atahualpa was killed near the town of Andamarca. Xerez (1985 [1534]) places Andamarca four leagues from Conchucos. Estete (1872 [1535]:93) also writes that Andamarca was where the road to Pachacamac

Huascar Inca], the straight and true line of the Incas, Lords of these kingdoms, who were raised and crowned through the ceremonies that they used among themselves from Manco Inca [*sic*], [the] first Lord of Cuzco, who gave birth to this noble family, until Huascar, who represented the last generation of legitimate kings, ended and finished. As this history has shown, there were twelve Incas and lords.

By the same order, Huascar's brothers, Titu Atauchi, Tupa Atau, and Huanca Auqui, died with him. Also killed were [Apu] Chalco Yupanqui, the high priest [of the Sun], Rahua Ocllo, the mother [of Huascar] and [the] legitimate wife of Huayna Capac, Chuqui Huipa, [the] wife of Huascar, and all the other captains and principals who had been imprisoned at Cuzco. This was another barbarous act of cruelty, similar to those committed by Quisquis and Chalcuchima when they defeated them [in Cuzco].[743]

I do not know any heart of diamond that remains unmoved by the deaths, destructions, misfortunes, and desolation that were brought on and befell the house and lineage of King Huascar Inca. These were the result and consequences of the lies and discord sown between these two brothers by Ullco Colla, [the] *cacique* of the Cañari, and captain Atoc, who perhaps desired to incite wars between them. It is possible that Atahualpa [would] never [have] had [the] intention or thought of rebelling against his brother Huascar, if they [had] not provoked him, or [if he] had not have been moved to deny his obedience after feeling [Huascar's] anger against himself and the fear that he would *[f.130r]* kill him, as he had done to the other brothers who had gone from Quito [to Cuzco] with the body of his father. Although until he saw himself provoked and that he was being ordered from Quito [to Cuzco], [Atahualpa] never gave signs of what he had in mind, if he even had it, but everything he did resulted in greater misfortune and misery for the two brothers. Despite ordering the death of Huascar Inca, as we have seen, in Andamarca, Atahualpa did not win, not by a nose, [as he] died in Cajamarca. Although his death provided hope for eternal life [through baptism], as we shall see in chapter 63.[744]

---

joins that of the highlands going to Cuzco, and that it was three leagues from Pombo (Pomabamba). Diego de Trujillo (1948 [1571]) states that Andamarca was three leagues from Huamachuco.

743 Cabello Valboa (1951 [1586]:473) provides similar information on the death of Huascar and his close kin.

744 Folio 130v is blank.

[F.131R] CHAPTER 61

The Coya Chuqui Huipa, [the] wife of Huascar Inca

To maintain the organization that we have established in this book, where we discuss the life and deeds of an Inca followed by those of his wife, I will provide only a brief account of this Coya here. [This is because] we have [already] mentioned his wife, the Coya Chuqui Llanto, also known as Chuqui Huipa, in the life of Huascar Inca and her marriage and [other] events, where they are combined with those of her husband's.

Of all the queens who [reigned] over these provinces, if we were to designate any as wretched and unhappy,[745] it would be the Coya Chuqui Llanto and her mother, Rahua Ocllo, since they saw with their own eyes the many misfortunes [and] unfortunate deaths that we have described, caused by Quisquis and Chalcuchima. They witnessed as many [tragedies] as any Inca saw, heard, experienced, or lived through in their lifetime.

Chuqui Huipa was a woman of pleasant disposition and beauty, despite being somewhat dark, which was true for all her lineage. When she left her house, she wore lavish and ornate clothing and was accompanied by a vast number of principal Indians and her servants and [was] surrounded by many elegantly dressed ñustas. Her palace walls were painted with different colors, as she was particularly fond of that, and the tapestries and draperies were made of very fine *cumbi*[746] with different figures that were carefully crafted in those times. This lady died with her husband, Huascar Inca, and her mother, Rahua Ocllo, in Andamarca, as ordered by [Atahualpa]. Therefore, it can be said with certainty she did not experience the greatness and power of her kingdom. Because of her violent death, there is little information concerning her burial. [However,] they would have buried her with her husband where she was killed, [but] without the solemnity according to their queens.[747]

---

745   Guaman Poma de Ayala (2004 [1615]:142) provides a drawing of Chuqui Llanto crying.
746   This word is underlined (Murúa 2008 [1616]:131r).
747   Folio 131v is blank.

[F.132R] CHAPTER 62

How Atahualpa mourned for his brother Huascar
and [how] Chalcuchima was captured

After the captain ordered the pitiful deaths of Huascar Inca, his mother, wife, and brothers, he dispatched messengers to Atahualpa, his lord, telling him that his order had been carried out and that [the] hindrance posed [by Huascar Inca] had been removed. Upon hearing the news in prison, Atahualpa was overcome with sadness and tears, displaying profound emotional distress by weeping and feigning mourning. When this news reached the Marquis Pizarro, he went to see [Atahualpa] to understand why he was sad and weeping. He asked [Atahualpa] why he was crying, dressed for mourning, and so upset. In response Atahualpa stated that he had received news of his brother's, Huascar Inca's, death from a certain illness while traveling to [Cajamarca]. Upon hearing this, the Marquis told him that Huascar could not be dead, because he knew that he was in good health and near Cajamarca, and that [Atahualpa] should not believe whoever had told him such a lie, and that he would see [Huascar Inca] very soon and they would be happily [reunited] and could discuss important matters together. With this, the Marquis departed, [but] questioned what [Atahualpa] had told him and made inquiries into whether [Huascar Inca] was dead. Numerous individuals came forward to tell the Marquis the truth of what happened and how [Huascar Inca], [along] with his mother, wife, brothers, and other Indians and captains who came as prisoners with him had been killed by order of Atahualpa himself. They refuted the notion that [Huascar Inca] had perished from an illness and regarded it a lie and a trick, just like Atahualpa's weeping. Among those who told the Marquis Pizarro of this event was a bastard Indian named Huaritito,[748] [a] brother of Huascar Inca, who had been there. He divulged this, wanting to revenge his brother's death, or to prevent the death from being covered up.[749]

The Marquis Pizarro deeply regretted the death of Huascar Inca, especially as it took place before he met him. Undoubtedly, had he arrived [f.132v] [in Cajamarca], he would have been willing to do whatever the Marquis wanted and would have given an infinite quantity of gold and silver in exchange for being set free and have revenge against his brother Atahualpa. Furthermore, he would have revealed the most important secrets of this kingdom, including the many places where the

---

748 Cabello Valboa (1951 [1586]:474) writes "Guari Titu." Sarmiento de Gamboa does not mention this witness.

749 Cabello Valboa (1951 [1586]:473–474) provides similar information on Atahualpa's and Pizarro's conversation.

Indians, leaders, and governors had hidden and kept the treasures of the *huacas* and the Inca, which were vast. While some treasures have been discovered to this day, many others remain hidden, as it is not known where they are buried.

[Furthermore,] it would have been of great benefit for pacifying the land, because on seeing himself free by the hands of the Spaniards, Huascar Inca [would have] ordered everything be sorted out as it would have been advantageous for him to have them on his side. The Marquis, along with his captains and soldiers, deeply regretted his death, as they had expected to receive more riches from him since he was the natural lord and king who possessed everything, which was the main reason and goal for all those who had come with the Marquis.

The Marquis also learned that Chalcuchima, under orders of Atahualpa, was coming toward Cajamarca with a large army. In order to present this, he dispatched a Spanish soldier along with an *orejon* Indian named Ancamarca Mayta, to reach Captain [Hernando de] Soto and Pedro del Barco and tell them to turn back immediately upon receiving this order, and try by any means to seize Chalcuchima, disband his army, and bring him before the Marquis, as he wanted to confront him with Atahualpa. The soldier and the *orejon* walked with such speed that they caught up with Captain de Soto, and together with his forces, they proceeded toward the Jauja Valley, where they had learned Chalcuchima was located.[750]

When they arrived at Jauja, they found Chalcuchima, who was gathering many Yauyos and Huancas.[751] Not content with the cruelties and deaths that he had inflicted on Huascar Inca, all his relatives, friends, and favorites in Cuzco, he now wanted to severely punish the Yauyos and Huancas for being *aylluscas*, who were [designated] to Huascar's chamber and reserved for his use only. There Ancamarca Mayta, who had come with the Spaniards on orders of the Marquis *[f.133r]*, discussed many issues with Chalcuchima. Eventually, they told [Chalcuchima] that the Marquis Don Francisco Pizarro, who had come from very distant lands, had a great desire to see him, and that is why he sent for him and [why] they were there to get him.

To this, Chalcuchima replied with some disdain, "How does the Apu (which means lord) know of me, that he should send for me from so far away?" In response, Ancamarca Mayta, showed great ferocity and arrogance, indicating little regard for Chalcuchima, saying, "What are you talking about? It is not enough that you have killed all our brothers and relatives in Cuzco, but now you want to kill these poor people and your thirst for bloodshed. Will your cruelties never end? Will you never stop killing so many innocent people?" After saying these words,

---

750   Cabello Valboa (1951 [1586]:474) provides similar information on the search for
        Chalcuchima.
751   Cabello Valboa (1951 [1586]:474) also mentions these groups.

[Ancamarca Mayta] emboldened by the favor and encouragement he received from the Spaniards, raised his hand, and slapped [Chalcuchima], telling him: "Let's go!" and "There is no need to wait any longer because Atahualpa, your lord, is a prisoner under the power of the Marquis."

When [Ancamarca Mayta] insulted Chalcuchima, it was the first time that such a thing had ever happened to him, so he stood up from where he was sitting and grabbed [Ancamarca Mayta], and the two wrestled, struggling to overpower each other. No one in Chalcuchima's army, who were there in great numbers, dared to help him in any way as they were fearfully watching the Spaniards, the likes of which they had never seen. [The fight continued] until the Spaniards intervened and separated them. After they had made peace, Ancamarca Mayta spoke in a loud voice, filled with confidence and self-assurance, to the Huancas and Yauyos, "Arise, brothers, and prepare yourselves with what everything needed to go to see the Marquis Don Francisco Pizarro. There is no other Inca or lord, but he who holds Atahualpa prisoner, and we must all obey him." The Huancas and Yauyos were very pleased with these orders, [feeling] like they had escaped a difficult death and had been saved from the deadly hands of their principal enemy. So, they arose, leaving Chalcuchima and his people, who were amazed by Ancamarca Mayta's words and actions. They could not believe that there was an Indian or an *orejon* in the world who would dare to lay his hands on [Chalcuchima]. However, the circumstances and times had changed, as we see such things daily.[752]

When Chalcuchima returned to *[f.133v]* his seat, burning with anger, and saw that the *orejon* spoke so freely and that the Spaniards favored him, he did not dare to move or contradict what was said. So, he kept silent, feeling great pain and rage in his heart, as he was not accustomed to hearing such things and was amazed to learn that Atahualpa was a prisoner. The next morning, Chalcuchima went with his people to the *pampa*,[753] saddened by what they had seen. Captain [Hernando de] Soto, Pedro del Barco, and the other Spaniards also went out to meet Chalcuchima. They told him to get ready to go to where the Marquis Pizarro was, as he was waiting for him, and that the Marquis Pizarro had specifically sent them to bring him. Chalcuchima replied that he did not want to go so quickly and that he would prepare himself slowly and take the things that he had prepared for his lord, Atahualpa. [He suggested] that they should go to the Marquis, and he would come later. Upon hearing this and seeing his unwillingness to go, and fearing that he might gather people against them, Captain de Soto and the other Spaniards decided that it was best to take him by force. So, they grabbed him without anyone in his army, who

---

752   Cabello Valboa (1951 [1586]:477) provides similar information on this encounter.
753   This word is underlined (Murúa 2008 [1616]:133v).

were watching, daring to prevent it. They tied him up, put him on a horse that they had prepared, and left Jauja to return to Cajamarca, where the Marquis awaited them. They took great care to guard him, to prevent him from fleeing.[754] Many of his servants and captains, some as prisoners and others on their own volition, went along with him, to see how the affair would end.[755]

[F.134V] CHAPTER 63[756]

How the Marquis Pizarro confronted Chalcuchima with Atahualpa and how he ordered Atahualpa killed

~~The apostle Saint Paul saw that greed was the source and fountain of all evils. It incites and insists on everything.[757] It pulls people by the hair as if they are blind. Those who truly have it in their hearts justify and encourage all unjust and perverse things. They do not respect any law or follow any commandments. They kill their own brothers, violate their faith, break friendships, overshadow truth, and undermine and discard justice. We see a good example of this in the present chapter regarding what the Marquis Don Francisco Pizarro and the Spaniards did to the unfortunate Atahualpa.~~[758]

Captain [Hernando de] Soto, Pedro del Barco, Ancamarca Mayta, the *orejon*, arrived at Cajamarca, with Chalcuchima as a prisoner. There, they put him in a separate prison from where Atahualpa was because the Marquis Pizarro wanted to judge and confront him, which was best done with Atahualpa being present. [The Marquis Pizarro] questioned one, and [then] the other, with each one trying to exculpate themselves and charge the other with guilt for all the damages and deaths that had occurred and taken place. Atahualpa denied commanding [Chalcuchima] to go to Cuzco, or to kill so many people there, or to commit such cruelties and

---

754   Estete (1872 [1535]:89, 90) and Hernando Pizarro (1872 [1533]), who were both at Jauja, suggest that Chalcuchima agreed on his own to travel to Cajamarca. In contrast, Cabello Valboa (1951 [1586]:477–478) provides similar information on the capture of Chalcuchima as Murúa; however, he also notes that the horse used to carry the captured Chalcuchima belonged to Captain de Soto.

755   Folio 134r is blank.

756   This is one of the most heavily redacted chapters by Remón (Adorno 2008:107) in the *General History of Peru*, showing that the execution of Atahualpa by Pizarro was still a difficult event to defend by the Crown.

757   Here Murúa interrupts the historical narrative to intercede with some spiritual thoughts.

758   Crossed out by Remón (Adorno 2008:107; Murúa 2008 [1616]:134v).

destroy so many principal lineages. Chalcuchima replied: "Lord, speak the truth, and do not try to shift the blame on me, for I am not responsible. When you began your differences and arguments with your brother, Huascar Inca, you went out against his captains with an army and ordered us to follow you. You took the litters of your father, Huayna Capac, and the vestments that were in the storehouses. Did you do that because you were afraid? Tell us, Lord, the truth of what happened and what you ordered when I went out with your army in the company of Quisquis, [and what you ordered] me to do. Do not try to blame everything on me now, for I did what you ordered me to do."

Hearing this, the Marquis Don Francisco Pizarro ordered both of them to return to prison, and this was done. [At this time] the *curacas* and governors of the provinces who had been coming *[f.135r]* on Quisquis's command to give allegiance to Atahualpa as their king and Inca were already arriving at Cajamarca. They were carrying the gold and silver vessels and other fine crockery that [Atahualpa] had urgently requested to pay his ransom and have him released from the prison, where he was being held. Everything was deposited in the room until the agreed-upon amount was reached. When the arriving *caciques* and governors found [Atahualpa] imprisoned and realized they could not speak with him, they were greatly troubled and sought permission from the Marquis to see him in his cell. [After the permission was granted] they talked with [Atahualpa] about the ransom and other matters. Atahualpa told them to beg the Marquis to let him out to eat, drink, and relax with them for a while, as he had been imprisoned for days, and the ransom was quickly arriving. Some say that he tried this with the intention of escaping and fleeing from the Spaniards, who were not offering him any special treatment, as the gold and silver were not arriving as quickly ~~as their greed and insatiable hunger~~[759] [as] demanded. The *caciques* and the others went to the Marquis and, with much humility, begged and asked him for this favor. He granted it with good will but ordered [that] some armed soldiers accompany [Atahualpa], carefully monitoring him to prevent any evil plan, treachery, or escape. So, [Atahualpa] left with the [Spanish] soldiers to eat and drink with his own [men] according to their custom[s]. As they enjoyed themselves, the night grew late, so the soldiers returned him to his prison, where he remained for a few days.[760]

Some of the Spaniards involved in the conquest say that [Atahualpa] wanted to rebel. However, this accusation was likely spread by Felipillo, the Marquis's translator and interpreter, because it was rumored that he had sex with one of Atahualpa's women and he, and perhaps she, was scared that if [Atahualpa] were released from

759 Crossed out by Remón (Adorno 2008:107; Murúa 2008 [1616]:135r).
760 Cabello Valboa (1951 [1586]:475) provides similar information on the actions of Atahualpa.

prison, he would be punished.[761] Others say that Atahualpa knew [of the affair], [and that] he threatened Felipillo, so he began to spread this rumor. The Spaniards were uncertain [about what would occur], given Quisquis's great army in Cuzco and the delayed arrival of the gold and silver to fill *[f.135v]* the ransom room. Even if [the ransom] had arrived the next day, they would have still deemed it late. [As a result] they become incited and killed the unfortunate king.

The Marquis Pizarro began collecting information against [Atahualpa] ~~as if he had been appointed as Atahualpa's judge by the Pope and Emperor Don Carlos~~[762] and judged him responsible for the death of his brother ~~as if being the supreme lord Atahualpa was obliged to give an account of it to the Marquis or any lord of the world.~~[763] They accused him of wanting to flee and incite a war against the Spaniards ~~as if his desire to flee was not completely legitimate~~[764] ~~since his imprisonment did not occur during a just war, as there was none, nor could there have been [one] against him since he had not done anything to offend the Spaniards when they arrested him. Nor had he prevented the preaching of the Holy Gospel by the religious who were with the Marquis, nor had he done anything to justify a war against him with a reasonable cause. So, if he had been able to flee from prison, he would have done so rightly, and those who detained him against his rights sinned. However, since they were all blind and Felipillo, the interpreter, guided them with fear and passion, everything was interpreted to his liking and according to his desires.~~[765]

With great courage, Atahualpa denied that he wanted to rise up or rebel, nor did he plan to harm the Spaniards in any way, and he asked them not to believe Felipillo. Furthermore, he [stated that] if he had ordered his brother's death, he had the right to do so because his brother had forced him to war for no reason. He had never intended to offend him or deny him his obedience. In addition, [Huascar Inca] had sent [men] to Quito to seize him, and if he had been caught, they would have killed him, just as he had done to his other brothers who were killed without cause. Because of these things, he had a right to defend himself, from the continuous provocations of his brother, Huascar Inca, who had sent captains to destroy him. ~~But as the judges,~~[766] interpreters, and other ministers ~~involved they can call as~~

---

761   Betanzos (1996 [1557]:272–274) and Cabello Valboa (1951 [1586]:475) provide descriptions of Felipillo's affair with one of the wives of Atahualpa. The role that Felipillo played in the death of Atahualpa was first proposed by Zárate (1981 [1555]:133), making the translator an easy victim to place blame on. Felipillo was later killed by Diego Almagro in 1536 (Hemming 1970:82).

762   Crossed out by Remón (Adorno 2008:107; Murúa 2008 [1616]:135v).

763   Crossed out by Remón (Adorno 2008:107; Murúa 2008 [1616]:135v).

764   A mistake has been corrected. "To" is written above the word.

765   Crossed out by Remón (Adorno 2008:107; Murúa 2008 [1616]:135v).

766   Crossed out by Remón (Adorno 2008:107; Murúa 2008 [1616]:135v).

~~such~~[767] were blinded by passion and greed, the wretched Atahualpa did not benefit from the justifiable reasons he raised, nor the truth, ~~nor the unreasonableness of what they did to him~~[768] so they condemned him to death.

[f.136r] [Atahualpa] heard the sentence with good spirits. He was then foretold by a religious of the inestimable and precious goods that he would enjoy in Heaven, and that the salvation of his soul hinged on sacred baptism, [which is the] principal means to enjoy God and the door to the other sacraments; [Atahualpa] asked with great willingness [to be baptized] and it was done.[769] He became a Christian,[770] accepting the character of Christ, the Lamb of God. With this, he washed away all the stains and faults with which he was infested, and beautified his soul with grace.

Some Spanish conquistadors suggested that he be sent to Spain to the emperor Don Carlos, our lord, which was the lesser evil, since his life would be spared. However, it did not help that [Pizarro] was determined that [Atahualpa] should die. Some say that he made a will. Whatever occurred, he woke up one morning garroted and with his tassel on his head, which was, as we have said, the royal insignia and crown.[771]

~~Just art Thou, O Lord, and fair are Thy judgments. From the evils that men with perverse inclination and depraved will do, thou brings, forth an infinity of good things. It could be that this king, by his death, paid for the offenses he had committed against thee. Being cleansed by Thy grace today, he may be rejoicing while those who murdered him may be perpetually burning in hell. Through one single act, they committed so many injustices. First, they captured someone with whom they had no reason or cause to wage war. Second, they did not free him. Third, they set themselves up as judges of individuals over whom they did not have, nor would never have, authority. Fourth, they engaged in the tyranny of processing passionately. Fifth, they exacted a ransom that would have been outrageous even if the war had been just and the imprisoned ruler justly captured. When the time came, they demanded the largest and highest ransom ever heard of or paid, since God created the earth until the present day, for the imprisonment of any king, emperor, or private citizen. It is said that they [demanded] three or four million in gold and silver,~~

---

767   Crossed out by Remón (Adorno 2008:107; Murúa 2008 [1616]:135v).

768   Crossed out by Remón (Adorno 2008:107; Murúa 2008 [1616]:135v).

769   Cabello Valboa (1951 [1586]:482) provides similar information on Atahualpa's conversion. The conversion was not voluntary, since Atahualpa was told that he would be burned at the stake if he did not convert (Betanzos 1996 [1557]:275; Pizarro 1921 [1571]:219; Sancho de la Hoz 1917 [1534]:17–18; Xerez 1985 [1534]).

770   On the last page of his chronicle, Santa Cruz Pachacuti Yamqui Salcamaygua (1993 [ca. 1613]:268) notes that Atahualpa was christened Don Francisco.

771   Within Murúa's description of Atahualpa's death, it is worth noting that Murúa was trained within the Mercedarian Order, which is dedicated to the redemptions of captives.

~~without counting the spoils that they had taken in the battle in which they captured him. Their actions were also tyrannical.~~

~~They were obligated to restore him to complete liberty as they had promised, even if he had been the evilest man in the entire world. Seneca says that even to those who do not have faith or the word, one's bond should be kept with them if they have been promised something.~~[772]

~~All of us who live in the Indies see and know that from the first to the last of [136v] all those [involved] in the unfortunate and tragic death of the king [Atahualpa], which was so unjust and evil, died unfortunate, sad, and early deaths without any hope of ransoming their salvation. For example, the Marquis Don Fran[cis]co Pizarro was stabbed to death in the City of Kings. Those who killed him took his body out [and] dragged it through the streets with great ignominy. Furthermore, we all see the children, grandchildren, and descendants of those who were there [in Cajamarca] now poor and unfortunate, and many of them miserable and dejected, despite the fact that their fathers and grandfathers won the richest and most extravagant kingdom of the globe. This seems to be a just judgment and punishment by God, who is punishing the wickedness, greed, and injustices of the fathers upon their children and descendants.~~[773]

~~The Marquis Pizarro and the Spaniards divided the ransom of gold, silver, and other things among themselves as if it had been theirs, obtained and won in a just war and with fair title. They took, enjoyed, and sold it, but they were obliged to restore it to Atahualpa's heirs, to whom it belonged. In the absence of such arrangements, their successors and those who inherited and had access to his goods and estates after his death have the same obligation to return it and make restitution. But they have carelessly bickered among themselves for everything, and not a dime has been restored to this today. That is why God has a hell fit for the punishment of such evils and injustices.~~[774]

When Atahualpa died, some of the Indians and leaders who were present and who belonged to Huascar Inca's group were pleased, as they were not fond of Atahualpa. They considered him an intrusive tyrant who was neither a true king nor a natural Inca. However, his death weighed on other governors and leaders, particularly those from the provinces of Quito who favored him and followed his wishes, causing them great emotions and weeping. He was buried [in a grave] according

---

772   Crossed out by Remón (Adorno 2008:107; Murúa 2008 [1616]:136r). Also, this censored section is especially difficult to translate. We have deferred to Adorno's (2008:108) translation.

773   Crossed out by Remón (Adorno 2008:107; Murúa 2008 [1616]:136r–136v).

774   Crossed out by Remón (Adorno 2008:107; Murúa 2008 [1616]:136v).

to our custom, but after a few days, two of his former captains, Rumiñavi[775] and Unanchuillo, who had been his most distinguished servants and who were there at his death, secretly dug up his body from its burial place ~~and they fled~~ and they fled[776] with it to Quito, which had been his principal seat.[777]

The death of the valiant king Atahualpa occurred in the year *[f.137r]* 1533.[778] He was young when he died, handsome and tall, with a truly royal, magnanimous spirit and a liberal disposition toward his own people. This is why he was able to sustain himself and be followed with great willingness by his own [people] when he rebelled against his brother. He was very neat, careful with personal adornments, and [had] many women. Five thousand were found in the [Cajamarca] bath alone, but it is not known who the royal Coya and his legitimate [wife] was.[779] Although he left children, they must have [all] died because there is no information on any of them except one, called [blank],[780] who was married to Blas Gómez, a Spaniard.[781]

---

775 Guaman Poma de Ayala (2004 [1615]:163 [165], 379 [381]) includes two drawings of Rumiñavi.

776 A dittograph has been crossed out.

777 See Zárate (1981 [1555]:135) for a more detailed description of the removal of Atahualpa's body. Betanzos (1996 [1557]:274–275) suggests that Cusi Yupanqui removed the body but that he was later killed by Rumiñavi. Also see Cobo (1979 [1653]:171).

778 Atahualpa was killed on 26 July 1533 (Hemming 1970:78). Sarmiento de Gamboa (2007 [1572]:202) writes that Atahualpa was thirty-six at the time of his death and that Huascar was forty when he died. Huascar had succeeded his father at thirty-one and was Inca for nine years, six in peace and three in war. Because [Huascar] had no male heir with Chucuy Huypa and the carnage of Quisquis and Calcochima in Cuzco, few of his lineage survived. Sarmiento de Gamboa (2007 [1572]:202) did, however, have contact with Alonso Titu Atauchi, Huascar's nephew and the son of Titu Atauchi.

779 Betanzos (1996 [1557]:180–181) notes that at the birth of Tocto Ocllo's and Yanqui Yupanqui's daughter, Cusi Rimay Ocllo, it was determined that she should marry Atahualpa when she came of age and would be his principal wife. Betanzos (1996 [1557]:204) also describes the wedding for her and Atahualpa. She was with Atahualpa in Cajamarca when he was captured by Pizarro. After Atahualpa's death, Cusi Rimay Ocllo was baptized Angelina Yupanqui and had two sons with Francisco Pizarro. Sometime after the death of Pizarro, Angelina Yupanqui married Betanzos, and she is believed to have been one of his major informants on the history of the Incas. As such, Betanzos's chronicle is sympathetic to Atahualpa and describes Huascar harshly. Betanzos (1996 [1557]:195) also notes that Angelina Yupanqui had a brother named Cusi Yupanqui, who was in Cuzco when Huascar declared war against Atahualpa. But he soon changed sides in the civil war and helped to oversee his sister's marriage with Atahualpa. Not surprisingly, in Betanzos's chronicle, Cusi Yupanqui plays a critical role in the civil war.

780 This space is left blank in the document, suggesting that Murúa was still trying to find the correct name. One of Atahualpa's daughters, who was baptized María, first married Pedro de León and later Blas Gómez (Hemming 1970:598).

781 Murúa seems misinformed, as several of the wives and children of Atahualpa survived

The rich clothes and wealth of the house of Atahualpa were of infinite and great value. The Spaniards took and enjoyed all of it.[782,783]

[*F.138R*] CHAPTER 64

How Marquis Pizarro went to Cuzco and
there named Manco Inca as Inca

After the conclusion of the justice or better said injustice[784] of Atahualpa, [the] king of these kingdoms, by the Marquis Don Francisco Pizarro, [Sancho de] Villegas and Martín Bueno[785] arrived in Cajamarca with the riches that they had taken from the House of the Sun in Cuzco, which were inestimable. They also brought the gold statues of Palpa Ocllo,[786] which they gave to the Marquis. On seeing such a vast amount of gold, silver, and many precious things that were brought from Cuzco, [Pizarro] felt a great desire to go there and seek more, because he believed this could not be all of it and there must be more.[787] So as he was growing richer with gold and silver, his desire to find and have more grew. It was like the dropsical—the more he drinks the thirstier he becomes, and the more he desires to drink. It is known that the wealth and treasures brought by [Sancho de] Villegas and Martín Bueno, were on the order of Atahualpa, who sent Indians with them to rescue him, because

---

the tragedy of Cajamarca. Seven of his children, five boys and two girls, were in Tomebamba and Atahualpa placed them in the care of Francisco Pizarro (Sancho de la Hoz 1917 [1534]:18; Xerez 1985 [1534]), certainly with the hope that as their caretaker, Pizarro, would protect them in later life. However, Pizarro did little for Atahualpa's children beyond placing most of them in monasteries or convents to be raised (see Hemming 1970:345, 557, 598). Zárate (1981 [1555]) suggests that Rumiñavi took care of Atahualpa's children for a short period, immediately after the death of Atahualpa.

782   It should be noted that Cabello Valboa (1951 [1586]) and Sarmiento de Gamboa (2007 [1572]) end their chronicles with the death of Atahualpa. Molina's now lost *History of the Incas* presumably ended with this event as well. If this is correct, then from this chapter forward, Murúa must have used other sources while composing his chronicle.

783   Folio 137v is blank.

784   Crossed out by Remón (Adorno 2008:107; Murúa 2008 [1616]:138r).

785   As noted, the first Spaniards to visit Cuzco were Martín Bueno, Pedro de Moguer, and Juan de Zárate.

786   Cabello Valboa (1951 [1586]) and Molina (2011 [ca. 1575]) are the only other chroniclers who mention this figure. It is said to have been a golden object believed to be one of the wives of the Sun.

787   See Sancho de la Hoz (1917 [1534]:131) for an account of the ransom of Atahualpa and the amounts given to each man.

otherwise, Quisquis and his captains, who were in possession of Cuzco with a powerful army, as noted above, would not have consented to have it removed.

When Atahualpa died, the Marquis Pizarro asked him whom he could put and name in his place as Inca and Lord of the land, so that he might govern it and serve the Spaniards. Because his brothers, Titu Atauchi and Huanca Auqui, were dead and there were other sons of Huayna Capac, who were valiant men of experience and government, who could succeed him, Atahualpa suggested Tupac Hualpa, his brother and a son of Huayna Capac, who was there [in Cajamarca] with the Spaniards [and] was the most appropriate of all those who were still alive. After Atahualpa's death, the Marquis named Tupac Hualpa as Inca, and commanded him to prepare himself to leave for Cuzco with the necessary items to rule, so that the land would not suffer without an Inca and governor. [Tupac Hualpa] left Cajamarca to go to Cuzco, but he died of an illness in Jauja, after only three months of power and command. With his [death], the succession *[f.138v]* of the Incas, Lords of this kingdom, came to an end, and the tassel belonged to the emperor Don Carlos, may he be glorified.[788] The Marquis Don Francisco Pizarro, claimed the tassel and took possession of this kingdom in his royal name, although he [later] named, for the good and utility of the land, Manco Inca, a brother of Huascar Inca and Atahualpa, [and a] son of Huayna Capac, as Inca, as will be seen.

The Marquis Don Francisco Pizarro left Cajamarca[789] and made his way slowly toward Cuzco. Nothing remarkable happened to him on the way, nor did he have any difficulty or opposition in [his journey].[790] All the nations of the provinces through which he passed came out with great readiness to give him obedience and to obey him, because they were frightened of the war that had taken place between Huascar Inca and Atahualpa, and of the destruction of the villages and crops as well as the many deaths caused by Quisquis and Chalcuchima when they did not come out to receive and give them obedience. They were glad about the Spaniard's arrival, who seemed to rescue them from intolerable servitude and misery.

As the Marquis was approaching Cuzco, the *orejones* and principal Indians were determined to raise Manco Inca Yupanqui as [the new] Inca and king since Tupac Hualpa, who had been named by the Marquis, as previously mentioned, was dead.

---

788   Guaman Poma de Ayala (2004 [1615]:117) includes a similar sentence. Sancho de la Hoz (1917 [1534]:52–54) also describes the debate that took place concerning who should be the next Inca.

789   Pizarro was with Tupac Hualpa when he died in Jauja. Having no other heirs to the tassel, Pizarro was forced to continue toward Cuzco without an appointed Inca. Nevertheless, he was fortunate to encounter Manco Inca just before arriving in Cuzco.

790   Murúa is incorrect as there were various battles between the Spaniards and different Indigenous forces between Cajamarca and Cuzco.

They wanted to do obtain the Marquis's permission, as they saw that everything depended on his will and that he ordered things as he pleased. [However], they kept this hidden because they were afraid of Quisquis, who was in Cuzco and did not want him to find out.

So [the *orejones*] waited for [Pizarro] to approach [Cuzco] and when he was at the Apurímac, which is a famous river thirteen or fourteen leagues from Cuzco, Manco Inca secretly left Cuzco with the main *orejones* and Indians. At the descent of Vilcaconga, which is the slope above Limatambo, they met with the Marquis Pizarro. There, Manco Inca and the *orejones*, with much humility, gave obedience in the name of the emperor Don Carlos. As a sign of peace and friendship, Manco Inca gave the Marquis a very precious gold shirt, a garment which is called a *capac uncu*, which means, "rich and powerful shirt," which was worn by the Incas during their coronation as kings.[791]

After the Marquis received [these gifts] with much affability, love, caring, and kindly gestures, Manco Inca and the *[f.139r]* others complained to him about the deaths and cruelties ordered by Atahualpa's captains, Quisquis and Chalcuchima, including killing a vast number men and women from the most principal and important, royal lineage[s] of the Incas.[792] They also urged [Pizarro], having come to this land as a messenger of the Pope and Emperor, to defend them from Quisquis's power in Cuzco, as he [still] possessed it, and to punish him for evil deeds that he had committed against them by killing so many innocent people, and that the land could not be safe or at peace as long as Quisquis remained in it with his army.

Seeing how willingly and fondly Manco Inca Yupanqui, [along] with the *orejones*, serviced the emperor, and how humbly they came out to give obedience, the Marquis named [Manco Inca] in front of the conquistadors who were with him, the *orejones*, other *curacas*, and chiefs of all the provinces that followed him, as the Inca. He commanded everyone to obey and respect him as their lord and as a son of the king Huayna Capac, who had been king of the entire land. With much contentment and joy, they obeyed [the Marquis] and gave [Manco Inca] their obedience, showing great pleasure in it. So, from that time on, they had [Manco Inca] as Inca. Continuing his journey toward Cuzco, the Marquis entered Jaquijhuana,[793] which is four leagues from [Cuzco]. Manco Inca Yupanqui was carried in his litters, the

791 The *History and Genealogy of the Inca Kings of Peru* (Murúa 2004 [1590]:46v) includes a drawing of Manco Inca giving obedience to the Spanish Crown.

792 Sancho de la Hoz (1917 [1534]:99–101) provides a detailed description of a conversation that may have taken place between Pizarro and Manco Inca.

793 Sancho de la Hoz (1917 [1534]:89, 96) writes "Sachisagagna," and Murúa writes "Sacsahuana." These are references to Jaquijhuana, which is now part of the Pampa de Anta (see also Pizarro 1921 [1571]:246).

insignia of the Inca, as they were accustomed to do, and was surrounded by the most principal *orejones* and *curacas*.

When the Marquis Pizarro saw that Manco Inca was well intentioned and carried out his commands with great eagerness and care, providing the Spaniards with everything necessary for the trip, including food, he treated him with love and familiarity. In the presence of the Spaniards and Indians, he called him "son" and gave him all possible honor so that the land would become pacified and the Indians would readily obey. To please [Manco Inca] even more and make him and the other *orejones* and principals on his side understand how much he regretted the damage that Chalcuchima had done and the deaths he had ordered in Cuzco to those of his *[f.139v]* lineage, and to secure their love and subjection, there, in Jaquijhuana, [Pizarro] ordered Chalcuchima to be taken out of the prison where he had been kept. In the presence of Manco Inca and all his people, he had [Chalcuchima] burned in a great bonfire, a punishment that he well deserved. With this, [Pizarro] appeased and gained their [good]will. There the Marquis said to the *orejones*, that henceforth they should not be afraid. He was there in the name of their lord, Emperor Don Carlos, and Huayna Capac, to favor and protect them from their enemies. And that just as he had burned Chalcuchima in their presence, he also hoped to capture Quisquis to avenge them. He wanted them to understand how much he loved and cared for them. With this, they were convinced of his subservience and respect, and they served him with great diligence.[794]

[F.140V] CHAPTER 65

How the Marquis Pizarro and Manco Inca battled Quisquis and defeated him, and [then] seized Cuzco

At dawn the next day, after justice was served to Chalcuchima, the Marquis Pizarro agreed to walk to Cuzco, which was only four leagues away. As mentioned above, Quisquis was there with a large army of all nations who had been with him since he defeated Huascar Inca. Upon hearing the news that the Marquis was determined to enter Cuzco and Manco Inca Yupanqui was with him, and that all the Indians obeyed [Manco Inca] as Inca and lord at [the Marquis's] command, [Quisquis] wanted to defend the entrance [of the city] and to try his luck by fighting [the Marquis] before he could enter Cuzco, and to destroy him if possible. So, [Quisquis] left Cuzco with his army, which they say was more than a hundred thousand Indians, in war

---

794 Folio 140r is blank.

formation, carrying weapons and wearing fancy clothes, including ones they had obtained from the spoils of the many armies that they had defeated since leaving Tomebamba, as well as the riches they stole in Cuzco. [Quisquis] awaited him in Paucarpata, which is on the royal road, with great spirit and bravery.

Upon being informed of this, the Marquis commanded the Spaniards to regroup with him and the followers of Manco Inca joined him. Those who had come from Cajamarca and those who had joined the Marquis from the provinces [would be under] his [command]. As they slowly advanced [the two armies] encountered each other and engaged in a cruel and difficult battle that lasted a long time, until the Marquis, by the grace of God, was able to promulgate the gospel among these uneducated nations, defeated and destroyed Quisquis, at the cost of many of his own men. [Quisquis] with the remainder of his army, retreated to Ccapi,[795] where he strengthened himself and spent several days regrouping and gathering more supporters.[796]

After achieving victory, the Marquis, the Spaniards, and Manco Inca Yupanqui, entered *[f.141r]* Cuzco, where they were warmly welcomed by the townspeople, as they were now freed from the tyranny of Quisquis and because Manco Inca entered with him.[797] The Marquis Pizarro took [the] Casana, which were the houses of Huayna Capac, for himself. His brother, Hernando Pizarro, took [the] Amarucancha, which were the houses of Huascar Inca. Gonzalo Pizarro, another brother, took the houses of Tupa Inca Yupanqui, known as Cora Cora, while the other conquering Spaniards were spread among the [other] main houses of the city.[798]

A few days later, wanting to secure the region and recognizing that this would not be possible with Quisquis only eight leagues away, the Marquis Pizarro sent a Spanish captain[799] with soldiers and Manco Inca, who brought many *orejones* and Indians with him. When they arrived in Ccapi, they found Quisquis participating in the solemn celebration of *Inti Raymi*,[800] which was observed in June, after the

---

795   Ccapi is located approximately forty kilometers southwest of Cuzco, across the Apurímac River.
796   Sancho de la Hoz (1917 [1534]:102–104, 108–109) provides a detailed description of this battle as well as the subsequent hunt for Quisquis.
797   According to Sancho (1917 [1534]:104), Pizarro entered the city of Cuzco on 15 November 1533.
798   All of these named buildings were situated around the central plaza of Cuzco (see Bauer 2004:103–137; Pizarro 1921 [1571]:250).
799   Juan Pizarro (1921 [1571]:204) provides a remarkable account of this with one of the royal mummies just before the Spaniards left Cuzco in search of Quisquis.
800   This word is underlined (Murúa 2008 [1616]:141r). Since, according to Sancho de la Hoz (1917 [1534]:104), Pizarro entered the city of Cuzco on 15 November, Murúa may be mistaken. It is possible that Quisquis was celebrating Capac Raymi, which was held on the December solstice, rather than Inti Raymi, which was held on the June Solstice.

sowing and feasts had been concluded. They fought bravely with him and slowly defeated him. With his army depleted and knowing he could no longer sustain himself in that land, [Quisquis] gradually retreated to Quito via the royal road. The Spaniards and Manco Inca returned to Cuzco, where the Marquis was.

All the *caciques* of the provinces from Chile to Quito were [in Cuzco] and they raised and recognized Manco Inca Yupanqui as Inca and lord and gave him the tassel in Santo Domingo, which previously had been the Temple of the Sun. On behalf of Emperor Don Carlos, the Marquis Pizarro appointed him as Inca and commanded [that] all nations obey and respect him, just as they had done for his father, Huayna Capac, and his brother, Huascar Inca, before he died. All the *curacas* recognized him as Inca and hailed him as lord.

When this was finished, the Marquis, his brothers, and Manco Inca agreed to go after Quisquis, who was fleeing to Quito on the royal road, as said, to prevent him from inciting the land *[f.141v]* and the provinces to rebel. So, the Marquis went with Manco Inca, and chased Quisquis until Jauja.[801] There the Marquis's daughter, Doña Francisca Pizarro, was born to his wife, Doña Inés Quispicizac,[802] who was a daughter of Huayna Capac. Later, Doña Inés married Francisco de Ampuero, a citizen of the City of Kings, and in Spain, Doña Francisca Pizarro[803] married her uncle, Hernando Pizarro, brother of the Marquis, her father, who has [already] been mentioned in this story and will be [mentioned] again.

In Jauja, the Marquis realized that Quisquis was far ahead and that it would be very hard to catch up, so he returned to Cuzco with Manco Inca. He was there for a few days, working to pacify the Indians and collecting more silver. Don Diego de Almagro, the companion of the Marquis, then went from Cuzco to conquer Chile, which was believed to be even richer than Peru in terms of gold.[804] He took

---

801   Jauja was established as the "capital" of Spanish Peru and housed some of the vast wealth collected in Cajamarca and Cuzco. Within two years, the capital was relocated to the coast to the City of Kings (i.e., Lima).

What might be called the Jauja campaign was far more complex than is told here: see Hemming (1970:137–150) for a detailed description. In the view of Cuzco, the retreat of Quisquis to the far north marked the end of the occupation of Atahualpa's forces and was an unexpected victory. However, the reality of the Spanish occupation soon became evident.

802   Also known as Quispe Cusi, and later as Inés Huaylas Yupanqui, she would later bear two children with Pizarro: Francisca, born in Jauja, and Gonzalo, born the next year but dying young. Later, she would have two sons and a daughter with Ampuero.

803   Doña Francisca Pizarro departed for Spain in 1550.

804   Pizarro returned to Cuzco and there agreed that Diego de Almagro should undertake the conquest of Chile. Almagro was unsatisfied with his share of the new kingdom and wished to invade new lands. Almagro's expedition into Chile is largely seen as a failure, as his men suffered greatly, and they recovered little wealth.

with him four hundred Spaniards, as more people were arriving as the fame of Peru's riches grew every day. Manco Inca ordered that Paullu Topa,[805] his brother, go with Don Diego de Almagro to Chile and that [the] Villac Umu[806] go with him.

At this time, knowing about the location and the fertility of the Lima Valley, two leagues from the seaport of Callao,[807] the Marquis decided to establish a city there to increase its importance for navigation. He left Cuzco in good order under the Captain Hernando Pizarro, Juan Pizarro and Gonzalo Pizarro, his brothers, and many other captains and soldiers. As [he] passed through Jauja, where he had previously established a city, many left to join him to establish and populate the City of Kings[808] on the banks of the Rimac River. However, he left some Spaniards in Jauja as a fort, to ensure the security of that area, which [was also] fertile and populated with many Indians.

When the Marquis Pizarro left Cuzco, as described above, [f.142r] Manco Inca was already beginning to move against the Spaniards with evil intentions and the spirit of rebelling, due to the ill treatment and discomfort they inflicted on his people every day; almost worse than how they had been treated by Quisquis and Chalcuchima because the overall greed of the Spaniards was so great; especially that of the captains and that of the Marquis's brothers. A week never passed when they did not make the unfortunate [Manco Inca] gather a mound of silver and gold as if they were stones taken from a stream. Even with this, they were never satisfied, because they all gambled with each other and spent it. Even worse, they took his women and daughters away by force before his eyes. These insults and grievances cooled Manco Inca's goodwill and love for the Spaniards.

When the Marquis learned of these things in the City of Kings, where he was at that time, he wished for them to be avoided, so he wrote a strongly worded [letter] to his brothers to treat Manco Inca, the *curacas*, the important people, and the other Indians well. However, his letter had little effect on their behavior, as they had begun to treat them worse, causing them more harm and misfortune.

At this time, [the] Villac Umu, a principal Indian who had gone with Paullu Topa and Don Diego de Almagro to Chile, fled again and told Manco Inca many lies. He reported that all the Spaniards who had gone to Chile were dead and that they were useless, except for eating, drinking, and stealing, and that they were already

805 More commonly known as Paullu Inca or simply Paullu.
806 The Villac Umu (Murúa writes Vilaoma) was the title for the head priest of the Temple of the Sun. The Villac Umu was generally a close relative of the ruling Inca. The *History and Genealogy of the Inca Kings of Peru* contains a drawing of a Villac Umu (Murúa 2004 [1590]:111V).
807 Murúa describes the port of Callao in book 3, chapter 15 of his chronicle.
808 Pizarro founded the City of Kings on 6 January 1535.

distributing women among themselves. Upon hearing this news and feeling deep restlessness, Manco Inca became even more upset and asked [the] Villac Uma for more information about what had happened in Chile and along the way to Don Diego de Almagro. As I noted, he had lied, since [Diego de Almagro] and the Spaniards were not dead.

Despite this, Manco Inca decided to send messengers throughout the provinces from Quito to Chile, telling the Indians that in order to free themselves from Spanish oppression, he would instruct them within four months *[f.142v]* to rebel against the Spaniards and to kill them without sparing any, along with the many Blacks and Indians of Nicaragua who had come to these parts in the company of the Spaniards who were scattered throughout their villages. Upon receiving this order from Manco Inca, they willingly offered themselves to the [cause] across the kingdom because everywhere, the Indians were discontent with bad treatment and abuse of Spaniards. All of this was born out of the Spaniards' arrogance and pride, which increased every day with the acquisition of riches, whether lawfully or unlawfully, seized from among the Indians, without considering the true account that they would have to give in the court and judgment of God, whose ears hears the cries of poor Indians.[809]

[F.143V] CHAPTER 66

How Manco Inca left Cuzco and rebelled and laid siege [to the city] with his captains

As mentioned earlier, the letters of the Marquis Pizarro were of little use in improving the treatment of Manco Inca. Hernando Pizarro, his brother, treated Manco Inca with terrible insolence, becoming worse every day. He would take [Manco Inca] prisoner without cause and then release him, demanding gold and silver. Despite his sorrow, [Manco Inca] always gave him everything he could, but he was never content. Furthermore, [Hernando Pizarro] mistreated the *curacas* and [other] important people every day, making himself more feared and abhorrent, as they could no longer suffer or tolerate him, and it became increasingly difficult to repair [the damages] caused by him.

One day, [Hernando Pizarro] seized Manco Inca to extort gold and silver. He tortured him with a rope and, to inflict more pain and grief separated him from his women. The Inca suffered all this, waiting for the right time to act, but it was hastened

---

809   Folio 143r is blank.

when his captains, [the] Villac Umu, Anta Alca, and other relatives and chief *caciques*, became increasingly restless by what [they] saw and suffered. They felt they had nowhere to go and were unable to move forward or backward, and so they urged Manco Inca to act, saying: "Lord, it is better that we defend ourselves and die than spend our lives under such subjection and misery, being treated even more harshly than the Blacks of the Spaniards. Let us rise up at once and die for our freedom and for our children and women, who are taken from us every day and affronted."

Moved by these appeals, Manco Inca told them to leave Cuzco and to go to Yucay, where they could meet more easily. After arranging this, [Manco Inca] requested permission from Hernando Pizarro and his brothers to go to Yucay to relax. He also requested that he send some Spaniards with him so he could celebrate with them, as well as an interpreter so that he could speak with the Spaniards who accompanied him. This request for soldiers was to better disguise their plans and intentions.

[f.144r] Hernando Pizarro and his fellow brothers and captains did not suspect Manco Inca, nor did they understand the injuries inflicted upon him, so they consented to Manco Inca's visit to Yucay, and they sent a Huancavilca Indian, named Antonillo, with him as an interpreter. With Hernando Pizarro's approval, he left Cuzco without any intention of returning, and all the Indians of the provinces followed him. The Cañari and Chachapoyas, who now reside in Cuzco, were among the groups who joined Manco Inca in largest numbers. However, when Manco Inca left for Yucay, some who did not wish to go with him remained, either out of a desire to serve His Majesty or due to personal passions and animosities among them. [These included] Pazca, Huaipar, Osoptor, Cayo Topa, sons of Auqui Tupa Inca, and the nephews of Huayna Capac. Don Juan Jona, Don Luis Utupa Yupanqui, and Don Pedro Mayo Rimachi also stayed, as did many other Indians born in Cuzco.

Finding himself in Yucay, free from the hands and oppression of Hernando Pizarro and his brothers, Manco Inca discussed the matter with his captains and advisors, [and] made a general call to all the provinces and their peoples. When many had arrived, Manco Inca seriously discussed the uprising with the leaders and strategized on the most efficient and effective way to carry it out so that the Spaniards would be unable to defend themselves or escape from his grasp. [However], they were unable to keep their plans a secret, and Hernando Pizarro and his brothers discovered their plot.

Upon learning of the uprising, Hernando Pizarro dispatched some Spaniards to go after Manco Inca and bring him back [to Cuzco], without revealing that they were suspicious. However, Manco Inca was forewarned, and when they arrived, he refused to come. He attacked the Spaniards with great courage and bravery, causing them and the Indians who came with them to withdraw. Unsatisfied, [Manco Inca] chased them, forcing them to flee to Cuzco.

Manco Inca realized that his intentions were now known and that war was inevitable. He sought to bring it to a swift end by eliminating Hernando Pizarro and the other conquerors who were in Cuzco. So, within three or four days, Manco Inca dispatched a large force *[f.144v]* with Inquill as general and his representative, [the] Villac Umu and Paucar Huaman, and as captains from Yucay to quickly surround Cuzco. The siege was so hard and difficult, that Hernando Pizarro and the Spaniards found themselves in real difficulty, unable to even obtain water as ~~the Indians~~[810] the Indians prevented them from accessing it. Since [water] is critical for life, and Cuzco had so little, they resorted to extreme measures, using spears and harquebuses [to obtain it]. Furthermore, Inquill set fire to the parts of the city he could, presenting a new difficulty and challenge. The siege lasted two grueling months, with daily fighting and the Indians preventing [the Spaniards] from getting food or other supplies.

As the siege dragged on, Hernando Pizarro, his brothers, and the other captains realized no help was forthcoming from Lima. Although they had sent word [to Lima], they were uncertain if it would arrive or not, so they decided with Pazca, the general of the Indians of the city and allies, to go out and fight the Indians who had them surrounded. With reckless fury and boldness, they attacked them on two sides, to either break the siege or die trying. They first broke [through] on the side of Carmenca[811] and, with luck, they defeated the people of Chinchaysuyu, who were on that side with their captains Curi Atao and Pazca. On breaking through, [the Spaniards] chased them, killing and wounding, without letting them regroup even though they wanted to. [The Spaniards] chased them to where the town of Ticatica[812] used to be, where the main water source of Cuzco is located. From there, they traveled around the base of the hill of Senca,[813] reaching the fortress [of Sacsayhuaman]. From there, they saw that [the] Villac Umu and Paucar Huaman, who had bravely resisted the Spaniards, were fighting with great spirit down in the city.

[Villac Umu and Paucar Huaman] looked up and saw that the Spaniards were in Chuquipampa,[814] *[f.145r]* which was next to the fortress. They assumed that [the Spaniards] had already defeated the Chinchaysuyu forces, and that if they descended, [the Spaniards] would attack their rear and kill them all. Knowing that

---

810   A scribal dittography has been corrected.

811   The area of modern Santa Ana.

812   Ticatica is on the mountain slope to the west of Cuzco, above what is now called Santa Ana. Murúa mentions Ticatica again in book 3, chapter 10 of his chronicle.

813   The mountain of Senca is to the northwest of Cuzco. It was a shrine within the Cuzco Ceque System (Bauer 1998:62, 72).

814   Chuquipampa was a large flat area beside the fort of Sacsayhuaman, also a shrine within the Cuzco Ceque System (Bauer 1998:54). It is the same location where Quisquis and Chalcuchima killed many people associated with Tupa Inca Yupanqui.

the enemy was above them, they lost courage, stopped fighting, and retreated with good order. They fortified themselves within the fortress, as it was well constructed for both defense and attack.

Once [the Villac Umu and Paucar Huaman] were inside [the fort], the Spaniards withdrew, but from there they caused great damage to the Spaniards and the Indian allies. Hernando Pizarro, seeing the good fortune and success that God had given him in breaking his enemies [lines] and forcing them to raise the siege, decided along with his companions and Pazca, [the] general of the Indian allies, the Blacks they had, and the Indians of Nicaragua, to surround the fortress and try to drive [the] Villac Umu and his men out. So, he encircled them on all sides, and they remain there for four days.

Before I proceed, I want to repeat something that both Spaniards and Indians consistently recount as true. They say that at the height of the fighting, a man on a white horse appeared, fighting on behalf of the Spaniards, slaughtering the Indians, and causing them to flee. Many Spaniards were certain that it was Mancio Sierra [de Leguizamo],[815] a prominent conqueror of Cuzco. However, an investigation later revealed that Mancio Sierra [de Leguizamo] had not fought there but was elsewhere and that no one else had a white horse except for him. So, this is believed to have been the Apostle Santiago, singular patron and defender of Spain, who appeared there, [and] because of this, the city of Cuzco has him as its protector.[816] It is also reported by the Indians that a *[f.145v]* woman blinded them with handfuls of sand while they were fighting and advancing hard on the Spaniards, and as they could not stand before her, they all fled. [This woman] is thought to have been Our Lady, Protector and Mother of Sinners, who wanted to help the Spaniards in that situation.[817] As a result, the Holy Church of Cuzco regards her as its patroness and titular. God is powerful in favoring his own, and even more so, when they have little hope of human favor and help. [In such instances, God] arrives on His own accord. Praise God. Let us give Him perpetual thanks for His infinite mercies.[818]

---

815   Mancio Sierra de Leguizamo played an important role in the invasion of Peru, and Pizarro (1921 [1571]:322) mentions him fighting during the siege of Cuzco. Sierra de Leguizamo is famously known for asking for forgiveness for the conquest in his will (see Stirling 1999).

816   Several writers suggest that Santiago appeared at the height of the siege and helped turn the course of the battle, including Guaman Poma de Ayala (2004 [1615]:404 [406], 405 [407]).

817   Betanzos (1996 [1557]:290) suggests that it was Santiago's horse that created so much dust that the local forces could not fight. Many writers also suggest that the Blessed Virgin Mary appeared on the top of the Spanish church, and Guaman Poma de Ayala (2004 [1615]:403 [405]) includes a drawing of Santa Maria de Francia throwing dust to blind the fighters.

818   Folio 146r is blank.

How the Indians in the fortress killed Juan Pizarro, and [how] the Spaniards finally captured it

After four days of siege, [the] Villac Umu and Paucar Huaman saw that the Spaniards were pressing them hard and driving them with such ferocity that escape was impossible. Furthermore, food was becoming scarce for their many people, and it was difficult to get food or help [from outside the fortress], since the passes were taken by the Spaniards and Indian allies. So, they decided to leave the fortress and save themselves as best they could by breaking through the enemies' [lines]. They waited [until] the Spaniards became careless and, one afternoon, shortly after dinner, almost at the hour of vespers, they suddenly left the fortress in mass and attacked their enemies. Breaking through, they all rushed down the slope toward [the] Saphi [River] and [then] up [the other side] to Carmenca. Although the Spaniards and their Indian allies pursed them, they escaped and fled to Yucay, which is four leagues from Cuzco. There, they reported to Manco Inca all the unfortunate events that had taken place on the hill with the Spaniards including the battles and encounters that had occurred between them. Upon seeing the disorder and retreat of his people, Manco Inca was greatly saddened and angered. He treated and scolded them harshly, dishonoring and insulting them, calling them cowardly chickens who had fled in fear of a few Spaniards. [Manco Inca] then angrily ordered some of the captains, who he knew had fled first and had not fought as they should have with their enemies, to be killed.

Some of the *orejon* captains, who prided themselves on being brave and valiant, along with other Indians of valor and courage, remained *[f.147r]* in the fortress, not wanting to leave, even though they could. They wanted to show how little they cared for their enemies, and not let the Spaniards know that they feared them. So, they fortified themselves as best they could, entering the main towers, and defended themselves with courage and bravery, against the Spaniards and the other Indians who were helping them.

When Hernando Pizarro saw that [the] Villac Umu[819] and his men had fled and that very few Indians remained in the fortress, no more than two thousand, he gathered all the Spaniards and their Indian allies and attacked the fortress from all sides simultaneously. Those inside defended themselves with reckless obstinacy for a long time, putting themselves in danger without any fear of death or the harquebuses that were being fired at them. Despite all this, the Spaniards overran the first two

---

819   The Villac Umu was captured and killed several years later.

defenses and a tower by sheer force of arms. As the Indians were still determined to defend themselves and did not want to abandon the places they had occupied, the battle lasted a long time. With the Spaniards unable to penetrate further into [the fortress], Juan Pizarro, a brother of the Marquis Pizarro and a valiant and brave captain, took a ladder that they had and was the first among his companions to climb it to enter a tower.

As [Juan Pizarro] was entering the [tower], they threw a large stone that struck him on the head, causing him to fall along with the ladder.[820] As the Indians saw the confusion this caused among the Spaniards, they seized the opportunity to leave the fortress. [They did so], with such courage that they disarmed the Spaniards and drove them out of the defenses and tower they had seized, winning them back and killing many Indian allies with great fury and rage. The Spaniards were deeply saddened by the loss of Juan Pizarro. Carrying him as best they could, they took him to Cuzco below. But the blow *[f.147v]* had struck his head with such force that it had split open, and lacking sufficient cures, he died. This caused great sorrow to his brothers and friends.[821]

After the Spaniards withdrew, the Indians inside the fortress threw out the remaining enemies. However, Pazca, the general of the [Indian] allies, ordered that they take the doors, entrances, and exits of the fortress with many Indians. They blocked the entrances in such a way that no one could enter with urgently needed provisions or reinforcements. [Thus] they were trapped, and they remained all night. In the morning, the Spaniards returned with the help of their [Indian] allies to assault the fortress. They did so with such determination that they finally entered it, defeating and killing many of them their enemies, [forcing them to] surrender. Thus [the Spaniards] remained [as] lords of the fortress and they rejoiced at the successful conclusion of the difficult siege and the challenges that the Indians had placed upon them. They can truly say that they owed their victory to the mighty hand of the Lord, who delivered them from danger, because the Indians seriously challenged them, fighting every day, and they suffered greatly from hunger.

Once the Spaniards were safe and rested from their work and the threat [they faced], Hernando Pizarro issued orders for them to divide into squads[822] and, with many Indian allies, they were to prevent the damage they expected from the people who were gathering in the provinces. Thus, some went by way of the Collao to fight with

---

820   Zárate (1981 [1555]:152), Pizarro (1921 [1571]:308, 312), and Titu Cussi Yupangui (2005 [1570]:107) also describe the death of Juan Pizarro, with the former two noting that he was not wearing a helmet that evening since he had been struck on the head earlier in the battle.

821   Juan Pizarro survived long enough to make a will (Hemming 1970:199).

822   A mistake may have been corrected (Murúa 2008 [1616]:147v).

the Indians who were on their way to Cuzco, catching them unaware and thwarting them. Another group of Spaniards went to Condesuyu and had a great battle where they defeated the Indians advancing from those provinces toward Cuzco, [forcing] them to retreat. Others went along Chinchaysuyu road and did the same.

After returning to Cuzco, it appeared to [the Spaniards] that the most important *[f.148r]* thing remained unaddressed, which was to go to Yucay where Manco Inca was, sad and depressed from the tragic events that had befallen his people during both the siege and elsewhere and knowing that everything was unfolding contrary to his wishes, and his plans were unraveling. [The Spaniards] tried to go to Yucay to capture him and bring an end to the war, thereby pacifying the Indians and the provinces who found themselves leaderless and lacking Inca, under the power of the Spaniards. Thus, many well-equipped Spaniards left Cuzco, accompanied by Indian [allies], and traveled to Yucay, expecting to find him there. However, [Manco Inca] had been warned of their departure and why they were coming, so he had gone to Calca. When [the Spaniards] did not find him [in Yucay], they decided to quickly follow him, knowing where he had gone. They caught sight of him, almost capturing him within their grasp. However, Manco Inca and with those that were with him skillfully escaped. They valiantly defended themselves from the heights, using stones and boulders, that they disarmed the Spaniards and killed many of their Indian allies.

When Manco Inca saw his enemies thwarted, he attacked them with a courageous spirit, rallying his own [people], making [the Spaniards] run more than walk, as they say. [Manco Inca] pursued them, and they urgently fled to Cuzco without stopping. Throughout the entire night, he allowed them no respite or a chance to catch their breath; the Indians pursued the exhausted Spaniards. Realizing that they could not destroy them, Manco Inca withdrew with his Indians to [Ollantay]tambo. There, he gathered many people, fortifying himself in case the Spaniards should come after him.[823]

[F.149R] CHAPTER 68

How Manco Inca sent Quizo Yupanqui to encircle
the City of Kings and what happened to them

It is undeniable that the rebellion and uprising of Manco Inca Yupanqui were forced and motivated more by the grievances and abuses of Hernando de Pizarro and his brothers, than by [Manco Inca's] own volition. [This is] because a generous

---

823   Folio 148v is blank.

and noble spirit feels offenses even at the slightest provocation. If the Marquis Don Francisco Pizarro had promptly ended the excesses and extremes of his brothers and other Spaniards, Manco Inca would not have rebelled, numerous Indian lives would have been spared, and Manco Inca would not have found himself in the dire predicament he faced. However, if one mistake is not corrected, countless others follow, and what could have been easily rectified in the beginning, becomes more difficult or impossible as the root and foundation of the evil grows, as we shall see.[824]

After Manco Inca had fortified himself in [Ollantay]tambo, as previously mentioned, and amassed thousands of Indians from different regions, he realized that if he took Lima and killed the Marquis, who was there with many people, Cuzco would lack the support of reinforcements from [the coast] and would soon fall into his hands. So, he decided to attack Lima first, and he sent Quizo Yupanqui,[825] Ylla Tupa, and Puyu Vilca to the city. Quizo Yupanqui was in charge as Captain-General. He received orders from Manco Inca that all the people of Chinchaysuyu, together with his own men, were to surround Lima and kill the Marquis Pizarro and all the Spaniards who were with him. So, he left [Ollantay]tambo, and while traveling along the Royal Road near the Chulcomayo River, *[f.149v]* he suddenly came upon many Spaniards who were carelessly going to Cuzco. Having heard that the siege of Cuzco was over and that the captains of Manco Inca had been thwarted, they believed that everything was now pacified and that there was nothing to fear. [Quizo Yupanqui] attacked and killed them, seizing many spoils including silk, cloth, garments, and various things from Spain such as clothing and wine, and even two Black men and women [slaves] that they were taking to Cuzco. Delighted by this good fortune and the loot that he had so easily seized, he sent everything to Manco Inca, who received it with great joy. With such a good beginning, it seemed to [Manco Inca] that his plan was moving forward according to his wishes.[826]

After Quizo Yupanqui sent the spoils to the Inca, he went forward, gathering many people by decrees and force wherever he went, making a larger and more fearful army. He continued toward Jauja, where, as previously mentioned, the Spaniards occupied a village near Hatun Jauja. However, before they arrived [the Spaniards] learned that they were coming to kill them. Yet they exhibited no fear or respect, declaring: "[Let] those dogs come here where we are waiting for them,

---

824   Here Murúa departs from the historical guide he was using to provide what he deemed was an appropriate introduction for the chapter.

825   Guaman Poma de Ayala (2004 [1615]:161 [163]) also mentions a Quizo Yupanqui. Zárate (1981 [1555]:162, 165) writes the name as Tizoyopangui.

826   Titu Cussi Yupangui (2005 [1570]:111) is even more specific, writing, "They brought my father many heads of Spaniards, as well as two Spaniards who were alive, and one Black and four horses."

and we will tear them to pieces, even if they are twice as many as they are now. It is their fault that [the Incas] lost Cuzco." With this, [the Spaniards] made no effort to strengthen or protect themselves in an *usnu*[827] that was there, establish guards or sentries, or [even] send out spies to warn them when the Indians were near, as one would expect them to do so. However, their hubris and arrogance proved to be their downfall. As [divine] punishment and as an example to others to respect their enemies, God allowed them to die.

Quizo Yupanqui arrived at daybreak [and was] on the Spaniards so suddenly that they were surrounded before they knew it. They had no place *[f.150r]* [to go] or time to get dressed, as many were [still] in bed. In the chaos, they went to the *usnu* that was there [using it] as a fortress. Amidst the confusion that one can imagine since they never believed that the Indians had the courage to attack, the Spaniards armed themselves with whatever weapons they could lay their hands on. They began to defend themselves with resolute Spanish spirit, and even more given the dire circumstances, since nothing less than their lives hung in the balance.

The fighting lasted from the [early] morning, when the Indians attacked, until the evening. In the end, the few fell into the hands of the many, and the Indians killed them all, along with their horses and Black servants. None were able to escape the fury of death, except for one solitary Spaniard. He saw the direction that fate was heading and that it was madness to remain with all his companions dead. Understanding that he could not save his life by fighting, he ran.[828] He fled on horse and the Indians, not wanting him to escape with information, followed him without resting or letting him rest for a moment, all the way to Anchacocha. In the end, with God's help, he escaped danger, and the Indians returned to enjoy the spoils of the dead Spaniards tearing their bodies apart with barbaric cruelty.

The Spaniard walked with great care to Lima, which was three long days away, and reported the news to the Marquis Pizarro, who was profoundly saddened by the death of the Spaniards. He [immediately] began to prepare defenses, gathering as many [Spaniards] as possible and rallying the Indians to defend themselves so that what had happened [in Jauja] would not occur there.

[After] Quizo Yupanqui finished destroying [Jauja], he collected and sent the most precious clothes and weapons of the Spaniards to Manco Inca, telling of his resounding victory *[f.150v]* and the death of all the Spaniards. Manco Inca received the presents with great joy and pleasure, [envisioning] a promising ending to the current actions with the killing of all the Spaniards across the kingdom, leaving him as the peaceful and legitimate[829] ruler. In gratitude for what he had done, [Manco

---

827   This word is underlined (Murúa 2008 [1616]:149v).

828   This was Cervantes de Maculas (Hemming 1970:207).

829   There may be a correction here (Murúa 2008 [1616]:150v).

Inca] sent Quizo Yupanqui a very beautiful Coya from his own lineage along with litters on which he could travel with more authority. [Manco Inca] also ordered [Quizo Yupanqui] to immediately go to Lima and destroy it, leaving nothing standing. And that he was to kill all Spaniards wherever he found them, with the expectation of the Marquis, who should be captured alive. Quizo Yupanqui should bring him [as a] prisoner or send him to where [Manco Inca] was so that he could then advance on Cuzco and seize Hernando Pizarro and the others and kill them all.

Quizo Yupanqui, filled with pride and gratitude upon receiving the Coya and the litters, all of which were indications of great favor and generosity, spent a month resting in Jauja and gathered people of Jauja, Huancas and Yauyos, to go to Lima [to attack] the Marquis. This was a grave error. Had [Quizo Yupanqui] chosen to leave without letting his large army rest, traveling, and crossing the *puna*[830] of Pariacaca,[831] and had suddenly attacked Lima, he would have certainly taken and devastated it. He would have caught the Marquis unaware and alone, depriving him of the chance to prepare himself and gather as many people as he did, and he could have done whatever he wanted. But God blinded Quizo Yupanqui's judgment, preventing him from continuing what had initially begun so well.

Quizo Yupanqui left Jauja with his army, and on approaching Lima, he ordered his forces to attack in three locations, so that they would better achieve his goal. The Huancas, Angaraes, Yauyos, Chocorvos, and Chauircos would enter by the royal road that ran along the coast via *[f.151r]* Pachacamac, where there was a famous temple, renowned[832] in this kingdom. Quizo Yupanqui would travel through the Mama [Valley] and enter Lima at the lower part of the river. Meanwhile, those from Tarma, Otavalo, Huánuco, and Huaylas would arrive via the road to Trujillo, which is also on the coast. Divided in this way, they surrounded Lima at dawn and then attacked and fought bravely with the Spaniards. They advanced so far that they entered inside the city, causing great havoc, and killing many Spaniards and an infinite number of Indian allies. Had fortune not favored the Spaniards, or, to put it better, if it had been God's decree for the sake of the numerous souls present there to be granted an opportunity for salvation, the war would have concluded on that day with the devastation of Lima. However, while Quizo Yupanqui was fighting at the height of the battle, he was shot in the knee by a harquebus.[833]

830   This word is underlined (Murúa 2008 [1616]:150v).
831   The highland area directly east of Lima.
832   A spelling error has been corrected (Murúa 2008 [1616]:151r).
833   Guaman Poma de Ayala (2004 [1615]:392–393 [394–395]) includes a drawing in his chronicle of Quizo Yupanqui being killed by his uncle, Luis de Avalos de Ayala, with a lance. In contrast, Pedro Martín de Sicilia claimed to have killed Quizo Yupanqui with his lance (Hemming 1970:575). Regardless of how he died, the attack on Lima quickly dispersed after his death.

Being wounded, he withdrew, and seeing their general retreat, so did the others. They disbanded [and] retreated to the hill of San Cristóbal,[834] located a quarter of a league from Lima, [but] within sight of it. Moreover, their mission for the day was achieved since the Huancas, along with the others who came with them, failed to arrive on time, halting [their progress]. Had they arrived [as planned], there would be no memory of the City of Kings nor of the Spaniards. However, in the end, it was all part of God's plan. Quizo Yupanqui was taken to Pumpu,[835] and from there, he went with his army to Chinchaycocha, where he died of the wound. In this way, his army dissolved, leaving the Marquis and the City of Kings free [of threat].[836]

[F.152R] CHAPTER 69

When Manco Inca learned of the death of Quizo Yupanqui, he sent messengers to the Marquis, who went to Cuzco

[When] Quizo Yupanqui died, Ylla Tupa and Puyo Vilca remained in his place as captains. Upon witnessing the death of their general and the collapse of their [army], they agreed to retreat to Jauja. So, they left along with the remnants of their army, and they sent messengers from Jauja to Manco Inca, informing him of the death of Quizo Yupanqui. When he learned this, [Manco Inca] felt immense sorrow and sadness, knowing how much he needed such a brave and fortunate captain and how his own ideas and plans were now foiled. [Manco Inca] appointed [Ylla Tupa], good spirit son of Quizo Yupanqui whom he had left [behind], a captain. He gave him the litters that had been given to his father, to honor him as much as possible and to encourage others to follow him and not leave him. He then dispatched Ylla Tupa, ordering him to guard all the high passes on the roads so that it was impossible for Marquis Pizarro to ascend toward Cuzco. At that point, the sole and most important task was to prevent [Pizarro] from joining his brothers and the other Spaniards who were in Cuzco.

To better conceal his [rebellion] and prevent the Marquis from ascending [to Cuzco], which he feared greatly, [Manco Inca] dispatched messengers to the Marquis, apologizing for what [Quizo Yupanqui] had done. He said he was not to be held responsible for those actions since he had neither left Cuzco nor intentionally separated himself from [Pizarro's] brothers, nor had he wished to attempt anything

834   San Cristóbal is now considered within central Lima.
835   Murúa writes this name as Bombon.
836   Folio 151v is blank.

against the Marquis, whom he loved very much, but was forced and compelled [to do so] due to the ill treatment and humiliations by his brother, Hernando Pizarro, and the other captains and Spaniards. He had sought his freedom and escaped the *[f.152v]* subjection and servitude in which they placed him, all to get gold and silver for them, [as they] never had enough of it. Furthermore, they dishonored his wives and daughters. And that until death, he would follow [Pizarro] with all his strength.

When the Marquis heard what the embassy of Manco Inca had to say, he consented to travel from Lima to Cuzco with many soldiers. He stated that, without a doubt, he would pacify Manco Inca with respectful treatment and [persuasive] arguments, and he would calmly and peacefully take him [to Cuzco]. Despite the passes being controlled, [Pizarro] and his forces crossed them unhindered. Once he arrived in Cuzco, [Pizarro] discussed with his brothers the way in which he would escort [Manco Inca to the city].[837] [Pizarro then] left Cuzco with many people armed with weapons and went to [Ollantay]tambo, where Manco Inca was. He announced that he was going in peace to meet, talk, and offer a plan to restore calm and bring an end to the hostilities and uprisings between him and the Spaniards. [Pizarro] sent a message to [Manco Inca], informing him that he was coming to meet him, as he had sent [an embassy] to Lima saying that he was not angry with him, but only with his brothers, who had mistreated him.

Upon hearing this, Manco Inca feared that they wanted to seize him and kill him, so he refused to discuss peace or talk with the Marquis. When he saw [Pizarro] approaching [Ollantay]tambo with his forces, [Manco Inca] went out to the road prepared for battle and fought with so much determination that the Marquis, and the others in his company, found themselves in a difficult situation. To avoid a complete loss with no one escaping alive, they were forced to immediately leave their tents and beds, cross the river, and retreat to Yucay. They remained here halted several days, trying to decide what was the best course of action. [The Marquis] sent messengers from [Yucay] to Manco Inca expressing much love and expressing remorse for the past events involving his brothers and now with him himself. He [explained] that his intention was not to capture him nor take him by force, but only to meet and talk with him *[f.153r]* about peace; and to arrange a trip so that [Manco Inca] could come peacefully with his Indians to Cuzco, as he had done before the rebellion, and the Marquis requested that he should come to Yucay where they could discuss it.

Being suspicious that this was a trick to capture him, Manco Inca never wanted to leave [Ollantay]tambo and go to Yucay to [meet with] the Marquis. Although every day [Manco Inca] sent messengers with presents and gifts, in a thousand forms,

---

837   Zárate (1981 [1555]:161) describes the problems that the men of Lima faced in arriving at Cuzco and breaking the siege.

complaining about Hernando Pizarro and his brothers and captains, and [reporting] that he had left Cuzco and rebelled out of fear, and that he was afraid to go to the Marquis, because they could harm him, as they had done without reason before.

While they were exchanging messages and embassies, Manco Inca secretly sent Tiso, appointing him Captain-General, to the Collao to gather as many people as possible. [Tiso] immediately left with his orders, and the people obeyed him and organized themselves while he remained in the Collao awaiting new orders from Manco Inca. With this, the Marquis realized that Manco Inca did not wish for peace through negotiations or flattery, so he decided, along with the other [Spanish] captains, to quickly quell [the rebellion] and fight [Manco Inca] with all the people he had. So, the Marquis departed Yucay with this goal and proceeded to [Ollantay]tambo, where the Inca was located. In the [ensuing] battle, he disarmed him and forced him to retreat to Amaibamba.

There, Manco Inca called a meeting with those of his council and the captains who were with him. They decided to go to the province of the Chuis, as they were aware of a fortress there called Oro[n]cota that his grandfather, Tupa Inca Yupanqui, had built. Determined to go, he set out with his army, and they went from Lares to Hualla[838] and from there he arrived at Pillco[pata].[839] There, he found many Blacks and Nicaraguan Indians of the Marquis, and he ordered them all killed without any mercy. While there, he learned from his spies that the Indians living in nearby villages had served him unwillingly and that they were united *[f.153v]* with the Spaniards, his enemies. Upon verifying this information, he ordered them all killed, making an exemplary punishment to instill fear and to discourage others from serving the Spaniards, even if compelled to do so, wanting them to flee if they were captured.

Having concluded this, [Manco Inca] gradually returned with all his people to Hualla, where he rested for a month. From there he returned to Amaibamba, where he had left, and he once again began sending messengers to the Marquis Pizarro, expressing his desire to demonstrate his good intentions and his willingness to serve his Majesty as a loyal subject in order to bring peace to the land, and that he would come in peace to where [Pizarro] was, if his brothers, who had done him so many wrongs, were killed. Or if he could not kill them because they were his brothers, that they needed to be banished from Cuzco and the kingdom, so that they could never again cause him any harm or trouble.

When the Marquis, heard the embassy, he gave his word that he would drive his brothers out of the kingdom, that no harm would come to him under his care, and he would be respected and obeyed by the Indians in Cuzco just like before, and no

---

838   Hualla is a town north of Lares.
839   The town of Pillcopata is east of Hualla.

one would cause him pain or suffering if he mollified and returned and was obedient. [However], the Marquis sent this message to lure Manco Inca safely to Cuzco where he would then do with him as he pleased, having no intention of fulfilling the promise or guarantee that he gave him.

Believing that the Marquis made his promise with simplicity and openness and that he would send his brothers away as he told him, which was what he most desired, Manco Inca came in peace with his people to Cuzco. He was already in Huamanmarca,[840] apparently having forgiven the past. When he learned that [Manco Inca] was approaching, the Marquis sent Spaniards and Indians to secretly capture and seize [Manco Inca] and bring him to [Cuzco].

When these people reached Manco Inca, he became doubtful and suspicious *[f.154r]* of their intensions. Realizing the truth and what the Spaniards were going to do, he switched to defense. [The Spaniards], seeing that he was ready to defend himself, attacked, and [Manco Inca] retreated to Chuquichaca as best he could.[841] There, with the arrival of additional reinforcements, he grew courageous as there were only a few [Spaniards] pursuing him. So, he turned on them, charging in such a manner that they were forced to retreat, fleeing with great haste. He pursued them as far as [Ollantay]tambo, where he rested and stayed for some days.

During this time, the Marquis was disappointed that Manco Inca would not return in peace, and [recognized] that it made no sense to wait for his peaceful return, since he was still angry about the last time, when he left his brother, Hernando Pizarro, in Cuzco with orders that if there was an occasion when Manco Inca was careless,[842] he should capture him. [So, the Marquis] then proceeded to Arequipa.[843] There, being convinced of the fertility of that settlement, he populated it with Spaniards, assigning them *encomiendas*, and subsequently traveled down to the City of Kings.[844]

---

840   The site of Huamanmarca (Huayopata District, La Convención Province, Department of Cuzco).
841   Chuquichaca was a major bridge that crossed the lower Urubamba River, providing an entrance into the Vilcabamba region. Control of the bridge, and thus access to the Vilcabamba region, remained a major concern for the Incas and the Spaniards for the next forty years.
842   A spelling error has been corrected (Murúa 2008 [1616]:154v).
843   The foundation of Spanish Arequipa occurred on 15 August 1540.
844   Folio 154v is blank.

[F.155R] CHAPTER 70

When Don Diego de Almagro returned from Chile, he tried to negotiate with Manco Inca, and what happened to him[845]

After Marquis Don Francisco Pizarro left Cuzco for Arequipa, Manco Inca learned about it. Even though he was in [Ollantay]tambo, he and his [people] continued to move freely and boldly about. During this time, Don Diego de Almagro, along with Paullu Topa and all the people that had accompanied them, arrived from Chile. No Spaniards were missing, although many Indians had perished in the wilderness due to the snow. As previously described, finding [the Cuzco region] in revolt greatly troubled Almagro, and he attempted to find a solution without bloodshed.

Paullu Topa sent a message to his brother, Manco Inca, informing him of his and Don Diego de Almagro's return from Chile, where they had endured countless hardships and misfortunes, including hunger and treacherous roads. [Paullu Topa expressed] great concern [that Manco Inca had rebelled] and [was now an] enemy of the Spaniards, and that if he wanted to ease [the situation] it would be easy for him to seek revenge on those that had offended him. Don Diego de Almagro had told [Paullu Topa] that he, along with his soldiers, including the four hundred Spaniards under his command, would support Manco Inca and kill the Marquis and Hernando Pizarro and the other brothers and captains on [Pizarro's] side.[846] If they joined forces, this could be easily achieved, and then live in peace, free from insults. Manco Inca was very pleased to hear this. He believed that he could take revenge on Hernando Pizarro, whom he deeply resented for having tortured him with a rope, and in this way, they would drive his enemies out of the land. Therefore, [Manco Inca] told his people *[f.155v]* about the return of the Spaniards and[847] Don[848] Diego de Almagro from Chile and that they would join him to destroy the Marquis and the others. So, they should prepare themselves [for battle].

To solidify their friendship and the agreement they had discussed, [Manco Inca] sent messengers and many presents to Don Diego de Almagro. [The messengers]

---

845   Parts of chapter 70 and chapters 72–85 first appeared as translations in Bauer, Halac-Higashimori, and Gabriel E. Cantarutti (2016:43–108). They are presented here, with small changes, with permission of the University Press of Colorado. Most importantly, we have improved the specific dates of the Spanish invasion of Vilcabamba with the use of Ziółkowski's date converter (https://inca-calendar.icm.edu.pl/index.php/date-converter/).

846   Cobo (1979 [1653]:173) and Pizarro (1921 [1571]:269–270, 294, 347) suggest that Manco Inca requested that Almagro kill two of his remaining brothers, one of which was named Octo Xopa.

847   The word "and" has been inserted into the manuscript (Murúa 2008 [1616]:155v).

848   A word was inserted into the manuscript here, and then crossed out.

reported that he was willing to do everything his brother, Paullu Topa, had requested on his behalf and that united, Don Diego would be helped in everything. By driving Hernando Pizarro out [of the kingdom, Don Diego] would remain as lord and governor of the land, similar to the Marquis, and that they would meet in some place of mutual agreement. When Don Diego de Almagro and Paullu Topa heard this, [they sent a reply saying] they wanted to see Manco Inca. They departed from Cuzco and went to Patachuayla, the designated meeting place.

As Manco Inca traveled along the road, he suspected that Don Diego de Almagro and Paullu Topa wanted to catch him unguarded and seize him because they were coming with many people. So, [Manco Inca] told his people: "These [Spaniards] must want to capture us through deception. Let us [attack] before they betray us just like the Marquis surely wanted to kill us. Let us kill them." Thus, his forces advanced, and they attacked Don Diego de Almagro, his men, and Paullu Topa, and engaged in battle.[849] They overwhelmed them, forcing them to flee. They chased them until the river, where the Spaniards found some rafts they used to cross to the other side, ensuring their safety and saving their lives on that occasion. When Manco Inca reached the river and found Arampa Yupanqui there, he asked him: "Why did you give the rafts to my enemies? Undoubtedly, you are allied with them and secretly supporting them." And with this [Manco Inca] immediately ordered him killed. [f.156r]

Don Diego de Almagro arrived in Cuzco with Paullu Topa, almost running from Manco Inca's trick. They pitched their tents in the plaza. Within two days, Don Diego de Almagro seized Hernando Pizarro and Gonzalo Pizarro as there were ongoing disagreements about the city's government and to whom it belonged: [Don Diego de Almagro] or the Marquis Don Francisco Pizarro. Diego de Almagro sent [the Pizarros] under guard to Lima, instructing them to return to Castile because their insolence and arrogance had caused Manco Inca to rebel. Perhaps [Don Diego de Almagro] did this with the intention of changing the Inca's outlook. By seeing that he had banished the Pizarros from Cuzco and sent them to Lima, he would come in peace.[850]

From [these events], bloody passions were kindled between Pizarros and Almagros, which cost the kingdom so much, impeding the spread of the Holy Gospel and the Indians' acceptance of Holy Baptism and causing the deaths of so many Spaniards and Indians.

The kingdom began divided into two factions, with some pledging their [allegiance to] one side and others to the opposite side, causing so much blood to flow

---

849   Zárate (1981 [1555]:155) also briefly discusses the communications between Manco Inca and Almagro.

850   Murúa is mistaken; Hernando Pizarro was taken to Lima, but Gonzalo remained imprisoned in Cuzco (Zárate 1981 [1555]:166).

that recounting it brings tears to the eyes. Eventually, Hernando Pizarro returned to Cuzco, and a bloody battle took place in the Salinas,[851] which are half a league from the city, near the parish of San Sebastián,[852] between Hernando Pizarro and Don Diego de Almagro, who was accompanied by those who had gone with him to Chile.

Following Don Diego de Almagro's defeat and capture, Hernando Pizarro wanted to eliminate this obstacle so that the absolute and unequaled control of the kingdom remained with his brother, the Marquis. He made [Diego de Almagro] stand trial, which God knows, and sentenced him to death. [Hernando Pizarro] ignored that he had [earlier] been Don Diego de Almagro's prisoner and that he had treated him with courtesy and clemency, sending him to Lima. [Hernando Pizarro] executed the sentence, and Don Diego de Almagro was publicly beheaded in Cuzco, evoking great pity and sorrow among his friends and enemies. He left a mestizo son, named Don Diego de Almagro,[853] like his father. I will speak briefly of this as *[f.156v]* my intention in this book is solely to record the descent of the Inca Kings of this kingdom and their rightful possessions. The details of the Spaniards' affairs, which others have already discussed, can be read in their writings.[854]

I will only mention that before and after the battle of Las Salinas, the Indians who were in Cuzco and its [surrounding] region, who had not joined Manco Inca, went to recognize Paullu Topa, as the son of Huayna Capac, in his house.[855] The Spanish neighbors and *encomenderos* wanted to avoid difficulties that could occur if [the Indians] grow accustomed to this, and to prevent Paullu Topa from gaining too much power, ordered that only his servants could go to his house. So, from then on, the Indians did not go to his house nor [offer him] reverence. In the end, the Spaniards believed that by doing so, they would eliminate the incentive for Paullu Topa to rebel like his brother.

---

851 There were once large salt pans upslope from the town of San Sebastián. This is where the "Batalla de las Salinas" occurred on 6 April 1538 (Zárate 1981 [1555]:172). During this battle, Diego de Almagro was captured, and his captain, Rodrigo Orgóño, was killed. Almagro was executed in Cuzco in July 1538.

852 There is a small chapel in San Sebastián dedicated to those who died in this battle.

853 Zárate (1981 [1555]:187) writes: "When Hernando Pizarro had captured and executed the Adelantado Don Diego de Almagro at Cuzco, he sent to Los Reyes a son of Don Diego's by an Indian woman, who was called like his father Don Diego de Almagro. He was a good lad of fine spirit and had been well educated, both to ride, in both styles, which he did most skillfully and gracefully, and also to read and write, at which he was more proficient than was necessary for a gentleman." This young man later served as the inspiration for a second civil war between the Spaniards of Peru.

854 Murúa notes that he had read other accounts of the Spaniards in Peru.

855 Zárate (1981 [1555]:157) suggests that Diego de Almagro invested Paullu Inca as Inca, after which he was given the palace of Colcampata.

Manco Inca remained relentless during this period, actively causing havoc, [committing] robberies, and destroying everything he could. When this news reached the Spaniards, [who] wanted to be done with him for once and for all, since he was disturbing the kingdom, they went out to where he was. They fought bravely, wounded him and killing, pursuing him as far as the province of Vitcos, which is in Vilcabamba. Paullu Topa followed them, and one day they managed to corner [Manco Inca], seizing his litter and *tiana* (which is the chair upon which he sat). However, he escaped into the forested mountains, where he hid with many Indians.[856] The other [warriors], who were unable to follow him, were exhausted and lacked the determination to continue. [So] they went to Cuzco, and from there, each returned to his own land. The Spaniards, knowing that Manco Inca had slipped from their grasp, also returned to Cuzco.

Manco Inca then went to his Huamanga[857] with his forces, where he inflicted as much harm as possible. Understanding that he would not stop, [the Spaniards] tried sending [troops] to capture him again.[858] Gonzalo Pizarro, [Francisco de] Villacastín,[859] Captain Orgoño *[f.157r]*, Captain [Pedro de] Oñate,[860] and Juan Balsa [the elder][861] entered [the Vilcabamba region]. Although they killed many relatives of Manco Inca and [other] important people who were with him, thirteen Spaniards and six horses were killed. Captain [Francisco de] Villacastín went with many Spanish soldiers and Indians, whose captains were Inquill and Huaipar.[862]

---

856   The first Spanish raid into Vilcabamba occurred in 1537 under the leadership of Rodrigo Orgoño and Rui Díaz. Indigenous forces were supplied by Paullu Inca (Pizarro 1921 [1571]:365).

857   The city of Huamanga, now called Ayacucho, is described by Murúa in book 3, chapter 25 of his chronicle.

858   The second raid into the Vilcabamba region occurred in 1539 under the leadership of Gonzalo Pizarro. Rodrigo Orgoño was not a member of the raid since he had been killed during the battle of Las Salina. During the second raid, the wife of Manco Inca, Cura Ocllo, was captured and later killed by Francisco Pizarro (Betanzos 1996 [1557]:291–293; Pizarro 1921 [1571]:396–406).

859   Francisco de Villacastín, who had fought with Gonzalo Pizarro in the civil war, died in prison in Cuzco soon after the battle of Jaquijahuana (1548).

860   Pedro de Oñate may have also entered the Vilcabamba region in 1537, as Cusi Titu Yupanqui was placed under his care after the raid. Oñate died in 1542 during the failed revolt of Diego de Almagro (the younger).

861   Since Juan Balsa (the elder) was a follower of Almagro, he may have entered the Vilcabamba region with Rodrigo Orgoño in 1537. His son, Juan Balsa (the younger), a cousin of Tupac Amaru, entered the Vilcabamba region in the raid of 1572.

862   Inquill and Huaipar were both sons of Huayna Capac, although they held a lower status than Manco Inca and Paullu. Both are mentioned by Titu Cussi Yupangui (2005 [1571]:108) as fighting on the side of the Spaniards in the 1536 siege of Cuzco. Titu Cussi Yupangui (2005 [1571]:123) also indicates that both brothers were killed during the 1539 raid into Vilcabamba.

Manco Inca gathered as many people as he could [and] suddenly attacked the Indians, killing them all, and he found and captured Huaipar. Inquill, who had escaped, fled and fell off a precipice. To install fear among the remaining troops, [Manco Inca] ordered that Huaipar be executed in front of his sister, who was the wife of Manco Inca.

Later, a battle was fought[863] [in which Francisco de] Villacastín and the Spaniards defeated Manco Inca and captured his wife.[864] She was captured because she remained in their hiding place, angry, and did not want to[865] follow her husband because he had killed her brother, Huaipar, in front of her, as mentioned above. [Francisco de] Villacastín and Gonzalo Pizarro took her to [Ollantay]tambo, where the Marquis Pizarro was, having recently returned from the City of Kings. In an act of unusual cruelty, unjustly inflicted upon a woman bore no responsibility for her husband's uprisings and rebellion, [Francisco Pizarro] ordered her and other captains of Manco Inca be shot with arrows. [Manco Inca] cried and expressed great sorrow, grief, and despair at the death of his wife, because he loved her very much. Consequently, he retreated to the site of Vilcabamba.[866]

[F.158R] CHAPTER 71

How all the high provinces rebelled and selected Quinti Raura as lord, and [how] Hernando Pizarro went out against them

The *Collas*[867] and all the other provinces were in upheaval due to the efforts of Tiso,[868] a general of Manco Inca, whom as previously mentioned, [Manco Inca] sent to gather people and to incite rebellion in Collao. When [these provinces] saw that Manco Inca was losing and the Spaniards were killing and abandoning many people, they decided to rise up from the Vilcanota [River] to Chile. They refused to obey Manco Inca and did not recognize the Spaniards, whom they were against because of their tyranny and oppression. Thus, they decided to name Quinti Raura, a native of the Pacajes, as their principal lord of all. He was an important *curaca* of great worth, who willingly and courageously accepted [the position], promising to expel the Spaniards and set the people free, [even] more than they had been in the

---

863   This battle took place at Huayna Pucara (Lee 2000; Pizarro 1921 [1571]:397 404).
864   This was Cura Ocllo, who goes unnamed by Murúa.
865   A spelling mistake has been corrected here.
866   Folio 157v is blank.
867   The word "Collas" is underlined in the original manuscript (Murúa 2008 [1616]:158r).
868   Zárate (1981 [1555]:174) also mentions this general.

time of the Inca. As part of the customary ceremonies and solemnities they undertake to confirm supreme lords, he crossed the Desaguadero [River][869] and fasted where there are now some ruins.[870]

Having heard about the commotion and uprising, Hernando Pizarro left Cuzco with many Spaniards, with Paullu Topa joining his company, along with Indian allies, to pacify the situation.[871] Upon reaching the Desaguadero [River], Quinti Raura emerged with his army to meet them. Hernando Pizarro gave battle, displaying great courage and daring. In [the battle] many Spaniards and Indians of Paullu Topa were killed, and Hernando Pizarro narrowly escaped being killed, along with many others, when they were unable to cross the Desaguadero [River] in time. Seeing [f.158v] this [dire situation], Paullu Topa ordered the construction [of rafts], so that all the Indians and Spaniards could easily cross in safety, and Paullu Topa, himself, charged with his own [men] against the Collas, forcing them to withdraw from the Desaguadero [River].[872] Then, Hernando Pizarro and the Spaniards arrived and joined them.

Realizing their imminent defeat, the Collas fortified themselves in a pass and gave battle again. However, in the end, they were thwarted by the courage of the Spaniards, who fought bravely that day. Some of the defeated Collas sought refuge in the lake while others returned to their lands. Quinti Raura, who never had the chance to enjoy his newly given authority and command, was captured in this battle, and the Spaniards burned all nearby settlements. Hernando Pizarro cruelly punished the prisoners and all the chiefs he could get his[873] hands on those had rebelled, aiming to teach them obedience and discourage future rebellions.

When he was finished, Hernando Pizarro continued with his troops to the province of Charcas, where Tiso, [the] general of Manco Inca was, [hoping to] catch him off guard. However, [Tiso] had been warned of Hernando Pizarro's approach, along with Paullu Topa and his many soldiers. In response, [Tiso] made a formidable army of Chuis, Charcas, and other nations from that region, extending as far as Chile. He also gathered a number of Cora Coras and set out to meet Hernando Pizarro. They fought at Tapacarí, where the Spaniards won, while General Tiso and the Indians were defeated and retreated. Hernando Pizarro then advanced with

---

869   Desaguadero is a marshy area that drains Lake Titicaca, currently marking the boundary between Peru and Bolivia.

870   This may be a reference to the ruins of Tiwanaku. If so, it is interesting that the people of the Collao returned to Tiwanaku for the coronation of their own king.

871   Zárate (1981 [1555]: 174) briefly mentions this expedition.

872   Pedro Pizarro (1921 [1571]:387–389) describes the battle of Desaguadero. However, he suggests that Gonzalo Pizarro was in charge. Hernando arrived after the troops were in Cochabamba.

873   A textual error has been corrected (Murúa 2008 [1616]:158v).

his men to Cochabamba, where he established his royal camp and rested since his people were tired from the journey and the battle.

One morning, while feeling at ease before dawn, the Spaniards found themselves unexpectedly surrounded by Indians, who had most likely been hiding nearby. They had placed an infinite number of thick and strong trunks around the camp as barricades, preventing the Spaniards from *[f.159r]* utilizing their horses, which were their most effective assets in battle. Both Hernando Pizarro and Paullu Topa realized that they were in grave danger because they were completely surrounded, unable to enter or exit the camp. If they remained there, they would perish of hunger and their houses from [lack of] pasture. Tiso on that occasion had assembled and had brought a large number of Indians with the promise of killing all the Spaniards; freeing and saving themselves from their abuses. He incited and motivated all those provinces to rebel, with promises and even threats made on behalf of Manco Inca, in whose name he had come, as previously described.

Hernando Pizarro and the Spaniards realized that they were surrounded and that their only option was to break through the timbers and palisades with as much force as possible and attack the enemies waiting outside with their weapons. They made plans for some to break [through] while others fought from within. Thus, the Spaniards and Paullu Topa with his Indian allies began dismantling the barricades and move forward in spite of Tiso's Indians, who defended them with great courage and ferocity with all their strength. The fighting continued all day and night, without either side resting, with both sides showing remarkable tenacity rarely witnessed in indigenous battles in this kingdom. However, in the end, through the will of God and with the assistance of Paullu Topa's Indians, the Spaniards defeated Tiso and his men with great effort, making them flee. This prolonged and fierce battle resulted in many deaths.

Knowing his luck had run out and realizing he was disarmed, Tiso retreated to Pocona with those who chose to follow him and then continued on to Chichas. Hernando Pizarro and Paullu Topa, wanting to quickly finish [the fighting] for once and for all, swiftly followed him, but no matter how hard they tried, they could not catch up with him. Thus, they returned to Pocona *[f.159v]* to rest, which they greatly needed because of the toil and efforts of the hard-fought battle. While in Pocona, Paullu Topa sought to convince Tiso, who was in Humahuaca with his people, to submit to the authority of His Majesty through acts of goodwill and persuasive words. [Paullu Topa] sent his ambassadors to inform [Tiso] that he knew he had little choice, and with Manco Inca having fled to Vitcos, [Manco Inca] could not leave or help him. Paullu Topa said it would be much better for [Tiso] to come peacefully than to continue fighting. Furthermore, if he liked, he would speak to Hernando Pizarro and gain a pardon for Tiso and his people, thereby ensuring their safety and peace.

Upon hearing this message of Paullu Topa and his sound logic, Tiso expressed his willingness to come to Hernando Pizarro and pledge obedience to him, on the condition that he would be pardoned and guaranteed protection from harm. Hernando Pizarro assured him, and with this Tiso slowly arrived, accompanied by all the *caciques* and principals of the provinces of the Charcas and Chuis, along with the others who had rebelled and fought alongside him in the war. They arrived with great fanfare where Hernando Pizarro and Paullu Topa were waiting for them in formation with their weapons of war. There, Tiso and the *curacas* humbly bowed, first to Hernando Pizarro and then to Paullu Topa, who warmly received them.

When this was concluded, Hernando Pizarro had his Spaniards seize Tiso and the other *curacas* who had come with him. Without causing any harm, he gave Tiso to Paullu Topa as a prisoner, telling him to keep him well and treat him as his friend and confederate. He also pardoned the other *curacas*. With this *[f.160r]* the land was pacified, and the Indians returned to their villages as before, without any rumors or revolts among them. Having placed [the region] in order and harmony, Hernando Pizarro[874] returned with Paullu Topa to Cuzco, bringing Tiso[875] and other *caciques* of the Collao as prisoners. They were kept in Cuzco for some time, ensuring that the provinces remained calm and united. By removing the governing figures from their sight, the Indians were less likely to initiate uprisings and rebellions, as it is the leaders who instigated such conflicts.[876]

[F.161R] CHAPTER 72

How Manco Inca killed many Spaniards who were coming to capture him, and [how] Diego Méndez and others entered where [the Inca was] living in peace

This was the situation when [Manco Inca] received news that the Spaniards were entering through Ruparupa, intending to capture him, because they thought that an expedition against him would fare far better if they came in from behind[877] rather than through the usual trail, which [the Indians] had fortified.[878] Since he

874   Later Hernando Pizarro was sent to Spain to explain the killing of Diego de Almagro, and Gonzalo Pizarro was sent to Vilcabamba to deal with Manco Inca (Pizarro 1921 [1571]:387).

875   Although Tiso kept his word, he may have been later killed by the Spaniards (Titu Cussi Yupangui 2005 [1571]:124).

876   Folio 160v is blank.

877   That is to say, from the west rather than from the east.

878   Much of this paragraph overlaps with information provided in Cobo (1979 [1653]:173–176).

knew they were coming, he sent Paucar Huaman and Yuncallo along with many Indians to defend the entrance at the most difficult pass along the trail by which [the Spaniards] were coming. These two captains went to find the Spaniards, who totaled one hundred sixty, not including the many Indian allies accompanying them. They gave battle in Yuramayo, which is behind Jauja [and] toward the Andes.[879] The Spaniards were tired and worn down from the rough trails and forested slopes they had cut and traversed, crossing rivers and enduring countless hardships typical of such *[f.161v]* expeditions that diverge from the well-traveled route and lack readily available supplies. Since the Indians came rested and eager to fight, they defeated [the Spaniards] without much difficulty, killing all who could not escape.[880] Only a few [escaped], [enduring] great hunger and dangers, crossing a thousand cliffs, until they reached to Christian lands.

Among Manco Inca's forces, Yuncallo died in this battle, causing immense sadness and pain [for the Inca]. He was a brave, wise, courageous Indian, and was greatly missed. Also, [the Inca] had great affection for him, due to his unwavering loyalty throughout all their trials and tribulations. Having killed so many Spaniards, Paucar Huaman gathered all the spoils he found on the battlefield and joyfully returned to Vilcabamba with his [forces]. Manco Inca received him with great honor and applause. Subsequently, Manco Inca's captains and followers engaged in periodic expeditions along the royal roads of Abancay, Andahuaylas, Limatambo, Curahuasi, [Ollantay]tambo, and other locations, where they knew they targeted isolated Spaniards to kill them and steal their possessions. In this way, no place was safe [for the Spaniards] nor could they travel unless there were many together.

Manco Inca discussed with his followers the following: that they [should] go to Quito, a fertile and abundant land where the Spaniards would be less able to harm them. There, they could more easily fortify themselves against their opponents. Furthermore, those provinces had an infinite number of people, more than up here [i.e., in the Cuzco highlands], because the Spaniards had not depleted [their numbers] as they had [done] to [Manco Inca's people]. After discussing it with his captains, who agreed, he put [his plan] into effect. He left Vilcabamba with his entire army and everything he had, including those taken from the Spaniards. When they arrived at Huamanga, where there were then few Spaniards, they robbed and destroyed it, committing *[f.162r]* every ill deed they could.[881]

It appears that both Murúa and Cobo extracted their information from the same text.

879   Murúa is referring to the area east of Jauja, toward the Amazonian area.

880   This may be a description of the 1538 battle of Oncoy, which took place in the Province of Andahuaylas.

881   Cobo (1979 [1653]:174) provides a similar description of Manco Inca's attack on Huamanga.

On his arrival, Manco Inca decided that there were already too many Spaniards in [Huamanga], and [more] were arriving from Castile every day, and thus increasing their numbers. Therefore, [he decided] it would not be wise for him to continue as they could come out from Lima and other places in large numbers and wait for him in a suitable location for their horses, where they could defeat and capture him. So, he decided it was more advantageous to return to Vitcos, where he had started. After telling his people this they left and, upon arriving, he stated that they should stay in Vilcabamba, as it was unsafe to go any other place, as the Spaniards occupied everywhere else.

This was the time when the widespread and notoriously known rebellions caused by the sorrowful death of Don Diego de Almagro [the elder] were occurring in the kingdom. They were led by Captain Juan de Herrada[882] and his associates, who sought to avenge [Almagro's] death in the City of Kings.[883] They had Don Diego de Almagro, [the younger], the son of the deceased, under their care. One day, they left young Don Diego locked in their house, as they feared for his safety due to his tender age. They then proceeded to the houses where the Marquis Don Francisco Pizarro lived on the central plaza, which are now royal palaces [and] where the Viceroy and the [Royal] Audiencia reside.

[Pizarro] had just finished eating with Captain Francisco de Chávez,[884] who was his compatriot, when [the rebels] entered the dining room. He entered a side room, where he defended himself at the door with a halberd for a considerable time, as he was [a] man of great courage. Realizing that any delay would attract the attention of the city's inhabitants, thwarting their plans, the conspirators pushed a Black man to the front, forcing him to enter the room. As the Marquis struck him with his halberd, they were able to enter, where they killed [Pizarro] and Captain Francisco de Chávez. They removed the body of the Marquis, dragging it through the plaza. As a result, many people gathered [and] all those allied with Don Diego de Almagro's faction accepted [f.162v] his son as their leader.

[Cristóbal] Vaca de Castro, [a member] of the Royal Council of the Emperor, our lord, and the Order of Santiago, then arrived and took control of those who remained loyal to His Majesty.[885] [Vaca de Castro] confronted Don Diego

882   Juan de Herrada had traveled with Diego de Almagro to Chile and was placed in charge of his son after Almagro was killed in Cuzco.
883   For detailed descriptions of the assassination of Pizarro, see Zárate (1981 [1555]:189–192) and Pizarro (1921 [1571]:418–423). Zárate (1981 [1555]:192) states that Pizarro was killed on 26 June 1541.
884   Francisco de Chávez was one of the most powerful Spaniards in Peru at this time. Chávez is also mentioned by Pizarro (1921 [1571]:421) and Zárate (1981 [1555]:190) as having been killed in Lima along with Francisco Pizarro.
885   Cristóbal Vaca de Castro was already in route to Peru when he learned of the death of

de Almagro, the younger, in Chupas, two leagues from Huamanga, with the king's army. There, Captain Francisco de Carvajal,[886] who later served as Gonzalo Pizarro's Field Marshal against Your Majesty, participated and contributed greatly to the victory. The battle took place, and Don Diego de Almagro's [forces] were defeated. [Almagro] fled to Cuzco, but was taken prisoner, and Vaca de Castro meted out justice to him, beheading him. There were other events that occurred that I do not intend to discuss at length, as I am solely focusing on, as I have said, the succession of the Inca Indians.

When Don Diego de Almagro, the younger, was defeated, Diego Méndez, [a] mestizo, along with Barba Briceño y Escalante and other soldiers, fled the battle of Chupas. They were thirteen companions in all and found themselves in opposition to Your Majesty. Realizing that those who were responsible for the rebellion were assiduously being captured, they fled into the mountains until they reached Vilcabamba, where Manco Inca was. [He] warmly welcomed them with great generosity for all they had suffered. They told him that many Spaniards would enter there to serve him, and with them, he could reclaim his land and defeat and cast out the Spaniards who were in it. They told this to flatter and please Manco Inca, as they feared he would have them killed. [However,] he treated them well in every respect, without intentions of causing harm, which reassured them and alleviated their fears.[887]

Several days later, Manco Inca discovered through the spies he had in Cuzco and other places that a *curaca* named Sitiel had mocked Manco Inca in front of many Christians. [Sitiel] had told Caruarayco, the *cacique* of Cotomarca:[888] "We are going to Vilcabamba to capture Manco Inca and Caruarayco will be Inca *[f.163r]* and lord, and all will obey him. Manco Inca also will serve him and bring him the *tiana* (which is the seat where the *curacas* and important leaders sit)."[889] When Manco Inca learned of this, he was deeply hurt, and began to devise a plan to avenge the impudence and mockery displayed by Sitiel. He considered it a great affront that one of his Indian vassals had the audacity to say such a thing, whether in the presence of the Spaniards or anyone else.

Francisco Pizarro. Emperor Charles V had sent him to restore order to Peru after the death of Diego de Almagro (the elder).

886   Francisco de Carvajal was an aging but highly effective military leader. He fought on the king's side in the Almagro uprising but turned against the king and fought alongside Gonzalo Pizarro a few years later.

887   Cobo (1979 [1653]:174) also describes Diego Méndez fleeing from the battle of Chupas into Vilcabamba and being welcomed by Manco Inca.

888   Cotomarca is located along the Abancay-Limatambo road, near the community of Mollepata. It is about a three days' walk from Vitcos.

889   Cobo (1979 [1653]:175) also mentions "Carbayayco," the Lord of Cotamarca.

[Manco Inca] said to[890] Diego Méndez and the others, "We are going to capture those people so that they may know our mettle and not underestimate us." Diego Méndez and the others agreed and willingly offered [their assistance]. However, Manco Inca changed his mind, saying, "We are not going there because you are still tired from the arduous trip you have made. It will suffice if the bravest of my people go. They will capture him." Thus, in accordance with this, he sent all the captains who were with him and all the Indians as well, such that only five hundred [warriors] remained as his guard. [The Inca] ordered them to quickly proceed before they could be detected and to attempt to bring Sitiel and Caruarayco back alive, so that he could exact revenge upon them as he pleased. With this, they set out to fulfill their order with the utmost speed.[891]

How Diego Méndez and the other Spaniards treacherously killed Manco Inca

No one would deny that ingratitude is an ugly and abominable[892] vice. To do good to the one who wronged me is a Christian act that follows in the footsteps and example of Christ, our Redeemer, who taught this through [his] words and deeds until the end of his life. All men who have [even] a little understanding of natural law, reward good with good. However, to [not] reward he who helped me, who freed me from risk and danger, who gave me food and drink when I was in need, who covered my nakedness, is [an act] of a malignant soul, blind and barbaric in understanding. Even wild animals recognize and respect those who have helped and done them good. We have a thousand examples of this in books, and as the Spanish philosopher Séneca stated, in calling someone ungrateful, with this name alone, they had spoken the worst of him, since all the shame and insults possible are included and subsumed in this single term.

I mention this because of [the actions of] Diego Méndez, Barba [Briceño y Escalante], and their companions. They had fled [a situation] from which they, like others who committed a sinful crime, would not have escaped with their lives if they had been caught. Yet, instead of treating them as enemies who had done so much harm to [him], Manco Inca helped them. He took them in, gave them food

---

890 The word "to" has been inserted into the manuscript (Murúa 2008 [1616]:163).
891 Folio 163v is blank
892 A spelling error has been corrected (Murúa 2008 [1616]:164r).

and drink and kept them in his company. He helped them in every way possible. [Yet] they repaid [Manco Inca's] hospitality and welcome by taking his life, under the false hope that [the Spaniards] would show them mercy. They did not consider the ugly and vile act too base to be imagined by noble hearts, they had committed against those who had, in fact, helped them. *[f.164v]*

After dispatching his captains and people, Manco Inca remained with the Spaniards, treating them with great kindness and courtesy. He provided them with a table, where they were served plentiful food and drink.[893] He gave them many gifts, as though they were in their hometowns. [However], it appeared that the Spaniards grew resentful of these many acts of kindness and became tired of their stay. They wanted to leave the interior and go to Cuzco. Yet they did not know how to do it safely without being captured by [Cristóbal] Vaca de Castro. They discussed among themselves a terrible betrayal, of killing Manco Inca by any means possible. Once they had killed him, they planned to flee [from Vilcabamba], as they believed that having contributed to pacifying the region by having killed him, it was certain that Vaca de Castro would pardon them and show them mercy. After deliberation, Diego Méndez was in favor of killing [Manco Inca] at the earliest opportunity, before the Indians who had gone to capture Sitiel and Caruarayco returned, because once they returned it would be more difficult [to achieve], as there would be so many people with Manco Inca. Therefore, they continued to wait cautiously for an opportunity to carry out their harmful and wicked act.

One day, while Manco Inca and Diego Méndez were playing a game of *bolos*,[894] Diego Méndez[895] won some money from Manco Inca, which was then paid to him. After playing briefly, [Manco Inca] said he did not want to play anymore, as he was tired. He ordered food brought to him, and Manco Inca said to Diego Méndez and the others, "Let us eat." They agreed and happily sat down and ate what had been brought to the Inca. [However, Manco Inca] grew suspicious of the Spaniards when he saw them behaving cautiously and carrying concealed weapons. As a result, he became worried that they might intend to commit treason, as he had few companions [to protect him]. So, when they finished eating, he told [the Spaniards] to rest *[f.165r]*, as he wanted to relax for a while with his Indians.

893 Cobo (1979 [1653]:175) also speaks of this banquet.
894 A tossing game played with balls tied together with string. Also see Salazar (2016 [1596]:178).
895 Guaman Poma de Ayala (2004 [1615]:407 [409]) and Pizarro (1921 [1571]:437–438) provide short descriptions of the killing of Manco Capac by Diego Méndez. Betanzos (1996 [1557]:292–296) provides a far more detailed account of Diego Méndez's time in Vilcabamba. He also records the names of two other Spaniards involved, Gómez Pérez and a man called Cornejo. Cobo (1979 [1653]:175) also provides some overlapping information about the Manco Inca being killed by Méndez.

[The Spaniards] said that they would leave, but [instead] started to playfully engage with each other, trying to amuse Manco Inca, who delighted in their joviality. They entertained themselves in this manner for a while until, Manco Inca, having drunk, rose to share a drink to the captain of his guard—a customary gesture of high regard among them. Manco Inca then drank another glass, given to him by one of his Indian women standing behind him. At this moment Diego Méndez, who was carefully waiting to seize the opportunity if it arose, saw that [the Inca's] back was turned, attacked with great ferocity from behind, and stabbed him with a dagger.[896] Manco Inca fell on the ground, and Diego Méndez proceeded to stab him two more times.[897] The unarmed Indians who were there were surprised by this unforeseen event and attempted to shield Manco Inca from further harm. The other Spaniards [then] drew their swords and counterattacked to free Diego Méndez. They swiftly made their way to the stables and saddled their horses. They took the gifts they had there and hastily loaded their *ato* as best they could. They then took to the trail to Cuzco without stopping anywhere, marching all night without sleeping. The mountainous terrain made it difficult to find the path, so they became lost, stumbling from one place to another and experiencing delays.

After Diego Méndez and his companions wounded Manco Inca and fled, the principal Indians who were [in Vitcos], [overwhelmed] with an understandable sorrow and grief, did not dare follow the Spaniards with the people that Manco Inca had there. They were fearful that the betrayal had been orchestrated in collaboration, and more people from Cuzco were en route to aid [the Spaniards]. Instead, with utmost *[f.165v]* haste, they sent word to Manco Inca's captains and people who had gone to capture Sitiel and Caruarayco, telling them that Diego Méndez and the other Spaniards had stabbed the Inca and fled toward Cuzco. [The captains were told] that they should drop everything and quickly return in hopes of capturing the Spaniards before they could escape, because if [they] did not return, the Spaniards would get away. The Indians who went to relay this [information] had the good luck of encountering [the captains] on the road, as they were already returning, bringing Caruarayco [as a] prisoner.[898] They had also captured Sitiel at the same time, but he proved to be fleetfooted and had slipped through their fingers.

Upon hearing the devastating news, the captains, along with hundreds and hundreds of other people, [headed toward Vitcos]. The bravest and quickest among

---

896   Cusi Titu Yupanqui, the son of Manco Inca, was by his father's side during this attack and barely escaped with his life.

897   The *History and Genealogy of the Inca Kings of Peru* (Murúa 2004 [1590]:47v) includes a drawing of Diego Méndez killing Manco Inca.

898   Pizarro (1921 [1571]:438) and Cobo (1979 [1653]:176) state that the Inca captains returned on the day that Manco Inca was killed.

them ran ahead at great speed and arrived at where Manco Inca was, mortally wounded but still alive. Seeing their lord in this condition, [and] wanting to avenge him and tear to pieces those responsible for this betrayal [the captains] turned to where they knew the Spaniards had gone. They were so eager in their pursuit that they caught up to them the next day.

[The Spaniards] had taken shelter in a large *galpón*⁸⁹⁹ along the trail, and were resting, thinking that no one was following them and that they were safe. The Indians who were following them arrived at where the Spaniards were resting, [with] their horses [sheltered] inside, before dusk. However, the Indians chose not to attack them immediately, as they wished to prevent any of the Spaniards from escaping while there was still daylight. So, they hid in the woods, without showing themselves until the middle of the night. Then, after gathering a large quantity of firewood from the woods where they had hidden, they encircled the *galpón*, and stacked the firewood at the doors, trapping [the Spaniards] inside so they could not escape. They then set it on fire with straw. When the Spaniards heard the commotion, they woke up. As some of them tried to escape through the *[f.166r]* fire, the Indians speared them, while the others burned there along with their horses. Nothing and no one inside the inside *galpón* escaped, as it was completely burned.⁹⁰⁰

After accomplishing this and finding solace in the avenging of their lord, Manco Inca's murder, they returned to Vitcos. There, they found him barely alive, as the medicines they had given had proven insufficient to heal him.⁹⁰¹ [The Inca] was pleased when he learned that the Spaniards were dead, with none having escaped, and his murder punished.⁹⁰² [The Inca] told them not to grieve for him so as not to distress the local populace and incite rebellion. [Manco Inca] named his eldest son, Sayri Tupac, as heir despite his youth. He [also named] Atoc Supa, an *orejon* captain from Cuzco who was there with them, as interim governor until [Sayri Tupac] came of age to assume the mantle of leadership.⁹⁰³ [Atoc Supa] was a man of valor, great prudence, and bravery in war, and [Manco Inca] told them to obey him. [He also told them] not to abandon the Vilcabamba region, and that his curse would fall

---

899   This word is underlined (Murúa 2008 [1616]:165v).
900   Betanzos (1996 [1557]:296) mentions that most of the Spaniards were killed when the building in which they were hiding was set on fire. Also see Cobo (1979 [1653]:176).
901   Cobo (1979 [1653]:176) notes that Manco Inca was still alive when the search party returned.
902   On 12 May 1565, Diego Rodríguez de Figueroa (2016 [1565]:158) passed Vitcos on his way to Pampaconas to meet with Cusi Titu Yupanqui. As he did so, he saw the heads of Méndez and six other Spaniards still hanging after they were executed for having killed Manco Inca.
903   Cobo (1979 [1653]:176) tells of the naming of Sayri Tupac as Inca and the appointment of Atoc Supa as his regent.

upon them if they did anything to the contrary, as he had discovered and founded the region through such hard work and sweat from his people, and so many of them had died in conquering it, and they had defended it from the Spaniards with such courage and determination. After conveying these instructions, [Manco Inca] died. They embalmed his body according to their customs, displaying as much emotion as they were allowed to show. Following his orders, they took his body, without displaying tears or sorrow, to Vilcabamba, where they remained under the governorship of the *orejon* captain Atoc Supa.[904]

This marked the end of Manco Inca Yupanqui's [life], [the] son of Huayna Capac, [the former] universal Lord of this kingdom. From the moment he left Cuzco, due to the harassment and tyranny[905] of Hernando Pizarro and his [men], [Manco Inca] endured countless hardships and misfortunes as he [traveled] from one place to another, followed and pursued by the Spaniards. At times, he suffered defeat; at others, he emerged victorious, and he escaped on thousands of occasions to maintain his liberty. What the Marquis Pizarro, his brothers, and other captains failed to do despite their vast numbers of soldiers and Indian allies, Diego Méndez, a mestizo, whom Manco Inca had taken in, aided, and hosted in his house along with his companions, achieved[906] and concluded. This serves as a stark reminder of the depths to which betrayal can lead.[907]

[F.167R] CHAPTER 74

How Sayri Tupac traveled to Lima and swore obedience to Your Majesty, and of his death

[When] Manco Inca Yupanqui died, as discussed above, his son, Inca Sayri Tupac Inca Yupanqui, succeeded him in office, although his dominion and lordship only encompassed the province of Vilcabamba and those Indians and *orejones* who were with him. [This was] because the Spaniards were steadily increasing their strength and influence every day, gradually taking possession of the kingdom. As a result, the Inca had become secluded in that corner [of the realm]. Devoid of strength and

---

904   Betanzos (1996 [1557]:298) also mentions the mummification of Manco Inca. Cobo (1979 [1653]:176) writes, "The Indians embalmed his body, and after carrying it to Vilcabamba, they put it in the temple of the Sun."

905   The word "tyranny" has been underlined by a series of dots (Murúa 2008 [1616]:166r).

906   A spelling mistake has been corrected here.

907   Folio 166v is blank.

authority, he was content with the small parcel of land they had left him, primarily due to its ruggedness rather than goodwill.

The Chunchu Indians from the far side of the large river commonly called the Marañón, and [other groups] from other provinces that remain largely unknown to the Spaniards, also came to support him. In this manner, without formally taking the governorship, Sayri Tupac came under the tutelage of [the] *orejon* Ato[c Supa].

During this time, the famous wars between the Spaniards took place. [These wars] resulted from the implementation of the New Laws by His Majesty, the Emperor, our lord, established for the Kingdom of Peru and New Spain, upon the insistence of Don Fray Bartolomé de Las Casas, [a] cleric of the Order of Santo Domingo [and the] bishop of Chiapas.[908] He was an apostolic man [and a] vigorous defender of the liberty of the Indians. He dedicated many years in Spain advocating for their aid and protection, exposing the harm inflicted upon them by the Spaniards and *encomenderos*. [He revealed] the insolence and tyranny with which [the Indians] were oppressed and humiliated, the greed and covetousness through which they were defrauded of their lands, [and] the contempt with which they were treated as if they were wild forest animals.

Through these [actions] and abuses, the governors and Lords of the *repartimientos* severely impeded the spread of the Holy Gospel and the indoctrination and teaching of these unfortunate [people]. [They treated them] as if they had not been created in the image and likeness of God and [as is their salvation] had not been secured *[f.167v]* through the blood of the most innocent lamb. In response [Las Casas] wrote a book wherein he chronicled thousands of events that occurred in this kingdom,[909] events never seen nor heard among barbarians, all driven by the pursuit of money, gold, and silver—and more gold and more silver. The Spaniards' greed was insatiable, as if even mountains turned into gold and silver would not satisfy their desires. Using persuasive and theological reasoning, [he] argued that the Indians were not as barbaric as they had been made out to be. Some [Spaniards] defamed them, daring to claim that they were not true human beings, with the intent of seizing their lands and [unlawfully] stripping them of their rightful possessions.

In the end, due to his Holy zeal and unwavering diligence, [Las Casas] achieved so much that the emperor, our lord, passed the new laws. [They were] highly beneficial and sacred, aimed at the advancement and conversion of the natives of

---

908   Fray Bartolomé de Las Casas (1474–1566), the bishop of Chiapas, fought against the exploitative practices of the Spaniards in the Americas and lobbied the Crown to institute measures to protect the Indigenous peoples.

909   This is a reference to Las Casas's *Brevísima relación de la destrucción de las Indias* (1550), which was published about ten years after its first reading.

this kingdom.[910] To enforce them, [the emperor] appointed Blasco Núñez Vela, a gentleman from Ávila, as the Viceroy of this kingdom, and he ordered the Royal Audiencia [to uphold] his authority, protect the oppressed poor, and restore justice, which had been trampled upon and neglected. This was the only [kind of justice] known in this kingdom.

Viceroy Blasco Núñez Vela implemented the New Laws, which plunged the kingdom into turmoil. Because [these laws] were [intended to] curb the insolence of numerous wealthy and powerful men, who had become inflamed and arrogant by the accumulation of gold and silver. [However, these men] were unwilling to obey [the laws] nor accept their authority, [which was] based upon sound reasoning. Gonzalo Pizarro rebelled in Cuzco, where he was [living], with the intention of traveling to Castile with [the] five hundred thousand pesos he had.[911] Assuming the title of *procurador*, he traveled to Lima and then to Quito, where he fought the honorable and loyal Viceroy. [Pizarro] defeated [the Viceroy] and decapitated him, placing his head on the gallows as [a] trophy of [the Viceroy's] loyalty [to the Crown].

To restore peace in Peru, President Pedro de la Gasca arrived from Spain in 1548. He defeated Gonzalo Pizarro at Jaquijahuana,[912] four leagues from Cuzco. He then beheaded him and pacified the region. With the belief that [Peru] would remain calm and at peace, [the Viceroy then] returned to Spain.

[*f.168r*] [However,] new disturbances soon emerged, born of unbridled ambition and the greed of many dissatisfied individuals, whose insatiable desire for rich *repartimientos* had not been fulfilled. Even if each one were given the entire kingdom, it would not have been enough to quell their insatiable appetite. Don Antonio de Mendoza [then] came to this kingdom as [the new] Viceroy, having already governed in New Spain.[913] God took him [to Heaven] at the most opportune time for the kingdom's greater punishment.

In the city of La Plata, in the province of the Charcas, Don Sebastián de Castilla rebelled.[914] However, within a few days the very same people who moved and incited him to this [act] killed him. Francisco Hernández Girón rebelled in Cuzco, at first successfully, [but he] was ultimately defeated by the king's army, governed by the Judges [of the Royal Audiencia], in Pucará.[915] [He] was captured by Captains

---

910 In 1542, Emperor Charles V instituted what are generally called the New Laws, a detailed reassessment of the *encomienda* system in use in the Americas.

911 Pizarro and other *encomenderos* offered to pay the king 500,000 pesos to release them from the obligations of the New Laws.

912 Murúa writes Sacsahuana, which we have written as Jaquijahuana.

913 Antonio de Mendoza was the first viceroy of Mexico (1535–1550) and the second viceroy of Peru (1551–1552).

914 Sebastián de Castilla rebelled in 1553.

915 Francisco Hernández Girón rebelled in 1553 and was defeated the following year.

[Juan] Tello and [Miguel de la] Serna along with the people of Huánuco in Jauja, and put to death in Lima. The rebellions and seditions raised by the malcontent were [then] over. As a book has [already] been written about them, I touch upon all these things only briefly, since my intention is to discuss only the Incas.⁹¹⁶

At that time, Your Majesty sent Andrés Hurtado de Mendoza, the Marquis of Cañete, as Viceroy of this kingdom. Seeing Peru peaceful and moods calmer, he tried to convince Sayri Tupac to [pledge] obedience to Your Majesty and surrender the province of Vilcabamba so that the gospel could be preached and the Indians would convert to the fellowship of the Catholic Church.⁹¹⁷ To accomplish this, he sent Diego Hernández, [the] husband of Doña Beatriz Quispe Quipi Coya,⁹¹⁸ daughter of Huayna Capac, along with Juan Sierra [of Leguizamo],⁹¹⁹ Alonso Juárez,⁹²⁰ and others as messengers [to] beg [Sayri Tupac] to come out in peace and to give obedience to Your Majesty.⁹²¹ When they departed on this mission, as stated in the *Chronicle of Peru*,⁹²² Sayri Tupac had not [yet] received the tassel,⁹²³ so he did not send a reply until he received it and had time to see if the embassy was well intentioned.

Once reassured, he discussed the matter with his captains. After many discussions, decisions, and disputes, among [*f.168v*] the sorcerers he had with him, and

916   This is most likely a reference to Diego Fernández de Palencia's *Historia del Peru* (1963 [1571]).
917   Much of the information in this paragraph comes from Fernández de Palencia (1963 [1571]:73, 76, 79). Cobo (1979 [1653]:179) also provides much of the same information.
918   Also known as Beatriz Huayllas Ñusta, she was a powerful woman in Cuzco, being the daughter of Huayna Capac. She had first been paired with Mancio Sierra de Leguizamo and then Pedro Bustinza. After Bustinza's death, she married Diego Hernández, who had once been a tailor, a status she considered beneath her. Nevertheless, her brother, Paullu, convinced her to enter the marriage (Garcilaso de la Vega 1966 [1616]:1229–1230; Hemming 1970:291).
919   Juan Sierra de Leguizamo was the son of Beatriz Quispe Quipi Coya and Juan Sierra de Leguizamo and thus the cousin of Sayri Tupac. As a close relative, Juan Sierra de Leguizamo is believed to have held a critical role in gaining Sayri Tupac's trust (Garcilaso de la Vega 1966 [1616]:1435–1436). In this journey, Juan Sierra de Leguizamo traveled with his stepfather, Diego Hernández.
920   Alonso Juárez would later play an important role in the conquest and occupation of the Vilcabamba region.
921   Juan de Betanzos was also among those that entered the Vilcabamba region to negotiate with Sayri Tupac. Betanzos's chronicle ends with a description of this event. The Dominican friar Melchor de los Reyes was also a member of the group (Cobo 1979 [1653]:179).
922   This is a direct reference to Diego Fernández de Palencia's *Historia del Peru*. Fernández de Palencia (1963 [1571]:76) writes, "pido su mandado al Inca y a todos sus capitanes (porque a la sazón aun no babia recibido la borla de señor)."
923   The royal tassel (*mascapaicha*), the insignia of the royal Incas, was worn in the middle of the forehead. Sayri Tupac was considered too young to wear the tassel and was under the tutelage of Atoc Supa.

a lukewarm response from many of his [captains], he decided to leave and go to Lima.[924] Therefore, he embarked [on his journey], taking three hundred prominent Indians, *caciques*, *orejones*, captains, and his sister named Cusi Huarcay. They arrived in Lima, where the Marquis of Cañete received him, doing him a great honor.[925] Several days later, Sayri Tupac [voluntarily] renounced and relinquished his privileges and rights to [the kingship], in favor of Your Majesty, the emperor, our lord. In [the king's] name, the Marquis of Cañete granted [Sayri Tupac] a favor, [giving] him the *repartimiento* and Indians that had formerly belonged to Francisco Hernández Girón,[926] which was known to yield seventeen thousand pesos *ensayados*, for his maintenance.[927]

After spending several days in Lima, Sayri Tupac returned to Cuzco, where the Indians of Chinchaysuyu and Collasuyu received him as their Inca, as ordered by the Marquis of Cañete. He wore [the] tassel and traveled by a litter as his ancestors had done.[928] The *orejones* from Hanan Cuzco and Hurin Cuzco also obeyed him, as he represented the descendant of his grandfather Huayna Capac. All the Spaniards liked and respected him, calling him Inca.

[While in Cuzco] Sayri Tupac and his sister, Cusi Huarcay, were baptized, as the Marquis of Cañete had ordered. [Juan] Bautista Muñoz, the corregidor of the city of Cuzco at the time, oversaw the baptism, to which they gladly consented. Upon being baptized, Sayri Tupac took the name Don Diego de Mendoza,[929] out of respect for the Viceroy, while his sister was christened Doña María Manrique.

---

924   Sayri Tupac left the Vilcabamba region via Andahuaylas. Juan Sierra traveled more quickly to prepare the viceroy in Lima for meeting the Inca (Cobo 1979 [1653]:180). Cusi Titu Yupanqui reports that this journey to Lima nearly bankrupted his brother Sayri Tupac.

925   Sayri Tupac arrived in Lima on 5 January 1558 (Hemming 1970:294). Guaman Poma de Ayala (2004 [1615]:440 [442]) provides a drawing of the Marquis of Cañete talking face to face with Sayri Tupac. The *History and Genealogy of the Inca Kings of Peru* (Murúa 2004 [1590]:49v) contains a similar drawing.

926   Francisco Hernández Girón's holdings included the repartimientos of Jaquijahuana, Pucará, Quipa, Guayla, and Yucay. Sayri Tupac's holdings included the wealthy *repartimiento* of Yucay, which encompassed the former country estate of his grandfather Huayna Capac. Originally, the Yucay *encomienda* was taken by Francisco Pizarro after the conquest and was later passed to his two sons before being claimed by Hernández Girón. Also see Cobo (1979 [1653]:180).

927   Certain parts of this paragraph concerning the departure of Sayri Tupac from Vilcabamba reflect information presented in Fernández de Palencia (1963 [1571]:76, 79).

928   Garcilaso de la Vega (1966 [1616]:1443) states that Miguel Astete gave Sayri Tupac the very fringe that was worn by Atahualpa when he was captured in Cajamarca.

929   Garcilaso de la Vega, who was in Cuzco and witnessed the baptism, indicates that Sayri Tupac took the name Diego after the patron saint of the conquistadors. The name "de Mendoza" came from Viceroy Andrés Hurtado de Mendoza.

After their baptism, [the issue of] their marrying was discussed, as they were siblings. It was an inviolable custom of the Incas to marry their sisters, ensuring that the heir to the throne would be the child of an Inca and Coya of royal blood through [both] the paternal and maternal line. Therefore, it is said that the bishop of that city, Don Juan Solano, granted them special dispensation to marry. Others [suggest] that the archbishop of *[f.169r]* the City of Kings,[930] Don Jerónimo de Loayza, [a] learned and esteemed man of great prudence and conduct, provided this dispensation through the apostolic authority and mandate of Pope Julius III.[931] Although it is extremely difficult to gain such dispensations ~~for its validation, as there are many ancient and modern scholars of theology who know for certain that such matrimony is prohibited by natural law. However, to secure their future, they contracted it of their [own free will] without faults or coercion and~~[932] [Written in the margin: "It is certain that if there was no dispensation (the marriage) was done with (the) authority and commission of the Pope."[933]]

The marriage resulted in the birth of their legitimate daughter, Doña Beatriz Clara Coya, who eventually became the wife of Martín García [Oñaz] de Loyola, [a] Knight of the Order of Calatrava and [the] captain of Viceroy Don Francisco de Toledo's guard.[934] Unfortunately, Sayri Tupac was not able to enjoy the tranquility and peace he found in Cuzco among his kin [for long], since he lived for only one year after he and his sister were baptized and married.[935] It is said that that [Francisco] Chilche, [a] Cañari [and the] *cacique* of Yucay, poisoned him. He was in prison in Cuzco for a year in Cuzco for this crime.[936] But in the end, he escaped without any new revelations.

At the time of his death, Sayri Tupac made a will in which he declared his brother, Tupac Amaru, who was in Vilcabamba [and] was the legitimate son of Manco Inca,

---

930   Cobo (1979 [1653]:180) states that it was the archbishop of Lima who granted the dispensation. Guaman Poma de Ayala (2004 [1615]:442 [444]) provides a drawing of the wedding between Sayri Tupa and Cusi Huarcay.

931   If papal dispensation was granted, it seems more likely that it was under Pope Paul IV (1555–1559) or Pope Pius IV (1559–1565) than Pope Julius III (1550–1555). Nevertheless, Ocampo Conejeros (2016 [1611]:130) provides similar information: "The marriage was later ratified by the Papal Bull of Paul III, which was [carried out] by the Lord Don Fray Jerónimo de Loayza, who was the first archbishop of this archbishopric of Lima."

932   This crossed-out section and the margin notes are difficult to read; however, Adorno (2008:104) has transcribed them.

933   The margin notes are written by Murúa (Adorno 2008:104).

934   Ocampo Conejeros (2016 [1611]:124) describes Loyola in almost the same words, writing, "Martín García Oñaz de Loyola, [who was the] Captain of the Lord Viceroy's Guard [and] Knight of the Order of Calatrava."

935   Sayri Tupac died in 1560 or 1561.

936   This charge against Francisco Chilche is also mentioned by Cobo (1979 [1653]:180).

their father, as his successor in the lordship.[937] The news of Sayri Tupac's death and the appointment of his brother Tupac Amaru as his legitimate successor reached Vilcabamba. [Upon hearing this] Cusi Titu Yupanqui,[938] the bastard[939] brother [of Sayri Tupac] and son of Manco Inca, [took advantage of] being older than Tupac Amaru, who was still young, and he seized the litter and rulership, proclaiming himself lord with the intention that his son would succeed him. [Cusi Titu Yupanqui] ordained Tupac Amaru as a priest and sent him to guard his father's body in Vilcabamba, where Manco Inca was kept. And thus, it was until we return.

In chapter 93, I will also tell of a remarkable event that happened to Prince Sayri.[940,941]

*During the rule of Cusi Titu Yupanqui, two clerics of the
Order of Saint Augustine entered Vilcabamba and what
happened to them, and of the death of the Inca[942]*

Cusi Titu Yupanqui was inducted as the Lord of the Incas in Vilcabamba. He did not leave from there, staying with the *orejones* and Indians of that province. Several

937   At the same time, the great estate of Yucay passed down to his only daughter, Beatriz Clara Coya. Her inheritance rights became the focus of the Acobamba treaty negotiations between Titu Cusi Yupanqui and the Spaniards (Covey and Amado Gonzales 2008; Guillén Guillén 1977a, 1977b; Nowack 2004).

938   Murúa writes this Inca's name as Cusi Titu Yupanqui rather than Titu Cusi Yupanqui. This unusual name order (Cusi Titu rather than Titu Cusi) is also found in the 1595 and 1599/1600 depositions concerning Ortiz's death (Bauer et al. 2014), indicating that Murúa was copying from these documents. This also shows that Murúa was still collecting new information for his chronicle after 1600. To be consistent, I also use Cusi Titu Yupanqui, except when referring to his famous report. In those references, I use the name Titu Cusi Yupanqui, since this is the name order used in those transcriptions of his work.

939   Ocampo Conejeros (2016 [1611]:120) includes similar details in his chronicle.

940   This last sentence was later added by Murúa (Adorno 2008:101,102). Chapter 93 discusses the descendants of Sayri Tupac.

941   Folio 169v is blank.

942   Most of this chapter is based on information provided by Juana Guerrero from the town of Socospata (Vilcabamba) in 1595. At that time, she was being interviewed concerning the death of Diego Ortiz. Said to be in her fifties, Juana Guerrero had been the wife of Martín Pando, a man who had lived in the Vilcabamba region for more than a decade as a translator and secretary to Cusi Titu Yupanqui. Juana Guerrero ratified her statement in another interview, held in 1599 (Bauer et al. 2014:80–84).

years passed during which the Count of Nieva[943] and the President [Lope García de] Castro[944] governed, until the cautious and prudent gentleman, Don Francisco de Toledo, became the Viceroy of this kingdom. At this time, two clerics of the Order of Lord Saint Augustine entered the province of Vilcabamba to preach to the Indians and to instruct them in the Catholic faith. One of them was named Friar Marcos [García],[945] and the other [was named] Friar Diego Ortiz,[946] [a] native of Seville.[947] With a fervent desire to save souls and set them on the path to Heaven, they started on their Holy work, as instructed by their prelate. They preached and provided religious education to Cusi Titu Yupanqui and the Indians who were with him.

The Indians willingly listened to [the friars] because, in general, many of them rejoiced at having priests and clerics to instruct them in the faith of Christ, our redeemer, since there were no Spaniards among them. These two clerics administered catechism and baptized [the Indians], and many of them learned the necessary things to receive the sacrament of Holy Baptism.

One of these [clerics], Friar Marcos, baptized Cusi Titu Yupanqui Inca and gave him the name Don Felipe.[948] After some time had passed, Friar Marcos decided to leave the province, and he requested permission from his prelate to [return to] the city of Cuzco. Upon receiving permission, [Friar Marcos] left [the province] where the Inca [resided] without informing him where he was going. He did so

---

943 Diego López de Zúñiga y Velasco was the count of Nieva and was viceroy of Peru from 1561 to 1564.

944 Lope García de Castro was interim viceroy of Peru from 1564 to1569.

945 Marcos García entered Vilcabamba in 1568 for the baptism of Cusi Titu Yupanqui.

946 Diego Ortiz entered Vilcabamba in September 1569 (Titu Cusi Yupanqui 2005 [1571]:134).

947 The reference to Diego Ortiz brings with it a complex history. As will be described by Murúa, Ortiz was killed following the sudden death of Cusi Titu Yupanqui in about 1571. What Murúa does not mention is that the Augustinian Order, starting as early as 1582, began to collect information on the death of Ortiz (Bauer et al. 2014; Hemming 1970:476; Levillier 1925:344). Their efforts increased in 1595 and in 1599–1600 as they began a failed effort to nominate Ortiz for sainthood. Interviews were conducted in the Vilcabamba region as well as in the city of Cuzco. Both Murúa, and much later Calancha (1981 [1638]), had access to these investigations while writing their chronicles. Murúa copied much of the information in various testimonies from the 1595 and 1599–1600 interviews into his work. The original reports have recently been printed (Bauer et al. 2014; Bauer Halac-Higashimori, and Gabriel E. Cantarutti 2016:193–218). Much of the information in this chapter comes from those reports (Bauer et al. 2014:63, 66, 77, 79, 81, 82, 101).

948 Murúa is confused; Titu Cusi's son was baptized Felipe Quispe Titu in the town of Carco on 20 July 1567 by the Augustinian prior Antonio de Vera. The name Felipe was certainly selected to honor the king of Spain. Cusi Titu Yupanqui was baptized Diego de Castro Titu Cusi Yupanqui in late August 1568 by Juan de Viver (Titu Cusi Yupanqui 2005 [1571]:133).

because he feared that [the Inca] would send someone to kill him, as he had shown signs of ill will.

When Cusi Titu Yupanqui discovered that Father Fray Marcos *[f.170v]* was leaving, he sent Indians after him to bring him back. On his return, [the Inca] roundly scolded him with great arrogance, asking him why he was leaving the land without permission. In response, [Fray Marcos] explained that he was not leaving but was merely traveling around. He told [the Inca] this because he realized that [Cusi Titu Yupanqui] would later have him killed. Cusi Titu Yupanqui told him not to leave until another cleric replaced him. Later, his companion, Friar Diego Martín, arrived and they stayed in Puquiura for about a month with the Inca, who had already abandoned the goodwill with which he had received Holy Baptism. [He] took the two clerics with him to [the town of] Vilcabamba and, along the way, he made [them] wade through a river where the water reached to their waist. [He] did this with cruel and perverse intentions, aiming to create the impression that the trail was difficult and the land rough and rugged, discouraging them from staying with him or remaining in that province.

Not content with this, when they arrived at the town of Vilcabamba Cusi Titu Yupanqui ordered pairs of *Yunga* Indian women to come out dressed as friars and talk with the clerics. [He did this] to mock and ridicule [them], as he held them in low regard. When they reached the town, [he] did not want [the clerics] to lodge within it, fearing that they would see the *huacas* and *mochaderos*[949] he had there or reprimand him for the rites and ceremonies that he performed.[950]

After spending eight days with the Inca, the clerics returned to the town of Puquiura, leaving him in Vilcabamba. They had been [in Puquiura] a month when some Indians approached the clerics, informing them that next to Vitcos, in a place named Chuquipalta, there was a house dedicated to the Sun, [and] a large[951] and wide stone above a spring.[952] [They said] that this [stone] caused many evils that

---

949   Holy places.

950   It was during this visit that Titu Cusi Yupanqui (2005 [1571]) dictated his famous letter to Lope García de Castro in which he told of his father's life and that of his own. The account was recorded by Martín Pando and signed by both Marcos García and Diego Ortiz on 6 February 1570 in the Inca town of Vilcabamba. It is believed that the two clerics returned to Puquiura soon afterward.

951   In her 1595 testimony, on which most of this chapter is based, Juana Guerrero (Bauer et al. 2014:81–84) describes "a white rock above a spring" ("una piedra blanca encima de un manantial de agua"). The phrase "white rock" is correctly copied by Calancha (1981 [1638]), but Murúa altered the description and wrote "large and wide stone above a spring" ("una piedra grande y basta encima de un manantial de agua").

952   In 1911 Bingham correctly inferred that the modern site of Ñusta España (also called Yurak Rumi) was the ancient shrine that Juana Guerrero, later copied by Calancha (1981

terrified and frightened them, and had killed many Indians. Therefore, they said the Devil was in that stone and, for this reason, they had stopped worshiping it and offering gold *[f.171r]* and silver, as they had done in the past. They pleaded with the two clerics, begging them to go and exorcise the stone, so that it would no longer harm or frighten them, thus freeing them of its danger.

Upon hearing this, the clerics, accompanied by many Indians and young men from the parish, went [to Chuquipalta] carrying a [great] amount of firewood, and they burned the stone. Since this event, nothing was ever seen to cause fear among the Indians again, nor did they experience any harm. This served to further confirm the faith among those who embraced it. They understood that the Devil had fled and was afraid of the clerics, the Holy words that they spoke, shunned the cross and did not return to where Holy water had been sprinkled.

Within eight days of this [event], Father Fray Marcos left Puquiura for Cuzco, and Father Fray Diego remained behind, administering the Holy Sacraments, and preaching the Gospel to the Indians because he knew the common language of the Indians very well, so they willingly listened to him.[953]

[Soon afterward], a Spaniard named [Antonio] Romero[954] entered the province on his own, claiming to be a miner in search of mines. (It was later revealed that the province indeed held very rich deposits when Don Francisco de Torres y Portugal, Count of Villar, governed this kingdom, [in] the year 1587.)[955] This Spaniard requested permission from Cusi Titu to search for silver and gold mines, which was granted. He went from place to place in search of mines and eventually found them. He returned to the Inca very happy, bringing [samples] of the metals to show the abundance of gold and silver that could be mined. When the Inca saw this, he grew concerned, because he realized that if news spread about the presence of gold and silver deposits in the province reached the Spaniards in Cuzco, many of them

[1638]), called Chuquipalta. This shrine and its connection with the former Inca city of Vitcos became the focus of a series of preliminary reports that were published in the following year (Bingham 1912a, 1912b, 1912c). The destruction of this shrine by burning was confirmed by excavations in 2008 and 2009 (Bauer, Aráoz Silva, and George S. Burr 2012; Bauer, Fonseca Santa Cruz, and Aráoz Silva 2015).

953   Cusi Titu Yupanqui subsequently banished Marcos García from Vilcabamba, an event that is not mentioned by Murúa.

954   Antonio Romero is also mentioned by Salazar (2016 [1596]).

955   Cusi Huarcay left Vilcabamba with Sayri Tupac in 1557 and remained in Cuzco until her death. In 1586, she wrote to Viceroy Torres y Portugal (Hemming 1970:476–477; Levillier 1925:54–55, 229–236). In the letter, Cusi Huarcay, who had lived in the Vilcabamba region for many years with Sayri Tupac, revealed the names and approximate locations of various mines, and she requested permission to return to the Vilcabamba region to reopen them. While denying the request, the viceroy wrote enthusiastically to the king in 1587 and 1588, suggesting that the wealth of the region was large and that he would investigate the matter.

would enter. [They] would send soldiers to conquer the province and seize control of the entire region, and the Indians who [*f.171v*] lived there in seclusion would lose their freedom and kingdom.

Consequently, he ordered that the Spaniard be killed, and his head cut off and thrown in the river. At that time, the Inca was in Puquiura. When Father Fray Diego heard the commotion in the Inca's house, he rushed there to see what the matter was and [if] he could help. When [Father Fray Diego] learned that they were killing the Spaniard, he begged the Inca not to do so. When Cusi Titu Yupanqui heard him, he sent word to Father Fray Diego not to go to or enter his house and to let him kill the man. And if [Fray Diego] kept interfering, he would have him killed, like the Spaniard.

Realizing that he was already dead, and he could not change [the situation], [Fray Diego] returned home, overwhelmed with sorrow, regret, and remorse for being unable to administer man's last confession. In a final act of compassion, he sent a young man from the parish to speak with the Inca. Since the Spaniard was already dead, he implored [the Inca] to give him the body so that [he] could be buried and given a Christian burial. The Inca sent word that he did not want to give [the body] to him, no matter how much he insisted, and he ordered that it be thrown in the nearby river.

Unsatisfied with this, the father was determined to diligently search for the body in the river, [so] he secretly went out at night with some young men, and he looked for the body in order to bury it. However, he could not find it. When the Inca heard of the father's activities, he sent a message to the father to stop searching for the Spaniard's body and warned him against leaving his house because if he [did so, the Inca] would have him killed. With this, the father halted the Holy work that he was doing.

God did not allow Cusi Titu Yupanqui to escape unpunished for the murder of the Spaniard, the threats he made against the good cleric, [or] the scorn and mockery that he had ordered [through] the Indian [women] dressed in friars' habits. Within five days of these events, the Inca went to a *mochadero* that he had [in Vitcos], where [the] mestizo Diego Méndez had killed his father, Manco Inca. He was in mourning there with other Indians, and when he grew tired [*f.172r*] [he] returned to his house. That night, tired and perspiring, [he] ate a lot and drank a large quantity of wine and *chicha*. As a result, on that very night, he contracted a deadly illness, which included terrible pain in his side, along with pronounced bleeding through his mouth and nose. The illness worsened as his mouth and tongue became swollen. This disease was so severe that he died within twenty-four hours, leaving the Indians in a state of deep sadness and inconsolable grief.[956]

---

956   Folio 172v is blank.

[F.173R] CHAPTER 76

How the captains of Cusi Titu Yupanqui Inca captured and killed Father Fray Diego in a very cruel manner

Everyone meets their end according to their deeds. This we have seen in [the case of] Cusi Titu Yupanqui Inca, [the] son of Manco Inca, who [mis]treated the clerics who entered the province where he lived to aid him and put his soul on the path[957] toward eternal bliss.[958] When Cusi Titu Yupanqui died, one of his *mamacona* Indian concubines, Angelina Polan Quilaco,[959] who was with him when he passed away, [become] possessed by an evil spirit that entered her heart. [This evil spirit] had [long] held [the province] under his will and, in the palm of his hand, and it wanted to kill the revered friar, by whose words and actions he was now losing ground in the conquest of that province. [She] came out screaming to the captains and Indians who were there with the Inca to capture the friar since he, along with Martín Pando,[960] his mestizo secretary, had poisoned and killed the Inca. Motivated [by] that infernal Indian, the captains who were there, especially Guandopa, Macora, Sotic, [and] Palloc,[961] mindlessly and recklessly rushed, with many others, to the priest's house. [However, it went] unnoticed that the revered father had not entered the priest's house, nor had he been close enough to him to give him the poison when he became ill. They seized him and, in an instant, put a rope around his neck and used another to tie his hands and forearms behind [his back]. Their forceful and violent actions dislodged some of his ribs, causing excruciating pain. They brought him out onto a patio, hurling countless offensive words,

---

957   A spelling error has been corrected (Murúa 2008 [1616]:173r).

958   Much of the information presented in this chapter is taken from the 1595 testimonies of Alonso de la Cueva and Juana Guerrero (Bauer et al. 2014:80–89) concerning the death of Ortiz. As noted earlier, Juana Guerrero had been the wife of Martín Pando at the time of Pando's and Ortiz's death, but at the time of the testimonies she was married to de la Cueva. Alonso de la Cueva was among the Spanish soldiers who entered Vilcabamba in 1572, and he witnessed the exhumation of Ortiz's body several months later. He is mentioned in numerous Vilcabamba-related documents (see Maúrtua 1906).

959   Angelina Polan Quilaco, one of Cusi Titu Yupanqui's wives, was baptized by Marcos García at the same time as the Inca in 1568 (Hemming 1970:321). A resident of Lucma, she was around fifty years old when she was interviewed on 25 January 1595 by Antonio de Monroy Portocarrero concerning the death of Ortiz. In an unusually short statement, she indicated that she knew nothing of Ortiz's death (Bauer et al. 2014:68). However, several other people interviewed suggested that she had added to the panic following the Inca's death.

960   Ocampo Conejeros (2016 [1611]:122–124) also mentions Pando in his chronicle.

961   Variations of these names appear in several 1595 testimonies (Bauer et al. 2014).

slapping and *[f.173v]* clubbing him for killing their Inca. To cause him even more pain, they left him exposed all night in the cold; naked, wearing *only*[962] loose, white trousers, while surrounded by many Indians. Periodically, [these Indians] would drench the ropes with water so that they would cut him and exacerbate his pain.

In the morning, the captains and other Indians gathered, and the father, still bound, asked why they were subjecting him to such cruel abuse, for he was their father, who had nurtured and taught them with much love and concern for their well-being. [He said] that if the Inca was dead, they [should] tell him [and] he would pray to God for him and his soul; or if he was alive but ill, he would say masses for his health so that he would recover. In response, they told him that Cusi Titu Yupanqui, their Inca and lord, was dead, [and] that [Ortiz should] perform Mass to resurrect him, since he had said and preached that his God could resurrect the dead. The Holy Father responded, saying that he was [but] a sinful priest [and] that only God could resurrect the dead. Nevertheless, he agreed to say Mass and commend [the Inca's soul] to God, trusting His divine will. At this point, they instructed him to proceed with the Mass.

Due to the torments endured by the father that night, the pain caused by the tightly tied ropes, and especially his dislocated ribs, the father could not move. So, one of the captains, who had been tormenting him, knocked him to the ground. Standing on the father's chest and forcefully pulling his hands, he kicked him repeatedly in his chest to set his bones back into place, causing even greater pain. With this mistreatment and cruelty, they took him to the church that the priests had built in the town of Puquiura. There, he approached the altar and donned his robes to begin the Mass, which he started very slowly [and] with profound devotion. It lasted such a long time and he shed so many *[f.174r]* tears that he soaked the missal and corporals with them. He released loud sighs and moans throughout the Mass, fully understanding the Indians' broken hearts and their evil plans to kill him afterward, such that every time he uttered *"Dominus Vobiscum,"* they threatened him with their spears, gesturing their intent to kill him.

When he had finished saying Mass, [the Indians] returned, screaming, and shouting, to seize and bind him once again. When they asked why he had not resurrected the Inca as they had demanded, he replied that only God, the Creator of All Things, could do that. However, [the Inca] had not been revived because it was not in accordance with God's will, as it was not fit for the Inca to return to this world. [With this,] they then took [Ortiz] out of the church and tied him around the waist to a cross that was in the cemetery. They then brutally whipped him for a very long time, warning him that he would walk with them into the interior to Vilcabamba.

---

962   This word is underlined.

Exhausted and tormented, the good friar implored them, for the love of God, to give him something to eat, as he was hungry and very thirsty. They went to his house and brought two crusts of cake that he had in a pouch. However, he could not swallow as he began to eat, as his thirst had increased with the strain and pain, so he asked them for water. Instead of water, the Indians brought him a cup containing urine and saltpeter, mixed with other bitter and repugnant concoctions. As the revered father tasted it and realized that it was so bitter and foul-smelling, he spit it out, refusing to drink it. Then, many of those ministers of Satan stood up from where they were sitting and threatened him, pressing their spears against his chest and commanding him to drink it immediately or be killed. *[f.174v]* Therefore, he lifted his hands to Heaven with great humility, and drank it, saying: "For the love of God, what more do I deserve than this?" He spoke these words in the common language of the Indians, ensuring they all understood him. Consequently, they untied him from the cross, [and began] walking to Marcanay.[963]

After they untied him, he sat down next to [the cross] to rest. However, he was unable to get up as quickly as the Indians demanded. An Indian named Juan Quispe, to show and amuse everyone with his boldness, or, better said, his insolence, raised his hand and struck the Holy Father. In His omnipotent majesty, God chose to punish the insolence and lack of respect [that Quispe] had for his minister, so little by little, his hand and arm withered, serving as a clear demonstration of[964] divine justice. This Indian lived many years longer than the others who were with him[965] and publicly displayed the wonders of God through his withered arm and hand and how deeply He feels the offenses committed against His priests, as we will later explain.[966] To lead [Ortiz], they pierced his cheeks and pulled a rough rope of pampa grass through them, using it like a bit, causing much blood flow from his wounds. So, they departed with him, walking barefoot and naked, in only a white tunic.

They shoved him, [hit him with] sticks, and slapped him along the trail, uttering a thousand hurtful words. On the first day of this journey, there was such a heavy downpour that the trail turned into a stream. Because of the mud, water, and the readiness with which they kicked, slapped, and pushed him, he occasionally fell to the ground, but they immediately made him stand up. In the meantime, with

963   The specific location of the settlement of Marcanay is unknown (see Lee 2000).
964   A spelling error has been corrected (Murúa 2008 [1616]:174v).
965   The story of Juan Quispe is frequently recounted by writers interested in the death of Ortiz. Juan Quispe himself testified in the town of San Francisco de la Victoria de Vilcabamba on least two occasions, in 1595 and again in 1599 (Bauer et al. 2014). Surprisingly, his withered arm is not mentioned during either of these depositions.
966   Ocampo Conejeros (2016 [1611]:121, 122) also writes of Juan Quispe and suggests that Ortiz was thirty-three at the time of his death.

remarkable patience and profound humility, all he would say was: "Oh, God!" There is no doubt that on this occasion, the Almighty Lord came to His priest's aid *[f.175r]* with supernatural aid and assistance so that he [endured these trials] with joy and patience, in imitation of Christ, our Savior. He would lift his eyes to Heaven and, with great humility, ask for forgiveness for his sins. The Indians mocked and ridiculed him for this and resumed [beating] him.

When they arrived at their resting place that day, they put him in a cave beneath a rock, where water constantly dripped on him. [Ortiz] meekly asked the Indians why they treated him so harshly and cruelly since he was fond of them and loved them like his children. [He] had educated and taught them, and he had stayed in the province for their own benefit, when he could have gone to Cuzco. The Indians replied that he was a deceitful liar who had failed to resurrect the Inca. Thus, subjecting him to a thousand tortures and torments along the way, they took him to Marcanay. There, they dragged him across the ground with his hands and feet bound and tied him to a pole. After stripping him of the habits he usually wore, they terribly [and] savagely whipped him and inserted native palm thorns into his fingertips. They forced him to inhale foul-smelling substances, leaving him breathless and unable to speak. Finally, they finished him off with a blow to the back of his neck from a copper axe.[967] [With this act] his Holy soul ascended to enjoy, in the presence of God, the reward merited by his Holy zeal, patience, and humility with which he suffered death at the hands of those whose spiritual well-being he had come to oversee. They should have guarded his physical life by any means possible, so he could have been a spiritual refuge for their souls in a land so lacking in priests. However, since they did not value the blessing they had, it is not surprising that they took his life, thus to better it in Heaven.[968]

[F.176R] CHAPTER 77

Of the cruelties that the Indians committed against the body of the revered Friar Diego Ortiz

When the Indian *caciques* had concluded their terrible cruelty and inhuman sacrilege, staining their dirty hands with the blood of the one who was anointed by God and their own spiritual father, who had paid with his sweat and toil to stay among them

---

967 Testimonies from 1599 suggest that the final blow came from a man named Manacotaba (Bauer et al. 2014).

968 Folio 175v is blank.

to win them into His divine grace, their diabolical intent and fervor were still not content or[969] satisfied. Not content with taking the father's life, they further pleased the Devil, who moved invisibly among them, soliciting their evil. As it seemed to him that with [Ortiz's death], he had secured victory and he could return to rejoice in possessing their souls. So, [they] seized the body and trampled it, as an even greater demonstration of their rage.[970] Laying [it] on the ground, they ordered all the Indians who were there, men, women, and youth, to walk upon him[971] to further scorn and mock him. So, they stepped and trampled upon him, thus satisfying their barbaric cruelty. They then made a very deep and narrow pit, placing him in it head down and feet up. To inflict further iniquity upon the lifeless body, they drove a palm lance through his anus, passing it through his entire body to his head. They filled [the grave] with earth, saltpeter, and *collpa*, a [type of] colored earth used for dyeing, and they poured a lot of red *chicha* and other things over him, according to their diabolical rites and ceremonies. Thus, they covered his body in the pit that they [had] made under the roots of a massive tree. These blind and unfortunate souls then left screaming and shouting, overjoyed at having fulfilled their infernal desires, oblivious of the great punishment that divine justice had in store for them for having killed the priest. [*f.176v*]

The reason for placing his body in the pit feet up and head down was that, according to what those same Indians said,[972] since the Holy Father had lifted his eyes to Heaven with every step, beseeching God for forgiveness for his sins and strength to endure those torments and hardships, the barbarians believed that God, through his importuning and groans, would hear him and take him out of the pit if his head was raised. Therefore, they placed him head down, preventing him from looking up to Heaven and calling out to God. Oh, how blind they are, devoid of reason or understanding![973] Did they not realize that He who could lift him out of the pit with his head up could also do so with his head down? Is God's power limited in some way? Shouldn't it be understood that if I could see him from Heaven in one position, I could also hear him and rescue him if he were in the opposite position? However, their malice and wickedness blinded them, and the Devil, who led [them] to this heinous sacrilege, left them senseless and devoid of judgment to recognize the iniquity they were perpetrating[974] against Christ, our Lord.

---

969   A textual error has been corrected (Murúa 2008 [1616]:176r).

970   Much of the information presented in this chapter is derived from the 1595 testimonies of Alonso de la Cueva and Juana Guerrero (Bauer et al. 2014:80–89) regarding the death of Ortiz.

971   This act resembles the practices of the Incas with war captives.

972   This refers to the taxonomies that Murúa was copying.

973   Here, Murúa inserts his own voice within the information that was taken from Alonso de la Cueva's testimony.

974   A textual error has been corrected (Murúa 2008 [1616]:176r).

Having done this, a sense of confusion and sadness, born of their sin, began to fall on them. The *caciques* and captains realized how unjustly they had laid their hands on a priest and how, contrary to reason, without any cause or provocation, they had taken the life of an innocent [person]. Fearing the impending punishment that loomed in their hearts, they held a meeting of all the sorcerers and diviners in the province. Together, they inquired about what would happen and occur in the future as a consequence of the death of Father Friar Diego Ortiz, as it weighed very heavily upon them.

For several days, the diviners and sorcerers deliberated among themselves over the answer, asking questions of the Devil, to whom they were beholden. Ultimately, they concluded that the Creator of All Things was deeply angered *[f.177r]* by what they had planned and done; laying their hands on and taking the life of that priest, who was innocent of the offense that had been attributed to him. [The diviners foretold] that as a result of this egregious sin, much adversity and misfortune would befall them, and that God would punish and destroy this generation of the Inca and all his people.

This response left the Indians even more confused and distressed over the deed they had committed. Adding to their fears, the following evening, a large house where they and the Inca held their drunken revelries, and where the aforesaid matter had been discussed, suddenly caught fire. As they rushed to extinguish the burning house, which was impossible to stop no matter how hard they tried, they saw[975] a large snake moving through the flames, from one place to another, without being burned. Witnessing the unburnt serpent frightened and terrified everyone, [so they therefore] departed from there even sadder and more pensive.

The *curacas* and captains decided to consult again with the priests of their *huacas*, and the diviners and sorcerers. Once gathered, they asked about the significance of the burned house and the sight of a large unscathed snake moving through the fire. The diviners responded that they foresaw a period of immense misfortune, calamity, and a cruel war of fire and blood would descend upon that province. It would destroy everyone because the blood of the priest they had killed cried out before God for vengeance over his unjust death.

Believing that [by] removing any memory *[f.177v]* of the priest, they could shield themselves from these evils and threats, they scraped the earth from the altar where he had said Mass, where he used to sit down and walk about, and where he prayed the Divine Office[976] in their church. Collecting the scraped-up earth, they cast it into the river to remove any trace of [his presence]. Some of the more daring

---

975   A textual error has been corrected (Murúa 2008 [1616]:177r).
976   The Divine Office, also known as the Liturgy of the Hours, is a series of prayers recited throughout the day.

individuals distributed his habits among themselves, making *chuspas*, small bags that they carry hanging on their left side, used to carry the coca they chewed.[977] [They] took the vestments he wore during Mass and, taking them to a place a few days from there that is called the Gallows of the Inca, threw them onto the ground and trampled upon them, expressing their disdain for the Christian religion and the priests who celebrated [Mass] with [those vestments].

But You, Lord, are just! Your judgments are righteous and justified. In punishing sinners, You provide the world with an exemplification of Your essential attribute of justice, [demonstrating] that You uphold and fulfill Your Holy word. You have declared that no one [may] touch Your Christians or [Your] anointed ones.[978] Therefore, these barbarians, lacking supernatural faith, paid the price through the punishments that You imposed on those who harm Your priests or speak ill of them. They themselves acknowledge the countless hardships and misfortunes that befell them for committing such a great evil. Because a little over a year later, the Spanish entered the very town where this sacrilege was committed, leveling, depopulating, and burning it, such that it has not been rebuilt to this day.[979] It appeared as though the divine curse and heavenly fire had descended upon it and upon everyone who was involved in the death and martyrdom of the revered friar. It is widely known that they all quickly met with miserable ends, suffering various sad and misfortunes deaths.[980] Only Juan Quispe, the man who slapped the friar, and whose arm had withered, lived for more than thirty years *[f.178r]*, [serving] to further shame him and demonstrating Divine Justice. This has served as a lesson to many to abstain from sin and to respect and venerate the priests and ministers of the Gospel of Christ.

Their misfortune did not simply end there, for God later sent them pestilence, hunger, massacres, hardships, and misery. And the vermin of the earth, [serving] as ministers and executors of divine punishment, decimated their food, *chacras* and crops, making it abundantly clear that [these afflictions] came from the heavens. They cursed at one another, particularly those who had advised and encouraged the killing of the revered Father who educated them. They clearly recognized that, as the most culpable, these curses and hardships were primarily directed at them.

977 The making of *chuspas* from Ortiz's clothes is mentioned in several testimonies describing the death of Ortiz (Bauer et al. 2014).

978 Once again, Murúa interjects his voice within information provided in the Ortiz testimonies.

979 Murúa is speaking of the Inca town of Vilcabamba (Bauer, Fonseca Santa Cruz, and Miriam Aráoz Silva 2015).

980 Murúa is referring to the 29 December 1599 testimony of Angelina Llacsa Chuqui, in which she described the deaths of many of the Inca captains who participated in the killing of Ortiz (Bauer et al. 2014:137–138).

There was an Indian among them named Don Diego Aucalli,[981] who wholeheart-edly converted to God as a consequence of all this. He turned to the Lord, asking for forgiveness for his sins, transforming his life, and performing the works of a good Christian. [He] became a preacher [among] his people, persuading them to repent and teaching them that it was the true [way] and the path to Heaven, as their superstitions and idolatry were lies and the deceit and trickery of the Devil. And if they did not [believe this], they should remember God's retribution upon those who killed His priest. [They should] take note because, although the Inca had martyred and cruelly tormented his pontiffs and diviners in the past, hanging them and leaving them like that for four or five days until they finally died, they had never [before] witnessed such signs, hardships, and calamities as those they experienced after having committed the crime of killing the priest.

Glory be to the omnipotent Lord of Heaven, who extracts redemption from the sins and missteps of sinners, and, through His punishments [f.178v], instills fear and true repentance from sin[ners].

One cannot assume or conclude [that] they suddenly conspired to kill[982] the good Father Friar Diego for having mistreated and shamed the Indians. First, because the punishment we have described, sent from the exalted one's hand onto those who killed [Friar Diego], highlights their injustice and lack of reason. Second, [as] the Spaniards entered and taught the Mañarí Indians, [who live] more than two hun-dred leagues inland, the Christian doctrine, they were told that Father Friar Diego had taught them the same things and had preached to them when they went to Vilcabamba to see Cusi Titu Yupanqui Inca. [They say] he was a very good priest who, with great love and sincerity, gave them gifts from his home, and when they fell ill, he healed them with great care. He himself made porridges for them to eat, visited and consoled them. He frequently told them that God sent hardships and illness as a consequence of [their] sins so that they would remember Him, mend their lives, and refrain from the offenses they committed against Him.

Upon learning of his death and the cruel manner in which it occurred, being infidels, they showed deep emotions, even to the point of crying. They believed this was why so much harm had befallen the Inca and his generation. It was because of the memory of the good Father that they did not harm the Spaniards who entered [their territory], fearing that another [punishment] might befall them, and they, therefore, welcomed them in peace. They gave [the Spaniards] food for the journey and many Indians who would accompany them [back] to Vilcabamba.[983]

---

981   Diego Aucalli is said to have been the personal servant of Cusi Titu Yupanqui and to have overseen the Inca's mummification. His conversion is described by Alonso de la Cueva (Bauer et al. 2014:85–90).

982   A textual error has been corrected (Murúa 2008 [1616]:178v).

983   Murúa speaks of events to come during the 1572 Spanish raid into the Vilcabamba region.

All that I have conveyed regarding the death and events [of] this *[f.179r]* revered cleric has not been [derived] solely from one person's knowledge or from confusing accounts from the aforementioned Indians, who are prone to lying. Instead, this [information] and all that occurred next when the Spaniards took control of that province and transferred [the] remains [of Friar Diego Ortiz] to the church of San Francisco de la Victoria[984] are based on an investigation conducted by the clerics of the Order of Saint Augustine with the Indians who were present, as well as with Juana Guerrero, [the] wife of Martín Pando, [the] secretary of Inca Cusi Titu Yupanqui, who witnessed it all firsthand when she was in the province, and with many Spaniards who heard the news of it and swore to it.[985] Furthermore, the subsequent events that occurred later, as will be told in chapter 84, provide clear evidence of the unjust death and revered martyrdom of this Holy cleric. It occurred in the year 1570 or [15]71, as the Indians often make mistakes when it comes to tracking time.[986]

[F.180R] CHAPTER 78

How Viceroy Don Francisco de Toledo sent messengers to Cusi Titu Yupanqui and how they were killed

As previously mentioned, Don Francisco de Toledo, commander of Acebuche of the Order of Alcántara, brother of Don Juan de Toledo, Count of Oropesa, governed these kingdoms during the time when the events that we have discussed occurred. [These events included] the deaths of Inca Cusi Titu Yupanqui and Father Friar Diego Ortiz, an Augustinian cleric. [Toledo] wanted to succeed in governing and administering this kingdom, as disorder and injustices still remained and persisted. He sought to conduct a general inspection of the entire Indian kingdom and reduce them into towns under Christian policing and order, as this was the only way for them to be fully indoctrinated and for them to learn the things of our Holy Catholic faith, and to extirpate for their ancient rites and ceremonies. Through the presence of priests and ministers, as experience has shown to be most effective for the salvation of the souls of these natives, [the Indians] would abstain from many vices, such as drunkenness and other harmful and abominable [sins]. In contrast, [where] the

---

984 San Francisco de la Victoria de Vilcabamba is also mentioned in book 3, chapter 24 of his chronicle.

985 Murúa directly mentions the Augustinian's testimonies that he had access to regarding the death of Ortiz (see Bauer et al. 2014).

986 Chapter 84 describes the reburial of Ortiz in the town of San Francisco de la Victoria de Vilcabamba and recounts several miracles that occurred afterward. This information was taken from the Ortiz testimonies (see Bauer et al. 2014). Folio 179v is blank.

reductions[987] have been dismantled, the towns have grown under the influence of individuals with little conscience or fear of God, corrupted by the Indians. This decline in the spiritual well-being of these souls has been observed and continues to be seen, with many dying without confession or sacraments for this reason.

The Viceroy decided to personally visit ~~visit~~[988] the cities of this kingdom to witness firsthand what would be helpful for good governance. [He] passed some laws and ordinances through which justice would be administered. The Indians were not to be troubled or humiliated by their *encomenderos* or any troublemakers living among them. They should pay their tributes and taxes *[f.180v]* equally and justly, without the excesses and irregularities of the past, [with] reliable counts and quantities established for everything. [Toledo] put [this plan] into effect, which was very pleasing to God and of much service to the king, our lord. [Moreover,] it was good and useful throughout the kingdom. If today everything remained as he had ordered, commanded, and reformed, there would be nothing to wish for, and peace and justice would prevail. Therefore, the Viceroy set out, and after visiting Huamanga, he went up to Cuzco, the principal city of this kingdom. In ancient times, it had been the place and residence of the Incas, [the] natural lords of [this kingdom], although now it has lost its former glory. When he arrived, he familiarized himself with the [regional] government and issued many necessary orders for its functioning and purpose.

Among other things, he proposed that it would be good to relocate Cusi Titu Yupanqui, who governed in Vilcabamba on behalf of his brother Tupac Inca, similar to what the Marquis of Cañete had done with Sayri Tupac, [who was also] his brother. [Toledo] was unaware of [Cusi Titu Yupanqui's] death because the Indians of Vilcabamba had carefully concealed it, preventing anyone from that area or here in Cuzco[989] to leave or enter. After discussing and conferring with many people who had information of the interior [i.e., Vilcabamba] and had experience in the affairs of this kingdom, he decided to send an ambassador to discuss the matter with [Cusi Titu Yupanqui] urging him to come out in peace, as Sayri Tupac had done, [so] that that land would come under the domain of Your Majesty, like the rest of the kingdom.

[The Viceroy] selected Atilano de Anaya,[990] a highly esteemed nobleman [and] citizen of the city of Zamora in Spain. He believed that the negotiations would be easier [if conducted] through him because [Anaya] knew [Cusi Titu Yupanqui]. Anaya had

---

987   During Toledo's administration, thousands of small, scattered villages were "reduced" into larger towns.
988   A scribal dittography has been corrected.
989   The wording of this passage suggests that it was written while Murúa was in Cuzco.
990   Salazar (2016 [1596]:180–181) and Cobo (1979 [1653]:181) also mention the journey of Atilano de Anaya.

been responsible for collecting the tributes and taxes on behalf of the Incas in the *repartimientos* of Yucay and Jaquijahuana under the Inca's orders, overseeing the tax money and other things for him. So, [Toledo] ordered him to prepare to go to the province of Vilcabamba to [meet] Cusi Titu Yupanqui, who, as previously mentioned, ruled as the absolute lord in place of Tupac *[f.181r]* Amaru, his legitimate brother.

Once all the necessary items and funds were ready, just before the beginning of Lent,[991] [Anaya] left Cuzco accompanied by many Indians.[992] When Atilano de Anaya arrived at the entrance of Chuquichaca, which is twenty leagues from the town of Puquiura, where the previously mentioned cleric was killed, and crossed the bridge, the captains, Paucar Unya and Colla Topa, both *orejones*, as well as Curi Paucar,[993] [a] Yauyo,[994] who had been stationed there by the Inca to prevent anyone from entering or leaving, approached him.[995] They asked what he was bringing the Inca and why he had come on this occasion. They asked if he had brought the taxes and tribute list from Yucay since it had been four or five years since they had received them.[996] Without giving him a chance to respond and fearing that he or one of the other Indians accompanying him might learn of the death of Cusi Titu Yupanqui, which had occurred over a year before and was [still] being kept secret, they fatally speared [Anaya] and the Indians with him. They also took the money, tribute, and other items the Viceroy had sent for the Inca. Only four or five Indians and one Black man named Diego, who belonged to Atilano de Anaya, escaped, fleeing when seeing what was happening. With great haste and good fortune, they quickly left the bridge and arrived in Cuzco, where Viceroy Don Francisco de Toledo was, to deliver the news.[997] They arrived on the fifth Sunday of Lent,[998] commonly referred to as Lazarus Day, in the year 1572.

Upon receiving the news, the Viceroy was deeply saddened and profoundly affected by the death of Atilano, a man of great honor and esteem. Moreover, as [Atilano] had been sent as ambassador, the fact that the Indians, [acting] like

---

991   According to Ziółkowski's date converter, in 1572 Lent started on Ash Wednesday, 20 February, and the fast ended on Holy Thursday, 3 April.

992   Ocampo Conejeros (2016 [1611]:123) suggests that Fray Juan de Vivero and Diego Rodríguez de Figueroa traveled with Anaya until Ollantaytambo.

993   Curi Paucar is also mentioned by Ocampo Conejeros (2016 [1611]:123).

994   All three of these captains were later captured by Antonio Pereyra and Martín García Oñaz de Loyola in the town of Panquis soon after the fall of Vilcabamba.

995   Ocampo Conejeros (2016 [1611]:123) also provides a detailed account of the death of Atilano de Anaya; however, many specifics differ from those provided by Murúa.

996   In 1565, Cusi Titu Yupanqui agreed to leave Vilcabamba sometime in the future, after receiving the tribute from the Yucay encomienda. It is plausible that he believed that Atilano was carrying those funds since he served as the guardian of Beatriz Clara Coya, who had inherited the Yucay encomienda.

997   Ocampo Conejeros (2016 [1611]:123) also describes the arrival of Diego in Cuzco.

998   According to Ziółkowski's date converter, the fifth Sunday of Lent was on 23 March in 1572.

barbarians and without respect, had broken *[f.181v]* the inviolable law afforded to ambassadors by all the nations of the world, compelled [Toledo] to quickly punish Inca Cusi Titu Yupanqui and everyone with him and to level and reduce that province to the service and obedience of Your Majesty, thus bringing the matter [of the Incas] to a close. [Therefore,] he sent Juan Basco and Tarifeño, harquebusiers of the Royal Guard, who were close to him along with others, including Father Diego López de Ayala,[999] who was the priest of the [Ollantay]tambo and Amaibamba valleys at the time, and Diego [de la] Plaza, [a] mestizo [and the] son of Juan de la Plaza, one of the first conquistadors of this kingdom, who was in the Amaibamba Valley at that time. They were joined by Don Pedro Pazca,[1000] [the] Indian leader of the abovementioned valley, accompanied by many Indians, and they proceeded to the bridge of Chuquichaca to search for Atilano de Anaya's body. They eventually found it, as the Inca's captains who had killed him were only interested in robbing him of his possessions. They had thrown him down a ravine, a long way from where they had killed him, so that he would not be easily found. After they retrieved the body, they took it to the church of Amaibamba Valley, two leagues from the bridge, where they buried him, ten days after he had been killed.

It was evident that the unwarranted killing of Ambassador Atilano de Anaya was God's will. It provoked the anger of Viceroy Don Francisco de Toledo, to take revenge and deliver a more comprehensive punishment for the murder of Father Fray Diego, which they were concealing, fearful of what had happened. Consequently, by sending Juan Basco and the others, the Viceroy proclaimed a full-scale war and he began gathering forces to move against Tupac Amaru and the other *[f.182r]* Incas who were hiding with him. On Quasimodo Sunday,[1001] they assembled, and he sent Governor Juan Álvarez Maldonado,[1002] a citizen of the city of Cuzco, along with nine soldiers, to go to the bridge of Chuquichaca.[1003] These [soldiers] included Gabriel de Loarte, nephew of Doctor [Gabriel] Loarte, chief justice of Lima; Captain Juan Balsa, a nephew of the Incas [and the] grandson of Huayna Capac, and the legitimate son of Coya Doña Marca Chimpo[1004] and Pedro [Ortiz] de Orué. [They also included] Martin de Orué and Alonso de la Torre de Landatas,

---

999   After the fall of Vilcabamba, Diego López de Ayala became the first vicar of the region.
1000 Pazca played an important role in the fall of Sacsayhuaman, fighting on behalf of the Spaniards. He was a cousin of Manco Inca.
1001 According to Ziołkowski's date converter, the first Sunday after Easter, also called Low Sunday, was April 13, 1572.
1002 Ocampo Conejeros (2016 [1611]:124) also mentions that Juan Álvarez Maldonado was in Cuzco when Toledo arrived and that he participated in the Vilcabamba raid.
1003 Sarmiento de Gamboa, who was among the Spaniards sent with Juan Álvarez Maldonado, states that these troops left Cuzco on Thursday, 15 April 1572.
1004 Coya Doña Marca Chimpo was Huayna Capac's daughter and a sister of Manco Inca.

sons of Captain Pedro Ortiz de Orué,[1005] [a] citizen of Cuzco, Juan Zapata, servant of the Viceroy, [and] Juan de Ortega and Galarza, *alguaciles* of Cuzco. [The Viceroy] ordered them to rebuild the bridge, as he understood that the Indians had burned it, and when it was [re]built, they were to guard it with fifty Cañari Indian allies, and not leave it until the Viceroy sent them [additional] troops.

Thus, they left on the Monday after Quasimodo,[1006] and [the Viceroy] appointed Governor [Juan Álvarez] Maldonado, a native of Salamanca, [as the] *maese de campo* for having loyally served Your Majesty during the period of the rebellions. Juan Álvarez Maldonado remained at the bridge for a month and a half, guarding it with great vigilance, having built it anew.[1007] During this time, the Indians saw that [the Spaniards] had rebuilt and were guarding [the bridge], and they realized that [the Spaniards] must be waiting for reinforcements to enter Vilcabamba. Deeming it was wise to do everything possible to dismantle and burn [the bridge], one hundred Indians armed with spears and arms and adorned with medallions and many feathers on their heads, as was their custom in war, came forward three times to converge at the bridge. To conceal their true intentions, they told [the Spaniards] to wait if they wished to speak with Inca Cusi Titu Yupanqui, as they would send word to him. [They did this] to hide news of Inca's death and that of the Augustinian cleric who had been them in Puquiura indoctrinating them. In this way, they gained time to harvest the maize and potato *chacras* as well as other fields of *oca* and legumes that they had planted, knowing that if the Spaniards entered, they would steal them, and [they] would have to have food brought to them. After harvesting the crops, [the Indians] placed them in secure, safe places so that they could use them during the war that they already surmised [was coming].[1008]

How Viceroy Don Francisco de Toledo sent Martín Hurtado de Arbieto as general against Tupac Amaru and the battle against him

After the *maese de campo*, Juan Álvarez Maldonado, had been at the bridge for a month and a half, as previously mentioned, Don Antonio Pereyra, a Portuguese gentleman [and] citizen of Cuzco, arrived with twenty soldiers.[1009] Within eight

---

1005 Pedro Ortiz de Orué held the encomienda of Maras (Glave 2017).
1006 According to date Ziołkowski's converter, this event occurred on 14 April 1572.
1007 The raid into Vilcabamba was postponed until the beginning of the dry season.
1008 Folio 182v is blank.
1009 Ocampo Conejeros (2016 [1611]:124) also mentions that Antonio Pereyra was in Cuzco when Toledo arrived and that he captured several leading Inca nobles during the

days, Doctor [Gabriel de] Loarte, Alcalde of the Court of the [Royal] Audiencia
of Lima, and Doctor Friar Pedro Gutiérrez [Flores], of the Order of Alcántara,[1010]
who at that time served as the chaplain of Viceroy Don Francisco de Toledo, and
who was later become [a member] of the Supreme Council of the Indies, also
arrived at the bridge. They brought with them two hundred fifty men—citizens
and soldiers—all distinguished and brave. These valiant and gallant men came well
equipped with weapons and uniforms. At the bridge, by orders of the aforementioned Viceroy, from whom they had received their instructions, they organized the
captaincies: Martín Hurtado de Arbieto[1011] was appointed as the general and head
of all the forces. Don Antonio Pereyra and Martín de Meneses[1012] [were named]
as infantry captains. Ordóñez de Valencia, native of Zamora, [was named] captain of artillery. Captain Antón de Gatos [was named] as Sergeant Major of the
entire army. Mancio Sierra [de] Leguizamo,[1013] [Martín] Alonso de Mesa,[1014] and
Hernando Solano [were appointed] as advisors on military affairs. They were citizens of Cuzco [and] among the first conquistadors and discoverers of this kingdom.
They [were] men of great fortune and valor, having served Your Majesty on many
occasions and had expended much during them.

Captain Julián de Humarán, a citizen of the city of [La] Paz and a permanent *regi-
dor* of the city of Cuzco, went as quartermaster of the army responsible for procur-
ing all the necessary food and providing the required weapons and ammunition.[1015]
Martín García [Oñaz] de Loyola, a Biscayan gentleman, *[f.183v]* [and] captain of

---

Vilcabamba raid. Years later, in 1589, he was asked by the viceroy to investigate Martín
Hurtado de Arbieto's administration of the Vilcabamba region, and he filed a damning
report of widespread corruption (Maúrtua 1906:181–192).

1010   Ocampo Conejeros (2016 [1611]:116) notes that Fray Pedro Gutiérrez Flores baptized
Melchior Carlos Inca.

1011   Martín Hurtado de Arbieto had been advocating for the invasion of Vilcabamba for many
months.

1012   Ocampo Conejeros (2016 [1611]:124) also mentions that Antonio Pereyra and Martín
de Meneses participated in the Vilcabamba raid and were both present in Cuzco when
Toledo arrived.

1013   By this time Mancio Sierra de Leguizamo was one of the few surviving members of
Pizarro's original expedition (see Stirling 1999). Ocampo Conejeros (2016 [1611]:124)
noted he participated in the final Vilcabamba raid.

1014   Martín Alonso de Mesa was an elderly veteran who, like Mancio Sierra de Leguizamo, had
been with Pizarro at Cajamarca. Ocampo Conejeros (2016 [1611]:124) also includes him
as a member of the Vilcabamba raid.

1015   Soon after the fall of Vilcabamba, Julián de Humarán fell ill and was replaced by his second in command, Francisco Pérez Fonseca (Maúrtua 1906:140–169). Ocampo Conejeros
(2016 [1611]:124) also notes that Humarán was in Cuzco when Toledo arrived and that he
participated in the raid on Vilcabamba.

the Viceroy's guard, who later became [a member] of the Order of Calatrava, also went. He took with him in his squad twenty-eight outstanding soldiers, sons of citizens and conquistadors of this kingdom, along with some other prominent gentlemen who wanted to fulfill their obligations and serve Your Majesty on this expedition. Among them were Don Jerónimo Marañón[1016] and Don Francisco de Mendoza, commonly called "the Paraguayan" since he was born there. He was [the] brother of Don Diego de Mendoza, whom Viceroy Don Francisco de Toledo later beheaded at Chuquisaca.[1017]

To wage war more effectively and to intimidate the Indians by attacking them on multiple fronts, the Viceroy sent Gaspar Arias de Sotelo.[1018] A native of Zamora, [he was] one of the most prominent gentlemen of the kingdom, a close relative of Viceroy Blasco Núñez Vela. He also had served Your Majesty as man of great courage and self-confidence on all occasions since the rebellion of Gonzalo Pizarro. Captain Nuño de Mendoza[1019] accompanied him, along with many other citizens of Cuzco and as many as one hundred soldiers. [They were] under orders that if Martín Hurtado de Arbieto were to die on the expedition, Gaspar Arias de Sotelo would become the *General Supremo*.

They entered [the Vilcabamba region] through Cochacajas and Curamba,[1020] which are on the Royal Road from Lima to Cuzco before arriving at Abancay, [Arias de Sotelo's] *encomienda*. Traversing the steep mountains and tortuous trails, he reached Pampaconas,[1021] a very cold place twelve leagues from Vilcabamba (the

1016 Later, in 1578, Jerónimo Marañón testified on behalf of Francisco Valencia, providing information about the events that occurred during the Vilcabamba campaign (Maúrtua 1906:106). Ocampo Conejeros (2016 [1611]:124) also mentions Marañón being in Cuzco when Toledo arrived.

1017 Diego de Mendoza served as the governor of the Mojos region. He rebelled against the Crown (1573–1575) but was defeated and killed by royalist forces.

1018 At this time, Gaspar Arias de Sotelo was the *encomendero* of Abancay, so it is logical that he chose to enter Vilcabamba via this route. Arias de Sotelo had been a member of a 1565 convoy to Vilcabamba led by Matienzo (Lohmann Villena 1941). Ocampo Conejeros (2016 [1611]:124) also states that Arias de Sotelo entered the Vilcabamba region via Curahuasi.

1019 Nuño de Mendoza was the *encomendero* of Curamba (Toledo 1975 [1573]:207), which borders on the Vilcabamba region and Abancay. Cusi Titu Yupanqui (2005 [1571]) writes that several Andeans attempted to escape his oppressive oversight and fled into the Vilcabamba region. Ocampo Conejeros (2016 [1611]:124) also states that Nuño de Mendoza entered the Vilcabamba region via Abancay.

1020 Cochacajas was a *tambo*, and Curamba was a major Inca settlement. Both installations are on the road between Abancay and Andahuaylas (Bauer, Kellett, and Aráoz Silva 2010:96–100).

1021 The forces of Gaspar Arias de Sotelo and those of Martín Hurtado de Arbieto met in Pampaconas. The town of Pampaconas is mentioned multiple times in the history of the Vilcabamba region. Perhaps most important, it is where Rodríguez de Figueroa (Bauer,

old),[1022] where the Incas had their seat and court. The citizens and advisors decided to halt there to discuss and consider[1023] what they would do next.

The Viceroy also dispatched Indian war allies to help the Spaniards on the expedition. Don Francisco Cayo Topa[1024] went as the general of the Cuzco *orejones*. He was in charge of one thousand five hundred Indian combatants from all the provinces surrounding Cuzco. *[f.184r]* General Don Francisco Chilche,[1025] [the] *cacique* of the Yucay Valley, led the Cañari[1026] and *mitimaes*.[1027] As mentioned above, he had been suspected of poisoning and killing Sayri Tupac, for which he was in prison in Cuzco for a year. He was in charge of five hundred well-armed Indian fighters.[1028] The army crossed the [Chuquichaca] bridge unimpeded and marched in good order until [they] were three leagues from Vitcos[1029] and Puquiura, where there is a difficult pass full of undergrowth through a steep mountain called Quinua Racay and Coyaochaca.[1030] At this point, Martín García [Oñaz] de Loyola, who had [only] twenty-eight men, was reinforced with thirty additional soldiers from the three companies of Don Antonio Pereyra, Martín de Meneses, and Ordóñez[1031] de Valencia.

On the second day of Easter,[1032] the Inca captains Colla Topa and Paucar Unya, [both] *orejones*, and Curi Paucar, [a] Yauyo, along with other captains, gathered their forces at the abovementioned place and passage of Coyaochaca. Due to the

---

Fonseca Santa Cruz, and Aráoz Silva 2015) first met with Cusi Titu Yupanqui (also see Bingham 1914a).

1022   This location is now known as Espíritu Pampa (Bauer, Santa Cruz, and Aráoz Silva 2015; Hemming 1970; Lee 2000).

1023   A textual error has been corrected (Murúa 2008 [1616]:183v).

1024   Francisco Cayo Topa is mentioned elsewhere by Murúa, and he played an important role in the final Vilcabamba campaign.

1025   Francisco Chilche, the leader of the Cañaris in the Cuzco region, appears to have played a major role in several important events that directly benefited him, including the death of Sayri Tupac and the capture of Tupac Amaru.

1026   During the time of Huayna Capac and his father Tupa Inca Yupanqui, many Cañaris were relocated from their homeland in central Ecuador and resettled in the Cuzco region. They became close allies of the Spaniards.

1027   In addition to the Cañaris, individuals from many other ethnic groups had relocated by the Inca into the Yucay region.

1028   Ocampo Conejeros (2013; 2016 [1611]:124–125) suggests a small battle took place for control of the bridge.

1029   Vitcos is now called Rosaspata (Bauer, Santa Cruz, and Aráoz Silva 2015).

1030   Coyaochaca is mentioned by Salazar (2016 [1596]:184). Also see Lee (2000).

1031   Ocampo Conejeros (2016 [1611]:124) also includes Ordóñez de Valencia as a member of the Vilcabamba campaign.

1032   According to Ziółkowski's date converter, the second day of Easter (also known as Pentecost) in 1572 was May 26.

difficult and rugged terrain that favored them, they believed it was an opportune place to defeat and destroy the Spaniards. So, they arranged themselves in their customary battle formation. Given the narrow trail and the mountain, Martín García [Oñaz] de Loyola, who was leading the vanguard along with Don Francisco Cayo Topa and Don Francisco Chilche, along with five hundred Indian allies, initiated the battle. Because the Indians had put many palm points and strewn thorns on the ground, [and] set many snares of creepers to entangle and trip the Spaniards, so that they would fall when attacked, [Loyola] divided his men into three units.[1033]

Both sides engaged in fierce combat, and Martín García [Oñaz] de Loyola was nearly killed. As [he was] fighting, an enemy Indian, who was so large and strong that he resembled a half-giant, emerged and grabbed [García Oñaz de Loyola] by [*f.184v*] the shoulders, rendering him immobile. However, one of our Indian allies named Currillo came to his aid with a sword. He struck at [the enemy's] feet, knocking him down, and with a second blow, he splayed his shoulders, such that he fell down dead. Thus, on account of this Indian, Captain Martín García [Oñaz] de Loyola was spared from death. Currillo's courage and speed in killing the half-giant with just two strokes of his sword and saving his captain was undoubtedly a noble feat worthy of remembrance.[1034]

The battle lasted two and a half hours, with great resolve on the part of the Indians and demonstrations of courage and bravery. However, at the height of the conflict, an Inca captain named Parinango, a very brave and courageous Indian who was the general of the Cayambes,[1035] was shot with a harquebus, and fell dead, along with Maras Inca, another captain, along with many other spirited Indians. With this, [the Inca forces] became discouraged and retreated, resulting in a Spanish victory. This battle took place on the third day of Easter[1036] at three in the afternoon. As the defeated Indians slowly retreated into the hills and forest, many [Spaniards] were allowed to escape.

After resting for two days after their victory, General Martín Hurtado de Arbieto ordered [the Spanish army] to continue searching for a safe path through the mountains, understanding that there could be Indians hidden in the interior who knew the paths and trails. During the last battle, as the Indians were withdrawing, they threw

---

1033   Sarmiento de Gamboa, testifying in 1578, also notes that Loyola divided his troops into three groups and highlights the moment when Francisco Ordóñez de Valencia killed an Inca captain with a shot from a harquebus (Maúrtua 1906:111).

1034   Ocampo Conejeros (2016 [1611]:125) also provides a detailed description of Martín García Oñaz de Loyola's rescue when he was attacked on the trail.

1035   The Cayambes were an ethnic group from central Ecuador, many of whom had been brought to the Cuzco region during the time of Huayna Capac.

1036   According to Ziółkowski's date converter, the third day of Easter of the Holy Spirit in 1572 was May 27.

boulders from a mountainside at the soldiers, killing [two] Spaniards named Gonzalo de Ribadeneyra and Gonzalo Pérez.[1037] These [soldiers] were buried on the trail itself, with [their graves] marked with crosses, as they were unable to find a more convenient or suitable burial place. As the general wanted to do everything to prevent his troops from being killed in an Indian ambush, the Spanish soldiers and their Indian allies searched from place to place, seeking a way out of the narrow mountains.[1038]

[F.185V] CHAPTER 80

A trail was discovered through which the army entered the Puquiura Valley, and other things that occurred

They searched for a path for three days after the aforementioned battle until a mestizo soldier named Juanes de Cortázaga, [the] son of Juanes de Cortázaga, a citizen of Arequipa, discovered a safe and unobstructed route. Greatly pleased with this, the general moved the army in an orderly fashion, and everyone left with their supplies. They reached the Puquiura Valley, where the Inca had his residence and where the Augustinian fathers had a church, as we have mentioned. [This was also] where Cusi Titu Yupanqui had died and [where] they had their small villages. In this valley, they found maize fields ready to be harvested.[1039] Since the army was short on food, the Spaniards and Indians rejoiced and were able to resupply themselves, particularly due to the abundance of native livestock, [such as] rams and sheep.[1040]

After resting, the army advanced toward Pampaconas, which, as previously mentioned, is a bitterly cold place, where they found a large quantity of potatoes, legumes, and ninety-seven Castilian cows, sheep, and pigs that the Incas had, as well as salt mines.[1041] From this unpleasant place, they traveled to Vicos Calla, where the Incas had silver mines, as they later discovered. [These mines] were operating and continue to be worked to this day.[1042] The Field Marshal, Juan Álvarez

---

1037 Ocampo Conejeros (2016 [1611]:126) also mentions the deaths of these two men, and specifically names Ribadeneira.

1038 Folio 185r is blank apart from four thick pen strokes.

1039 Ocampo Conejeros (2016 [1611]:125) also describes how the Spaniards were resupplied with local rations.

1040 This refers to llamas and alpacas.

1041 The salt mine of Qollpacasa and the remains of an Inca platform can still be seen at Pampaconas.

1042 The possible mineral wealth of the Vilcabamba region greatly interested the Spaniards, and the existence of mines is frequently mentioned in early descriptions of the region.

Maldonado,[1043] charged forward to seize the plunder, yelling: "*Arcay tucui nocap*," meaning "Take everything, for it is mine" ([referring to] the livestock, food, and clothing). He [then] fell off his horse into a swamp.

They arrived at Pampaconas the following day, three leagues by trail [from Vicos Calla]. Due to the rugged terrain, densely forested mountains, and steep slopes, the army stopped for thirteen days, as many soldiers and Indians had fallen ill with measles. [The stop] allowed them to rest and for the ill to recover. *[f.186r]* It also [allowed] them to gather more information and news of the route, which was unfamiliar to them.[1044]

On the eleventh day of the army's rest, an Indian who had surrendered during the previous battle of Coyaochaca escaped with a cloak and dagger stolen from a soldier. This Indian intended to warn Tupac Amaru, as well as his uncle, nephew, and their captains, about the Spaniards' situation and whereabouts. [However,] he was caught, returned, and hanged that same day by the guards and sentinels, serving as a lesson to others who had surrendered that they [should] not attempt to escape. This Indian was named Canchari.

On the thirteenth day, the army left from there and passed through the forested slopes and gorges, with a great deal of effort on everyone's part. Along the trail, they came across sacrificed *cuyes*, which are like Castilian rabbits, at three or four places. It is common for the Indians [to make such offerings] during times of war, famine, or pestilence and while attempting or conducting difficult and arduous negotiations. [This is done] in order to appease their *huacas* and seek signs revealed in the *cuyes*, of what events will befall them, whether they will be prosperous or unfortunate [and] sad, or happy and joyful.[1045] They had done this in the places and areas through which the army was advancing.

When [the Spaniards] arrived at a passage called Chuquillusca,[1046] which is a jagged cliff running alongside a wide river, making it nearly impossible to traverse, the soldiers and their Indian allies had to either crawl or hold onto each other's hands, facing great difficulties and risks to proceed. Upon seeing this, a Portuguese soldier

1043 Juan Álvarez Maldonado would later lead an unsuccessful expedition into the Manu region.
1044 While the forces of Martín Hurtado de Arbieto were resting in Pampaconas, they were joined by the troops of Gaspar Arias de Sotelo, who had entered the Vilcabamba region by way of Curamba.
1045 This refers to the Andean practice of killing an animal and then examining the internal organs for indications of future events.
1046 Gonzalo Pizarro and his forces had conducted a raid into the Vilcabamba region, some thirty years before, between April and July of 1539. In that raid a major battle took place at Chuquillusca, where between thirteen and thirty-six Spaniards were killed with boulders that were rolled down the steep mountain slope.

named Pascual Juárez hoisted a bronze *versete*[1047] over his shoulder and managed to get through this difficult path. It was so steep that fifty Indians could not have safely passed with the *versete*, and many would have fallen [*f.186v*]. According to all the soldiers who were part of the army and saw him, he performed a heroic act and a valuable service to God, our lord, and to Your Majesty. By firing the [*versete*] and a small *culebrina*,[1048] they scattered the Indians, preventing the Spaniards from being trapped in such a difficult pass. [This was] because the enemy was within sight of the Christians, shouting, screaming, firing arrows, [and rolling] boulders. And at every difficult spot where the Cañari Indian allies broke rank, leaving the protected company of the Spaniards and the harquebusiers, they would return with spear wounds inflicted by their enemies. Although we know that the Cañari were skillful with their spears, their enemies had more experience, given that there were days when they never relinquished their weapons and were familiar with the route, knowing where they could easily take advantage of our [troops]. Thus, they were occasionally able to inflict damage.

The following day, as the army marched toward Tumichaca, an Inca captain named Puma Inca approached the Spaniards in peace and with signs of goodwill that did not appear to be counterfeit or disguised.[1049] This captain was always with Incas Tupac Amaru and Quispe Titu, never leaving their side. They had discussed among themselves [about] giving obedience to General [Hurtado de] Arbieto, as they wanted end the war and battles with the enemy, opting instead for peace. [This was] because on his deathbed Manco Inca, [the] father of Tupac Amaru, had ordered them [to do so] or suffer his curse if they acted otherwise. He understood that they could not sustain themselves in that land if the Spaniards entered in force against them. Because the Incas had made these decisions, Curi Paucar and the other captains of the Sun, Colla Topa and Paucar Unya, [both] *orejones*, had decided to kill them, as they were unwilling to make peace, and instead wished to continue the war and defend themselves to the death. [*f.187r*]

Some [people] say that [these captains] were [also among] the most insistent on killing the revered father Friar Diego Ortiz, as previously detained, and that Martín Pando, a mestizo who was secretary of Cusi Titu Yupanqui, helped them. Furthermore, they say that after [Pando] helped them carry out that evil deed, the captains made him commit idolatry. Wicked and cowardly, or of little faith, like the Indians among whom he lived, [Pando] committed idolatry. Thus, on this occasion, the Spaniards discovered a small pit in his house where he made his sacrifices, [a

---

1047 A small artillery piece.
1048 A small cannon.
1049 A textual error has been corrected (Murúa 2008 [1616]:186v).

practice] that, in fact, most of the mestizos of this kingdom commit.[1050] ~~While a few mestizos have shown signs of virtue in their childhood and youth, upon reaching adulthood, they have returned to the customs and inclinations inherited from their ancestors and nurtured by their mothers' breasts. Because in their disposition and inherent nature, they are generally all the same as~~[1051] this Martín Pando ~~who~~[1052] after having finished committing idolatry, referred to as a *"pago"* by the Indians, received his rightful punishment; this unfortunate [individual] was killed as payback and compensation for his sin and abominable crime.

On the day Captain Puma Inca came out in peace, as mentioned above, the army with the General [Martín Hurtado de Arbieto] and other captains arrived at Anonay, where they halted and spent the night. They camped with great care and precaution, fearing the Indians would suddenly appear, as they found numerous palm thorns, tipped with a poisonous herb, strewn on the ground so that those who stepped on them would certainly die. [However, Puma Inca] warned of this, so that they would be careful and walk cautiously.

In the name of the Incas, Tupac Amaru and Quispe Titu, Captain Puma Inca offered obedience to General Martín Hurtado de Arbieto, stating the Incas' desire for peace and mercy. He asked the general to punish the rebels, as they were afraid that Curi Paucar and the other *orejon* captains *[f.187v]* would kill them. [The rebels] were impeding [the Incas], and because of this they did not dare come out in person to offer obedience ~~and obedience~~[1053] to the general. [The situation] was therefore beyond their control, and the death of Atilano de Anaya was in no way their fault, nor had they given the order [to kill Anaya], since they were in the interior at that time. Instead, Curi Paucar and the other *orejon* captains had acted independently, to conceal the death of Cusi Titu Yupanqui, their brother and father. Puma Inca [also] told of how the captains had built a well-supplied and fortified fort, called Huayna Pucara. He provided a sketch and [explained] the means by which it could be overtaken without endangering any Spaniards or Indians during the assault. At this time, the enemy [forces] were within sight of the army, briefly showing themselves in contempt of our [troops].[1054]

1050   A textual error has been corrected (Murúa 2008 [1616]:187r).
1051   Crossed out by Remón (Adorno 2008:111, Murúa 2008 [1616]:187r).
1052   Crossed out by Murúa (Adorno 2008:102; Murúa 2008 [1616]:187r).
1053   A dittography has been corrected by Murúa (Adorno 2008:102; Murúa 2008 [1616]:187r).
1054   Folio 188r is blank.

[F.188V] CHAPTER 81

How, with the counsel of Puma Inca, the fort of Huayna Pucara was taken by force

The following day, the army rose and marched two leagues in good order toward Huayna Pucara, where the enemy had fortified themselves.[1055] They rendezvoused at a place called Panti Pampa.[1056] The Spanish army halted there to discuss how to take the fort and to prepare the necessary things for the assault, which was expected to be difficult and dangerous. There were so many disagreements among the captains and citizens over where to station the army that they almost came to blows. Since most, if not all, of those present were prominent and distinguished, rich and powerful, estate owners serving Your Majesty, at their own expense, they were losing respect for the *maese de campo*. However, the general, who was lagging behind, arrived and defused the situation, and the army settled down as best they could. The enemy was now in sight, practically near the army's camp, steadily advancing.

The *orejon* captain, Puma Inca, who we said had come to swear obedience, informed the general and the other advisors and captains who were holding counsel about the route and path that the army, along with their supplies, had to traverse the next day. This captain provided answers to all that he was asked as well as truthful and accurate advice, which was of great importance. It is well known that their victory and the taking of the fort were based on his advice.[1057] [This is] because he told them that [Huayna Pucara] was very large [ridge], measuring a league and a half, almost nearly two, in the shape of a crescent moon. The path they needed to follow was very narrow, traversing a rocky and forested [mountain], with a large and wide river running beside it. This [route] became even more dangerous and treacherous during combat with the enemies *[f.189r]*, who held the heights along that league-and-a-half stretch along the knife-edge ridge where only one person could pass at a time.

1055   The battle for Huayna Pucara was a key event in the 1572 raid into Vilcabamba. The site of Huayna Pucara, now called Tambo, was first identified by Lee (2000). It had previously been the location of another battle in 1537. Puma Inca may well have remembered the details of that earlier encounter.

1056   Panti Pampa is located between Pampaconas and the area of Tambo.

1057   In 1537, a battle had taken place in this same location as where Spanish troops pushed deep into the Vilcabamba region. After suffering heavy loses, the Spaniards managed to secure the heights above the fort and the Inca retreated (Pizarro 1921 [1571]:396–404). The Spaniards then spent several months in the region. However, in 1572, they avoided casualties thanks to advance warning from Puma Inca about the fortification. It seems that Puma Inca had knowledge of the battle that had taken place there decades before.

The Indians had constructed a strong fort made of stone and clay, where they had many piles of rocks to be thrown by hand and with slings. Furthermore, there were large rocks with levers along the entire ridge above the fort. If any youth were to push these large rocks, they would come tumbling down. The [Indians] would have certainly done this when the Spanish army and their Indian war allies were walking in double file with all the supplies along the crescent ridge. If God had permitted the enemy to execute their prepared plan, not a single person from the entire army, neither Indian nor Spaniard, would have been left alive, as the boulders would have killed everyone, crushing them as they came rolling down. Anyone who escaped with their life would have been forced to throw themselves into the river, where they would quickly drown, pulled under by the weight of their weaponry and clothing. If anyone survived both the boulders and the river, they would have then been killed by arrows because there were five hundred Chunchu Indians from the Andes, archers who would have spared no one on the other side [of the river] to finish them off. So, Puma Inca's warning proved invaluable to the Spanish army that day as they set out on their mission to conclude the war.

The next day, Monday, all the soldiers and gentlemen of the army prepared themselves and performed all the duties that befit Christians in such circumstances: confessing, [partaking] communion, and preparing their arms. It was understood that, without a doubt, the [upcoming] battle and taking of the fort would be dangerous, given its location and the precautions taken by the enemy within it. General *[f.189v]* Martín Hurtado de Arbieto, accompanied by General Gaspar [de] Sotelo, went out to the army, joined by all the citizens and captains. He started calling out the soldiers he selected from the troop rosters. [Once] there were about one hundred fifty, he ordered them to ascend a high and steep ridge [that extended] a league and a half along the hilltops, and they departed as ordered.

It must have been after six in the morning [when] they began climbing the hill, which was so steep and difficult that they had to crawl, holding onto one another until, finally, by the grace of God, they safely reached the summit at about one in the afternoon. Commanding the summit, they revealed themselves to the enemy, who was well organized, as is customary in war. Being skillful and experienced [at fighting] in this terrain and seeing the Spaniards above them, and [thus] subject to [the Spaniards'] will, they realized it was unwise to wait for them there below. They slowly withdrew to the fort of Huayna Pucara, leaving behind the boulders and rocks they had arranged to kill the Spaniards.

The general advanced slowly with the army and supplies, stopping occasionally to allow those taking the heights to reach the top. [He waited] until the Spaniards and their Indian allies signaled from the heights, firing their harquebuses. The artillery was gradually fired against the fort to frighten their enemies, who were retreating there. Meanwhile, [the Spaniards] struggled to reach [the fort], but the rough, overgrown, and narrow trail detained [them]. But in the end, with the help provided by those above [the fort] and the skillfulness of those below, God granted [victory]. As they drew near, [the Spaniards] shouted "Santiago!" [and] attacked the fort. After discharging a formidable volley of harquebus fire, they captured [the fort]. The Indians displayed courage and daring for a time, although without posing a threat to the exhausted [troops], as the road and the climb to the fort were so difficult and hard.

[*f.190r*] The following day, Tuesday, thirteen prominent soldiers, who were formally [positioned] on the heights near the Chuquichaca bridge, set out. Don Francisco Chilche, [the] *curaca* of Yucay [and] general of the Cañari, went with them. They arrived at Machu Pucara,[1058] where Manco Inca had defeated Gonzalo Pizarro, [Francisco de] Villacastín, Captain Ordóñez [de Valencia], and others.[1059] When these prominent [soldiers] came to a halt, the enemy advanced in numbers to attack them. At first, there was so much shouting and howling that it caused confusion, such that a servant of Don Jerónimo de Figueroa,[1060] a nephew of Don Francisco de Toledo, [accidentally] set fire to a doublet he was wearing. If [Figueroa] had not thrown himself into a nearby stream, he would undoubtedly have been hopelessly burned.

That day, the advancing army arrived at Marcanay, where they found many unharvested maize fields along with large quantities of bananas, *ají*,[1061] *yuca*, cotton, and guavas. This made the army extremely happy, as they were starving and in need of food, and they were able to replenish themselves with these supplies. However, a mestizo soldier named Alonso Hernández de la Torre, [the] son of Francisco Hernández de la Torre, a respected figure in this kingdom, broke [ranks] and took some sugarcane to eat. As a result, the *maese de campo*, Juan Álvarez Maldonado, beat him to prevent further disobedience from the other soldiers, who were [beginning to] scatter [and] break ranks due to their lack of militarily training. [Álvarez Maldonado did this] because the Indians could potentially be [lying] in ambush, ready to suddenly attack those who strayed from their squadron, causing much damage. As we have seen on infinite occasions, an entire army can be destroyed for not remaining vigilant of the enemy.[1062]

1058 Old Fort.
1059 This battle took place in Vilcabamba region in 1539.
1060 Ocampo Conejeros (2016 [1611]:124) also mentions the involvement of Jerónimo de Figueroa in the Vilcabamba campaign.
1061 Chili peppers.
1062 Folio 190v is blank.

[*F.191R*] CHAPTER 82

How General Martín Hurtado de Arbieto entered Vilcabamba and sent [his forces] after Quispe Titu, and they apprehended him

The next morning, which was the day of Lord Saint John the Baptist, 24 June 1572, General Martín Hurtado de Arbieto ordered the entire army to be organized by companies each with their captains and Indian allies. Generals Don Francisco Chilche and Don Francisco Cayo Topa, along with their other captains, marched in an orderly fashion, carrying the artillery and their flags. They entered the town of Vilcabamba on foot, [as] the terrain is very rough and craggy and not suited for horses, at ten in the morning. They found the entire town sacked, such that if the Spaniards and Indian allies had done it, it could have been no worse, for all the Indian men and women had fled into the mountains, taking with them whatever they could. They burned and destroyed the rest of the maize and food in the *buhíos* and storage houses, where they typically keep them, and they were [still] smoldering when the army arrived. The House of the Sun, where their major idol was kept, was also burned.[1063] [The Indians] believed that if the Spaniards failed to find food or any sustenance quickly, they would soon turn around and leave the region rather than stay and settle it, as occurred when Gonzalo Pizarro[1064] and [Francisco de] Villacastín entered [the region]. The lack of food forced [the Spaniards] to turn back and leave the land in their control, which was the Indians' intention when they set fire to everything they could not take and fled.

The army rested in the town of Vilcabamba for one day, allowing soldiers to recuperate [*f.191v*]. The next day, seconds after their arrival, General [Hurtado de] Arbieto summoned Gabriel de Loarte, Pedro de Orué (Inca de Orué),[1065] Captain Juan Balsa (the uncle of the Incas Tupac Amaru and Quispe Titu) and Pedro Bustinza (also an uncle), and other outstanding friends and comrades. Juan Balsa and Pedro Bustinza were [the] sons of the two Coyas, Doña Juana Marca Chimpo and Doña Beatriz Quispe Quipi, daughters of Huayna Capac, and[1066] with them [came] other important friends and companions.

1063 Excavations at the site of Espíritu Pampa (Vilcabamba) have found evidence of this massive burning event (Bauer et al. 2015).

1064 Here, Murúa suggests that Gonzalo Pizarro reached the city of Vilcabamba during the 1538 raid into the region.

1065 Like Juan Balsa and Pedro Bustinza, Pedro de Orué (the younger) was of mestizo descent and was closely related to the ruling Incas in Vilcabamba. His father was Pedro de Ortiz de Orué, and his mother was María Tupac Usca.

1066 At this point Murúa's first scribe concludes his work and the second scribe begins.

The general ordered them to pursue Inca Quispe Titu in the rough mountain of Ututo,[1067] as he had been told that Inca Quispe Titu was fleeing with some followers toward Pilcosuni, a province on the other side of the Andes, toward the Marañón River. This group hastily departed to pursue Quispe Titu Yupanqui, marching through the hills mentioned above. This was arduous work, as there was no water or food apart from what they had taken from Vilcabamba. After six days, Captain Juan Balsa, who was leading the vanguard, with Pedro de Orué as second and Gabriel de Loarte as rear guard, came upon Quispe Titu Yupanqui with his wife, who was within days of giving birth, along with eleven Indian men and women who served him, as the rest of [his] retinue had scattered. After capturing him, they turned back toward Vilcabamba. They descended in two [days], what had taken them six days to ascend. It is said that they encountered numerous rattlesnakes in that mountain, but by the grace of the Divine Majesty, no one was bitten, as they [cause] great harm. The exhaustion and toil they, of necessity, had experienced during the journey transformed into relief and joy due to their good fortune. Thus, they arrived at the town of Vilcabamba and handed [Quispe Titu] over to the general at the Inca's very own house.[1068] [f.192r] Imprisoned, they stripped [Quispe Titu and his wife] of all their belongings and clothes, such that neither he nor his wife was left with a change of clothes nor any of their belongings. Despite the warm climate, they suffered from cold and hunger.

The climate of this region is such that honeybees, similar to those in Spain, build hives under the eaves and at the rear of the *buhíos*, and maize can be harvested three times a year. The fields benefit from the fertility of the soil and the timely irrigation they receive. Abundant crops of *ají*, coca, sugarcane for honey and sugar production, as well as yucas, *camote*, potatoes, and cotton thrive there. The town covers, or better said, used to cover an area half a league wide, similar in layout as Cuzco. It extended over a distance where they raised parrots, chickens, ducks, local rabbits,[1069] turkeys, pheasants, curassows, guans, *guacamayos*, and a multitude of other colorful birds—a magnificent sight to behold. The houses and *buhíos* [were] roofed with high-quality straw. There are many guavas, *pacay*, peanuts, *lucumas*, *papayas*, pineapples, *paltas*, and various other wild fruit trees.

The house of the Inca had an upper and lower floor [and] was [roofed] with tiles,[1070] and the entire palace [was] adorned with a wide variety of paintings in their

---

1067 Ututo is located on the Inca road between Pampaconas and the Inca city of Vilcabamba.

1068 There is a set of buildings at the site of Espíritu Pampa that are widely believed to have been the houses of an Inca.

1069 That is to say, guinea pigs.

1070 Both Bingham (1914b:196–197) and Savoy (1970:97–98) noted the remains of Spanish tiles in the ruins of the site of Espíritu Pampa. Hemming (1970) later used the presence of

style, which was quite a sight to see. There was a plaza that could hold many people, where they celebrated and even raced horses. The doors of the house were of fragrant cedar, which is plentiful in that land, and the *zaquizamíes*[1071] [were made] of the same material. In this way, the Incas did not miss the pleasures, grandeur, and opulence of Cuzco in that distant land, or better said, land of exile, because the Indians brought them anything they desired from the outside to ensure their joy and pleasure; and they enjoyed themselves there.

At the time General [Hurtado de] Arbieto sent those [troops] we have mentioned *[f.192v]* in search of Inca Cusi[1072] Titu Yupanqui, whom they captured. He sent Captain Martín de Meneses in a different direction to search for Inca Tupac Amaru. [Meneses] and his company set out and they reached [a place] six leagues inland called Panquis and Sapacatin. There, they discovered the golden idol of the Sun,[1073] along with much silver, gold, precious emeralds, [and] a wealth of old clothing. Rumor has it that the total value of all this exceeded a million [pesos]. All of it was divided among the Spaniards and their Indian allies, even the two priests who were traveling with the army received their shares. While some theologians and learned men believed that the [taking] of such spoils was unjust, and that they should not profit from them, the law of unbridled greed prevailed over natural and divine law. Thus, they took everything, including many silver and gold pitchers and vessels that the Incas themselves had used. Some [of these items] had either escaped the hunger of the Spaniards and the Pizarros in Cuzco at the beginning [of the conquest] or had been hidden away and retrieved later. They had even crafted certain items to replace the many that they had lost and had been lawlessly seized by the Spaniards with little regard for God. It was as if the Incas and Indians were no longer the rightful owners of their possessions; instead, all rights of ownership had been forfeited and granted to whoever could seize them by force. So, everyone took whatever they could, and thus, their possessions [were] ill-gotten goods.

[General Hurtado de Arbieto] sent Captain Don Antonio Pereyra in another direction in pursuit of Inca Tupac Amaru and to do everything possible to capture him and the other captains who had fled with him, because [with them as] prisoners, the war would end, and the land would be peaceful and tranquil. Don Antonio

---

these tiles, as well as this passage by Murúa, to identify Espíritu Pampa as the Inca town of Vilcabamba. This identification was later confirmed by Lee (2000).

1071 Arabic: gables or attic.

1072 Murúa made a mistake here. Instead of "Cusi Titu Yupanqui," it should read "Quispe Titu Yupanqui."

1073 Guaman Poma de Ayala (2004 [1615]:449 [451]) includes a drawing depicting the Spaniards leading Tupac Amaru and carrying this idol. Toledo later sent this idol to Spain (Nowack and Julien 1999).

Pereyra set out and displayed such remarkable skill that he caught up with and apprehended Colla Topa and Paucar Unya, [the] *orejon* captains mentioned earlier, along with the traitor Curi Paucar. He was the cruelest of all the Inca captains and was the most insistent on continuing the war and rejecting the possibility of peace and obedience. *[f.193r]* He had done the most harm and [was] the principal cause of Atilano de Anaya's death.

[Pereyra] also apprehended many other Indian enemies who were hidden in the mountain of Sapacatin and returned to Vilcabamba with the prisoners. Along the way, a snake bit Curi Paucar's young son, who was being carried on his [father's] shoulders. The venom was so strong that the child died of the bite within twenty-four hours. Following this, they arrived at Vilcabamba, where [Pereyra] turned in the prisoners.

Captain Don Antonio Pereyra, devoid of greed, did not take any of the [seized] spoils for himself. He served on the expedition with great valor, being the son of Captain Lope Martín, who had also distinguished himself in Your Majesty's service during Pizarro's rebellion. After traveling to Spain in the company of President Pedro de la Gasca, [Lope Martín] returned to this kingdom and [served Your Majesty] in the uprising and revolution of Francisco Hernández Girón. He [faithfully] followed the royal standard on various occasions, proving himself in all. He was taken prisoner by Francisco Hernández [Girón], during the battle of the Hoyas de Villacuri, six leagues from Ica. [Hernández Girón] later ordered his beheading.[1074] This is how he ended his days in Your Majesty's service, true and loyal. His body was later taken to Lima and buried in the main church, where Your flag hung over the main chapel. There it remained for many years until time consumed it.[1075]

[F.194R] CHAPTER 83

How the general sent Captain Martín García [Oñaz] de Loyola, who apprehended Inca Tupac Amaru

After Captain Don Antonio Pereyra returned to Vilcabamba with the abovementioned enemy captains, General [Hurtado de] Arbieto, who was eager to apprehend Inca Tupac Amaru, believing that the war would not end until [the Inca] was captured and the Indians would remain restless as long as he was among them, decided

---

1074   Lope Martín was one of the richest men of the Cuzco region. He was captured and killed in 1554 by Hernández Girón (Pizarro 1921 [1571]:480–481).

1075   Folio 193v is blank.

to search for him again.[1076] Therefore, he dispatched General Martín García [Oñaz] de Loyola to search for [Inca Tupac Amaru] and his uncle, Huallpa Yupanqui, a former Inca general who was traveling with him. [Loyola] departed with forty soldiers along the Masahuay River of the Mañarí, [who were] Chunchu Indians [from the] province of the Andes.[1077] They walked forty leagues from Vilcabamba to where this river flows into or becomes the Marañón and flows toward the North Sea.[1078] [There], they found six light balsa rafts, which had been used by the Inca, his captains, and others to reach the other bank. Martín García [Oñaz] rested there.

At midday, while resting in the mountains full of huge trees and tall mangroves, [Loyola] and his soldiers saw five Chencho Indians bathing on the opposite side [of the river]. One of them, serving as a lookout, was fishing for *sabalo*[1079] with his arrow. These [fish] are very abundant in that river, and the Indians shoot them in the water with arrows. Captain [Loyola] devised a plan to capture some of those Indians to collect information and intelligence about the Inca, as no one else could know better. He ordered six soldiers to prepare themselves. [His plan was that] as the Indians went into the mountains, [the soldiers] would cross in pairs to the other side in the rafts and attempt to capture [the Indians] any way they could. They could see smoke [coming from] a *buhío* in the mountain, which was three hundred fifty fathoms long and had 20 doors, where they were cooking.

Although some soldiers refused, Gabriel de Loarte finally declared, "My comrades and I will cross [the river], and I am determined to bring back spoils." Thus, he, *[f.194v]* [along] with Pedro de Orué, Captain Juan Balsa, Cristóbal Juárez (a Portuguese), [Domingo de][1080] Tolosa (a Biscayan), and another individual boarded the rafts and crossed the river in pairs. Once on the other side, they entered the [*buhío*], and were lucky enough to find seven Chunchu Indians [within it], swiftly capturing five of them. The other two escaped because there were so many doors in the *buhío*, [but] they did not have time to grab their arrows, which were made of stingray tail spines. In the *buhío*, they found a lot of cooked maize and more

1076 Detailed information regarding the hunt for Tupac Amaru can be found in the various petitions sent by Martín García Oñaz de Loyola to the king of Spain, requesting rewards for his actions, as well as in the eyewitness testimonies of many of the men who accompanied him (see Maúrtua 1906:3–70).
1077 Murúa is attempting to describe lands unknown to him, and he is not sure of the relationship between the major rivers downstream from Vilcabamba. Tupac Amaru certainly reached as far as the Pichu River and may have arrived at the Mantaro-Urubamba confluence before attempting to flee on foot eastward into Pilcosuni territory.
1078 That is to say, the Atlantic Ocean.
1079 *Prochilodus lineatus.*
1080 The first name of this Spaniard is not known with certainty; however, a Domingo de Tolosa did testify on behalf of García Oñaz de Loyola in 1572 (Maúrtua 1906:52).

than fifty [dried] *sabalos*. They reassured the [captured] Chunchu with kind gestures, using an Indian who had spent [time] with them and knew their [language],
to speak with them. They told them not to be afraid [and] that no harm or offense
would come to them. They left the *buhío* with them, [traveled] through the mountains to reach the riverbank, where they saluted their companions on the opposite bank with their harquebuses. When the rafts returned, Captain Martín García
[Oñaz] de Loyola and his soldiers boarded them and crossed the river, where they
ate in great relaxation and contentment. They were pleased with the spoils they
had taken, because they found thirty loads of extremely fine clothing in the *buhío*
[belonging to] the Inca. [This included] much rare velvet, rich silk, bundles of cloth
from Rouen and Holland, basketwork, buskins, a large number of featherworks
from Spain and this land, and, above importantly, an abundance of gold and silver cups and table service [belonging to] the Inca. Everyone rejoiced over [seizing]
so many and such valuable spoils. They believed that Tupac Amaru could not be
very far from there, as there were so many items belonging to him guarded by the
Chuchu within the *buhío*.

Captain Martín García [Oñaz] de Loyola then requested, [speaking] with
the Chunchu through an interpreter, that their *curaca* appear [before him].[1081]
When Captain [García Oñaz de Loyola] gave them offerings and gifts, their
cacique, Ispaca, came to where he was and he warmly received him as the leader
of the Chunchu Mañarí Indians.[1082] [García Oñaz de Loyola] spoke with
[Ispaca], persuading him to reveal where Tupac Amaru was. To further encourage Ispaca, he gave him certain garments that [belonged to] the Inca himself,
along with Castilian feathers. [The captain] also reassured him, that no harm
would befall his land or his people. Fearful, Ispaca ●●●●●●●●●●●●● ~~Tupac
Amaru's fate~~ ●●●●●● ●●●●●●●●●●●●●●●●●●●●●●●●●●●●●● ●●●●
●●●●●●●●●●●●●●●●●.[1083] He said that [Tupac Amaru] had left there five days
earlier, traveling by canoe to go to the Pilcosuni, [which is] another inland province. [He also said] that Tupac Amaru's wife was somber and frightened as she
was days away from giving birth. Furthermore, [Tupac Amaru] was traveling very
slowly, helping to carry her *ato* himself, because he loved her so much. [García

---

1081 Murúa compresses two different events that occurred during the Spaniards' hunt for
      Tupac Amaru. The encounter between Ispaca and García Oñaz de Loyola occurred near
      the town of Momorí, many leagues downriver from where the Spaniards found the large
      stash of Inca goods (see Maúrtua 1906:3–70).
1082 Several individuals who were with García Oñaz de Loyola and who later testified on his
      behalf also mention the leader Ispaca (Maúrtua 1906:33, 40, 49).
1083 The Royal Censor, Pedro de Valencia, has rendered this sentence largely unreadable
      (Adorno 2008:115; Murúa 2008 [1616]:194v).

Oñaz de Loyola] gave the Inca's gifts to Ispaca, [but he] declined, stating that [by accepting them], he would be committing a grave betrayal of his lord. Later that afternoon, Martín García [Oñaz] de Loyola took this *cacique* and left in search of Tupac Amaru, so that [he] would not pull ahead and escape with his general, Huallpa Yupanqui. He left five soldiers and four Indians at the *buhío*, to guard the captured spoils, clothes, and tableware. They were [instructed] to send food forward, as there was ample food there stored for the Inca, but he had only stopped [to collect] Indians to carry his *ato*. [García Oñaz de Loyola] entered the forested mountains with thirty-seven soldiers, following the trail taken by the Inca. The provisions, including ten loads of maize, five of *maní*, three of sweet potato, and eight of *yucas*, followed behind for their sustenance.

Martín García [Oñaz] de Loyola walked for fifteen leagues before coming upon Tupac Amaru, who had veered from the path along an arm of the sea, as one can refer to that large river. Had Martín García [Oñaz] de Loyola not pressed on the day he received the news and the following day, he would not have ever been able to reach [Tupac Amaru] as [the Inca] was planning critical actions with his wife [to escape the Spaniards] that very day. [He was] imploring her to get into a canoe so they could travel forth by sea. However, she was terrified of going so far into open waters for more than one hundred fifty leagues, and this [hesitancy] led to their imprisonment and death. If they had gotten into the canoe and travelled the [water] route, *[f.195v]* it would have been impossible to catch them, as they had already received food and provisions for their trip to the opposite shore, placing them beyond the reach [of the Spaniards].

The capture unfolded in the following way: two mestizo soldiers, Francisco de Chávez, son of Gómez de Chávez, scribe of the Cuzco Municipal Council, and Francisco de la Peña, son of Benito de la Peña, also a public scribe in the same city, were walking in front at nine at night when they spotted a distant campfire. They gradually reached the location where Inca Tupac Amaru, his wife, and General Huallpa Yupanqui were warming themselves.[1084] Since they came upon them by surprise, [the Spaniards] were very courteous, not wanting to agitate them. They told [Inca Tupac Amaru] not to be upset as his nephew Quispe Titu was safe and well treated in Vilcabamba and was not in distress or being mistreated. Furthermore, that his relatives, Juan Balsa and Pedro Bustinza, sons of the Coyas Doña Juana Marca Chimpo and Doña Beatriz Quispe Quipi, his aunts, were coming for him. Because Francisco de Chávez was the first to reach the Inca and took some valuable vases from the Inca, he became known as "Chávez Amaru." While this was

---

1084 Murúa is mistaken; the Inca general Huallpa Yupanqui was captured one or two days before Tupac Amaru.

transpiring, Martín García [Oñaz] de Loyola, along with Gabriel de Loarte[1085] and the other soldiers, arrived and apprehended the Inca. After spending a night filled with apprehension and caution, they [began their] return to Vilcabamba the next morning, where they arrived safely without any mishaps.

Tupac Amaru Inca was very affable, well mannered, modest, eloquent, and intelligent. [He was] solemn and strong and did not show concern over the loss of his belongings, that Loyola, and all the other soldiers who had gone with him, had stolen from him, except for a feather adorned with gold thread, [made from the] tail of a *guacamayo*. [He] was also saddened when [García Oñaz de Loyola] gave a red blanket [so well made] that it was akin to satin from Granada, and a black velvet shirt, to the *cacique* Ande in his presence. With this, [Tupac Amaru] became irritated with Martín García [Oñaz] de Loyola and abruptly shoved him. The [Spaniards] stole more than one and a half million in gold, silver, Castilian clothes, silks, bars of silver, dishes, jars, precious stones, jewels, and clothes from him. Captain [García Oñaz de] Loyola [subsequently] turned Tupac Amaru and his wife over to General Martín Hurtado de Arbieto, who was granted the governorship of Vilcabamba by Viceroy Francisco de Toledo, and later took on the title of lord.[1086]

[F.196V] CHAPTER 84

How Governor Arbieto ordered the body of Father Fray Diego Ortiz to be removed from where the Indians had buried him

Governor Martín Hurtado de Arbieto [was] overjoyed at seeing such a fortunate end to the war, which had been considered very difficult due to the rough passes, grueling trails, and dense mountains found in that land, where the Indians had inflicted significant harm on the Spaniards. With Tupac Amaru Inca, his nephew Quispe Titu, his general and uncle Huallpa Yupanqui, as well as Curi Paucar and the other *orejon* captains they had captured, [Hurtado de Arbieto] was ordered

---

1085 Gabriel de Loarte, a lawyer for the Crown, had traveled to Cuzco with Toledo. Toledo named him the *corregidor* of Cuzco, a position he held for only a year. Later, he held a number of other important positions for the Crown in the Americas. Ocampo Conejeros (2016 [1611]:128) suggests that it was Gabriel de Loarte who sentenced Tupac Amaru to death in Cuzco.

1086 Murúa is mistaken; Viceroy Toledo granted Martín Hurtado de Arbieto the governorship of Vilcabamba, while García Oñaz de Loyola was given a bounty for capturing Tupac Amaru and Huallpa Yupanqui and was also granted permission to marry Beatriz Clara Coya. Also, folio 196r is blank.

by Viceroy Don Francisco de Toledo to prevent any Spaniard from leaving, as he wanted the land occupied. Therefore, [Hurtado de Arbieto] dispatched Gabriel de Loarte, Pedro de Orué, Martín de Orué, Juan Balsa, and Martín de Ribadeneyra to the Marcanay pass,[1087] where they remained on guard, preventing any soldiers from returning to Cuzco. [They did this because] if the Spaniards did not leave, the land could be settled more effectively, and towns would be established at the most convenient places and locations.

At that time, upon learning of the brutally cruel death that the Indians had brought upon the revered Father Fray Diego Ortiz,[1088] as previously described, the governor ordered and sent soldiers to search for his body, which the Indians had buried.[1089] Eventually, they found it, [buried] in the abovementioned way, beneath the roots of a large tree trunk. Upon exhuming him, they saw he had received a blow to the back of the neck from a *macana* and five arrow wounds inflicted by the Indians. [When the body was] removed from the pit and hole where he had been placed, God wished to demonstrate the innocence of His servant and priest, so despite having killed and buried by Indians some fourteen months earlier, his Holy body was dry [and] without any foul odor. His cheeks appeared rosy, as if fresh blood still flowed. [He appeared as he was] at the *[f.197r]* moment of his death, without any signs or evidence of decay or worms, [even though] the area where he was buried was hot and forested, as it rains during both the winter and summer. [At that moment], the mosquitoes disappeared in the Hoyara Valley and in Chucullusca until now.[1090]

The soldiers placed the body in a *petaca*[1091] and took it to the town of San Francisco de la Victoria, which was already[1092] called Vilcabamba. After it was inside a coffin, Governor Arbieto and Father Diego López de Ayala, the vicar of that province at that time, led a procession of all the Spaniards who lived [in the area]. They carried the coffin on a stretcher, adorned with a cross and a great quantity of wax.[1093] The governor, along with the most prominent [citizens] of the city, placed it upon their

---

1087 This is most likely the pass between Espíritu Pampa and the settlement of Concevidayoc.

1088 Here, Murúa returns to the 1595 and 1599/1600 reports on the death of Diego Ortiz for most of his information (Bauer et al. 2014).

1089 One of the soldiers who found the body was Alonso de la Cueva. Antón Álvarez may also have been present (Bauer et al. 2014).

1090 One of the miracles associated with the death of Diego Ortiz was the disappearance of mosquitoes from the region. They are said, however, to have returned after the Augustinians stole his body from the local church and took it to Cuzco in 1595.

1091 Nahuatl: wicker box.

1092 A textual error has been corrected (Murúa 2008 [1616]:197r).

1093 This information is taken from the 11 March 1595 testimony of Alfonso de la Cueva (Bauer et al. 2014:85–89).

shoulders, and with deep reverence, they laid [Fray Diego Ortiz] in the city church. The vicar conducted Mass and spoke in praise of the revered priest and his Holy zeal and intentions. The governor [made] another [speech] to the Indians, denouncing their terrible and abominable deed, pointing out the punishments that had befallen them by the hand of God.

When the Mass was over, they put the Holy body in a vault below the main altar.[1094] However, the most compelling evidence of the revered and religious father's favor with God in Heaven is what was described in the reports that were written many years later in Vilcabamba and the city of Cuzco.[1095] Reliable witnesses stated that several days after [the funeral], Doña Mencía de Salcedo,[1096] [a] natural daughter of the aforementioned governor, went to the vault where the bones and coffin were kept and could be touched because[1097] she had serious eye problems [f.197v] and was in danger of losing them. As she gazed upon the coffin and prayed with great devotion to God, his Divine Majesty granted her mercy, whereupon she was cured of the illness and ailment that had afflicted her [eyes].

Doña Leonor Hurtado de Ayala,[1098] [a] legitimate daughter of the governor, mentions this in her sworn testimony.[1099] She also states that Doña Juana de Ayala,[1100]

1094 After the body of Ortiz was discovered by the Spaniards, it was reburied in the village church in Hoyara (aka San Francisco de la Victoria de Vilcabamba). Some twenty-two years later, in 1595, the bones of Ortiz were stolen by Fray Pedro de Aguiar as he completed the first Augustinian effort to investigate the death of Ortiz. It is worth noting that although Murúa describes the death of Ortiz in great detail, he does not cover the theft of Ortiz's remains by the Augustinians.

1095 This is a direct reference to the Augustinians' reports that Murúa read sometime after 1600. During their 1595 and 1599–1600 investigations, the Augustinians recorded several miracles associated with Ortiz: the remarkable preservation of his body, the disappearance of mosquitoes in the region, and various healings. Murúa is careful to mention all of these.

1096 Francisco de Mariaca married Mencía de Salcedo Hurtado de Arbieto in 1582. He was killed a year later during a failed expedition to the Pilcosuni region under the leadership of Martín Hurtado de Arbieto. The miraculous healing of Mencía is mentioned in various testimonies taken in 1595 and 1599–1600, particularly those given by Martín Hurtado de Arbieto's wife and his other daughters (Bauer et al. 2014).

1097 A spelling error has been corrected (Murúa 2008 [1616]:197r).

1098 Also known as Leonor Hurtado de Mendoza.

1099 Murúa again makes a direct reference to the 1595 and 1599–1600 investigations into Ortiz's death. Witnesses interviewed in 1595 were Juana de Ayala Ponce de León, the wife of Martín Hurtado de Arbieto, as well as two of his daughters, Leonor Hurtado de Mendoza and Mariana Hurtado de Mendoza; and, in 1599, another daughter, Francisca de Arbieto (Bauer et al. 2014).

1100 Juana de Ayala Ponce de León and Martín Hurtado de Arbieto had one son, Juan Hurtado, and two daughters, Leonor Hurtado de Mendoza (who married Diego

her mother and the wife of the said governor, suffered from terrible pain in her molars. And whenever the pain got worse, she would place her cheeks and jaw on the coffin where the bones were kept, whereupon her pain would subside.

God, in His immense power, knows how to honor those who serve Him in life and death. Therefore, this priest, moved by his zeal for serving God and saving souls, followed the directives of his prelate, who sent him to enter [Vilcabamba]. He died in innocence in that province [whose inhabitants] were in servitude and enslaved by Satan. We must believe that Almighty God, [who] justly rewards the virtuous, [now] holds him in His glory, rewarding him for the work he accomplished. Therefore, all of us within this kingdom who are involved in converting these [peoples'] suffering souls must [undertake this task] with a saintly zeal, to earn God's honor. [We must] proclaim His Holy Name throughout these nations; leaving [behind] other vain and futile interests only leads to the loss of the honorable reward of our work.[1101]

[F.198V] CHAPTER 85

How Governor Arbieto sent Tupac Amaru and the other prisoners to Cuzco, and [how] the Viceroy administered justice to Tupac Amaru

A month after Martín Hurtado de Arbieto captured the Indians Tupac Amaru, Huallpa Yupanqui, and Quispe Titu, an order arrived from Viceroy Don Francisco de Toledo, stating that those who wished to leave for Cuzco could do so, as the land was peaceful and calm and there was no reason to fear rebellion since the [leading] Incas were now unable to do so. They were to be placed in prison in the city of Cuzco, alongside Paucar Unya and Colla Topa, [Tupac Amaru's] captains, and other important prisoners. The Viceroy ordered that they be brought before him so he could carry out his plans, as he was deeply hurt by the death of his ambassador, Atilano de Anaya.

While in route to Cuzco, Huallpa Yupanqui, [the] uncle of the Incas, fell ill with bleeding in his stomach. The illness worsened and he died a league before reaching

de Gamarra and, after his death, Miguel de Otaça de Mondragón) and Mariana Hurtado de Mendoza (who married Luis Catano de Cazana). Martín also had an illegitimate daughter named Mencía de Salcedo Hurtado de Arbieto (who married Francisco de Mariaca). Juana de Ayala Ponce de León's wife and her daughters were living in Cuzco in 1595 and 1599–1600 (see Bauer et al. 2014).

1101   Folio 198r is blank.

Cuzco. Consequently, he did not witness the pain and sorrow that would soon befall his nephew, Tupac Amaru.

They entered Cuzco in formation with the prisoners.[1102] Captain Martín García [Oñaz] de Loyola, who had captured Tupac Amaru, led him with a gold chain fastened around his neck, while his nephew, Quispe Titu, had a silver one.[1103] All the captains and soldiers marched along with him according to their rank, as ordered by the Viceroy. The prisoners of higher and lower status, along with the captains and principal *orejones*, [marched] alongside of them. Viceroy Don Francisco de Toledo was in residence in his mansion, which belonged to Diego de Silva,[1104] [a] citizen of Cuzco and native of Ciudad Rodrigo, [and a] gentleman of high standing *[f.199r]*. [Toledo] watched from a window as the people entered. His uncle, Fray García de Toledo, a member of the Order of Santo Domingo, was with him, along with his chaplain, Fray Pedro Gutiérrez [Flores], who later was [a member] of the Royal Council of the Indies.

When the Incas[1105] reached the window where the Viceroy was, Captain Loyola ordered them to remove their *llautus*, and Tupac Amaru [to remove] the tassel he wore as royal insignia. [However], they refused. Instead, they simply touched the *llautus* with their hands [and] bowed their heads toward the Viceroy. Some people say that when Captain Loyola told Tupac Amaru to remove his tassel because the Viceroy was there, he replied that he did not want to, as the Viceroy was merely the king's *yanacona*, meaning "servant."[1106] In his anger, Loyola dropped the gold chain with

---

1102   At times, Ocampo Conejeros is cited as an eyewitness to the execution of Tupac Amaru. He did not actually witness it; instead, he relied on information provided by the Mercedarian Nicolás de los Ríos. Ocampo Conejeros (2016 [1611]:131) writes, "And in this city a cleric of Our Lady of Mercy, named Father Fray Nicolás de los Ríos, heard and saw all of the events that I have recounted until now. He touched [the burial site] with his hands and walked upon it with his feet. [He is] a faithful cleric, and very familiar with the land of Cuzco, from whom Your Excellency could gain valuable information because he has a good memory and is a great authority, having been an eyewitness to all of these events." As various details provided by Ocampo Conejeros overlap with information recorded by Murúa, it is likely that they both independently used de los Ríos as an informant.

1103   The *New Chronicle* (Guaman Poma de Ayala 2004 [1615]:449 [451]) and the *History and Genealogy of the Inca Kings of Peru* (Murúa 2004 [1590]:50v) include drawings of Tupac Amaru being chained and led by García Oñaz de Loyola. Salazar (2016 [1596]187) also mentions the gold chain.

1104   Ocampo Conejeros (2016 [1611]:127) also notes that the viceroy was in de Silva's house, one of the largest and most prominent houses of the city. Diego de Silva was the godfather of Garcilaso de la Vega, and he describes the location of the house in his chronicle (Garcilaso de la Vega 1966 [1609]:429).

1105   This word has been changed from "Indians" to "Incas" (Murúa 2008 [1616]:199r).

1106   Guaman Poma de Ayala (2004 [1615]:450 [452]) and Murúa (2004 [1590]:51) provide similar accounts of the arrival and death of Tupac Amaru in Cuzco.

which Tupac Amaru was being led as prisoner and struck him twice, believing that he was serving Your Majesty and pleasing the Viceroy. Nevertheless, everyone present considered it an undignified [act] for a nobleman. Tupac Amaru and his nephew, Quispe Titu Yupanqui, were then imprisoned in the house of Don Carlos Inca, [the] son of Paullu Topa, which the Viceroy had turned into a fortress.[1107]

[The Spaniards] deliberated and discussed at length the case of the Incas, [debating] how to administer justice to them. Many people spoke and pleaded with the Viceroy to temper his anger toward them, but [their pleas] were of no avail. Many theologians argued that the Incas did not deserve death because they had not been baptized or initiated into the community of the Holy Roman Catholic Church, [and] they had always striven for [f.199v] peace and acknowledged and given obedience to His Majesty, our King Felipe. [They requested] that [the Incas] be allowed to remain in their land, live in peace, and receive the faith and Holy Baptism.[1108] [The theologians] presented many arguments on behalf of the [the Incas], but the Viceroy turned a deaf ear, determined to publicly deliver justice to Tupac Amaru by decapitating him in front of all in order to eliminate any [potential] future insurrection. Also, to convey to the Inca Indians and the other provinces that King Felipe, our lord, was their sole king, and that they must obey him without looking to anyone else in the kingdom.

Thus, [the Viceroy] ordered that the sentences be carried out against the Inca captains Colla Topa and Paucar Unya, and their hands were cut off. Curi Paucar, a Yauyo, who had consistently opposed the Spaniards and played the primary role in the death of Atilano de Anaya, was hung[1109] on the gallows in the plaza of Cuzco, putting an end to him and his evil deeds.

To execute Tupac Amaru, they erected a scaffold covered in black in the middle of Cuzco's public plaza.[1110] When [Tupac Amaru] learned of his impending death, he emotionally pleaded with the Viceroy to spare his life, asserting that he had committed no offense and that his death would serve no purpose. [He asked] to be sent to His Majesty to serve as his *yanacona*, meaning "servant"; however, the Viceroy

1107 Tupac Amaru was imprisoned in the former palace of the Incas, Colcampata, on the slope between Cuzco and Sacsayhuaman. Soon after the death of Tupac Amaru, Toledo seized the palace. Years later, after Carlos Inca's son, Melchor Carlos Inca, had sued the state, it was returned to his family. Ocampo Conejeros (2016 [1611]:128) also mentions that Tupac Amaru was placed in Colcampata.

1108 Ocampo Conejeros (2016 [1611]) and Salazar (2016 [1596]) provide additional information on the pleas offered to the viceroy to spare Tupac Amaru's life and the death of Tupac Amaru's captains.

1109 This word has been underlined with a series of small dots, marking a spelling mistake (Murúa 2008 [1616]:199v). The corrected spelling is provided in the margin.

1110 Ocampo Conejeros (2016 [1611]:129) also describes the location of the gallows.

did not take advantage of this offer. His hard heart was not moved with compassion or pity, even when Don Fray Agustín de la Coruña,[1111] an ecclesiastic who is known throughout this kingdom [for leading] an exemplary and saintly life, and who [later become] the bishop of Popayán, threw himself at the feet of the Viceroy, tearfully pleading for [Tupac Amaru] as he was innocent and did not deserve the planned execution, urging instead that he be sent to His Majesty in Spain.[1112] While [Tupac Amaru] was staying in the abovementioned houses of Carlos Inca, which are [in] the fort, he had requested to receive the Holy Baptism from [Agustin de la Coruña] *[f.200r]*, and my lord, the bishop, granted [his petition]. [Nevertheless,] the Viceroy resolutely refused his pleas, closing the door on his requests and appeals in this matter.

The city of Cuzco had never been seen in all its [prior] hardships or [during Manco Inca's] siege, so on the verge[1113] of being lost, as it was on the day that the sentence was issued, as an infinite [number] of Indians, [including] Incas and *orejones* from other provinces, came out to see the unfortunate Tupac Amaru decapitated. Dressed in mourning cloth,[1114] he was escorted, weeping, by Viceroy Don Francisco de Toledo's guard and halberdiers.[1115] It was [so crowded] no one could walk through the streets, and the balconies were filled with prominent lords and ladies who, moved by compassion, wept at seeing a young man, so broken, being led to die.[1116] It can truly be said that everyone, regardless of their status, grieved his death. Although the Viceroy and all who counseled him [to rule] against the sad Amaru, were widely cursed, [the Inca] ascended the scaffold. There, Bishop Don Fray Agustin de la Coruña, who had washed him with the water of Holy Baptism

---

1111 Augustine of Coruña was one of the first Augustinians to enter Mexico in 1533 and was ordained as bishop of Popayán, Colombia, in 1564. He was a longtime supporter of Native rights. He is also mentioned by Cobo (1979 [1653]:182) and Ocampo Conejeros (2016 [1611]:130) as pleading for Tupac Amaru's life.

1112 Ocampo Conejeros (2016 [1611]:128–130) also provides a detailed description of the priests who argued on behalf of Tupac Amaru.

1113 A mistake in the manuscript may have been corrected (Murúa 2008 [1616]:199v).

1114 Ocampo Conejeros (2016 [1611]:129) writes, "The Inca, dressed in white cotton, held a crucifix in his hands, rode on a mule adorned for mourning. [He was] accompanied on either side by the two clerics [i.e., Fray Melchor Fernández and Fray Gabriel Álvarez de la Carrera], as well as by Father Alonso de Barzana, of the Order of Jesuits, and Father [Cristóbal de] Molina, [a] cleric who preached to the natives, who had the Parish of the Hospital of Our Lady of the Remedies."

1115 Ocampo Conejeros (2016 [1611]:129) also notes that Tupac Amaru was surrounded by more than 400 armed Cañaris.

1116 Ocampo Conejeros (2016 [1611]:129) also describes the state of Cuzco at the time of the execution: "The roofs, plazas, and windows of the parishes of Carmenca and San Cristóbal were so full of people, that if you threw an orange, it would have been impossible for it to reach the ground, because the people were so packed and pressed together."

the day before, publicly confirmed before everyone that [Tupac Amaru] had been baptized, granting strength to him through the grace of that Holy Sacrament instituted by Christ into the Catholic faith.[1117]

They say that a notable and wondrous event [then occurred].[1118] The plaza was completely filled with a multitude of Indians who had come to witness the sorrowful and deplorable spectacle of their lord Inca's death, and the skies resounded and thundered with their cries and screams. His relatives, who were nearby, marked this sad tragedy with tears and weeping. Those on the execution platform ordered the people to be silent, upon which the poor Tupac Amaru raised his hand and clapped. Instantly, everyone fell silent, as if there were no living soul in the plaza, and not a voice or a sob could be heard. This was a demonstration and a clear sign of the obedience, fear, *[f.200v]* and respect that the Indians had for their Incas and lords. Thus, [Tupac Amaru], whom most had never seen before, as he had been secluded in Vilcabamba since childhood, managed to suppress the weeping and tears that spring from [the depths of] the heart, which are so difficult to conceal and hide, with a single clap. Then, the executioner blindfolded him, placed his head on the platform, and, with a cutlass, cut it off. In this way, the sad and broken young man ended his days and the male line descending from Manco Inca ended.[1119]

His nephew, Quispe Titu, was banished to the City of Kings by Viceroy Don Francisco de Toledo. Because the climate there is so hot and different from that of the mountains, where the young man had been raised, he died prematurely.[1120] [Toledo also] assigned some [of the Inca's] sisters and aunts to the houses of that

---

1117 Ocampo Conejeros (2016 [1611]:129) provides similar information.

1118 Ocampo Conejeros (2016 [1611]:129) also tells of this event: "When the executioner, who was a Cañari Indian, raised the sharp knife to cut off the head of Tupac Amaru Inca, a marvelous thing happened; all the native people raised such a great outcry and clamor that it seemed like Judgment Day. None of the Spaniards hid their feelings, publicly weeping; their tears falling with pain and sorrow. When the Inca heard this great outcry, he did nothing more than lift his right hand in the air and let it fall. As he remained serene with a lordly air, all of the outcries passed to a deep silence and not a living soul moved, neither those furthest away nor those who were in the plaza." This overlapping information suggests that Murúa and Ocampo Conejeros shared the same informant, who we believe was the Mercedarian Friar Nicolás de los Ríos.

1119 Guaman Poma de Ayala (2004 [1615]:390 [392], 451 [453]) provides similar drawings for the death of Atahualpa in 1532 and the death of Tupac Amaru in 1572. While the historic details of the two executions differed greatly, for Guaman Poma de Ayala they were almost identical events. The *History and Genealogy of the Inca Kings of Peru* (Murúa 2004 [1590]:51v) illustrates the death of Tupac Amaru in a drawing that is similar to that found in Guaman Poma de Ayala (2004 [1615]:451 [453]).

1120 Quispe Titu died in Lima in 1578.

city's citizens, [but as they faced] difficulties, misfortunes, and lacked shelter, they constantly moved from one place to another, eliciting much compassion and pity.

Manco Inca's body was retrieved from Vilcabamba, where he was murdered by the mestizo Diego Méndez, [along] with Briceño y Escalante and others who had escaped from the battle of Chupas, next to Huamanga, as previously mentioned. Viceroy Don Francisco de Toledo ordered it be burned in the heights of the old fortress called Sacsayhuaman.[1121] He gave this order to prevent the Indians who knew where he was buried from secretly removing and worshipping him.[1122]

As mentioned above, there was a legitimate daughter of Sayri Tupac, granddaughter of Manco Inca, and great-granddaughter of Huayna Capac, the universal Lord of these kingdoms, named Doña Beatriz Clara Coya de Mendoza. Her marriage to Captain Martín García [Oñaz] de Loyola, captain of his guard, was arranged by the viceroy.[1123] However, there were serious disagreements and lawsuits which lasted many years concerning the marriage, since Cristóbal Maldonado, a native of Salamanca, claimed to have married her first.[1124] The bishop of Cuzco and the archbishop of Lima issued rulings on these, all of which were confirmed by the ruling of the honorable Fray Juan de Almares, ecclesiastic of the Order of Saint Augustine. [He] was an erudite professor of composition at the Royal University *[f.201r]* of the City of Kings [and] an apostolic judge. [As a result, García Oñaz de Loyola] remained with her. [Later], Captain Martín García [Oñaz] de Loyola was appointed as the governor of the Kingdom of Chile. He went there with his wife and was killed in an unfortunate event along with seventy other men by Indians at the end of the year 1598.[1125] After her husband's death, [Beatriz Clara Coya] went to Lima, where she died within a year. She was survived by one legitimate daughter,[1126] who was taken to Spain, having inherited her mother's *encomienda*, which produced about ten thousand assayed pesos in rent. Consequently, this branch of the Inca lineage was destroyed and put to an end.

1121   Murúa writes "Quíspiguaman."
1122   In early colonial times it was not unknown for Indigenous people to exhume the mummified bodies of their ancestors that the Spaniards had confiscated and buried.
1123   The marriage between Captain Martín García Oñaz de Loyola and Beatriz Clara Coya de Mendoza was arranged on the very day that Tupac Amaru was put to death (Maúrtua 1906:65–67). This was clearly a reward for the capture of Tupac Amaru and provided Martín García Oñaz de Loyola access to the prized Yucay *encomienda*, making him one of the richest men in Peru.
1124   In a failed attempt to gain control over her estate in Yucay, Cristóbal Maldonado kidnapped and raped Beatriz Clara Coya de Mendoza in 1566.
1125   García Oñaz de Loyola was killed, along with about fifty Spaniards, near the end of December 1598 while attempting to put down a revolt of the Mapuches in Chile.
1126   Ana María Lorenza de Loyola.

There are many other descendants of Huayna Capac in the city of Cuzco, especially, as already mentioned, Paullu Topa, whose baptismal name was Don Cristóbal Paullu Topa. He served Your Majesty [faithfully] and had many sons and daughters with various women. His most important son was Don Carlos Inca, [who was] legitimate [and] married a noble[1127] Spanish lady, named Doña María de Escobar. Because of certain suspicions against him, Viceroy Don Francisco de Toledo imprisoned [Carlos Inca] for a long time and confiscated his income, causing him to become impoverished.[1128] Some say that [Carlos Inca] had a son named Don Melchor Inquill Topa, also known as Don Melchor Carlos Inca, [who] was crowned in front of many Incas and *curacas* who were in Cuzco.[1129] Even if this were true, it would have been more out of frivolity and ignorance than an intention to rise up against Your Majesty.

After the death of Don Carlos, [Melchor Carlos Inca], being of marrying age, made a marriage agreement with Doña Leonor Carrasco, [the] legitimate daughter of Pedro Alonso Carrasco,[1130] a Knight of the Order of Santiago [and] a man of spirit and courage. In May 1601, he was imprisoned in Cuzco on the orders of Juan Fernández de Recalde, a judge of the Royal Audiencia of the City of Kings. At that same time, Don García de Solís Portocarrero, a Knight of the Order of Christ and *corregidor* [of Huamanga], was also imprisoned in the city of Huamanga, for allegedly attempting to rebel against Royal service. It was rumored that he had an agreement with Don Melchor Carlos Inca. In the end, Don García [de Solís Portocarrero][1131] was decapitated by [the order of] Licentiate Francisco Coello, *[f.201v]* an Alcalde of the court of the City of Kings [and] a judge of the commission, who was sent [to

---

1127   We have translated the term "hija dalgo" as "noble."
1128   Carlos Inca eventually won his release from prison and regained some of his confiscated property. He died in Cuzco in 1582.
1129   Murúa and Melchor Carlos were contemporaries, and both lived in Cuzco during an overlapping period. Melchor Carlos Inca was born before Toledo arrived in Cuzco. The infant's father, Carlos Inca, asked the viceroy to participate in the baptism, which according to Ocampo Conejeros (2016 [1611]:116) was held on 6 January 1572. This royal patronage and the creation of the ceremonial *compadre* relation between Carlos Inca and Toledo, as well as an *ahijado* relationship between Melchor Carlos Inca and Toledo, did the Indigenous Cuzco line little good. Once Tupac Amaru was captured, Toledo immediately turned on Carlos Inca and his infant son. Melchor Carlos Inca inherited his father's reduced wealth in 1582. Leading an opulent lifestyle, he was in constant conflict with local and Crown authorities. Melchor Carlos Inca traveled to Spain in 1603 (see Hemming [1970] for a detailed account of Melchor Carlo Inca's life).
1130   Ocampo Conejeros (2016 [1611]:142) also mentioned that Alonso Carrasco was a member of the Order of Santiago.
1131   García de Solís Portocarrero was executed in the town of Huamanga in September 1601.

investigate] this matter by Viceroy Don Luis de Velasco,[1132] Knight of the Order of Santiago, who was governor of the Kingdom of [Peru] at that time.

According to the Royal Audiencia and the carefully and thorough investigations conducted in this case, Don Melchor Carlos Inca was not found to have made any agreement, nor to have known any details of [the conspiracy], nor did he participate in it. So, he was set free and declared [innocent] with utmost honor. [This] was publicized and declared throughout the kingdom. In that same year, by order of Your Majesty, he traveled to the Kingdom of Spain, where he received significant aid to cover his expenses. Several days after arriving at the court where Your Majesty resides, he was granted the favor of an annual income of seven thousand ducats. He was instructed to give up his holdings in Peru and to remain in Spain forever, where he is presently, and to bring his wife there.[1133]

Another son of Huayna Capac was named Illescas. The Indians also say that Rumiñavi, [the] captain of Atahualpa who arrived [in Cuzco] in the company of Quisquis and Chalcuchima, captured[1134] him. When Quisquis withdrew from Cuzco to Quito, [Rumiñavi] took [Illescas] with him, where where [sic] he cruelly and inhumanely killed him, intending to revolt. At that time, no one could oppose him, as [Illescas] was just a child. Displaying his wicked and perverse spirit, [Rumiñavi] fashioned a drum of [Illescas's] skin.[1135] However, [Rumiñavi] did not enjoy rulership long, as the Spaniards [soon] entered the province of Quito, defeated, and killed him, conquering it.

They say that Quisquis was killed by his own Indians because he refused to negotiate for peace with the Christians when they sought it. They [subsequently] saw [the Spaniards'] strength and how they subjugate the entire land. Thus, this entire generation perished, including the captains who had accompanied the renowned Huayna Capac in the war and conquest of Tomebamba.[1136]

1132   Viceroy of Peru between 1596 and 1604.

1133   Melchor Carlos Inca died in Alcalá de Henares in 1610. Apparently, Murúa did not know of his passing.

1134   A spelling error has been corrected (Murúa 2008 [1616]:201v).

1135   Guaman Poma de Ayala (2004 [1615]:163 [165]) provides a drawing of Rumiñavi killing and skinning Illescas.

1136   Folio 203r is blank.

A fable involving Pachacuti, the son of Manco Capac

Having dealt specifically with all the Incas who were lords in this kingdom, and having painstakingly collected the most reliable and trustworthy accounts from the great variety and different versions given to me by elderly Indians with their *quipus* and memories, it seems fitting to include and recount some [accounts] of the sons of the Incas. Although not all of them ascended to become rulers, as others were preferred because of their age, [these sons] were brave and distinguished themselves in the wars and conquests led by the Inca, serving as captains of his armies. The Indians remember and celebrate them to this day, recounting their noteworthy deeds with no less enthusiasm and pride than those of their kings and princes. Among these notable [sons], the first [to be mentioned is] Pachacuti, [the] son of Manco Capac, the lord who established and initiated this monarchy.[1137]

They say that [Pachacuti] was brave and feared. He aided his conquering the area around Cuzco, earning the name "lord" as he was more cruel than brave. The Indians say, that in his time it rained continuously day and night for an entire month, which frightened the inhabitants of Cuzco. Fearful, they believed that the land wished to turn over and destroy [them], which they call *"pachacuti"* in their language. At that time, a giant dressed in red appeared above Cuzco, at a place called Chetacaca, also known as Sapi. He held a trumpet in one hand and a staff in the other. Having arrived by water as far as Pisac, four leagues from Cuzco, Pachacuti went out to him on the road. He begged him not to blow the trumpet, as the Indians feared that this would cause the earth to turn. He agreed to Pachacuti's request, and they became close friends. As he did not blow the trumpet, that would have led to their destruction, they were saved [from] imminent danger. A few days later *[f.204r]*, he transformed into stone, hence earning [Manco Capac's son] the name Pachacuti, having [been] before called Inca Yupanqui.

[Pachacuti] was feared by his enemies for his extreme cruelty and by his own [people] for the punishments he imposed on them for minor infractions. Yet, due to the victories they achieved with him, he was revered and deeply loved. They gave him the title of Supreme Captain and gave him great and valuable gifts as if he were the Inca and king.

Cusi Huana[n] Churi, also known as Pachacuti, was the son of Manco Capac Pachacuti. Following [in] his father's footsteps and manner, he frequently went to war with his own [troops]. He was generous and magnificent among them, a superb

---

1137 Guaman Poma de Ayala (2004 [1615]:112) is the only other writer who mentions this son, although his description is very different from that of Murúa.

plunderer, and cruel to his enemies. Some Indians point to Cusi Huana[n] Churi as starting [the tradition] of ear piercing, as he had pierced [his own] during a war that he fought against his father. After this, all his descendants continued the tradition. However, others believe that the inventor of this [tradition] was Manco Capac,[1138] the first Inca. The Indian accounts vary, but regardless of its origins, [pierced ears] are an unmistakable sign of nobility and authority among them, signifying knighthood among [the] royal lineage and descendants of the Incas.

Whenever Cusi Huana[n] Churi drank, he would kneel and toast the Sun, seeking his blessing and permission to drink. He performed this ritual every morning at sunrise throughout his life, with his household members doing the same. He was married to a *ñusta*, who was a cousin, as was their custom, and had numerous other wives. It is believed that he fathered more than a hundred children; although their names are known, they are omitted here to avoid prolixity. They say he married some *ñustas* known as *yunacas*, who were principal women in Cuzco. He gave each of them one hundred and fifty female service Indians. These were among the war captives and other defeated Indians prisoners that Cusi Huana[n] Churi had defeated.[1139]

[F.205R] CHAPTER 87

Inca Urcon, son of Viracocha Inca, and of the stone in Cuzco which they call "tired"

Inca Urcon, the son of the great Viracocha Inca, was known as one of his most valiant sons. He saw himself as a great conqueror, and thus some [people] credit him with the conquests, dominations, and pacifications of Maras, Mullaca, Calca, Tocay Capac, Huaypomarca,[1140] and other towns as far as the Lucanas and the Canas. Two other achievements showcase his ingenuity. First, he ordered the transportation of very fertile and suitable soil from distant lands, some say from Quito, by a vast number of Indians for the cultivation of potatoes. This would have been during the life of Pachacuti Inca Yupanqui, his brother [and the] son and heir of Viracocha Inca, because at that time Tupa[1141] Inca Yupanqui, [the] son of Pachacuti Inca Yupanqui and [the] nephew of Inca Urcon,[1142] went to conquer Quito and its

---

1138   A spelling error has been corrected (Murúa 2008 [1616]:204r).
1139   Folio 204v is blank.
1140   The conquest of these towns is also mentioned in chapter 17.
1141   A spelling mistake has been corrected (Murúa 2008 [1616]:205r).
1142   A spelling mistake has been corrected (Murúa 2008 [1616]:205r).

provinces. If the soil was indeed from Quito, it was carried more than four hundred fifty leagues. It used to create a hill on the east side of the fortress in Cuzco, called Alpa Sunro. This name denotes that the soil was painstakingly collected by hand. The hill produced beautiful and flavorful potatoes that were only served at the table of the Inca for his enjoyment.

Second, during the construction of the impressive and remarkable fortress of Cuzco, [Inca Urcon] ordered that a massive and extraordinarily heavy stone, [measuring] three *estados* high and eight *pasos* long,[1143] be brought from Quito. The Indians say that when the stone arrived close to the fortress, where it is now, it cried out *"saycuni,"* which means "I am tired," and shed tears of blood. So, they left [the stone] in its current location,[1144] and they refer to it as "the tired stone."[1145]

I do not believe that they brought it from Quito, as they say, since it seems to me that no human effort could have moved it *[f.205v]* an untold number of leagues. The roads from Quito to Cuzco are rough and rugged, with hills, valleys, and ravines that are difficult to pass even today on horseback. Furthermore, the rivers are large and swollen, particularly the famous and celebrated Apurímac, located sixteen leagues from Cuzco, where there has never been anything more than a narrow, grass-rope bridge.

It is impossible for the stone to have crossed at [that bridge] nor could it have traversed the [steep] river slopes just before reaching the bridge, where countless beasts, loaded with silver and merchandise, have been lost by falling off the narrow road and into the river. So, if the stone came from where the Indians claim, there is no doubt that the Devil, known for his influence over them and who wished to have them under his domain by any means, helped them in this unproductive work to further attract them to his will and blindness. Inca Urcon, himself, paid for this work, and the Indians who were with him bringing the stone to Cuzco killed him, frustrated and tired by such futile work. [Or] perhaps [their anger was raised] by how poorly he treated them; maintaining a cruel oversight and punishing everyone, with no excuses, for failing to carry out his orders. The stone remained in that location without ever moving, and the Incas made no subsequent attempts to move

---

1143   A textual error has been corrected (Murúa 2008 [1616]:205r).

1144   This stone was included within the Cuzco Ceque System (Bauer 1998:56–59). Garcilaso de la Vega (1966 [1609]:470) also mentions that the stone wept blood. For more information on "tired stones," see Van de Guchte (1984).

1145   As noted earlier, Guaman Poma de Ayala (2004 [1615]:157 [159], 160 [162], 159 [161]) also mentions an Inca Urcon as the son of Pachacuti Inca Yupanqui who was responsible for moving stones from Cuzco to the northern provinces, and he includes a drawing of that Inca. Guaman Poma de Ayala's image of Inca Urcon moving stones appears to be based on an image contained within the *History and Genealogy of the Inca Kings of Peru* (Murúa 2004 [1590]:37v).

it, as the fable says it spoke and cried blood. Inca Urcon[1146] had no heir, which is remarkable since, in those times, the Indians, especially the sons and brothers of the Incas, had a multitude of women.

Others say that after the war, Viracocha Inca fought with the Chanka, as [described] in chapter 19, [Pachacuti] Inca Yupanqui, envious of the heroic deeds and accomplishments of his brother Inca Urcon, and realizing that his father, Viracocha Inca, intended to name him as his heir *[f.206r]* on account of his bravery, killed him during a battle in Cache. [Pachacuti Inca Yupanqui] told [Inca Urcon] to lead from the front and he then ordered a captain to kill him from behind. It is said that Viracocha Inca, his father, died of grief from this, though others [claim] he disappeared. All this confusion arises from the multitude of accounts that the Indians have concerning the wars and successions of their Incas.

Additionally, there were two courageous and brave captains named Apu Mayta and Vilcaquiri.[1147] The Indians assert that the Inca sent one of these [captains], without specifying which one, to conquer the coast. When they arrived where the town of Cañete[1148] is now, they settled and, by order of the Inca, built the formidable stone fortress of Huarco, at great expense. They transported that region's main *huaca* to Cuzco, so that in this way,[1149] the entire province would contribute people and Indians to care for the *huaca*, and so that they would come to Cuzco to worship it. Apu Mayta and Vilcaquiri told the Indians that these same *huacas* and idols would assist them in winning all the conquests and wars that they undertook together.

They say that Inca Mayta, who was [the] son of Viracocha Inca and brother of Inca Urcon, was brave and daring, never wanting or requesting to rest. He followed his brother[s], Inca Urcon and [Pachacuti] Inca Yupanqui, and his nephew Tupa Inca Yupanqui when they marched to war. He participated in the conquest of Huancavilca, Cayambe, and Pasto alongside his brother[s] Cunayrachali, Curopanqui, and Capac Yupanqui, all sons of Viracocha Inca. They received many gifts of women, Indian servants, and clothing from their brother and father, in accordance with Inca customs.[1150]

1146 A mistake has been corrected (Murúa 2008 [1616]:205v).

1147 Guaman Poma de Ayala (2004 [1615]:153) also tells of two captains named Apu Mayta Inca and Vilca Inca.

1148 The town of Cañete and several other coastal cities south of Lima are described in book 3, chapter 19.

1149 A mistake has been corrected (Murúa 2008 [1616]:205v).

1150 Folio 206v is blank.

[F.207V] CHAPTER 88

Of Tupa Amaru, son of [Pachacuti] Inca Yupanqui and of a strange event

Tupa Amaru, the son of [Pachacuti] Inca Yupanqui and brother of Tupa Inca Yupanqui, was a famous captain with good fortune in both his marriage, as will be told in the following chapter, and throughout his life. As the Indians report, while [Tupa Amaru] and his brother were in Tiahuanaco, engaged in the war and conquest of the Collao, they received word that a Spaniard had traveled through the Collao. [He was] dressed as a poor beggar, and some even say that he was preaching the Holy Gospel to the Indians.

As he walked toward Cuzco, where the Inca was, he arrived at the village of Cache, where the Indians were drunkenly celebrating an important feast. Upon entering [the village], the poor man began to rebuke them for acting as they were, for getting so drunk, losing their minds like beasts, and even worse, the abhorrent vices that took place there. However, the Indians of the town, had never seen or heard of [a Spaniard], nor [had they] seen the type of clothes worn by this preacher. They were so used to and accustomed to their vice of eating and drinking excessively that they did not listen and readily and willingly continued [celebrating]. They laughed at the poor man, ridiculing and mocking what he told them. As barbarians without reason or understanding, they rejected him and started to stone him, so he left the town.

No sooner had he set foot outside of the [village], when, just like another Sodom and Gomorrah, a rain of fire descended from the Heaven, burning and scorching all who were in [the town]. No one escaped; all were consumed. The fallen and burned buildings can still be seen today, and all the land around the town is [scorched] yellow, due to the fire.[1151]

Upon witnessing *[f.207v]* such a fearful event, the Indians who were in the [nearby] *chacras* fled to Cuzco, where others of the same village were in the service of the Inca. [The Inca] ordered them to return and rebuild the town in a new location, a quarter of a league away, where there is now a royal *tambo* for travelers walking to Potosí, Chuquisaca,[1152] Collao, and other parts. This is what the Indians generally report, and the visible remains, ruins, and burned earth provide proof of what they say.

1151   There are many versions of the destruction of Cache (now called Rachi) recorded in the chroniclers. See, for example, Betanzos (1996 [1557]:7–10), Cabello Valboa (1951 [1586]:237), Cieza de León (1976 [1553–1554]:27–29), Molina (2011 [ca. 1575]:9–10), Sarmiento de Gamboa (2007 [1572]:51–52), and Garcilaso de la Vega (1966 [1609]:290–293).

1152   Later called La Plata, and then renamed as Sucre. Murúa provides additional details on the town of Chuquisaca in book 3, chapter 29 of his chronicle.

Many readers will be amazed by the accounts described in this chapter, and to most, it may seem like fiction. However, this is not all, as they are unaware of the events that occurred in our time in Carabaya, in the mines of Alpa Cato.[1153] There, Pedro de Bolumbiscar, a highly respected man married to Catalina de Urrutia, saw a man flying, apparently coming from the east. [The flying man] had his arms outstretched as if he were swimming. He had a white beard, was dressed in black with a pair of walking boots, and had a hat like ones worn at court.

Before Pedro de Bolumbiscar saw this fright, his wife asked him why the cats, dogs, chickens, and hens were cowering under the table and bed. Startled by this and the commotion, he stood up, gazed to the heavens, and saw the man described above. But not sure [of what he was seeing] and fearing that alone he would be an unworthy witness, although he was an honest man, [Bolumbiscar] called his wife, who, along with their household workers and servants, saw [the flying man] with equal clarity and even greater awe. As word of this event spread as common gossip, it reached the ears of the commissioner, who sent for [Bolumbiscar], who testified that it was true under oath.

In this same province and place, the [following] occurred to Thomas Plebe Genovés. [While] he was walking to Santiago de Buenavista[1154] with some merchandise with rams of the earth,[1155] he arrived at the slope called Guari Guari. [Although no one had] ever seen anyone riding there, because of the extreme slope, he saw a man walking alongside a black mule. Surprised by this strange [encounter], when they met, he asked [the man] where he was coming from and how the mule had gotten up there. [The man] replied that he had just arrived from Spain, from the city of Córdoba, that very day and he had left that city to see the richest land in the world, the hill where he was. That is why he had specifically brought that mule. Undoubtedly, this must have been the Devil who, having seen that greedy man, placed him on that unfertile and rough hill that cannot be cultivated. When they had finished talking, they took their leave, and the man mounted the mule and disappeared, leaving [Genovés] bewildered about this destination. However, before saying goodbye, the man told him that the place was called Guari Guari, and that the flood had deposited all the riches of the world there. The hill is very high and rough and is uninhabitable. Genovés is an honest man and resides in Sandia,[1156] located down in the valley.

A similar incident occurred to a religious in the coastal city of Trujillo, in the convent of San Agustín. As he was in his cell, a man arrived at the entrance riding a dark horse and asked for the cell of this religious. He asked the porter to take the

1153   This may refer to Santa Cota, a mining area in Carabaya, Peru.
1154   Santiago de Buenavista is in the Province of Carabaya, Peru.
1155   This is to say llamas.
1156   The town of Sandia is in the Province of Puno, Peru.

horse and upon reaching the religious, he begged to confess. He began by saying: "father, forgive me, for I left Madrid an hour ago with the intention of reaching Potosí today" (which is more than four hundred leagues [away].) The religious told him that he did not [take] confess[ion] from anyone who walked in such a hurry. The man, not wanting to wait for his horse, got up from the confessor's feet and vanished before his eyes.

This is enough for this chapter, as in the next one we will tell of other astounding events.[1157]

[F.209R] CHAPTER 89

In which the marriage of the prince and captain Tupa Amaru, and an admirable event that befell him with the ñusta Cusi Chimpo, his wife, will be told

As previously described in this history, Tupa Amaru Inca, was the valiant son of [Pachacuti] Inca Yupanqui, [the] brother of Tupa Inca Yupanqui, and the direct grandson of Viracocha Inca, the king and Lord of this western Kingdom of Peru and of the four provinces of Chinchaysuyu, Cuntisuyu, Antisuyu, and Collasuyu. Tupa Inca Yupanqui inherited this kingdom by direct succession. While he was in the great city of Cuzco, the capital of this vast kingdom, he constructed a temple in the fortress, as told in the life of his wife, Coya Mama Ocllo.

[Tupa Amaru Yupanqui] received important omens and predictions from the heavenly planets, as well as signs from the earth, seas, and elements of this region, foretelling grave evils that would befall the entire kingdom. Wanting to understand the meanings of those signs, Tupa Inca Yupanqui summoned all his magicians, augurs, enchanters, and sorcerers from across the empire. Presuming that their gods were angry, he hoped that all together, they could placate them with offerings and sacrifices, so that some of the oracles would reveal what those signs foretold.

They gathered with their customary solemnity and ceremony to perform numerous and diverse sacrifices. As a result, the Devil was pleased and responded through one of the idols that a time would come when an unknown and invincible, bearded people, the Spaniards, would emerge from the Southern Meridian sea and arrive on the coasts of Peru. These people would bring ruin to these kingdoms, their inhabitants, and their estates, subjecting them to perpetual subjugation and servitude.

1157   Folio 208v is blank.

[The Spaniards] would dominate them to such an extent that the memory of [their] lords, princes, and Inca Kings would vanish entirely.

Having heard this, the courageous King Tupa Inca Yupanqui assembled *[f.209v]* his courts and consulted with the members of his Royal Council, the wise *orejones*. They concluded, [that] to prevent such calamity, [they needed] to build a temple in Quinticancha,[1158] where the current convent of our Father Santo Domingo stands. After having consecrated it to the Sun and placing a golden figure of the Sun in it, [the building] became known as the Coricancha. Mancio Sierra [de Leguizamo] seized [this figure] when the Spaniards entered and gambled it [away].[1159]

Tupa Inca Yupanqui was shocked for several days by all that was revealed. The thought of this omen badly affected him and gave him such a serious illness that he was forced, by order of his doctors, the *hambicamayos*, to relocate to a place with pleasant weather, a quarter of a league from the city of Cuzco. This place is now owned by the Convent of Our Lady of Mercy, and its many and abundant lands are cultivated by the *yanaconas* of that convent. There, following the order of Coya Mama Ocllo, his wife, the great sorcerer and pontiff of the Inca, Villac Umu, humbly prayed, consulted, and asked his idols if his king and lord, Tupa Inca Yupanqui, would die of his illness. This included [many] sacrifices, as they had a large number of children and other materials for this purpose. The oracles responded that he would not die, which is to say, "*manan huañunca.*" Since then, this name has been given to that location and place, which it [still] bears to this day.[1160]

Due to the many versions that the Indians tell of the remarkable event involving the famous Prince Tupa Amaru in this place, it is necessary to investigate the truth of this event and to do it with brevity, a close friend of the wise and discreet. Nevertheless, that is difficult since it happened so long ago and is [recorded] in ancient *quipus* used by the Incas. These are cords with a wide range of colors and knots, on which they record their works and deeds *[f.210r]*. However, there are few [who] can now understand them, as [the ancient *quipus*] are different from those

---

1158   Sarmiento de Gamboa (2007 [1572]:73) also writes of a section of Cuzco called Quinticancha.

1159   In his will Mancio Sierra de Leguizamo states that he received the figure of the Sun from the Coricancha, writing, "I was given the figure of the Sun which was of gold and kept by the Inca in the house of the Sun, which is now the convent of Santo Domingo" (Stirling 1999:142). Garcilaso de la Vega (1966 [1609]:180) provides additional information, writing, "When the Spaniards entered the city, the figure of the Sun fell to the lot of one Mancio Sierra de Leguizamo, a nobleman, one of the first conquerors, whom I knew. He was still alive when I came to Spain. He was a great gambler, and though the figure of the Sun was large, he staked it and lost it in a night. Hence, we may say, following Acosta, from this [event] originated the saying: He played away the Sun before the break of day."

1160   See chapter 18 for additional information on the site of Manan Huañunca.

now in use. Furthermore, the inherent limitations and linguistic constraints of the Indians' language makes translation and communication difficult in a [language] as expansive as ours. [So], I have decided to limit some parts of this event and provide in-depth descriptions of others. As a result, I have interpreted what they say in their cords and *quipus*, which were among other [methods] that they record past events, histories, and the deeds of their ancestors in the Kingdom of Peru. The following is recorded within those [*quipus*] about the Captain and Prince Tupa Amaru [Inca].

Tupa[1161] Amaru Inca, our prince, was the son of [Pachacuti] Inca Yupanqui. During his father's reign, he proved his royal blood to all by conquering a great many lands. He was a courageous, prudent, and wise captain. For example, when his brother, Tupa Inca Yupanqui, was severely ill and was in danger [of dying] at Manan Huañunca, he realized that it was unwise to leave him [alone], so he went with him.

While [Tupa Amaru Inca] was away from Cuzco, he learned various games, including *tapta*, which is like backgammon, from none other than the *orejones*, his uncles, and other principal lords. [He was] so [engrossed in this game] that he disregarded his sorrows and romantic pursuits. It seemed that [the impulses of] youth held little sway over him. [Nevertheless, when] some *ñustas*, maidens of his sister-in-law Coya Mama Ocllo,[1162] who were like ladies of the queen, came to watch the game, the prince was not so absorbed in the game that he failed to raise his eyes to look at the *ñustas*. As they say, love is an intangible force that enters through the eyes and captures the heart. Suddenly, Tupa Amaru fell in love with Cusi Chimpo, the most beautiful [*ñusta*].

The ardent lover left his entertainment and game, knowing that the [pursuit] of love would be more pleasing. He averted his gaze to conceal what he felt in his heart in front of so many people. Being a shrewd and discreet prince, [Tupa Amaru] hid until the next day when he had a chance to see her. Because of his close relationship with his brother, he could move about freely within the palace, and the door was never closed to him [f.210v]. Bashfully, he expressed his feelings to the indifferent *ñusta*, who scornfully dismissed the discreet advances of her disadvantaged lover. She carelessly exposed her beautiful breasts, and occasionally she laughed and let him touch them. Although the Inca pretended to be indifferent, love's cruel arrows continued to pierce his heart. Nevertheless, he persevered to entertain her with sweet words. As result of the fire burning within him, he undoubtedly [won] her favor through these actions, despite his disadvantaged position.

The stubborn *ñusta*'s heart was as cold as ice [and] she truly despised the genuine love of such a valiant prince. Understanding his misfortune and seeing the

---

1161 The word "Tupa" was begun and then crossed out and then written again (Murúa 2008 [1616]:210r).

1162 Coya Mama Ocllo was married to Tupac Inca Yupanqui.

hardened disposition of his beloved *ñusta*, his eyes moistened with sadness. He decided to give up completely and allow fortune to take its course. A short distance away, he came across a spring where he sat to mourn his sorrowful fate. After a passionate sigh, he uttered the following words: "*husupa husupacac husupacainimpi husuc husutimpas yman husun*," which is like saying in our common language, "the lost one who is lost, is lost for being lost, should be lost, should be lost!"

Soon after he said these words, he decided to disappear. He would have done so if a spider had not appeared to him, which these Indians call *cusi cusi*,[1163] which they consider a good omen, as it indeed proved it be for this sad lover. He was admiring [the spider] when he saw two snakes attempting to mate, amid the fragrant flowers and herbs surrounding the beautiful spring. When the female refused and fled to various places, the clever male went to look for a flower. On finding it, he returned to the [female] snake and upon touching her with the flower, she remained still, as it has this natural effect.

Seeing this *[f.211r]* strange and admirable event, which mirrored his own desire, he let the snakes go. Filled with joy and contentment, he took the beautiful white flower, saying: "This has been a joyful and blessed day for me, as I have found an effective remedy and cure for my illness." He then returned to where his cruel yet beloved *ñusta* was, and as soon as he saw her, he touched her with the marvelous flower. The *ñusta* immediately felt its effect. Unable to stop the virtuous effect of the flower, her heart was pierced by a hidden arrow. Feeling transformed and delirious, she condemned her cruelty. With the gift of now being able to clearly see her beloved Inca, who stood before her, she turned her gaze toward him; as he had [always held] the most cherished place in her heart, she was determined to express her true emotions. Being wise and discerning, Tupa Amaru was moved by how love aided his victory in this [unusual] game. He set aside her past cruelty [and], recognizing the benefits of his fortune, he listened to the sweet voice of his beloved *ñusta*.

After deliberating this strange event, they stood, admiring each other for a brief period, exchanging glances, and contemplating their promising future. Sitting down in the shade of a tree, the prince rested his head on the lap of his beloved *ñusta*, surrendering his weary body to sleep. While asleep he was overcome by a dream, and he awoke, shouting: "Cruel and troublesome sleep, you will not stop me from enjoying what my soul greatly desires!" And with this, they quenched their desires.

As their love was unwavering and true, the two lovers married, and their hopes flourished. Because of this event they chose names, the prince calling himself Tupa Amaru, for his admiration of the snakes that bear this name. Furthermore, the spring

---

1163   *Arañas saltadoras* (Salticidae family).

[was named] Colque Machacuay,[1164] which means "silver snakes," and the prince had a temple constructed in this very place [adorned] with two silver snakes and a *kantu*[1165] flower, in memory of what occurred. The Indians [also] painted them on their clothes and buildings. Since then, the Incas have used [snakes] as emblems on their weapons.[1166] The name of the flower is not provided, but it is sufficient to say that for the unfortunate, the end of one hardship is the beginning of another.

It is worth noting that Tupa Amaru and his *ñusta* had many sons, who were very courageous during the conquest and wars of Huayna Capac, [the] son of Tupa Inca Yupanqui.[1167]

[F.212R] CHAPTER 90

Who Capac Huaritito and Cusi Tupa[1168] were

To account for every notable deed that I have learned about the Incas, their sons, and captains, I wanted to include the previous chapters and those that follow. Capac Huaritito was a son of [Pachacuti] Inca Yupanqui and brother of the valiant Tupa Inca Yupanqui, whom the Indians celebrate as the most famous and renowned of all their Incas and kings due to the great conquests that he made and the remarkable order and organization he established in this kingdom. All that the Spaniards found in [this kingdom], we owe to him, and since it was related to the political [order], and did not contradict our evangelical religion, it should have been preserved and observed. Without a doubt [if this had happened], these

---

1164 The spring of Colque Machacuay was a well-known feature of Cuzco, and Murúa mentions it again in book 3, chapter 10 of his chronicle. It was on the Cuzco Ceque System (Bauer 1998:128) and is described in detail by Garcilaso de la Vega: "Near the road there are two streams of excellent water which are channeled underground. The Indians do not know where the water comes from, for the work is a very ancient one and the traditions about these things are being forgotten. The channels are called Collquemacháchuay, silver snakes, for the water is as white as silver and the channels wind like snakes through the earth" (1966 [1609]:420–421).
1165 The common name for the Andean flower *Cantua buxifolia*.
1166 The coat of arms that Murúa (2008 [1616]:13r) includes at the beginning of his manuscript contains two snakes. A similar drawing can be found in *The First New Chronicle* (Guaman Poma de Ayala 2004 [1615]:83). Also, The word "proverb" is written in the margin of the manuscript (Murúa 2008 [1616]:211r).
1167 Folio 211v is blank.
1168 Murúa writes this name as Ausi Tupa; we have changed it to Cusi Tupa to conform with other writers.

vast provinces would [now] be appropriately governed, and the population would greatly increase.

Capac Huaritito had an invincible spirit, which he demonstrated in the wars fought alongside his brothers and other captains who were his companions, such as Colla Topa, Sinchi Roca, Huaillipo, Cusi Atauchi, and others. Some elderly Indians report that these captains, [along] with Tupa Inca Yupanqui, wanted to know what was to happen to them in [the] future and what events would befall their heirs. After days of great sacrifices and fasts, as is their custom, with weeping and animal offerings, which they killed for this purpose, the Devil answered them that very soon men with long beards and with clothes [that covered] their entire bodies would come to this kingdom. They would be so strong that they could cleave an Indian from top to bottom with their swords and inflict incredible slaughter and destruction on them. They would take and spill the blood of children and grandchildren, and they mistreat and rob them, trample and walk upon their idols and *huacas*, and destroy their rites and ceremonies. Upon hearing such an answer, [filled with] sadness and thoughtful, they cried out with pain and suffering, for they knew the persecution and toil that would [come]. In memory of this fearful answer *[f.112v]*, they composed a sad and melancholy song in the form of a dirge, which they sang as a prelude to the sad and mournful events they were to experience.

All these predictions were fulfilled to the letter, and it is possible ~~that the Devil, as a great astrologist, [foresaw] through the movements of the planets the signs that threatened these provinces, and seeing~~[1169] [Inserted: It is most likely that the Indians are lying, pretending that they prophesized what happened to them, or that the Devil saw that][1170] the Spaniards, with Columbus [as] the first discoverer and conqueror of the Indies as their guide, were attempting, preparing, and announcing the above [inserted: as a possible outcome][1171] to force them to begin anew the sacrifices of innocent children and other offerings, knowing the fierce spirit and insatiable greed of the Spaniards. [However, the Devil] does not know, nor does he have evidence of future events; this is reserved only to God Almighty, the wonderfully wise, and those He deems worthy enough to reveal it to, as He did many times to His prophets, announcing through them many events that were to come and punishments that he would render.

The second sacrifices and offerings they made to their gods and idols, as has already been mentioned in the last chapter and in this one, took place after the Inca had recovered from a grave illness. [It] always seemed [that] their idols, or rather the Devil, explained what had happened, thus keeping these miserable people under

1169   Crossed out by Remón (Adorno 2008:104; Murúa 2008 [1616]:212v).
1170   Inserted by Remón (Adorno 2008:104; Murúa 2008 [1616]:212v).
1171   Inserted by Remón (Adorno 2008:104; Murúa 2008 [1616]:212v).

the control of their idolatries. To this day, I know that few, if any, have escaped from his clutches.

Cusi Tupa, [the] son of Tupa Inca Yupanqui and [the] brother of Huayna Capac, was also brave and feared. He subdued certain provinces that had rebelled against his father with great courage and prudence. *[f.213r]* To this they add, that on orders of his father, he constructed an underground tunnel from the fortress high above the city of Cuzco to the Coricancha temple which ~~so~~[1172] he made so famous, which has already been described in the last chapter. They worshiped the Sun and had an infinity of other *huacas* and idols there. Today, the mouth of this tunnel is open, and it is called the Chincana, meaning "place where one is lost," like that much-mentioned labyrinth on the Island of Crete. However, it is now destroyed and in ruins, and there is no one who knows where it leads. Only the entrance of this tunnel [is known, and] those who venture a little way into it become lost and cannot find the way, forcing them to return. There is no longer any memory of [the exit] near the temple.[1173] They say that the Inca ordered it to be closed and hidden completely.

They [also] say that during the conquest of those rebellious provinces, Cusi Tupa fought with his people for twenty consecutive days, without resting a single day, until he finally subdued them and exacted severe punishments upon them. They say that these were the [provinces of the] Abachiris, Curiamunas, and Piriamunas, who are located next to the great province of Paititi, who [they] claim to be descendants of the Pacajes, Collas, Canas, and Canchis Indians, and who thus speak Aymara, although [their pronunciation is] more closed. They also say that in the great province of Paititi, there is a lake larger than that of the Collao,[1174] into which the Magno[1175] River from the slopes of San Juan del Oro[1176] flows, [and that] a large river is formed in the drainage below the lake, which flows to the province of the women known as Amazons. This [river] joins the Northern Sea and passes behind the Andes of Cuzco, where the Indians of the great province of Paititi claim to come from. They are descendants of Indians from the abovementioned city, who speak Quechua, and the principal *curaca* and governing is called Choco.[1177]

1172 Crossed out.
1173 Many early writers record the widely held belief in underground tunnels connecting special places in the Andes.
1174 Lake Titicaca.
1175 Perhaps Manu.
1176 San Juan del Oro is on the eastern slope of the Andes, northeast of Lake Titicaca, in the Province of Sandia, Department of Puno, Peru.
1177 Folio 214v is blank.

[F.214R] CHAPTER 91

The story and tale of Acoytapia, a shepherd, and Chuqui Llanto, [a] daughter of the Sun

To conclude [this first book] on the stories of these Indians and the events remembered and recounted by the elderly, [and] then move on to the ceremonies and customs of this kingdom [in book 2], I want to record here a remarkable story.[1178] Not far from Cuzco, there are two mountains called Sahuasiray and Pitusiray, which are next to the towns of Huayllabamba and Calca. According to their tradition, a shepherd named Acoytapia and a *ñusta* called Chuqui Llanto, who was dedicated to the Sun, were transformed into [these mountains].

In the high and snowy mountain called Sahuasiray, four leagues from Cuzco, above the Yucay Valley (famous for its many orchards and country house[s]), an Indian from Lares called Acoytapia tended the white sacrificial llamas that the Incas offered to the Sun. He was handsome, willing, and spirited. [He] herded his cattle all day, and when the cattle rested, the shepherd did so as well. He skillfully played a flute, softly and sweetly, free from any care or worries that could trouble him or anyone else.

One day, as he was dreamily playing the flute and enjoying its sounds, something happened that would lead to his downfall. He was startled by the arrival of two daughters of the Sun, who had accommodations and guards throughout the area.[1179] These Daughters of the Sun could roam freely across the mountain and rejoice in its meadows and springs, but they would return to their house at night. Guards and porters watched over the entrance, ensuring that they were not carrying anything harmful [f.214v]. [The two *ñustas*] unexpectedly came across the shepherd, who was singing, [and] asked him about the cattle and the pastureland where he was taking them. As they appeared suddenly, the shepherd, who had never seen them before, was amazed at such rare beauty and loveliness. Since the two *ñustas* were Holy, he was surprised and knelt before them, knowing that they were not human, and [that] such beauty could not be found in a mortal. In his confusion, he was unable to speak. Understanding his deep emotions by his expression, they told him not to be afraid, that they were the well-known Daughters of the Sun, who [inhabited] those mountains. To assure him, they took him by the arm, made him sit down, and [again] asked him again about his cattle.

Encouraged by the *ñustas'* friendliness, the fortunate shepherd stood up, kissing their hands, and again admired their beauty and grace. He tried to answer their

---

1178   The story of Acoytapia and Chuqui Llanto is told in the *History and Genealogy of the Inca Kings of Peru* (Murúa 2004 [1590]) along with several illustrations.

1179   A textual error has been corrected (Murúa 2008 [1616]:214r).

questions, [but] he gave so poorly composed and illogical answers, due to his fright and novelty [of the situation], that they caused [the *ñustas*] to be frightened as well.

Chuqui Llanto, the eldest, found Acoytapia's demeanor appealing and asked him various [other] questions to amuse herself: What was his name? Where was he from and who were his relatives? The shepherd's [answers] satisfied [the *ñusta*], increasing his confidence. As this occurred, Chuqui Llanto noticed that the shepherd wore a silver headband on his forehead, known as a *canipu* by the Indians, which shimmered and reflected pleasing light. She saw two very subtle mites[1180] in its base, and looking more closely, she realized that they were eating a heart. Pleased with this, Chuqui Llanto asked Acoytapia about the name of the silver band. Acoytapia replied that it was called *utussi*, although he did not fully understand its true meaning. However, it is important to note that what is commonly called a *canipu*, he called [*utussi*]. ~~Some believe that utussi is a word that was formerly used for genitals, but it is no longer used.~~[1181] The *ñusta*, having looked at it very carefully, returned it [to Acoytapia], *[f.215r]* along with her heart.

[Chuqui Llanto] took leave of the shepherd, with the name of the headband and the [image] of the mites etched in her memory. [As] she was thinking [about] how delicately and lifelike they were depicted eating the heart, [they were] gnawing and consuming hers. All the way [back], she talked with her sister of nothing else but the shepherd's gentle manner, the wonderful way he played his flute, and [their encounter] until they reached their palace and dwelling, where the *ñustas*, Daughters of the Sun, had their rooms.

At the entrance, the porters and guards thoroughly inspected them to see if they were carrying anything with them. They say some[1182] of those *ñustas* would occasionally hide their suitors within their *chumpis*, which we call sashes, or among their necklace beads, so the vigilant porters watched them with great care. When they entered the palaces, they found the women of the Sun waiting for them to dine, having cooked many different types of food that they eat in vessels of fine gold.

[However,] Chuqui Llanto, with a restless heart, did not want to eat with her sister and the others. Instead, she went to her room, claiming that she was tired and weary from walking through the mountains, but in truth, the memory of the shepherd weighed on her more than any fatigue. She would have gladly gone out again and walked through the mountains just for a glimpse of him. While the rest of [the *ñustas*] ate, Chuqui Llanto withdrew to her room. Nevertheless, she could

---

1180   Murúa uses the word "aradores," which Houtrouw (2019:176, 180) translates as "plowmen." While this is possible, we note that during the sixteenth century the term "aradores" was also used for "mites."

1181   Crossed out by Remón (Adorno 2008:107; Murúa 2008 [1616]:214v).

1182   A misspelling has been corrected (Murúa 2008 [1616]:215r).

not calm herself, as her heart burned with intense flames, which only intensified in the solitude, and she longed for the [next] day. The night was long and painful, [as she] struggled with her newfound love and with her determination to suppress it from the start. She [eventually] fell asleep, with tears bathing her face.

There were large and sumptuous palaces in this dwelling dedicated solely to the women and daughters of the Sun. Within them were an infinite number of elaborately carved chambers where the women and daughters of the Sun lived. They were selected from the four provinces of the vast Inca Kingdom, *[f.215v]* which were Chinchaysuyu, Cuntisuyu, Collasuyu, and Antisuyu. Each province had a specific type of woman, and for each, there were four springs of clear and crystalline water. [These fountains] emerged and flowed from the four parts [of the compound], and the women from the [different] regions were to bathe in their spring.

The springs had names. The Chinchaysuyu spring was called Sulla Puquio, meaning "spring of pebbles," [and] it was on the western side. The Collasuyu [spring] was called Llullucha Puquio, meaning "spring of grapes," and it was on the eastern side. That of Cuntisuyu, [was] called Ocoruru[1183] Puquio, [meaning] "spring of watercress," [and it was to the north]. The Antisuyu [spring] was called Siclla Puquio, meaning "spring of frogs," [and it] was to the south. The women and daughters dedicated to the Sun lived in that house, and bathed in these fountains.

[That night] as the beautiful Chuqui Llanto was deep asleep, she saw a nightingale flying from one tree to another, singing softly.[1184] Its sweet harmony claimed her, and after singing, [the bird] came to her and sat on her lap and began to talk. It asked why she was sad and sighing at times, [urging her] to not be sad or imagine anything that would cause her sorrow. The *ñusta* replied that she would certainly end her life very soon unless [the bird] gave her a remedy for her illness. The nightingale replied that he would give her the remedy she wanted, if she told him why she was sad. Chuqui Llanto then shared how much she loved Acoytapia, the shepherd who guarded the white cattle of her father, the Sun, and that she would soon die if she did not see him. However, if she were discovered by the women, the Sun, her father, would order her to be killed. The nightingale told her not to grieve [and] that she should go and position herself between the four fountains *[f.216r]*. [There, she should] sing about what she remembered. If the four fountains answered her, repeating the same words, her wish would be granted.[1185]

1183   A misspelling has been corrected (Murúa 2008 [1616]:215r).
1184   The coat of arms that Murúa (2008 [1616]:13r) includes at the beginning of his manuscript contains a nightingale.
1185   The *History and Genealogy of the Inca Kings of Peru* (Murúa 2004 [1590]:145v) contains an illustration, drawn by Guaman Poma de Ayala, that shows Chuqui Llanto sitting with the nightingale at the center of the four springs.

Having said this, the nightingale flew away, and the frightened *ñusta* awoke from her sleep and quickly dressed herself. Since everyone in the house was sound asleep, she was able to get up without being heard, and she went and stood in the middle of the four fountains and began to sing, remembering the silver band and the mites. She softly sang, "*micuc, usutu, cuyuc, utussi cusin*," meaning: "happy is the mite which moves eating the utussi."

The four fountains immediately began singing the same words to one another, responding to the nymph with great harmony and agreement.[1186] This filled the *ñusta* with joy, as it seemed her every wish would be granted, as the fountains had shown their favor toward her. So, she returned to her room for what little remained of the night, longing for the break of dawn when she could see her beloved shepherd Acoytapia.[1187]

The tragic end of the love affair between Acoytapia and Chuqui Llanto

To avoid a long last chapter that might annoy the reader, I have divided it in two, as the story and fable told by the elderly Indians is very long. After the two *ñustas* left for home, the shepherd Acoytapia remained with his cattle. Sad and pensive, he gathered them together and entered his hut, thinking about the beauty of the lovely *ñusta*, her clothes, and her spirit. His heart was filled with this newfound love, yet [he felt] despair on considering and remembering who she was, and the difficulty that her love might bring him. Daughters of the Sun, like her, were esteemed and revered by all the shepherds, and no one dared to even glance at them for fear of the severe punishment. With these thoughts, [Acoytapia would] occasionally play his flute, expelling deep sighs from the depths of his soul while bathing the earth in his warm tears. The only sound from him was a sad lament, which moved the stones. Even the sheep, not accustomed to hearing such a lamentation from their guardian, came to the door of the hut, seemingly wanting to help the lonely shepherd. After spending most of the long night thinking and weeping, at dawn, he was overcome by the evil force that was consuming his vitality and claiming the shepherd's life. Undoubtedly, his days would have come to an end if a remedy had not arrived quickly.

1186   The *History and Genealogy of the Inca Kings of Peru* (Murúa 2004 [1590]:146r) contains an illustration, drawn by Guaman Poma de Ayala, showing Chuqui Llanta sitting among the springs as they respond to, and repeat, her.
1187   Folio 216v is blank.

Acoytapia's mother was in Lares,[1188] where he was born. She was surely one of the individuals who is respected among the Indians as a fortune teller. This [woman] knew of the affliction and hardship her only son was suffering and that he would die if a cure did not arrive quickly. When the cause of his illness was revealed by the Devil, she took a colorfully painted staff that she treasured for such occasions, and quickly traveled *[f.217v]* through the mountains, guided by the one who made her aware of her son's suffering.

She arrived at her son's hut before the sun had risen. Upon entering, she saw him wounded and close to death, drenched in tears. She woke him and struggled to make him regain his senses. Acoytapia was astonished by seeing his mother, not understanding how she had arrived so quickly. His mother, who understood his illness, consoled him, assuring and encouraging him that she could provide a cure for his sadness. With this, she left the hut and gathered a quantity of nettles from nearby rocks, which the Indians believe alleviates sadness and gladdens the heart. She made a stew from them in her unique way.

Before she finished, the two sisters, Daughters of the Sun, arrived at the door of Acoytapia's hut. At dawn, Chuqui Llanto had dressed and, on a whim, set out through the green meadows of the mountains with her sister. She left her house and went to find her new love, as her heart could not guide her anywhere else. Weary from their journey, they sat by the hut's entrance. When they saw the elderly woman inside, they spoke to her, asking if she had any food, as they were hungry. The old woman knelt and told them that she only had nettles, which they willingly accepted and began to eat with pleasure. Chuqui Llanto looked around the hut, searching for her beloved Acoytapia, but by the time she and her sister arrived, he had hidden himself within the staff she had brought along. Not seeing him, Chuqui Llanto asked for him, [and] the old woman replied that he was with the cattle. Attracted by the beautifully worked staff, Chuqui Llanto, asked who owned such a stunning staff and its origin. The old woman explained that it once had belonged to one of the beloved women of Pachacamac, a renowned *huaca* in the coast, four leagues from the City of Kings, and that she inherited it.

Enamored by the staff, Chuqui Llanto persistently asked for it *[f.218r]*. At first, the old woman refused, which just increased [Chuqui Llanto's] desire. However, in the end, she gave it to her.[1189] Taking the staff in her hands, Chuqui Llanto grew even more fond of it. After spending time with the old woman, her desire to see Acoytapia intensified. So, she took leave of [the old women] and walked through the meadows, turning her restless and beautiful eyes from side to side, hoping to see him.

1188   A misspelling has been corrected (Murúa 2008 [1616]:217r).

1189   The *History and Genealogy of the Inca Kings of Peru* (Murúa 2004 [1590]:146v) contains an illustration, drawn by Guaman Poma de Ayala, showing Chuqui Llanto receiving the staff from Acoytapia's mother.

The two sisters went from one place to another the entire day without stopping, driven by Chuqui Llanto's desire to enjoy the sight and conversation of the shepherd, unbeknownst to her sister. As the sun began to set, and the shadows lengthened, they wearily turned back toward the palaces. Chuqui Llanto felt great sorrow at not having been able to see the one she was carrying within the staff. When they reached the gates, the guards carefully, as was their custom, scrutinized them. However, as they only saw the staff that they openly carried, they closed the doors, and [the sisters] entered their rooms. Chuqui Llanto did not want to attend dinner with her sister and the other daughters and women of the Sun. The fire in her heart prevented her from engaging with anyone, and she wanted to be alone to fan the flames. Placing the staff beside her bed, she lay down and, feeling alone, began to cry and sigh for the shepherd, until she eventually fell asleep around midnight.

At that moment, Acoytapia emerged from the staff where he had been hiding. Kneeling in front of the bed of his *ñusta*, he softly called her name.[1190] Startled, she woke up in great fear. Rising from her bed, she saw her beloved shepherd beside her [and] burst into tears. Stunned by all this, they embraced, and she asked how he had entered with the palace, which was sealed. He replied that he had entered, without anyone knowing it, within the staff that his mother had given her. Chuqui Llanto then covered him with the blankets of worked *lipi* and very fine *cumbi*, that she had on her bed [f.218v], and the two lovers slept together. When they sensed it was near dawn, Acoytapia re-entered the staff, [with] his *ñusta* watching.

After the sun had bathed the entire mountain range, Chuqui Llanto took the staff to enjoy Acoytapia's conversation alone and unhindered, leaving her sister in the palaces. She left, traveling through the meadows with the staff in her hand. When she arrived at a secluded ravine, she sat down with her beloved shepherd, who had already emerged from the staff, to talk. However, it so happened that one of the guards noticed that Chuqui Llanto had gone out alone, something she never did, and followed her ~~and in the end~~[1191] and in the end, although hidden [he] found her with Acoytapia on her lap. When he saw her, [the guard] began to shout. Acoytapia and Chuqui Llanto, knowing they had been discovered, [and] fearing that if caught they would be killed, as their crime could no longer be concealed, jumped up and fled to the mountains near the town of Calca.[1192] Exhausted, they [eventually] sat on a rock, drowsy with fatigue, thinking that they were safe and secure.

1190   The *History and Genealogy of the Inca Kings of Peru* (Murúa 2004 [1590]:146v) contains an illustration, drawn by Guaman Poma de Ayala, showing Acoytapia kneeling beside Chuqui Llanto's bed.

1191   A scribal dittograph has been corrected.

1192   The *History and Genealogy of the Inca Kings of Peru* (Murúa 2004 [1590]:147r) has an illustration, drawn by Guaman Poma de Ayala, showing Acoytapia and Chuqui Llanto fleeing.

They were awakened by a loud noise and they [quickly] rose to their feet. [Chuqui Llanto] grabbed one *ojota* in her hand while the other remained on her foot. They wanted to flee again, but as they looked toward the town of Calca, they were transformed into stones, one after the other. Today, these two statues can be seen from Huayllabamba and Calca from[1193] and from various other places. I have seen them many times.[1194] The mountain is called Pitusiray. This is the end of the story of the two lovers, Acoytapia and Chuqui Llanto, which the Indians celebrate and refer to as something that happened in ancient times, along with other fables that they recount.[1195]

[F.219V] CHAPTER 93

A remarkable tale told by the Indians about Sayri Tupac Inca and his wife and sister, Doña María Cusi Huarcay, [the] parents of Doña Beatriz Clara Coya

While some readers may argue that this chapter is misplaced and out of order, I did not want such strange and admirable events to go untold or be forgotten in silence due to my own laziness or carelessness. So, I will recount what these Indians say about Sayri Tupac Inca, [a] prince and wise captain who, as a young man of twenty, was [already] skilled in arms and who always accompanied his people from Yucay to his refuge in Vilcabamba. He was a noble youth and an unmarried gentleman, who brought his sister to service him. As noted in [a previous] chapter and history, her name was Cusi Huarcay. He fell in love with her because they were so close. We priests, who educate these Indians, must warn against this, so that no one goes anywhere with their sisters or female relatives, nor fathers with their daughters, and much less, mothers with their sons. Having served as their priest for many years, I learned of such occurrences and have punished them accordingly.

Because it is not my intention to dwell on these matters, I will return to my captain, [Sayri Tupac]. He was already so preoccupied with his newfound and forbidden affection that he lost focus on the wars and duties that he had. It would not

---

1193   A scribal error has been corrected.

1194   The *History and Genealogy of the Inca Kings of Peru* (Murúa 2004 [1590]:147v) has an illustration, drawn by Guaman Poma de Ayala, showing Chuqui Llanto having been converted into the mountain of Sauasiray above the town of Huayllabamba and Acoytapia having been converted into the mountain of Pitusiray above the town of Calca.

1195   Folio 219r is blank.

be exaggerating to say [that] he had lost his own mind. After spending a few days apart from the *ñusta*, Cusi Huarcay, his sister, this sad and distraught lover became painfully aware of his deep and intense strong affection for her. He did not dare to confess his profound attraction and love to his sister Cusi Huarcay, nor [could he] stop thinking about her night and day. Moreover, he could not ignore the exhausting fondness that he felt whenever he thought of her. As a woman, [Cusi Huarcay] wanted to know [about] her brother's strange behavior, so she asked, albeit with different *[f.220r]* assumptions, if he had fallen in love with any of the *ñustas* in the royal service of his mother, the Coya, or, if he had been taken captive or had experienced any other life changing event in the war that he was ashamed of and did not want anyone to know.

The lovesick [Sayri Tupac] was fraught with these questions [and] countless other thoughts. Nevertheless, he persisted in knowing the definitive and true answer from the discreet and beautiful *ñusta*. Kneeling, with fervent and bitter tears and sighs that emanated from his tortured soul, he humbly begged her to accept him as her husband and spouse. But the humble[1196] and earnest advances made by the good lover, Sayri Tupac, were of little use, as nothing that that discreet and wise Inca did or said was enough to change her mind. Being wise and discreet, he resolved to change his strategy and do something else. So, he left the renowned Yucay Valley, hoping to find a better and happier fate. When he arrived in the great city of Cuzco at Carmenca,[1197] he encountered an elderly and astute Indian sorcerer named Auca Cusi, to whom he confided his troubles. On account of the fame and reputation of the old man, he entered the famous and illustrious city with optimism.

[Auca Cusi was] an elderly Indian who, due to his great experience, knew various incantations. There was no one in the entire city or kingdom who surpassed his abilities, as he appeared to do things that defied both nature and custom. The mere mention of his deeds caused fear in people, and witnessing them caused [even greater] fear and fright. Upon hearing [Sayri Tupac's] desires and secrets, [Auca Cusi] was not moved by mercy, but rather by his confession. He decided to help [Sayri Tupac] with all his strength and to the best of his abilities, without anyone, not even his own sister, knowing about it, as the valiant captain was so infatuated with her.

The next *[f.220v]* day, the cunning and astute [Auca Cusi] visited the palace to see [Sayri Tupac]. The wise old man shared the visions he had, through his science and art, the previous night, offering great hope that [Sayri Tupac] would be united with his dear and beloved *ñusta*. The fortunate Inca Sayri Tupac gratefully thanked

---

1196   A spelling mistake has been made here (Murúa 2008 [1616]:220r).

1197   Carmenca is the area of Cuzco now called Santa Ana, where the road from Yucay enters the city.

[Auca Cusi] for his answer. To keep [Sayri Tupac] happy and to prevent him from losing hope, the old sorcerer recounted many other things that he had achieved on other occasions. They entertained themselves in this way [all] day until night came.

The next day, at the right time for the enchantment, old Auca Cusi went to the ravine and source of the Saphi [River], which is above Huaca Pongo,[1198] where the river enters the city. There, he found a small bird, [that is] called by these Indians "*kenti*"[1199] or "*causarca*"[1200] meaning "revived." It resembles a large bee with a long, slender beak adorned with beautiful feathers that shimmer in different colors in the sun, shade, and lights. According to the elders, [this bird] either dies or sleeps, in [a] warm place in October, captured by a small white flower with remarkable properties. They claim that [the bird] revives around April, which is why they call this bird "*causarca*." It is also known as "*kinti*" due to its colorful feathers. The root of the [white] flower has many other important virtues, and it is so pure that it closes [upon hearing the word] "*huaccho*," which means "dishonest."

The attentive old man prepared [a potion] with this small bird to achieve his goal, which was not known by anyone other than Sayri Tupac. Some suggest that its power comes from some planet, perhaps Venus or another star. As for the [flower] closing when the word ["huaccho"] is spoken, I can swear this is true, as I have seen it. So, the old man disguised himself [and] went to the unknowing *ñusta*. Using the properties of the small bird and the flower, he made a circle and a charm, whispering and commanding her with a calm and peaceful voice, to immediately go with him, without any delay, to where the prince Sayri Tupac *[f.221r]*, her lover and dear brother, was.

The *ñusta*, Cusi Huarcay, already under the charm's enchanted, happily agreed to do so with much joy and delight. She quickly arrived where her beloved Sayri was, and they immediately engaged in small talk, which meant little because it was more for amusement than importance. Prince Sayri Tupac, smiling at what they had discussed, told his dear and beloved *ñusta* that they should go into a fine and royal chamber to rest. Their affectionate and tender words were so kind and of such virtue and strength, that they fell deeply in love with each other. That night, they both promised that they would marry according to their own customs and traditions, and they married and later [found] peace and tranquility within the Holy Mother Church, as has been described in the chapter about them.[1201]

1198   Huaca Pongo was located where the Saphi River enters the city of Cuzco. It was on the Cuzco Ceque System (Bauer 1998).

1199   Hummingbird.

1200   From the Quechua *kausachun*: to live.

1201   This passage has been crossed out by Remón (Adorno 2008:107; Murúa 2008 [1616]:214v).

A few days later, the dear and discreet *ñusta* showed signs of being pregnant, a sight which greatly pleased those in her father's royal palace, especially her family and relatives, who had always considered her to be virtuous and composed. Concerned and worried, they frequently asked her if she was sick or pregnant, and [if so] by whom. With a cheerful and contented face, the honest *ñusta* answered that it was by Sayri Tupac, her beloved brother and husband. Her parents, the kings, and those of the palace, found this deeply shameful as they contemplated the consequences of such dishonesty and improprieties. Because of this, the vassals [of the Incas] frequently declared that marriage between [the royalty] was acceptable, as it is practiced among the kings and lords, as described above. [This marriage] occurred with the approval of their subjects and later, of the Holy Mother Church, [Inserted: as has already been described in chapter 74.][1202]

When [Sayri Tupac's] father, Manco Inca, died, the wedding took place at the same time as the king's funeral rites, as is customary among these people. It is common to begin a feast with great joy and laughter, and conclude it with tears, weeping, and moaning, transitioning from dancing and singing and to crying as the Indians note and recall some [sorrowful] event that has occurred.[1203]

[End of book 1]

1202 Murúa wrote the insertion (Adorno 2008:102, 103). In chapter 74, Murúa writes that the marriage of Sayri Tupac and his sister, Cusi Huarcay, was recognized by the church.

1203 Folio 221v is blank.

Glossary

Q: Quechua; S: Spanish

aclla [Q]: females selected for lifelong service to the state.

acso [Q]: shirt.

ahuasca [Q]: common cloth.

ají [Taíno loan word]: chili pepper.

Antisuyu [Q]: northeastern quadrant of the Inca Empire.

apu [Q]: lord.

aquilla [Q]: drinking vessel.

asnac uchu [Q]: pepper with strong favor (*rocoto*; *Capsicum pubescens*).

ato [Q]: herd or large transport bags.

audiencia [S]: judicial council.

ayllu [Q]: related family group, lineage, community.

ayllu [Q]: weapon made of three stones tied together with leather straps.

aylluscas [Q]: servants of an Inca.

Ayuscay [Q]: birth celebration.

buhío (Taíno loan word): large building made of wood.

cacique (Taíno loan word): regional lord.

camote (Nahuatl loan word): sweet potato (*Ipomoea batatas*).

cancha [Q]: courtyard or plaza.

canipu [Q]: metal ornament; marker of rank.

chacra [Q]: field.

champi [Q]: club with a metal head.

chaquira [Q]: beads.

chasqui [Q]: messenger.

chicha (Kuna loan word): drink made from fermented maize.

chumpi [Q]: belt.

chuspa [Q]: small woven bags to hold coca.

coca [Q]: coca (*Erythroxylon coca*).

Collao [Q]: region located between southern Peru and Bolivia.

Collasuyu [Q]: southeast quadrant of the Inca Empire.

collpa [Q]: type of yellow soil used as a colorant.

cori quinqui [Q]: nightingale (*Luscinia megarhynchos*).

corregidor [S]: royal administrator of a city or a large area of land.

Coya [Q]: queen; principal wife of an Inca.

cuchu [Q]: ball used in games.

cumbi [Q]: fine cloth.

Cuntisuyu [Q]: southeast quadrant of the Inca Empire.

curaca [Q]: leader.

cuys [Q]: guinea pigs (*Cavia porcellus*).

duho (Taíno loan word): wooden seat.

encomienda [S]: grant of Indigenous labor.

guacamayo (Taíno loan word): macaw.

guanaco [Q]: type of Andean camelid (*Lama guanicoe*).

guavas [Q]: type of fruit (*Psidium guavaja*).

hambicamayos [Q]: healers.

hanan [Q]: greater or upper part.

higujayas [Q]: hard stones.

huaca [Q]: scared place or object.

huaccho [Q]: poor or orphan.

huaraca [Q]: sling.

hurin [Q]: lesser or lower part.

ichu [Q]: type of grass.

kantu [Q]: type of flower (*Cantua buxifolia*).

kenti [Q]: hummingbird.

lipi [Q]: type of cloth.

llautu [Q]: royal headband.

lliclla [Q]: shawl.

llipta [Q]: a mass made of ash that serves as a catalyst in the extraction of alkaloids from coca.

lloque [Q]: left.

macanas [Taíno loan word]: wooden mace-like weapons.

machacuay [Q]: snake.

Mama Huarmi [Q]: reigning queen.

mamacona [Q]: noblewoman.

maní [Q]: peanuts (*Arachis hypogaea*).

mantur [Q]: knife.

mate [Q]: drinking vessels often made of gourds.

michoc [Q]: accountant; tax collector of the Inca.

mitima [Q]: resettled person.

mocha [Q]: act of reverence.

mochadero [Q]: a place of worship.

mote [Q]: cooked maize grains.

mullu [Q]: spiny oysters (Spondylidae).

ñusta [Q]: princess; noble daughter; daughter of the Sun.

oca [Q]: sweet potato (*Oxalis tuberosa*).

ojota/s [Q]: sandals.

orejón/orejones [Q]: high-ranking person from the Cuzco area who wore ear-spools.

otorongo [Q]: jaguar (*Panthera onca*).

pacae [Q]: a type of fruit (*Inga feuilleei*).

paltas [Q]: avocados (*Persea americanca*).

pampa [Q]: flat area.

papaya [Q]: fruit (*Carica papaya*).

petaca [Q]: (Nahuatl loan word: *petlacalli*): basket.

puquio [Q]: spring.

quipu [Q]: knots; accounting cords of different colors.

raymi [Q]: celebration.

sabalo [Q]: shad; type of river fish (*Prochilodus lineatus*).

sunturpaucar [Q]: insignia of the Inca.

suyu [Q]: large political division of the Incas.

tambo [Q]: rest stop for travelers.

taqui [Q]: dance.

tiana [Q]: seat.

tipqui [Q]: small pins.

tocapo [Q]: fine woven design made with different colors.

topacusi [Q]: drinking vessel of gold.

topos [Q]: unit of land.

Tucurico Apu [Q]: regional governor.

tupa cusi napa [Q]: gold drinking vessels.

tupayauri [Q]: scepter; insignia of the Inca.

tupus [Q]: large pins.

ultis [Q]: small vessel to hold *llipta*.

usnu [Q]: large platform.

vicuña [Q]: Andean camelid (*Vicugna vicugna*).

vizcacha [Q]: rabbit-like rodent (*Lagidium viscacia*).

yanacona [Q]: servants of the Inca.

yuca [Q]: tuber (*Manihot esculenta*).

Yunga [Q]: a hot and forested mountain region of Peru.

zaquizamíes (Arabic loan word): attic.

References

Acosta, José de. (1590) 2002. *Natural and Moral History of the Indies*. Edited by Jane E. Mangan and translated by Frances M. López Morillas. Durham, NC: Duke University Press.

Adorno, Rolena. 2008. "Censorship and Approbation in Murúa's History General del Perú." In *The Getty Murúa: Essays on the Making of Martín de Murúa's "General History del Pirú."* Edited by Thomas Cummins and Barbara Anderson, 95–124. Los Angeles: Getty Research Institute.

Adorno, Rolena, and Ivan Boserup. 2008. "The Making of *Murúa's History General del Perú*." In *The Getty Murúa: Essays on the Making of Martín de Murúa's 'General History del Pirú.'* Edited by Thomas Cummins and Barbara Anderson, 7–66. Los Angeles: Getty Research Institute.

Albornoz, Cristóbal de. (ca. 1582) 1984. "Instrucción para descubrir todas las guacas del Pirú y sus camayos y haciendas." In "Albornoz y el espacio ritual andino prehispánico." Edited by Pierre Duviols. *Revista Andina* 2(1):169–222.

Álvarez-Calderón, Annalyda. 2007. "La crónica de fray Martín de Murúa: Mentiras y legados de un mercedario vasco en los Andes." *Revista Andina* 45:159–186.

Amado Gonzales, Donato, and Brian S. Bauer. 2022. "The Ancient Inca Town Named Huayna Picchu." *Ñawpa Pacha* 42(1):17–31.

https://doi.org/10.5876/9781646426553.c002

Anderson, Barbara. 2008. "Introduction." In *The Getty Murúa: Essays on the Making of Martín de Murúa's "General History del Pirú."* Edited by Thomas Cummins and Barbara Anderson, 1–3. Los Angeles: Getty Research Institute.

Araníbar, Carlos. 1963. "Algunos problemas heurísticos en las crónicas de los siglos VXI XVII." *Nueva Coronica* 1:102–135.

Ballesteros Gaibrois, Manuel, ed. 1964. "Introducción." In *Historia general del Perú, origen y descendencia de los incas*, 5–29. Madrid: Instituto Gonzalo Fernández de Oviedo.

Ballesteros Gaibrois, Manuel, ed. 1987. "Introducción." *Historia general del Perú*. Madrid: Historia 16.

Barriga, Víctor M. 1942. *Los mercedarios en el Perú en el siglo XVI: Documentos del Archivo General de Indias de Sevilla, 1518–1600*. Arequipa: La Colmena.

Bauer, Brian S. 1991. "Pacariqtambo and the Mythical Origins of the Inca." *Latin American Antiquity* 2:1:7–26.

Bauer, Brian S. 1996. "The Legitimization of the Inca State in Myth and Ritual." *American Anthropologist* 98(2):327–337.

Bauer, Brian S. 1998. *The Sacred Landscape of the Inca: the Cuzco Ceque System*. Austin: University of Texas Press.

Bauer, Brian S. 2004. *Ancient Cuzco: Heartland of the Inca*. Austin: University of Texas Press.

Bauer, Brian S. 2006. "Suspension Bridges of the Inca Empire." In *Andean Archaeology*. Vol. 3. Edited by Helaine Silverman and William H. Isbell, 468–493. New York: Kluwer Academic Press.

Bauer, Brian S., Miriam Aráoz Silva, and George S. Burr. 2012. "The Destruction of the Yurac Rumi Shrine (Vilcabamba, Cusco Department)." *Andean Past* 10:195–211.

Bauer, Brian S., and Antonio Coello Rodríguez. 2007. *The Hospital of San Andrés (Lima, Peru) and the Search for the Royal Mummies of the Incas*. Fieldiana Anthropology. N.s. No. 31. Chicago: Field Museum of Natural History.

Bauer, Brian S., and R. Alan Covey. 2002. "State Development in the Inca Heartland (Cuzco, Peru)." *American Anthropologist* 10(3):846–864.

Bauer, Brian S., Jesús Galiano, Teofilo Aparicio, Madeleine Halac-Higashimori, and Gabriel Cantarutti. 2014. *La muerte, entierros y milagros de Fray Diego Ortiz: Política y religión en Vilcabamba, S. S XVI*. Cuzco: Ceques Editores.

Bauer, Brian S., Madeleine Halac-Higashimori, and Gabriel E. Cantarutti. 2016. *Voices from Vilcabamba: Accounts Chronicling the Fall of the Inca Empire*. Boulder: University Press of Colorado.

Bauer, Brian S., Lucas C. Kellett, and Miriam Aráoz Silva. 2010. *The Chanka: Archaeological Research in Andahuaylas (Apurimac), Peru*. Los Angeles: Cotsen Institute of Archaeology, University of California.

Bauer, Brian S., Javier Fonseca Santa Cruz, and Miriam Aráoz Silva. 2015. *Vilcabamba and the Archaeology of Inca Resistance*. Los Angeles: Cotsen Institute of Archaeology, University of California.

Bauer, Brian S., and Charles Stanish. 2001. *Ritual and Pilgrimage in the Ancient Andes: The Islands of the Sun and the Moon*. Austin: University of Texas Press.

Bayle, Constantino. 1946. "Introducción." In *Historia del origen y genealogía real de los reyes incas del Perú*. Madrid: Instituto Santo Toribio de Mogrovejo, Consejo Superior de Investigaciones Científicas.

Betanzos, Juan de. (1557) 1996. *Narrative of the Incas*. Translated and edited by Roland Hamilton and Dana Buchanan from the Palma de Mallorca manuscript. Austin: University of Texas Press.

Bingham, Hiram. 1912a. "Preliminary Report of the Yale Peruvian Expedition." *Bulletin of the American Geographical Society* 44(1):20–26.

Bingham, Hiram. 1912b. "A Search for the Last Inca Capital." *Harper's Monthly Magazine*. October, 695–705.

Bingham, Hiram. 1912c. "Vitcos: The Last Inca Capital." *Proceedings of the American Antiquarian Society* 22 (April):135–196.

Bingham, Hiram. 1914a. "The Pampaconas River." *Geographical Journal* 44(2):211–214.

Bingham, Hiram. 1914b. "The Ruins of Espiritu Pampa, Peru." *American Anthropologist* 16:185–199.

Borja de Aguinagalde, Francisco. 2019. "Un misterio resuelto: El autor de la Historia General del Perú, Fray Martín de Murúa (1566?–1615) de Eskoriatza." In *Vida y obra Fray Martín de Murúa*. Edited by Thomas Cummins and Juan Ossio, 194–261. Lima: EY.

Cabello Valboa, Miguel. (1586) 1951. *Miscelánea antártica, una historia del Perú antiguo*. Edited by L. E. Valcárcel, 11–483. Lima: Universidad Nacional Mayor de San Marcos, Instituto de Etnología.

Calancha, Antonio de la. (1638) 1981. *Corónica moralizada del Orden de San Agustín en el Perú*. Edited by Ignacio Prado Pastor. Lima: Universidad Nacional Mayor de San Marcos, Editorial de la Universidad.

Calvo Pérez, Julio, and Henrique Urbano, eds. 2008. *Relación de la fábulas y mitos de los incas, written by Cristóbal de Molina*. Lima: Universidad de San Martín de Porres Press.

Casas, Bartolomé de Las, see Las Casas, Bartolomé de.

Chávez, Sergio J., and Karen L. Mohr Chávez. 1975. "A Carved Stela from Taraco, Puno, Peru, and the Definition of an Early Style of Stone Sculpture from the Altiplano of Peru and Bolivia." *Ñawpa Pacha* 13:45–83.

Cieza de León, Pedro de. (1553–1554) 1976. *The Incas of Pedro Cieza de León*, Parts 1 and 2. Translated by Harriet de Onís and edited by Victor W. von Hagen. Norman: University of Oklahoma Press.

Cieza de León, Pedro de. (1553–1554) 1998. *The Discovery and Conquest of Peru*. Edited and translated by Alexandra Parma Cook and Noble David Cook. Durham, NC: Duke University Press.

Cobo, Bernabé. (1653) 1979. *History of the Inca Empire: An Account of the Indians' Customs and Their Origin Together with a Treatise on Inca Legends, History, and Social Institutions*. Translated and edited by Roland Hamilton. Austin: University of Texas Press.

Cobo, Bernabé. (1653) 1980. "An Account of the Shrines of Ancient Cuzco." *Ñawpa Pacha* 17(1979):2–80.

Cobo, Bernabé. (1653) 1990. *Inca Religion and Customs*. Translated and edited by Roland Hamilton. Austin: University of Texas Press.

Contreras y Valverde, López de Vasco de. (1642) 1982. *Relación de la ciudad del Cuzco*. Cuzco: Imprenta Amauta.

Covey, R. Alan. 2006. *How the Incas Built Their Heartland: State Formation and the Innovation of Imperial Strategies in the Sacred Valley, Peru*. Ann Arbor: University of Michigan Press.

Covey, R. Alan, and Donato Amado Gonzales. 2008. *Imperial Transformations in Sixteenth-Century Yucay, Peru*. Memoirs of the Museum of Anthropology. Ann Arbor: University of Michigan Press.

Cummins, Thomas. 2008a. "Introduction." In *The Getty Murúa: Essays on the Making of Martín de Murúa's "General History del Pirú."* Edited by Thomas Cummins and Barbara Anderson, 3–5. Los Angeles: Getty Research Institute.

Cummins, Thomas. 2008b. "The Images in Murúa's Historia General del Pirú: An Art Historical Study." In *The Getty Murúa: Essays on the Making of Martín de Murúa's "General History del Pirú."* Edited by Thomas Cummins and Barbara Anderson, 147–174. Los Angeles: Getty Research Institute.

Cummins, Thomas. 2019a. "Dibujado de mi mano: Martín de Murúa como artista." In *Vida y obra Fray Martín de Murúa*. Edited by Thomas Cummins and Juan Ossio, 278–305. Lima: EY.

Cummins, Thomas. 2019b. "Análisis de la producción de las imágenes en la Historia general del Pirú." In *Vida y obra Fray Martín de Murúa*. Edited by Thomas Cummins and Juan Ossio, 398–415. Lima: EY.

Cummins, Thomas, and Barbara Anderson, eds. 2008. *The Getty Murúa's Essays on the Making of Martín de Murúa's "General History del Pirú."* Los Angeles: Getty Research Institute.

Cummins, Thomas, and Juan Ossio, eds. 2019. *Vida y obra Fray Martín de Murúa.* Lima: EY.

Duviols, Pierre. 1962. "Les sources religieuses du chroniqueur péruvien fray Martín de Morúa." *Annales de la Faculté des lettres et sciences humaines d'Aix.* 36:267–277.

Estete, Miguel de. (1532) 1872. "Of the Journey Made by El Senor Captain Hernando Pizarro . . ." In *Reports on the Discovery of Peru.* Translated by Clements Markham, 74–94. London: Hakluyt Society.

Fernández de Palencia, Diego. (1571) 1963. *Primera y segunda parte de la Historia del Pirú.* Biblioteca de Autores Españoles (continuación), vol. 165. Edited by Juan Pérez de Tudela Bueso. Madrid: Ediciones Atlas.

Garcilaso de la Vega, Inca. (1609, 1616) 1966. *Royal Commentaries of the Incas and General History of Peru, Parts 1 and 2.* Translated by H. V. Livermore. Austin: University of Texas Press.

Glave, Luis Miguel. 2017. "Pedro Ortiz de Orué: El encomendero y la encomienda de Maras." *Revista Andina* 55 (2017):95–123.

Guaman Poma de Ayala, Felipe. (1615) 2004. *El primer nueva corónica y buen gobierno.* http://www5.kb.dk/permalink/2006/poma/info/en/frontpage.htm.

Guillén Guillén, Edmundo. 1977a. "Documentos inéditos para la historia de los Incas de Vilcabamba: La capitulación del gobierno español con Titi Cusi Yupanqui." *Historia y Cultura* (Lima) 10:47–93.

Guillén Guillén, Edmundo. 1977b. "Vilcabamba: La última capital del estado imperial inca." *Scientia et Praxis* (Lima) 10:126–155.

Hamilton, Andrew James. 2024. *The Royal Inca Tunic: A Biography of an Andean Masterpiece.* Princeton, NJ: Princeton University Press.

Hemming, John. 1970. *The Conquest of the Incas.* New York: Harcourt Brace Jovanovich Press.

Houtrouw, Alicia Maria. 2019. "Forbidden Love in the Andes: Murúa and Guaman Poma Retell the Myth of Chuquillanto and Acoytapra." *Getty Research Journal* 11:161–184.

Julien, Catherine. 2000. *Reading Inca History.* Iowa City: University of Iowa Press.

Las Casas, Bartolomé. (ca. 1550) 1958. *Brevísima relación de la destrucción de las Indias.* In *Obras escogidas de Fray Bartolomé de Las Casas.* Edited by Juan Pérez de Tudela y Bueso. Biblioteca de Autores Españoles (continuación), vol. 106. Madrid: Ediciones Atlas.

Las Casas, Bartolomé. (1566) 1988. *Apologética historia sumaria III.* Vol. 8 of *Obras de Bartolome de Las Casas.* Madrid: Alianza.

Lee, Vincent R. 2000. *Forgotten Vilcabamba: Final Stronghold of the Incas*. N.p.: Empire Publishing.

Levillier, Roberto. 1925. *Gobernantes del Perú*. Cartas y papeles, siglo XVI. Sucesores de Rivadeneira: Madrid.

Levillier, Roberto. 1940. *Don Francisco de Toledo, supremo organizador del Perú*. Vol. 2, *Sus informaciones sobre los incas* (1570–1572.) Buenos Aires: Espasa-Calpe.

Loarte, Gabriel de. (1572) 1882. "Información hecha en el Cuzco a 4 de enero de 1572." In *Informaciones acerca del Señorío y gobierno de los Incas hechas por mandado de Don Francisco de Toledo, Virrey del Perú, (1570–1572): Colección de libros españoles raros ó curiosos*. Edited by Marcos Jiménez de la Espada. 16:223–243. Madrid: Imprenta de Miguel Ginesta.

Loayza, Francisco de. 1943. "Introduction." *Relación de las fábulas y ritos de los incas*. Los Pequeños Grandes Libros de Historia American. Lima: Librería e Imprenta D. Miranda.

Lohmann Villena, Guillermo. 1941. "El Inga Titu Cussi Yupanqui y su entrevista con el oidor Matienzo, 1565." *Mercurio Peruano* 23(167): 3–18.

López de Gómara, Francisco. 1552. *Historia general de las Indies*. Zaragoza.

Markham, Clements R. 1873. *An Account of the Fables and Rites of the Yncas*. In Narratives of the Rites and Laws of the Yncas. 1st ser., 48:1–64. London: Hakluyt Society.

Maúrtua, Víctor M., ed. 1906. *Juicio de límites entre el Perú y Bolivia. Tomo VII (Vilcabamba)*. Barcelona: Henrich y comp.

Molina, Cristóbal de. 1571. *History of the Incas*. Now lost.

Molina, Cristóbal de. (ca. 1575) 2011. *Account of the Fables and Rites of the Incas*. Translated by Brian S. Bauer, Vania Smith, and Gabriel E. Cantarutti. Austin: University of Texas Press.

Morrone, Ariel J. 2019. "Entre altares y escritorios: Liderazgo étnico y poder local en la pluma de tres curas-cronistas del Lago Titicaca (1570–1650)." *Memoria Americana: Cuadernos de Etnohistoria* 27(1):51–86.

Murúa, Martín de. (1590) 2004. *Códice Murúa: Historia y genealogía de los reyes incas del Perú del padre mercenario fray Martín de Murúa*. Facsimile. Madrid: Testimonio Compañía Editorial.

Murúa, Martín de. (1616) 2008. *Historia general del Pirú*. Facsimile. Los Angeles, Department of Manuscripts, J. Paul Getty Museum.

Niles, Susan A. 1988. "Looking for 'lost' Inca Palaces." *Expedition* 30(3):56–64.

Niles, Susan A. 1999. *The Shape of Inca History: Narrative and Architecture in an Andean Empire*. Iowa City: University of Iowa Press.

Nowack, Kerstin. 2004. "Las provisiones de Titu Cusi Yupanqui." *Revista Andina* 38:139–179.

Nowack, Kerstin, and Catherine Julien. 1999. "La campaña de Toledo contra los señores naturales andinos: El destierro de los Incas de Vilcabamba y Cuzco." *Historia y Cultura* (Lima) 23:15–81.

Núñez Carvallo, Sandro Patrucco. 2008. "Cabello Valboa, Miguel." In *Guide to Documentary Sources for Andean Studies, 1530–1900*. Vol. 2. Edited by Joanne Pillsbury, 91–94. Norman: University of Oklahoma Press.

Ocampo Conejeros, Baltasar. (1611) 2013. "Descripción de la provincia de San Francisco de la Victoria de Vilcabamba." In *Baltasar de Ocampo Conejeros y la Provincia de Vilcabamba*. Edited by Bauer, Brian S., Madeleine Halac-Higashimori, 21–56. Cuzco: Ceques Ediciones.

Ocampo Conejeros, Baltasar. 2016. "Description of the Province of San Francisco de la Victoria de Vilcabamba." In *Voices from Vilcabamba: Accounts Chronicling the Fall of the Inca Empire*, edited by Brian S. Bauer, Madeleine Halac-Higashimori, and Gabriel E. Cantarutti, 109–150. Denver: University Press of Colorado.

Oré, Jerónimo de. 1598. *Símbolo católico indiano*. Seville.

Ossio, Juan M. 2001. "Tras la huella de Martín de Murúa." *Revista del Museo Nacional* (Lima) 49:433–454.

Ossio, Juan M. (1590) 2004. *Códice Murúa Historia y genealogía de los reyes incas del Perú del padre mercenario fray Martín de Murúa*. Facsimile. Madrid: Testimonio Compañía Editorial.

Ossio, Juan M. 2008a. "Murúa's Two Manuscripts: A Comparison." In *The Getty Murúa: Essays on the Making of Martín de Murúa's "General History del Pirú."* Edited by Thomas Cummins and Barbara Anderson, 77–94. Los Angeles: Getty Research Institute.

Ossio, Juan M. 2008b. "Murúa, Martin de." In *Guide to Documentary Sources for Andean Studies 1530–1900*. Vol. 3. Edited by Joanne Pillsbury, 436–441. Norman: University of Oklahoma Press.

Ossio, Juan M. 2019a. "Nuevas miradas a los textos escondidos en el manuscrito." In *Vida y obra Fray Martín de Murúa*. Edited by Thomas Cummins and Juan Ossio, 262–277. Lima: EY.

Ossio, Juan M. 2019b. "Los dos manuscritos de gray Martín de Murúa: Una comparación." In *Vida y obra Fray Martín de Murúa*. Edited by Thomas Cummins and Juan Ossio, 350–369. Lima: EY.

Pachacuti Yamqui Salcamaygua, Joan de Santa Cruz, see Santa Cruz Pachacuti Yamqui Salcamaygua, Joan de.

Palacio, Eudoxio de Jesús. 1999. *Provinciales del Cuzco de la orden mercedario 1556–1994*. Rome: Instituto Histórico de la Orden de la Merced.

Pärssinen, Martti. 1989. "Otras fuentes escritas por los cronistas: Los casos de Martín de Morúa y Pedro Gutiérrez Santa Clara." *Historia* (Lima) 13:45–65.

Pease G. Y., Franklin. 1992. "Tópicos sobre los incas en Martin de Murúa." *Mercedaria*
11:9–30.

Phipps, Elena. 2019. "Documentos tejidos: Colores, diseños y orígenes culturales de los textiles en el manuscrito de Murúa del Getty." In *Vida y obra Fray Martín de Murúa*. Edited
by Thomas Cummins and Juan Ossio, 398–415. Lima: EY.

Phipps, Elena, Nancy Turner, and Karen Trentelman. 2008. "Colors, Textiles, and Artistic
Production in Murúa's History General del Piru." In *The Getty Murúa: Essays on the
Making of Martín de Murúa's "General History del Pirú."* Edited by Thomas Cummins
and Barbara Anderson, 125–146. Los Angeles: Getty Research Institute.

Pizarro, Hernando. (1533) 1872. "Letter from Hernando Pizarro to the Royal Audience of
Santo Domingo." In *Reports on the Discovery of Peru*. Translated by Clements Markham,
113–127. London: Hakluyt Society.

Pizarro, Pedro. (1571) 1921. *Relation of the Discovery and Conquest of the Kingdoms of Peru*.
Translated and edited by Philip Ainsworth Means. New York: Cortes Society.

Placer, Gumersindo. 1987. "Fray Martin de Murúa y su Historia General del Peru: Ruta
del MS Wellington." *Boletín de la Provincia de Castilla de la Orden de Ntra. Sra.
De la Merced* 24(87):33–44.

Polo de Ondegardo, Juan. (n.d.) 2012. "De los errores y supersticiones de los indios." In
Pensamiento colonial crítico: Texto y actos de Polo Ondegardo. Edited by Gonzalo Lamana
Ferrario, 343–363. Cuzco: Centro Bartolomé.

Polo de Ondegardo, Juan. (1571) 2021. "Las razones que movieron a sacar esta relación y
Notables daños de no guardar a los indios sus fueros." In *Pensamiento colonial crítico: Texto
y actos de Polo Ondegardo*. Edited by Gonzalo Lamana Ferrario, 217–326. Cuzco: Centro
Bartolomé.

Porras Barrenechea, Raúl. 1986. *Los cronistas del Perú (1528–1650) y otros ensayos*. Edited by
Franklin Pease G. Y. Lima: Banco de Crédito del Perú.

Prado Tello, E., and A. Prado Prado., eds. 1991. *Y no hay remedio*. Lima: Centro
de Investigación y Promoción Amazónica.

Remón, Alonso. 1618. *Historia general de la orden de Nuestra Señora de la Merced, redención
de cautivos*. Madrid: L. Sanchez.

Rodríguez de Figueroa, Diego. 2016. "Diego Rodríguez de Figueroa's Journey into
Vilcabamba [1565]." In *Voices from Vilcabamba: Accounts Chronicling the Fall of the Inca
Empire*. Translated and edited by Brian S. Bauer, Madeleine Halac-Higashimori, and
Gabriel E. Cantarutti, 151–176. Boulder: University Press of Colorado.

Román y Zamora, Jerónimo. 1575. *Repúblicas del mundo*. Medina del Campo.

Román y Zamora, Jerónimo. 1595. *Repúblicas del mundo*. Salamanca.

Rowe, John Howland. 1944. "An Introduction to the Archaeology of Cuzco." In *Papers of the Peabody Museum of American Archaeology and Ethnology*. Vol. 27, no. 2. Cambridge, MA: Harvard University.

Rowe, John Howland. 1958. "The Age-Grades of the Inca Census." In *Miscellanea Paul Rivet Octogenario Dicata*. Vol. 2, 499–522. Mexico City: Universidad Nacional Autónoma de México.

Rowe, John Howland. 1985. "Probanza de los incas nietos de conquistadores." *Histórica* (Lima). 9:193–245.

Rowe, John Howland. 1987. "La mentira literaria en la obra de Martín de Murúa." In *Libro de homenaje a Aurelio Miró Quesada Sosa*. Vol. 2, 753–761. Lima: Talleres Gráficos P. L. Villanueva.

Ruiz de Arce, Juan. (ca. 1545) 1933. "Relación de servicios en Indias de don Juan Ruiz Arce, conquistador del Perú." *Boletín de la Real Academia de la Historia* (Madrid) 102:327–384.

Ruiz de Navamuel, Álvaro. (1572) 1882. "La fe y testimonio que va puesta en los cuatro paños . . ." In *Informaciones acerca del señorío y gobierno de los incas hechas por mandado de Don Francisco de Toledo*. Vol. 16. Edited by Marco de Jiménez de la Espada, 245–257. Colección de Libros Españoles Raros o Curiosos. Madrid: Imprenta de Miguel Ginesta.

Salazar, Antonio Baptista de. (1596) 2016. "Antonio Bautista de Salazar and the Fall of Vilcabamba." In *Voices from Vilcabamba: Accounts chronicling the Fall of the Inca Empire*. Translated and edited by Brian S. Bauer, Madeleine Halac-Higashimori, and Gabriel E. Cantarutti, 177–191. Boulder: University Press of Colorado.

Sancho de la Hoz, Pedro. (1534) 1917. *An Account of the Conquest of Peru*. Translated by Philip A. Means. Documents and Narratives concerning the Discovery and Conquest of Latin American, no. 2. New York: Cortes Society.

Santa Cruz Pachacuti Yamqui Salcamaygua, Joan de. (ca. 1613) 1993. *Relación antigüedades deste reyno del Piru*. Edited by Pire Duvils and César Lier. Cuzco: Institut Français D'Études Andines and Centro de Estudios Regionales Andinos.

Sarmiento de Gamboa, Pedro. (1572) 2007. *The History of the Incas*. Translated and edited by Brian S. Bauer and Vania Smith. Introduction by Brian S. Bauer and Jean Jacque Decoster. Austin: The University of Texas Press.

Savoy, Gene. 1970. *Antisuyu: The Search for the Lost Cities of the Amazon*. New York: Simon and Schuster.

Stirling, Stuart. 1999. *The Last Conquistador*. Sutton, UK: Thrupp.

Titu Cussi Yupangui, Diego de Castro. (1570) 2005. *An Inca Account of the Conquest of Peru*. Translated, introduced, and annotated by Ralph Bauer. Boulder: University Press of Colorado.

Toledo, Francisco de. (1573) 1975. *Tasa de la visita de Francisco de Toledo*. Introduction and paleographic version by Noble David Cook, and studies by Alejandro Málaga Medina and Thérèse Bouysse Cassagne. Lima: Dirección Universitaria de Biblioteca y Publicaciones, Universidad Nacional Mayor de San Marcos, Seminario de Historia Rural Andina.

Topic, John, Theresa Lange Topic, and Alfredo Melly Cava. 2002. "Catiquilla: The Archaeology, Ethnohistory, and Ethnography of a Major Provincial Huaca." In *Andean Archaeology 1: Variations in Sociopolitical Organization*, edited by William H. Isbell and Helaine Silverman, 303–336. New York: Kluwer Academic.

Trentelman, Karen. 2019. "Colorantes y paletas de los artistas en los manuscritos de Murúa." In *Vida y obra Fray Martín de Murúa*. Edited by Thomas Cummins and Juan Ossio, 330–349. Lima: EY.

Trujillo, Diego de. (1571) 1948. *Relación del descubrimiento del reyno del Perú*. Edited by Raúl Porras Barrenechea. Seville: Imprenta de la Escuela de Estudios Hispano-Americanos.

Turner, Nancy K. 2019. "Explicando una historia inacabada." In *Vida y obra Fray Martín de Murúa*. Edited by Thomas Cummins and Juan Ossio, 306–329. Lima: EY.

Urbano, Henrique. 2008a. "Ediciones de la 'Relación.'" In *Relación de la fábulas y mitos de los incas*. Edited by Julio Calvo Pérez and Henrique Urbano, lxxix–lxxx. Lima: Universidad de San Martin de Porres.

Urbano, Henrique. 2008b. "Introducción a la vida y obra de Cristóbal de Molina." In *Relación de la fábulas y mitos de los incas*. Edited by Julio Calvo Pérez and Henrique Urbano, xi–lxvi. Lima: Universidad de San Martin de Porres.

Urbano, Henrique, and Pierre Duviols, eds. 1989. *Fábulas y mitos de los incas*. Madrid: Historia 16.

Van de Guchte, Maarten J. 1984. "El ciclo mítico andino de la Piedra Cansada." *Revista Andina* 2(2):539–556.

Wachtel, Nathan. 1982. "The Mitimaes of the Cochabamba Valley: The Colonization Policy of Huayna Capac." In *The Inca and Aztec States, 1400–1800: Anthropology and History*, edited by George A. Collier, Renato I. Rosaldo, and John D. Wirth, 199–235. New York: Academic Press.

Xerez, Francisco de. (1534) 1985. *Verdadera relación de la conquista del Perú*. Edited by Concepcion Bravo. Madrid: Historia 16.

Zárate, Agustín de. (1555) 1981. *The Discovery and Conquest of Peru*. Translated by J. M. Cohen. London: The Folio Society.

Index

Buenos Aires, city of, 4, 19*n36*, 26, 28, 43*t*
Bustinza, Pedro, husband of Beatriz Quispe
  Quipi Coya, 293*n918*

Cabello Valboa, Miguel, relationship with other
  authors, 35, 37, 39, 40, 41*t*
Cacachicha Vicaquirao, son of Inca Roca, 84
Cache (Rachi), town of, 81, 98, 346, 347
Cahuamana, member of Huayna Capac's army,
  184
Cajamarca, town of: capture of Atahualpa at, 32,
  215, 233, 235, 240, 327, 328; Huanca Auqui in,
  212, 213; Huayna Capac in, 140, 164, 204, 212;
  Pachacuti Inca Yupanqui in, 103, 105, 109;
  Spanish actions in, 109, 183*n574*, 215, 233–237,
  240–246, 248, 249, 252–255, 258, 259, 294, 315
Calancha, Antonio de la, 37, 69, 297*n947*,
  298*n951*, 298*n952*
Calatayud, Zaragoza, 26
Calca, town of, 84*n227*, 94, 197, 267, 344, 356,
  361, 362
Calcochima, Captain of Atahualpa, 253*n778*
Callao, port of, 150, 260
Callavaja, region of, 180
Cañaracay, ruins of, 177*n560*
Cañar Capac, *cacique* of the Cañaris, 107, 231
Cañari, ethnic group, 199, 213, 295, 338, 339;
  Atahualpa, 119, 203, 208, 229, 243; *cacique*
  of, 197–199, 203, 243, 229; in Cusco, 262;
  Francisco Chilche, 295, 316, 324; Huayna
  Capac, 147, 154, 156, 159, 188*n581*, 208, 212;
  Tupa Inca Yupanqui fights, 106, 107; in
  Vilcabamba, 295, 313, 316, 320
Canas, ethnic group, 81, 171, 344, 355
Canchari, killed in Vilcabamba, 319
Canchis, ethnic group, 81, 171, 355
Cañete, city of, 293, 294, 310, 346
Canta Guancuru, *cacique* of lowland group, 116
Canto, *cacique* of the Cayambes, 162
Capac Huaritito, 128, 135*n429*, 353, 354
Capac Raymi, December solstice celebration,
  258*n800*
Capac Yupanqui, fifth Inca, 76, 78, 80*f*, 84, 86,
  92, 346; builds Pachacamac, 79; death of, 81;
  sons of, 82, 117, 135, 138
Capac Yupanqui, General, 102, 103, 105
Capan, captain of Huayna Capac, 156
Caquiamarca, town of, 94
Carabaya, province of, 120, 348

Caranqui, ethnic group in Ecuador, 141, 144, 150,
  154; fort of, 157, 160, 161
Caraz, town of, 102
Cari, *cacique* of Chucuito, 154
Caro Atoneo, Lord of Cajamarca, 235
Carlos Inca, Inca during Spanish rule, 177, 231,
  314*n1010*, 337, 338, 341
Carmenca, sector of Cuzco, 263, 265, 338*n1116*,
  363
Caro Atoneo, lord of Cajamarca, 235
Carrasco, Leonor, wife of Melchor Carlos Inca,
  341
Carrasco, Pedro Alonso, suspected of a rebellion,
  341
Caruamay Huay, Beatriz, daughter of the lord of
  Chinchaycocha, 231
Caruarayco, *cacique* of Cotomarca, 285–288
Carvajal, Francisco de, Chief of Staff for
  Gonzalo Pizarro, 285
Carrillo, Luis, linguist, 22, 42*t*
Casana, palace of Huayna Capac, 141, 190, 258
Casas, Bartolomé de las. See Las Casas,
  Bartolomé de
Castilla, Sebastián de, revolt lead by, 292
Castro, Cristóbal Vaca de. See Vaca de Castro,
  Cristóbal
Catano de Cazana, Luis, husband of Mariana
  Hurtado de Mendoza, 335*n1100*
Catiquilla, *huaca* of Cajamarca, 164
Cayambe(s), ethnic group, 144, 154, 156,
  160–164, 185, 317, 346
Cayara, fort of, 106
Cayo Topa, Francisco, *orejón*, 262, 316, 317, 325
Caytomarca, town of, 84, 94
Ccapi, town of, 258
Chachapoya(s), ethnic group, 103, 262, 299;
  huaca of, 164; Huanca Auqui, 212, 213;
  Huascar Inca conquest of, 191–195; Huayna
  Capac conquest of, 141, 146*n469*, 164, 179;
  Tupa Inca Yupanqui conquest of, 106, 121
Chahuaytire, ethnic group, 96
Chalco Mayta, captain of Huayna Capac, 167
Chalco Yupanqui, captain of Tupa Inca
  Yupanqui, 115, 176, 225, 228, 243
Chalcomarca, fort, 100
Chalcuchima, captain of Atahualpa, 122, 200, 211,
  215, 217–223, 342; actions in Cuzco, 224–235,
  240, 244, 255–257; capture of, 245, 248
Chacán. See Hurin Chacán

About the Authors

Brian S. Bauer is a Professor of Anthropology at the University of Illinois Chicago. He received his PhD from the University of Chicago. He has published numerous books on Andean prehistory, including *Voices from Vilcabamba*, and is particularly well known for his work on the Incas.

Eliana Gamarra Carrillo received her Licenciatura in Archaeology from the Universidad Nacional de San Antonio Abad del Cusco and is pursuing a master's degree of Art History at the Universidad Nacional Mayor de San Marcos. She has worked extensively in the Peruvian Ministerio de Cultura and the Ministerio de Relaciones Exteriores.

Andrea Gonzáles Lombardi is a PhD student at the Pontificia Universidad Católica del Perú and teaches at the Universidad Privada Antenor Orrego in Piura, Perú. She earned her MA from the University of Illinois Chicago, and her work focuses on the early contact between local groups and the Spanish empire in the Northern Andes during the sixteenth century.